Praise for earlier editions of

RECOMMENDED COUNTRY INNS® THE MIDWEST

"The top of the . . . crop for a getaway splurge."
—Chicago Sun-Times

"A delightful writer, Puhala gets into history and description, which enhances the reader's pleasure . . . lets you know what's available as far as facilities and activities . . . [and] lists things nearby each inn that are worth seeing or doing."
—Ohioana Quarterly

"Suggests . . . outstanding inns for quality, unique features, and value."
—Chevron USA Odyssey

"Puhala has opened a door to a Midwestern treasure house of travel gems—a spectrum of places not to be missed. One can almost smell the morning muffins and feel the sunshine."
—Wisconsin Division of Tourism

"Puhala has captured the essence of the inns: welcoming and warm as a fire's glow."
—Detroit Free Press

RECOMMENDED COUNTRY INNS® SERIES

"These guides are a marvelous start to planning the leisurely trek,
romantic getaway, or time off for reflection."
—Internet Book Review

The Recommended Country Inns® series is designed for the discriminating traveler who seeks the best in unique accommodations away from home.

From hundreds of inns personally visited and evaluated by the author, only the finest are described in detail here. The inclusion of an inn is purely a personal decision on the part of the author; no one can pay or be paid to be recommended in a Globe Pequot inn guide.

Organized for easy reference, these guides point you to just the kind of accommodations you are looking for: Comprehensive indexes by category provide listings of inns for romantic getaways, inns for the sports-minded, inns that serve gourmet meals, inns for the business traveler . . . and more. State maps help you pinpoint the location of each inn, and detailed driving directions tell you how to get there.

Use these guidebooks with confidence. Allow each author to share his or her selections with you and then discover for yourself the richness of the country inn experience.

EDITIONS AVAILABLE:

Recommended Country Inns®
New England · Mid-Atlantic and Chesapeake Region
The South · The Midwest · West Coast
The Southwest · Rocky Mountain Region

Recommended

COUNTRY INNS®

THE MIDWEST

Illinois / Indiana / Iowa / Michigan / Minnesota /
Missouri / Nebraska / Ohio / Wisconsin

Eighth Edition

by Bob Puhala
illustrated by Bill Taylor Jr.

The
Globe
Pequot
Press

GUILFORD, CONNECTICUT

ISSN 1078-5507
ISBN 0-7627-0984-7

Cover photo: Stuart McCall/Stone Images
Cover, text, and map design: Nancy Freeborn/Freeborn Design

Manufactured in the United States of America
Eighth Edition/First Printing

Dedication

For Debbie and my teenage daughters, Kate and Dayne.

Contents

A Few Words about Visiting Midwestern Inns

have a "magic number," just like all those sports teams closing in on a championship. It's 1,100. By March 2001, I had visited more than 1,100 country inns looking for the best overnights in the Midwest that can then be shared with you.

More than one thousand heartland inns, bed-and-breakfasts, historic hotels, guest ranches, farmsteads, and upscale retreats, all personally visited by me—and hundreds with wife Debbie, daughters Kate and Dayne, brother Mark, even Grandma and Grandpa in tow, so that I can offer you the cream of the crop: 240 fabulous nights away from home in the eighth edition of *Recommended Country Inns The Midwest.*

You can already tell I like numbers. Here's another one: Since I started this gig with the book's first edition in 1987, I've rambled over more than 22,000 miles of Midwest roads to discover these gems.

That's lots of traveling. But there's no other way to do it. No other way to evaluate inns without seeing them with my own professional traveler's discerning eye; talking to the innkeepers; probing guests for insights, impressions, and anecdotes; tasting the food; sleeping in the beds (or covered wagons or under the stars, whatever the case may be); walking the grounds; exploring the cities, villages, hamlets, and cow towns. In good weather and bad. Below-zero temperatures and searing heat. In high season and low season.

I get plenty of rewards for my hard work. I've visted historic lighthouses transformed into inns on Michigan's Upper Peninsula in the waning days of winter. Of course, in the Upper Peninsula, winter takes a lot longer to wane than in more southern climes of the Midwest.

Even in April, massive piles of snow reached the second-story windows of some homes. Also remaining were beautiful 14-foot-high snow caves, nature's handicraft sculpted along the Lake Superior shoreline.

And I'll never forget that ever hopeful town sign along a lonely Upper Peninsula road that was virtually buried under a white blanket of the fluffy stuff. The town's name? Florida.

There are other perks, too. River town inns perched atop high bluffs afford magnificent views of the heartland's mighty rivers: the Mississippi, the Missouri, the Ohio.

Elegant Victorian mansions charm me with sparkling woodwork, master craftsmanship, and opulent furnishings. Turn-of-the-twentieth-century summer houses, transformed into spectacular retreats, boast the fiery glow of Great Lakes sunrises and sunsets.

Log cabins located in North Woods and Ozark Mountain wilderness are steeped in pristine tranquillity. Some inns nestle on rivers with world-class white-water rapids; others, on historic estates and manors tucked deep in the rolling hills of Appalachia, offer genteel Southern hospitality.

And with Nebraska under my "Midwest" umbrella, some "inns" are rooted on cattle ranches and rangelands, which often stretch for thousands of acres over prime pasture.

Then there are the innkeepers—no two are alike. Some have fled big-city corporate life to pursue a dream. Others are ex-soldiers, homemakers, teachers, lawyers, farmers, engineers. They each graciously tackle the day-to-day task of running a hostelry mostly for the pleasure of making travelers feel as though there's a little bit of home waiting for them no matter where they go. They have to love their innkeeper role; the work's too hard to make sense for any other reason.

You're part of the fun, too. Inn-goers seem to be more friendly, interesting, and involved with the world around them, possessing a special drive to experience new things, explore the past, or relive a little part of history.

Let's not forget our animal surprises. I've made so many furry friends (with everything from a horse named Firmy to a llama called Dali) while on the road that I could start up my own ranch. And I had some other interesting animal adventures, too. Let's see . . . there was the black bear standing in the middle of the road in a remote corner of northwest Wisconsin that looked me right in the eye before scurrying back into the brush. I saw eagles soar over bluff tops and dive into icy waters for a wintertime meal, foxes slink through the woods, deer stand frozen in my headlights, hawks, coyotes.

Oh, yes—and those rattlesnakes that did a "shake, rattle, and roll" at Nebraska's Ash Hollow State Historical Park, on the Oregon Trail. I would've felt a whole lot better if I had had a six-gun strapped on my shootin' hip.

Of course, there are some glitches. Unlike the East Coast, where traditional country inns (a full-service restaurant with lodging accommodations for travelers) were a part of the landscape from Colonial times, the Midwest's definition of a "country inn" is pretty elastic. Here your choices include everything from historic log cabins and ranch bunkhouses to re-created Victorian resort hotels and small bed-and-breakfast inns.

You'll still have a great time, as long as you have an authoritative travel guidebook. A trusted guidebook with an excellent track record of directing people to those very kinds of establishments is one of the most important tools in planning a getaway. A trusted guidebook like this one. Just ask veteran inn-goers . . . and innkeepers, too.

So after more than a decade of "traveling together," I ask you to join me yet again and discover the Midwest's best country inns. Each has something special and exciting to offer: atmosphere, charm, romance, history, architecture, location, feeling. Maybe even a little soul.

I'm still surprised by how many of you I meet while out on the road. And how you've had my book in hand while telling me that you never realized there were so many "fabulous places" in the Midwest until you read about them in these pages. That means a lot to me. Thanks.

Several others have written to second my choices. Some have offered me anecdotes about their stays. A few of you have even added "inn-side" information about places you'd like to see in the book. Again, thanks.

No doubt I'll bump into more of you somewhere down the line. It might be in some little cow town in Nebraska or some upscale whirlpool and fireplace wonderland where romance is the only currency.

Just make sure you stop to say, "How's it going?"

—Bob Puhala

How to Use This Inn Guide

Country inns, historic hotels, and outstanding B&Bs are listed state by state and alphabetically by city, town, and village within each state. You'll find them in the following order: Illinois, Indiana, Iowa, Michigan, Minnesota, Missouri, Nebraska, Ohio, and Wisconsin. Preceding each state grouping is a map guide and handy index. There's also a complete alphabetical index at the end of the book.

Helpful guidebook features are the special inn indexes. These list particularly noteworthy inn activities, amenities, and features. They will help you select the inn that's right for you.

There is no charge of any kind for an inn to be included in this guidebook. I have chosen inns based on my professional experience and personal standards. I offer readers a choice among the finest, most interesting, and most historic accommodations available in the Midwest. I thank those of you who have written me in the past, and I continue to welcome comments, questions, and information about your favorite inn—whether or not it's included in my selections—or newly opened and soon-to-be-opened inns. Please address all correspondence to Bob Puhala, *Recommended Country Inns The Midwest,* The Globe Pequot Press, P.O. Box 480, Guilford, Connecticut 06437.

Rates: Inns often change rates without notice. The high/low prices I have quoted are meant to be used only as guidelines. They'll give you a reasonable idea of what a room might cost. For the most part, I haven't included tax rates or service charges, which add to your bill; neither have I described tipping suggestions. Inquire upon making reservations.

Menu Abbreviations: The following abbreviations are used:

EP: European Plan—room without meals
EPB: Modified European Plan—room with full breakfast
AP: American Plan—room with all meals
MAP: Modified American Plan—room with breakfast and dinner
BYOB: Bring Your Own Bottle

Note that meal plans change often. An inn offering certain quoted specialties may change chefs and, thus, their entire entree list. Other inns constantly adjust breakfast policies, some offering full breakfasts one season, then continental or buffet-style breakfasts the next. There are several inns offering lunch and dinner specials by reservation or request; this is noted under "Facilities and activities" in each inn description. Remember that it is always best to call ahead so that you know what to expect.

Innkeepers: Some inns remain in the same family for decades. Others change ownership more frequently. This might result in wholesale revisions of previous inn policies. Or inns might completely close their doors to the public as they convert to private residences. Be sure to call ahead to ensure that the inn of your choice still welcomes travelers.

Reservations and Deposits: Many inns maintain such a sterling reputation of excellence and service that they require reservations made months in advance. Even on average it's advisable to call at least one month in advance at most inns, especially if you're planning to visit during the high-volume travel season (usually summer). Smaller establishments may require even more advance notice. And if you wish to stay at inns during annual town festivals, call right now.

On the other hand, it's always possible that you'll be able to make spur-of-the-moment reservations—possible, but not always likely.

As for deposits, this is such a common requirement that I do not mention specific inn policies. Assume that, with few exceptions, you'll be required to pay a deposit to reserve a room, using a personal check or a credit card. Be sure to inquire about refund policies.

Credit Cards: Visa and MasterCard are accepted unless otherwise stated. Many inns accept additional credit cards, too. Others accept only cash or personal checks. Call ahead to be sure.

Business Travel: Establishments listed in the "Inns for Business Travelers" category are especially sensitive to the needs of the burgeoning class of business travelers. At a minimum, these inns, historic hotels, and bed-and-breakfasts offer corporate rates, meeting/conference rooms, and fax machines. They also provide writing desks, reading lamps, and telephones in guest rooms, and they may be able to arrange photocopying, computer access, or other business-related services.

Entries in this category also geographically place the inn in context to the city's or town's primary business district.

Children: Inns that offer special rates for children are duly noted. Several inns do not publicly advertise kid discounts, so ask about them. Also note that some inns specialize in quiet getaway weekends for couples; others are antique-filled treasures. I still cringe when my kids get close to my baseball trophies; imagine how innkeepers might feel if your little ones were steamrolling toward a precious Ming vase. My wife and I are used to all types of kid-related noises (at all hours of the night), but some people are not. I guess what I'm trying to say is—please use your discretion when choosing an inn. Make sure it's one that the kids will enjoy. (See the "Inns Especially Good for Kids" index for some help.) As we and thousands of other parents have discovered, traveling with children is often a joy, but it's also tough work.

Pets: Spot usually won't be allowed inside. The rule: No pets unless otherwise stated.

Minimum Stay: Two-night minimums on weekends and even three nights during holidays are requirements at several inns, as noted. This is a frequently changing policy.

Bed Size: Inns may use three-quarter beds, twins, doubles, queens, or kings. While a few historic selections may offer antique rope beds or other fanciful contraptions, exotica is usually not a worry. If you have a preference, make it known in advance.

Television, Telephones, and Air-Conditioning: Are you the type of person who loves to travel deep into the heart of the wilderness but still must get a nightly fix of David Letterman? Were you born to live in air-conditioned rooms? I've noted which inns offer the above amenities in guest rooms. (Other inns offer these amenities in common rooms only.)

Food for Thought: A number of B&Bs are included in my selections. Oftentimes, innkeepers will have area restaurant dinner menus for guests to look over. At the least, the innkeeper should inquire about your food preferences and suggest an appropriate local restaurant. Most of the time, choices range from casual to fine dining. If you have any special dietary requirements, you should realize that such requests often are considered by inn restaurants. If you're not a red-meat eater, you'll usually find seafood and fowl entree selections. Therefore, if I do not mention restaurants as part of my inn descriptions, be assured that your hosts can advise you.

Wheelchair Access: Inns that have wheelchair access are noted in each "Rooms" listing; there is also a special "Inns with Wheelchair Access" index at the back of the book. Wheelchair access to restaurants and dining rooms only is listed under "Facilities and activities."

Bad Habits: More inns than ever prohibit smoking in guest rooms or common areas. You will find a special "No Smoking Inns" index at the back of the book.

Key to Icons Used in This Book

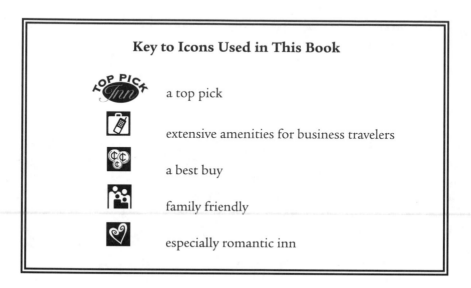

a top pick

extensive amenities for business travelers

a best buy

family friendly

especially romantic inn

Recommended

COUNTRY
INNS®

THE MIDWEST

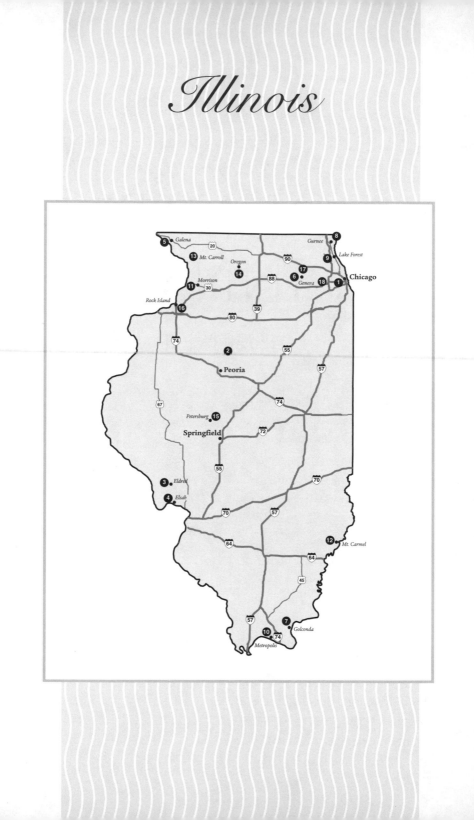

Illinois

Numbers on map refer to towns numbered below.

*A Top Pick Inn

The Gold Coast Guest House
Chicago, Illinois 60610

INNKEEPER: Sally Baker

ADDRESS/TELEPHONE: 113 West Elm Street; (312) 337–0361, fax (312) 337–0362

WEB SITE: www.bbchicago.com

E-MAIL: sally@bbchicago.com

ROOMS: 4; all with private bath, 2 with whirlpool, 1 extra bath with whirlpool tub. All rooms have TV/VCR. No smoking inn.

RATES: $129 to $229, single or double; continental breakfast and welcoming beverages. Parking available in high-rise behind B&B for $7 nightly/based on availability.

OPEN: Year-round

FACILITIES AND ACTIVITIES: Gathering room looking out into private garden, with chairs and barbecue in summer. Nearby: five-minute walk to shops on "Magnificent Mile" (North Michigan Avenue); including Bloomingdale's, Niketown, Water Tower Place (with Marshall Field's), Burberry's, and lots more tony shops. Also walk to "Loop" live theater, upscale boutiques on Oak Street. Short drive to Field Museum, Museum of Natural History, Adler Planetarium, Art Institute, Soldier Field (home of the Chicago Bears), Shedd Aquarium, Oak Street Beach.

*I*finally found a magnificent bed-and-breakfast in Chicago—right near the "Magnificent Mile." It's located in the very heart of the Gold Coast, one of Chicago's most exclusive neighborhoods. And give Sally Baker credit for her preservation efforts; she restored this stately 1873 brick townhouse, one of five historic buildings that used to line this portion of Elm Street. Now only three are left.

Sally's style is a very contemporary House Beautiful look, with some fine antiques spicing the classic design—along with decorating surprises. Guest rooms offer the best of both classic and contemporary design. Bedchambers on the second floor, reached by a winding spiral staircase, are among my favorite, especially one graced with a big bay window overlooking the street, along with its art deco armoire and original brick fireplace. Both second-floor rooms claim the inn's in-room whirlpools, too; there's also an extra whirlpool bath on the first floor. Sally explained: "That's for my guests from England who might have a room without a tub. The English must have their bath."

Breakfasts are taken in the second-floor dining room that hangs like a balcony overlooking the gathering room below. Fresh bagels, English muffins, cold cereals, yogurt, juices, and more are part of the morning treats.

HOW TO GET THERE: From the Kennedy Expressway (I-94), take the Ohio Street exit and continue down Ohio to Dearborn; turn left and proceed to Elm; turn left and continue to the inn.

"English" Spoken Here

Sally knows about "the English" because she lived in London for a year while working as a tour hostess for a major travel company. And Sally continues to travel the world via her guests, some of whom have come from as far away as India, Australia, and Guam.

See for yourself—she keeps a stickpin map of the world inside the foyer, tracking her guests' homelands. Sally even has photographs of most of her far-flung visitors.

The Hotel Inter-Continental 📱
Chicago, Illinois 60611

INNKEEPER: Rex Rice, manager

ADDRESS/TELEPHONE: 505 North Michigan Avenue; (800) 628–2468, (312) 944–4100, fax (312) 944–1320

WEB SITE: www.chicago.interconti.com

E-MAIL: chicago@interconti.com

ROOMS: 844, includes 40 suites; all with private bath; executive floors with butler service. Wheelchair accessible.

RATES: $169 to $249, single; $189 to $279, double; $299 to $700, suites.

OPEN: Year-round

FACILITIES AND ACTIVITIES: Boulevard Restaurant with great views of Michigan Avenue; swimming pool, fitness club. Executive floors boast butler service; coffee, tea, pastries served throughout the day; walk out of hotel onto Michigan Avenue; short walk to Water Tower shopping and "Magnificient Mile" shops.

*T*his hotel has to be one of the most historic and unusual in all of Chicago, built in 1929 of Indiana limestone and crowned by a Moorish-style dome. First it housed the Medinah Athletic Club; now restoration has breathed new life into its fabulous Egyptian-influenced architecture, which includes painted ceilings, arched entryways, marble inlays, winding staircases, and bronze and brass everywhere.

Guest rooms are done in the Biedermeier style, popular in the nineteenth century, and feature ebony inlays, Axminster carpets, and antique and reproduction furnishings.

For the ultimate luxury, book yourself into the Presidential Suite, located on the thirty-seventh floor of the historic South Tower. It overlooks both Michigan Avenue and the soothing blue waters of Lake Michigan. This is a two-level suite, with two full guest rooms and four baths. You can curl up with a special somebody in the luxurious living room, while gazing out onto city skyscapes thanks to spectacular floor-to-ceiling windows.

However, the benchmark of this architectural beauty is its junior Olympic-sized swimming pool, done in stunning mosaics and housed in an almost three-story-tall atrium. Brush up on your breaststroke—none other than Tarzan (Olympic gold medal winner Johnny Weismuller) is among the celebs who have stayed here and done laps in the pool.

HOW TO GET THERE: From I–94 (Kennedy Expressway), exit at Ohio Street and continue to Michigan Avenue; then turn right (south) and proceed to hotel.

Glory Hill 🏵
Chillicothe, Illinois 61523

INNKEEPERS: Bonnie and Jack Russell

ADDRESS/TELEPHONE: 18427 North Old Galena Road; (309) 274–4228

WEB SITE: www.gloryhill.midco.com

ROOMS: 2, with 1 suite; both with private bath, TV, radio.

RATES: $80 to $85, single or double; EPB.

OPEN: Year-round

FACILITIES AND ACTIVITIES: Formal dining room, veranda, in-ground swimming pool. Near Peoria and Wildlife Prairie Park, 1680 Fort Vrececour, Par-A-Dice Riverboat Casino, Wheels O' Time Museum, Lakeview Planetarium.

*L*et's see . . . we have a tree-lined lane, horse paddock, 150-year-old house—all the ingredients that add up to a charming country inn. And that's just what Glory Hill is, a step back into the era of down-home hospitality that was the hallmark in these parts in the mid-1800s. Built in 1844, Glory Hill stands as a proud reminder of what open land on the Illinois prairie once looked like. It's also had famous visitors, too. For example, did you know that Abe Lincoln slept here? In fact, he made Glory Hill a regular stopover when he traveled to and from the state capitol building in Springfield.

So why not spend a night in the Lincoln Room, graced with all kinds of Lincoln memorabilia. Or try out the Old Kentucky Suite, which features a romantic lace-canopied bed, two-person whirlpool, and plenty of other pampering touches.

HOW TO GET THERE: From Peoria, take Illinois 40 north to Hallock Hollow Road; turn right (east) and go to Old Galena Road; turn left (north) and proceed to inn.

Hobson's Bluffdale
Eldred, Illinois 62027

INNKEEPERS: Bill and Lindy Hobson

ADDRESS/TELEPHONE: Hillview Road; (217) 983-2854

ROOMS: 8, with 3 two-room suites, plus 1 cottage; all with private bath and air-conditioning.

RATES: $77 per person; $52 for children ages 9 to 14, $45 for kids 4 to 8, $25 under age 4; AP. $485 adults, sliding scale for children, for weekly farm vacations; includes all activities and recreation. Bed-and-breakfast only, $105 per couple. Three-night minimum stay Memorial Day, July 4, and Labor Day. Two-night minimum all other weekends, June through September.

OPEN: Year-round for B&B; farm vacations, March through November.

FACILITIES AND ACTIVITIES: Horseback riding and trail rides, cart rides, swimming in heated pool, hot tub, canoe day trips, hiking through private wooded bluffs, arrowhead hunting, wild blackberry picking, fishing in private pond or Illinois River, pontoon boat rides, hayrides, square dancing, ice cream socials, bonfire roasts, workshops in forestry, archaeology, pottery, ceramics, wildlife, and more. Nearby: water park.

*B*luffdale is a 320-acre farm (soybeans, corn, wheat, and a few pigs) run by the Hobsons; it's been in Bill's family since 1828. It was named by his great-great-grandfather for bluffs that run through the property. In fact, Charles Dickens was one of Bill's ancestor's friends and visited here in the 1840s. Dickens was picked up at the train station and brought in a spring wagon to the farm.

Bill and Lindy encourage everyone to help with regular farm chores—feeding the chickens and pigs, gathering eggs, moving geese, bottle-feeding calves, picking fresh blackberries, harvesting vegetables from the two-acre garden, and more. Lindy is the cook who takes all this delicious farm-fresh food and whips up great feasts. Family-style meals include eggs, French toast or pancakes, fruits, and home-baked breads for breakfast; maybe a picnic lunch packed for a trek through the woods; and supper-table specials such as fried chicken, baked ham, pot roast, and barbecued pork chops, topped off with oven-fresh sweets and homemade ice cream.

Overnight rooms are comfortable enough, done in bandana red and blues with brass lanterns and wide-plank floors. There's also a Log Cabin in the Woods, a private getaway that transforms the "ranch" into a secluded playground. Activities include archaeological digs (this is historic Native American country), Saturday night square dances, Sunday ice cream socials, Monday ball games, Friday night bonfire sing-alongs, and Tuesday afternoon cookout picnics at Greenfield Lake.

HOW TO GET THERE: From St. Louis, take Missouri 367 north to Alton, Illinois. Continue north on U.S. 67, then head north on Illinois 267. Turn west at Illinois 208 and continue to Eldred. At Eldred–Hillview Road (at the bottom of a hill, opposite the Standard gas station), turn north and proceed just over 3½ miles to the farm.

Green Tree Inn ⬡
Elsah, Illinois 62028

INNKEEPERS: Michael and Mary Ann Pitchford

ADDRESS/TELEPHONE: 15 Mill Street; (618) 374–2821

ROOMS: 9, including 1 suite; all with private bath and air-conditioning, phone on request.

RATES: $95, single or double; $115, suite; EPB.

OPEN: Year-round

FACILITIES AND ACTIVITIES: Dining room, gathering room, private balconies; nineteenth-century-style mercantile store featuring fine arts and crafts; paddle wheeler offering riverboat excursions. In the heart of historic Elsah. Short walk to Mississippi River. Jogging or biking on Great River Road. Nearby is 16-mile-long Vadalabene bike trail. About

40 antiques shops within 15 minutes' drive. Bald eagles winter along the river in great numbers from December through March. About 40 minutes from St. Louis.

*F*ound it hard to believe that this 1850s-style river-town building is just over a decade old. "We designed it to convey nineteenth-century charm," innkeeper Mary Ann Pitchford said. "And since the entire town is on the National Register of Historic Places, we had to be very exact in matching the spirit of this building with its authentic nineteenth-century surroundings."

My favorite bedchamber is the Federal Room, done in Federal blues, boasting a canopy bed that copies 1850s Mississippi style. Bedposts are draped with linens made in Lao Ping province in China. "It's interesting that the linens are handmade in China but are copies of American nineteenth-century lace," Mary Ann said. Austrian and Swedish lace also grace windows. The Federal theme is carried through with two wing chairs and handsome wall portraits.

A charming gathering room in the building's lower level is a picture of country quaint. Red-checked tablecloths cover tables and chairs specially made by local craftspeople for the inn. Mary Ann serves breakfast here—everything from tasty omelettes and homemade strawberry-tinged French toast or biscuits and gravy to pastries from the renowned local bakery.

HOW TO GET THERE: From St. Louis, take Missouri 367 north to U.S. 67 and continue into Illinois. At Illinois 3, turn west and proceed to Elsah. There are only two major streets in the town, Mill and LaSalle.

Maple Leaf Cottage Inn
Elsah, Illinois 62028

INNKEEPERS: Patty and Jerry Taetz

ADDRESS/TELEPHONE: 38–40–42–44 LaSalle Street, P.O. Box 156; (618) 374–1684

ROOMS: 4; all with private bath, air-conditioning, and TV; 1 with wheelchair access. Family cottage with 2 bedrooms and fireplace. No smoking inn

RATES: $75, single; $99, double; EPB. Family cottage, $375 weekly.

OPEN: Year-round

FACILITIES AND ACTIVITIES: Restaurant, 7-course dinner ($25 per person); lecture/luncheons on Elsah history and architecture 5 days per month. English country garden, herb garden. Located in heart of historic Elsah, nineteenth-century Mississippi river town. Near Grant River Road, jogging and biking along the 16-mile Vadalabene bike trail. Nearly 40 antiques shops within a 15-minute drive. Bald eagles winter along river from December through March. About 40 minutes from St. Louis. Limousine service to and from St. Louis Regional and Lambert International Airports. Will arrange for special trolley tours to St. Louis arch, Union Station, etc.; will arrange daily river and walking tours.

This cozy country inn occupies an entire village block, surrounded by blazing colors of a handsome English garden and facing the spectacular limestone bluffs that run down to the Mississippi River. Rooms can be overwhelming, fashioned with seemingly every country accent and craft imaginable and available. Yet, I found them to be some of the most relaxing and enjoyable lodgings I've encountered since I began inn-hopping years ago.

My favorite guests quarters here is the Wash House, a charming cottage (the first ever of the Maple Leaf Inn, which has been open to travelers for four decades). In 1891 it was the Maple Leaf's summer kitchen, but after a fire it became the family washhouse. Patty and Jerry Taetz have carried this theme through to perfection, with quaint country decor that showcases an 1888 wooden washing machine, old-fashioned scrub boards, and even a clothesline. A wonderful rail bed adds to country charm. There are historic photos of the original Maples hanging on the walls. (And a feather bed is offered in the fall and winter!)

Let's not forget Patty's incredible meals. Breakfasts might include a special recipe of heart- shaped

French toast, tarragon eggs, fruit cups, hot muffins, and gourmet coffee and teas. For dinner, consider boneless breast of chicken baked in herbs and butter, flounder stuffed with crab, Elsah Hills gravy, river-bluff rice with pecans, country green vegetables, and scrumptious garden-house cheesecake.

HOW TO GET THERE: From St. Louis, take Missouri 367 north to U.S. 67 and continue into Illinois. At Illinois 3, turn west and proceed to Elsah. There are only two major streets in Elsah, Mill and LaSalle; Selma intersects both.

Aldrich Guest House
Galena, Illinois 61036

INNKEEPERS: Sandy and Herb Larson

ADDRESS/TELEPHONE: 900 Third Street; (815) 777–3323

WEB SITE: www.aldrichguesthouse.com

E-MAIL: larson61036@hotmail.com

ROOMS: 5; all with private bath and air-conditioning.

RATES: $80 to $195, single or double; two-night minimums on weekends; midweek discounts; EPB.

OPEN: Year-round

FACILITIES AND ACTIVITIES: Double parlor, screened porch, gardens. Walk or drive to restaurants and historic attractions of the old lead-mining town of Galena, including U. S. Grant home and scores of antiques, specialty, and art shops; museums, historic homes.

*T*he Aldrich Guest House, an elegant 1853 Greek Revival mansion with Italianate touches, is part of the Galena legend of hometown-boy-made-good Ulysses S. Grant. Tales say that Grant mustered his Civil War troopers on the green next to the home. I sat on the inn's screened porch, gazing at the expansive yard, trying hard to imagine the stoic figure of the bearded general drilling his ragtag

army of Illinois farm boys, readying them for furious battle. Now you can also enjoy wonderful spring and summer blossoms, thanks to owner Sandy Larson's green thumb; get set for an explosion of tulips, lilies, and other perennials.

A broad fluted oak banister heads the stairway leading to the second-floor guest rooms. The Tiffany Ann is a favorite, with its iron-rail bed, white wicker chair, and violet-bouquet wall coverings. "It looks like spring in here," Sandy said. The Sherrie Lee is another Victorian-style beauty, complete with canopy bed, bay window, and a water closet featuring a claw-footed bathtub and old-fashioned pull-chain commode, adding a feel of authenticity to the historic house.

Breakfast here—served on fine china—is a treat: delicious stratas, soufflés, French toast, fruits, and more. And Sandy's home-baked pastries make you forget about your waistline. She also will recommend restaurants to suit your dinner tastes; I found Bubba's to be a Galena favorite. Other crowd pleasers are Fried Green Tomatoes, The Log Cabin, and Cafe Italia, one of my favorites.

HOW TO GET THERE: Take U.S. 20 (across the bridge toward U. S. Grant's house) to Third Street. Turn left and go to the end of the block to the inn.

Brierwreath Manor Bed and Breakfast
Galena, Illinois 61036

INNKEEPERS: Mike and Lyn Cook

ADDRESS/TELEPHONE: 216 North Bench Street; (815) 777–0608

WEB SITE: www.brierwreath.com

ROOMS: 3, including 2 suites; all with private bath and air-conditioning.

RATES: $100 to $110, single or double; EPB. Two-night minimum on weekends, holidays. Special packages, off-season rates available.

OPEN: Year-round

FACILITIES AND ACTIVITIES: Sitting room, upstairs breakfast buffet; wraparound porch. Nearby: historic sites, art galleries, antiques shops, restaurants. Short ride to Mississippi Palisades State Park; riverboat rides, riverboat museum, and other attractions in Dubuque, Iowa.

A homey atmosphere with soft sofas, comfy guest rooms, and a great wraparound porch perfect for people-watching in this historic lead-mining town—that's 1884 Brierwreath Manor. And it's only a half block from all the shops lining Galena's Main Street. "People love our porch," Lyn Cook said. "They do some sightseeing, come back and relax on the swing to recharge batteries, then go right back out again."

The Mayor's Room (named for the previous owner, who happened to be Galena's top honcho) offers lace curtains, a queen-sized bed, a shower big enough for two, and a gas log fireplace. An antique pedestal sink and the inn's other guest room fireplace grace the Country Charms Suite. My favorite is the Heirloom Suite, which has the inn's finest antiques, including an Eastlake dresser, armoire, and claw-footed bathtub. (Lyn supplies the bubble bath.)

A typical breakfast might include pecan French toast, ham, and watermelon slices. For early birds an upstairs buffet features a variety of teas and coffees that should hold you until breakfast. Galena is graced with several fine restaurants: the fun-filled Bubba's, all-you-can-eat walleyed pine and peel-and-eat shrimp at Benjamin's, and fine fettucine Alfredo at Cafe Italia.

HOW TO GET THERE: From Chicago, take the Northwest Tollway (I–90) north to U.S. 20, then go west to Galena. Turn north on Main Street, west on Franklin, and south on Bench Street to the inn.

DeSoto House 📱
Galena, Illinois 61036

INNKEEPER: Daniel Kelly

ADDRESS/TELEPHONE: 230 South Main Street; (815) 777–0090

WEB SITE: www.desotohouse.com

ROOMS: 55, with 4 suites; all with private bath, air-conditioning, TV, and phone. Wheelchair access.

RATES: $89 to $205; EP. Special discount weekend packages including a "bed-and-breakfast" weekend.

OPEN: Year-round

FACILITIES AND ACTIVITIES: Three full-service restaurants, tavern, indoor courtyard, courtyard specialty shops, free parking. On Main Street in historic Galena. Nearby: home of U. S. Grant; preserved Civil War architecture; specialty shops and museums.

BUSINESS TRAVEL: Located about 20 miles east of Dubuque. Corporate rates, conference rooms, fax.

*T*he massive 1855 structure—opened during the period when unprecedented lead-mining profits transformed Galena into a trade and commerce center rivaling Chicago—has undergone more than $8 million in restoration work. That kind of money is reflected in the elegance evident throughout the building, which was once billed as "the largest hotel in the West."

On my way to the guest rooms, I passed through an enclosed courtyard with high skylight windows that sent a rush of sun toward diners enjoying an elegant alfresco buffet in its open space. The guest rooms are decorated in various shades of soothing blues and beiges. Some of the furnishings include high-back chairs, dressers, and writing desks. Even the inside rooms have views, with windows overlooking the Grand Court.

The hotel offers breakfast and lunch in its indoor courtyard; or try a down-home country meal at the Steakburger Inn, a local breakfast favorite. For elegant formal dining, enjoy the hotel's General Dining Room, located on the lower level; it's a romantic showplace with exposed brick walls and original ceiling beams. Menu choices include the finest steaks and seafood. Then relax in the hotel's Einsweiler Library with a cognac nightcap in front of a roaring fire—an elegant way to end a day.

By the way, nine presidents have stayed at the DeSoto House, as well as the likes of Mark Twain, Ralph Waldo Emerson, Susan B. Anthony, and Horace Greeley. So a stay here puts you in pretty distinguished company.

HOW TO GET THERE: Take U.S. 20 to Galena. Turn north on South Main Street. The DeSoto House is halfway up the block, at the corner of Main and Grand.

Taken for Grant-ed

The first time I visited the DeSoto House, General Ulysses S. Grant was standing in front of the historic hotel. He was unmistakable with his heavy navy blue Union Army greatcoat, wide-brimmed hat, full beard, and ever-present cigar.

I walked up to him, aimed my camera, said, "Smile," and clicked the shutter. The general wasn't even startled. In fact, he said, "You need another shot? I'll strike my presidential pose for you."

Of course, Grant turned out to be a local actor who portrays the general at special functions, both at the hotel and in Galena. But the likeness is striking. Now, if only Abe Lincoln were standing with him—there's a photo!

DeZoya House & Davis Creek Woodland Cottage Bed and Breakfast
Galena, Illinois 61036

INNKEEPERS: Fred Tuttle and James Zalewski

ADDRESS/TELEPHONE: 1203 Third Street; (815) 777–1203

WEB SITE: www.dezoya.com

ROOMS: 4; all with private bath and air-conditioning.

RATES: $125, single or double; cottage: $175, one couple; $295 two couples; EPB. Two-night minimum on weekends if Saturday night is included.

OPEN: Year-round

FACILITIES AND ACTIVITIES: Sitting room, library, screened porch, lawn activities, garden. Short walk to Main Street shops and restaurants. Nearby: skiing, golf, fishing, riverboat rides, historical attractions, state park.

*I*f you want to stay overnight in one of Galena's more historic settings, try the DeZoya House. Built before 1830 by a local financier, the 4,000-square-foot structure is "the largest stone residence in Jo Daviess County." It's significant because it remains the only Virginia-style Federal home in Galena. And unlike most homes around here, it was built wholly at one time.

Owners Fred Tuttle and Jim Zalewski are from Wicker Park in Chicago (my old neighborhood), so we talked like old pals. Fred told me that the two guest rooms on the second floor feature unusual cypress floors (probably brought up the Mississippi River from New Orleans by riverboat) in addition to hand-carved four-poster beds. Two third-floor rooms, both with original plank floors, boast a sleigh bed (my favorite) and a pine cannonball bed.

The home rests on two acres, with Muddy Hollow Creek gurgling somewhere down the bluff. A screened porch is the center of conversation and games during summer months; guests also enjoy a small balcony that overlooks the property. Breakfasts might include a fancy fruit compote, quiche, strata, tomato tarts, and home-baked breads.

Also enjoy the 1835 brick cottage out by the creek; it's a great getaway with its own fireplace and screened porch.

HOW TO GET THERE: From Dubuque, take U.S. 20 east to Third Street, turn right, and continue all the way down the block to the inn.

Hellman Guest House
Galena, Illinois 61036

INNKEEPER: Merilyn Tommaro

ADDRESS/TELEPHONE: 318 Hill Street; (815) 777–3638

WEB SITE: www.galena.com/hellman

ROOMS: 4; all with private bath and air-conditioning.

RATES: $99 to $129, weekdays; $109 to $149, weekends. EPB. Two-night minimum weekends and holidays.

OPEN: Year-round

FACILITIES AND ACTIVITIES: Parlor, library, porch, patio, and gardens. Nearby: Main Street shops, antiques, restaurants, historic attractions. Short drive to Dubuque's riverboat rides, museums, Mississippi River.

*S*ome of the best views of Galena can be enjoyed from the Hellman Guest House, built on Quality Hill, offering views of Horseshoe Mound and overlooking church steeples, gingerbread turrets, turn-of-the-century merchant buildings, and surrounding bluffs. Just one glimpse of this spectacular scene convinced me that the entire town had actually been suspended in time.

Innkeeper Merilyn Tommaro fell in love with the house as soon as she laid eyes on it in 1986. The sun-filled attic, with its turret room, inspired the painter in her; she's converted it into her private art studio.

The 1895 home, built by a wealthy local merchant, has a magnificent interior. I can't remember being more impressed by what appears from the outside to be a modest home; the inside offers cherry and oak woodwork, stained and leaded glass, and an incredibly opulent foyer—complete with its own fireplace.

A huge window in the formal parlor reveals spectacular views of Galena. For a closer peek I fixed my eye to the brass telescope, a 1942 U.S. military surveyor's tool that brought the town within arm's reach.

Guest rooms are equally distinctive. The Hellman is the original master bedroom of the home. Besides Victorian antiques and a queen-sized brass bed, it boasts a tower alcove with more incredible views.

Other rooms are named for Hellman's daughters: Pauline offers a queen-sized iron-and-brass bed; Irene features a Victorian oak bed and sapphire-tinted accents; and Eleanor is a great afternoon sunroom, with a Victorian bath that includes a claw-footed bathtub. There's also a new luxury suite, complete with fireplace and whirlpool bath.

Yes, Merilyn allows guests to luxuriate in the spectacular view from the house's main tower. Get your camera ready; you won't want to miss this shot.

And breakfast treats . . . consider a fancy fruit plate, blueberry buttermilk pancakes, quiche, strata, even hobo hash. Of course, there are always oatmeal cookies for afternoon snacks.

HOW TO GET THERE: Although the house is located on Hill Street, guest parking is on High Street. From Dubuque, take U.S. 20 east into Galena and turn left on High Street (up the steep hill) to the inn's parking area (marked with a sign).

Inn at Irish Hollow ♥
Galena, Illinois 61036

INNKEEPERS: Tony Kemp and Bill Barrick

ADDRESS/TELEPHONE: 2800 South Irish Hollow Road; (815) 777–2010

WEB SITE: www.irishhollow.com

ROOMS: 5, with 1 suite; all with private bath; 4 cottages. No smoking inn.

RATES: $165 to $205, single or double; suite $105; cottages $245 to $295; full breakfast. Minimum two-night stay on weekends, three nights during fall color season.

OPEN: Year-round

FACILITIES AND ACTIVITIES: Guest parlor, front porch, horse-and-buggy rides, dinners available. Short drive to downtown Galena and shops, boutiques, and art galleries. Chestnut Mountain Ski resort and Mississippi Palisades State Park also nearby.

*T*his 1880 building, an old general store and post office, was virtually intact inside when Tony Kemp and Bill Barrick first bought it—all signs and scales and wooden display counters that would be so familiar to nineteenth-century farmers who frequented this way station 8 miles from the heart of downtown Galena. Today it is an elegant bed-and-breakfast that's also a romantic getaway.

It's still out in the country, amid the rolling hills of Galena's bluff country and lazy cattle grazing in undulating pastureland. But inside, the atmosphere is all romance.

Guest quarters offer all the amenities necessary for coosome twosomes. Imagine fireplaces, whirlpools, huge beds, and private balconies. There are even cottages that afford extra privacy for those who want to disappear for a weekend.

Breakfasts are served in "Country Gourmet" style, such as baked grapefruit halves, French toast with peach syrup, and crispy bacon strips. Then there's Irish Hollow dinners—anything from pork tenderloin au jus to holiday season banquets of scrumptious goodies. You'll be wanting to come back again before you even leave.

One of the inn's extra-special treats is its cottage experience. What's your travel fantasy this weekend? The French Maid's Cottage dates to the 1880s and is festooned with a wood-burning fireplace in the bedroom (as well as a four-poster bed), double whirlpool, and sitting room. Aalto's Thatched Cottage brings a little bit of the Auld Sod back to the Midwest, with its traditional thatched roof, authentic Irish furnishings, wood-burning fireplace, and something that my Irish grandparents probably never had in their home—a deluxe double whirlpool. Finally, you can imagine you're in jolly old England and the Cotswolds when you choose from two romantic and opulent Cotswold-style romantic cottages, boasting all-marble baths and whirlpools, wood-burning limestone fireplaces, king four-poster beds, English furnishings, and more.

HOW TO GET THERE: From Rockford, take Highway 20 west 3 miles past the town of Elizabeth and look for a scenic lookout tower. One mile past the tower, turn left onto Rodden Road. Continue 3 miles, always bearing to the right. The inn will be on your left.

Log Cabin Guest House
Galena, Illinois 61036

INNKEEPER: Jon Allen

ADDRESS/TELEPHONE: 11661 West Chetlain Lane; (866) VI-PINES (toll free)

WEB SITE: www.VictorianPinesLodging.com

ROOMS: 5 authentic 1800s log cabins; historic Coach House; all with double whirlpool bath, wood-burning fireplace, air-conditioning, TV, VCR, CD, and wet bar; 1 with wheelchair access.

RATES: Sunday through Thursday, $175; Friday and Saturday, $225 double; EP.

OPEN: Year-round

FACILITIES AND ACTIVITIES: Coffeepots, minirefrigerators in rooms. Nearby: historic barn, fields, woods. Short drive to historic attractions, specialty shops, museums, and restaurants of Galena.

*I*t's not often that Midwesterners get to step inside an authentic log cabin. Most have been destroyed by "progress." The few that remain usually belong to local historical societies, and most of these can be viewed only from the outside. That's why these cabins are so special.

One was built in 1865 by a Civil War veteran who came to the booming lead-mine frontier town of Galena to carve a fortune out of the ground. Two other cabins, dating from 1850 to 1860, were found north of Plattville, Wisconsin, dismantled there, then reassembled and restored on this historic homestead. I pulled open the old latch door to the soldier's cabin and found a room dominated by a huge stone hearth, with a massive stone floor covered by a braided rug. A large antique spinning wheel sat in one corner, and black kettles hanging from iron rails hovered over the remains of a toasty fire in the hearth.

Upstairs is a sleeping loft, furnished with two three-quarter-sized rope beds—real pioneer spirit, here. I tried one out, and it actually felt quite comfortable. (Owner Jon Allen explained that it's

all in how the ropes are strung.) A small corner crib adds more sleeping space for babies. Two other cabins are ideal romantic retreats that each accommodate one couple. Their stone fireplaces add to the coziness; so do the upstairs whirlpools.

HOW TO GET THERE: Take U.S. 20 west through Galena to Chetlain Lane and turn left. Go ¼ mile and you'll find the farmstead on the left.

Park Avenue Guest House
Galena, Illinois
61036

INNKEEPERS: Sharon and John Fallbacher

ADDRESS/TELEPHONE: 208 Park Avenue; (815) 777-1075

ROOMS: 4, including 1 suite; all with private bath and air-conditioning, 3 with gas log fireplaces.

RATES: $95, single or double; $125, suite; continental breakfast. Two-night minimum on weekends. Midweek discounts, off-season rates available.

OPEN: Year-round

FACILITIES AND ACTIVITIES: Two parlors, screened porch, gazebo, and Victorian garden. Short walk to Galena historic attractions, shops, and restaurants. Short drive to Dubuque riverboat rides, bluff scenery, Mississippi River.

*H*olidays play an important part at the Park Avenue, especially Christmas, when each room has its own decorated tree, and the house is festooned with more than 200 feet of garlands, 1,400 holiday lights, and 27 window candles.

Guest rooms are charming. The Miriam Room, named for the original owner's daughter, offers Victorian furniture, including a gray iron-rail bed. The Lucille Room is bright and cheery, with a queen-sized iron-rail bed and an Eastlake dresser. Sunlight lovers should choose the Anna Suite, boasting six huge windows, Victorian and Eastlake antiques, and an extra trundle bed.

Sharon and John Fallbacher are proud of their newest room. It's huge, gobbling up the entire back of this spacious house, and lavished with Victorian furnishings, a gas fireplace, and five sunny windows that overlook the inn's fabulous gazebo.

That gazebo, by the way, always elicits questions from guests. "People, especially from Chicago, seem to feel its ornate iron filigree design is familiar," Sharon said. Maybe that's because the gazebo is constructed from cast-iron elevator doors salvaged from the historic Marquette Building in the Windy City.

HOW TO GET THERE: From Dubuque, take U.S. 20 east to Park Avenue, turn left, and continue to the inn.

Pine Hollow Inn
Galena, Illinois 61036

INNKEEPERS: Sally and Larry Priske

ADDRESS/TELEPHONE: 3700 North Council Hill Road; (815) 777-1071

ROOMS: 5; all with private bath and air-conditioning. No smoking inn.

RATES: Weekdays: $95 to $110, single or double; weekends, $105 to $125, single or double; continental breakfast. Two-night minimum on weekends.

OPEN: Year-round

FACILITIES AND ACTIVITIES: Picnic basket lunches available. Dining room, porches. Hiking, birding, wildlife watching. Nearby: Galena Main Street shops, restaurants, historic attractions. Drive to Dubuque for riverboat rides on Mississippi, fishing, museums.

*T*his inn may be one of the best-kept secrets of northwestern Illinois. Located on a 110-acre Christmas tree farm in the heart of Galena's historic lead-mining district, it is a treasure for travelers who want to enjoy the splendor of country living while having Galena's treats only a three-minute drive away down Main Street.

My pa and I turned up Pine Hollow's long driveway, crossed Hughlett's Branch (creek), and stopped near a patch of black walnut trees that surround a picture-perfect country inn. Andy and Molly, a pair of golden retrievers, greeted us with wagging tails.

"Samuel Hughlett owned this valley in Galena's lead-mining heyday," owner Sally Priske explained, "and you can still find some 'sucker holes' in the ground." One old mining hole is now used as a den by coyotes.

In fact, this valley used to be called Hughlett's Bottom, and Sally contemplated that as the name for the inn. "But I decided there'd be too much explaining to do," she said with a chuckle.

Sally and husband Larry planted 9,000 evergreen trees that are ready for the "U-chop" Christmas season (selections include beautifully shaped Scotch and white pines). They originally had planned to build a shed for tree sales, then changed that to a warming hut, and finally settled on a country inn. "I still don't have that shed," Sally said.

This is a landscape and wildlife wonderland, with wild turkeys galore, blue heron, deer, and howling coyotes. Hike the bluffs for panoramic views of the countryside. Or poke around the valley for mining artifacts; an archaeological dig a few years ago turned up some historic items.

I prefer a guided tour with Andy, who beckoned me to follow him up a hill. "Guests have told me he's such a good leader, we should hang up a sign reading GUIDE DOG TOURS EVERY HOUR," Sally said.

Most country-charming guest rooms are huge, with four-poster canopy beds and wood-burning fireplaces. I like Number 3, which also has two skylights. Number 5 offers a beamed ceiling and a claw-footed tub, while Number 2's allure is a large whirlpool bath.

Sally's hearty country breakfast might include blueberry pancakes and sausage, sticky buns, and more.

HOW TO GET THERE: From Dubuque, take U.S. 20 east to Main Street and proceed 1½ miles north (Main Street changes into Dewey) to reach Pine Hollow. Turn left at the sign and continue up the driveway to the inn.

Queen Anne Guest House
Galena, Illinois 61036

INNKEEPERS: Diane Thompson and Frank Checchin

ADDRESS/TELEPHONE: 200 Park Avenue; (815) 777-3849

ROOMS: 5; all with private bath and air-conditioning. No smoking inn.

RATES: $85 to $95, single or double, weekdays; $95 to $125, weekends; continental breakfast. Special multinight and midweek discounts; EPB.

OPEN: Year-round

FACILITIES AND ACTIVITIES: Double parlor, library, video, entertainment room. Short walk to Grant City Park, Main Street shops and restaurants. Nearby: hiking, biking, state park, riverboat rides, horseback riding, skiing, golf.

*T*ucked away on a quiet corner in a residential neighborhood, this gingerbread-crazy showplace is impossible to ignore. Its elaborate turrets, knobs, fretworks, and overhangs combine to create a graceful snapshot of past elegance. Built in 1891 by William Ridd, an Englishman who became a prominent Galena merchant selling window, sash, and door treatments, it served as his showpiece. It seems he put extras everywhere to impress his customers.

A century later "customers" are still impressed. The house is a genuine "Painted Lady," boasting five different colors on its impressive gingerbread. Inside, stained, leaded, and beveled glass is everywhere; oak floors and woodwork lend more elegance; and the home has a very comfortable and relaxed atmosphere—thanks to its two friendly and gracious innkeepers, Diane Thompson and Frank Checchin.

Guest rooms are furnished with handsome antiques by Diane and Frank. "We like to think of the decor as country Victorian," Diane said. Make no mistake—she knows her stuff, as evidenced by her past work in the architectural salvage business. Of course, you might choose the inn's newest room—a grand suite with an inviting whirlpool on the second floor that's been completely refashioned from the traditional innkeeper's rooms.

"This is really going to be special," said Frank, "I can't wait for people to enjoy it."

A full country breakfast is served in the dining room atop a long antique farmer's harvest table that was handmade in Dubuque. But it's not just any breakfast—and sometimes one is served by candlelight. Count on home-baked muffins and breads, fresh fruit plates, juice, coffee, stratas, waffles, casseroles, and more.

HOW TO GET THERE: From Chicago, take the Northwest Tollway (I-90) north to U.S. 20 and go west to Galena. Turn right on Park Avenue (the street before the bridge) and continue to the corner of Park and Adams to the inn.

The Victorian Mansion
Galena, Illinois 61036

INNKEEPER: Robert George McClellan

ADDRESS/TELEPHONE: 301 High Street; (815) 777-0675

ROOMS: 8; all with private bath. No smoking inn.

RATES: $135 to $165, single or double, continental breakfast. Midwinter discount of 20 percent.

OPEN: Year-round

FACILITIES AND ACTIVITIES: Library, dining room, card room with TV. Nearby: historic attractions of Galena, U. S. Grant home, tours of historic houses; art, antiques, and specialty stores.

*I*nnkeeper Robert McClellan led me into his twenty-three-room 1861 Italianate mansion, long a prestigious address for entertaining important guests in this former boomtown along the Fever (Galena) River. We sat down in the library to chat about this incredible inn, furnished and preserved with museum-quality antiques so authentically displayed that it's as if a photograph of the home in the 1860s had come to life.

I noticed soldiers' boots standing next to a tall coatrack and Civil War–era Union Army greatcoats slung over the high backs of elegant chairs in the dining room. That's not surprising, because General Ulysses S. Grant was a confidant of the home's original owner, wealthy smelter Augustus Estey. A group of the general's cronies often gathered to discuss political issues of the day with the cigar-chomping soldier in the very library where Robert and I were sitting.

"See that black grate above you?" Robert asked, pointing to the ceiling. "Estey had that built into his library ceiling to suck cigar smoke out of the air."

Second-floor guest rooms exhibit exquisite antique furnishings. My favorite is the Grant Room, with its invitingly huge walnut bedframe, marble-topped bureau, and deeply colored floral-print carpeting. Robert's collection of antique *Harper's* political caricatures sniping at General Grant hang on the walls.

HOW TO GET THERE: Take U.S. 20 west to High Street and turn left. Go all the way to the top of a steep hill to the mansion, which stands on the left side of the street.

The Herrington Inn
Geneva, Illinois 60134

INNKEEPER: Dan Harrington, general manager

ADDRESS/TELEPHONE: 15 South River Lane; (630) 208-7433

WEB SITE: Herringtoninn.com

ROOMS: 63; all with private bath, whirlpool bath, fireplace, and private balcony or patio.

RATES: $79 to $249, single or double; continental breakfast. Special package rates available.

OPEN: Year-round

FACILITIES AND ACTIVITIES: Full-service dining room, high tea, sitting room, bar, riverside spa, outdoor gazebo-enclosed

whirlpool tub. Nearby: walk to historic town, shops, boutiques, river-walk; rent bikes for river trail rides.

BUSINESS TRAVEL: Located about 1 hour from downtown Chicago. Corporate rates, conference room, fax. Rooms with phone.

"Papa, it's right on the water," Kate said.

"Can we swim in the river, Pa?" asked Dayne.

"Let's go fishing," Kate added.

"Do they have canoes?" Dayne wondered.

I guess the girls liked the location of The Herrington, a handsome inn nestled on the banks of the Fox River. Housed in the restored Geneva Rock Springs Creamery, where milk was kept and chilled along the swift waters of the river in the 1870s, The Herrington is a luxurious day-in-the-country getaway only about one hour west of Chicago's stress-filled hubbub.

Walk inside double doors crested by Palladian windows to a luxurious sitting room, with a fireplace, wing chairs, and nooks and crannies perfect for late-night whispers. An old-fashioned bar is at the far end of the room; you can lounge here until your table is ready for gourmet meals prepared by the inn's chef. Some guest rooms have riverside views; others have courtyard vistas (with glimpses of the rushing waters). If you choose to be on the river, your balcony literally hangs over the water, a great treat for landlocked Midwesterners.

Another treat that the girls really looked forward to was the milk and cookies delivered at the end of the day by the staff. That glass-enclosed riverside gazebo in the middle of the courtyard sports another extra: a large

Swedish Days Fun

Come to Geneva during its annual Swedish Days in June for a family festival that's hard to beat. Colorful tents all over town are filled with artisans' handiwork and great bargains. There are carnival rides for both kids and the young at heart, as well as food galore. There's even a three-on-three basketball tournament for active (and really tall) sorts. Swedish Days offers a great chance to browse among historic Geneva's many boutiques, galleries, and specialty stores. It's one of my favorite Midwest fests.

whirlpool tub that allows you to take its soothing waters under the stars.

HOW TO GET THERE: From Chicago, take the Eisenhower Expressway (I-290) west to I-88 Aurora, exiting at Farnsworth Avenue; go north to Route 38 to the first left past the Fox River Bridge (River Lane).

The Mansion of Golconda
Golconda, Illinois 62938

INNKEEPERS: Don and Marilyn Kunz

ADDRESS/TELEPHONE: Columbus Avenue, P.O. Box 339; (618) 683–4400

ROOMS: 2; both with private bath and air-conditioning.

RATES: $110, single or double; EPB. Special "Room for Romance" package, dinner packages.

OPEN: Year-round, Friday and Saturday, except Christmas Eve and Day. Special package Thursday only.

FACILITIES AND ACTIVITIES: Full-service restaurant with wheelchair access. Lounge with TV, sitting room; patio, gardens. Nearby: a short walk to Ohio River, levee. A short drive to Shawnee National Forest, park, fishing, marina, houseboat and pontoon boat rental. Horseback riding, hiking; cross-country skiing in area during winter.

I wandered down to Ohio River country in southern Illinois, which boasts some of the most beautiful scenery in the Midwest. This historic corner of the state is also rich in legend, from the trailblazing George Rogers Clark expedition to the Ohio River pirates of the 1790s who preyed on flatboats from infamous Cave-in-Rock. Right in the heart of a small river town is The Mansion of Golconda. I was surprised to learn that one of the innkeepers of this 1895 mansion was from my old neighborhood back in Chicago.

Don and Marilyn Kunz have established a tradition of

fine dining and hospitality. The rose, gold, and blue dining rooms, furnished largely with period antiques, set the mood for what Marilyn proudly called "The Mansion's dining experience." In fact, former Illinois governor Jim Thompson dined here several times. "I had a chance to do some show-off cooking," Marilyn said. Another former governor, Jim Edgar, has also enjoyed the inn's cooking. Many diners drive more than 100 miles just to eat here.

Dinner means candlelight and elaborate meals. Selections include sautéed chicken livers, honey-crisp chicken, steaks, and fresh seafood. I recommend catfish Camille, a spicy, grilled touch of heaven; or the shrimp stuffed with cold crabmeat. Marilyn serves dinners on antique china platters, and loaves of steaming-hot bread on rough-hewn breadboards add to the homestyle "flavor" of the meal. You can't push away from the table without trying one of The Mansion's homemade desserts, which are prepared daily. The favorite of the moment: Almond Joy Pie—all custard, milk chocolate, and, of course, almonds.

HOW TO GET THERE: From north, east, and west, follow Illinois 146 into Golconda and turn right after the courthouse.

Sweet Basil Hill Farm ¢¢
Gurnee, Illinois 60031

INNKEEPERS: Bob and Teri Jones

ADDRESS/TELEPHONE: 15397 West Washington Street; (847) 244–3333 or (800) 228–HERB

WEB SITE: sweetbasilhill.com

E-MAIL: BasilHill@aol.com

ROOMS: 2 two-bedroom suites, 1 single room, 1 guest cottage with fireplace; with private bath and air-conditioning.

RATES: $95 to $175, single or double; EPB. No smoking inn.

OPEN: Year-round

FACILITIES AND ACTIVITIES: Large parlor, herb garden, hiking trails. Nearby: Gurnee Mills, Six Flags Great America. A short drive to Lake Michigan, Chain O'Lakes and Illinois Beach State Parks, Long Grove

Historic District, Temple Farms Lipizzans Horse Show, Wauconda Orchards, charter fishing, hike and bike trails, tennis, golf, dog and horse racing, and winter sports.

*Y*ou're the most colorful guests that have visited my sheep in more than two years," owner Bob Jones said to Kate and Dayne as they headed to the barn in their neon-colored ski jackets for a visit with his forty-head flock.

That's why Sweet Basil Hill Farm is one of my girls' favorite getaways—where else can they fuss over lovable barnyard creatures so close to our Chicago home?

Nestled on a hilltop amid seven and a half wooded acres, just 6 miles west of Lake Michigan and halfway between Chicago and Milwaukee, the inn is a wonderful retreat from big-city hassles.

Teri Jones, a photographer, herb lover, and wool spinner, personally greets guests at the door. Step inside and you're in a world of handsome English and American country antiques, gleaming wood floors, 8-foot-tall cupboards and armoires, and wicker rockers and Shaker chairs.

Debbie, my wife, loved our two-room suite, with its Laura Ashley linens, European feather comforters, and antique knickknacks. Daughter Kate found a crystal ball and told our fortunes before we could unpack the suitcases.

The downstairs Basil Room is another favorite, with its Shaker-style pencil-post canopy bed and Amish quilt.

Breakfast in the knotty-pine dining room is like dining inside a North Woods cabin. Seated at a long harvest table, we feasted on chicken, cheese, and broccoli pastry puffs; cinnamon and cranberry rolls; fresh juices; and warm apple-cinnamon dumplings. Then we hiked the back acres to visit with sheep, chickens, and llamas.

Get Bob to tell you the sheep's names (including Johann Sebastian Baa) and the story of how Half Jack got his moniker.

Those llamas (Fernando and Dali) love to rub noses with guests. Kate didn't hesitate going nose-to-nose with Fernando. Dayne waited until she saw that Kate didn't lose anything in the bargain.

Bob, a successful commercial actor, revels in giving tours of the place. That includes hikes to the inn's "hugging tree." "Hug it and you'll have seven years' good luck. Feel silly about it, and you get eleven years," Bob claimed.

The newest inn addition is a two-bedroom English cottage with its own stone fireplace and a flower garden out front. What a way to enjoy a day!

HOW TO GET THERE: From Chicago, take the Tri-State Tollway (I–94) north to the Illinois 132 (Grand Avenue) exit; proceed to Illinois 21, then turn right. Go to Washington Street, turn right, and continue about a half mile. The inn is on the left.

Deer Path Inn
Lake Forest, Illinois 60045

INNKEEPER: Michel Lama, general manager

ADDRESS/TELEPHONE: 255 East Illinois Road; (847) 234–2280 or (800) 788–9480, fax (847) 234–3352

ROOMS: 53, including 32 suites; all with private bath.

RATES: $155 to $195, rooms; $195 to $300, suites, single or double; EPB. Special packages available.

OPEN: Year-round

FACILITIES AND ACTIVITIES: Fine dining, Sunday champagne brunch in the English Room; the Hunt Room, an English-style pub, features jazz pianist entertainment, outdoor garden. Nearby: walk to Market Square, the first planned shopping center in the country; walking tours of Historic District. A short drive to Lake Forest beach, Ravinia Park, Chicago Botanical Garden (in Glencoe), Six Flags Great America.

Though there's been a Deer Path Inn since 1854, the current building made its debut in 1929. It immediately became a hit with Chicago's movers and shakers (who built impressive mansions on

the North Shore) and their visiting guests.

Certainly, the inn (located
in the Historic Market District
of Chicago's toniest suburb)
makes a statement with its
architecture. In fact, L. C. Jones
was sent overseas to study English inn designs; when he
returned he re-created the
ornate Elizabethan style of a
fifteenth-century manor house in Chiddingstone, Kent, complete with its
unusual three-gable roofline. You can see a print of the original Chiddingstone
in the inn's foyer.

The inn's ambience is quiet and sedate, much like that of a select, old-
money European hotel. Fine English period furnishings, antiques, and artifacts (including pewter chandeliers suspended from heavily timbered
ceilings), shining dark woods, stone fireplaces, leaded windows, and rough-
plastered walls elicit a baronial feel of a country manor.

Many of the guest rooms (all named after properties of the National
Trust of England) are oversized, and several are graced with fireplaces. The
inn's signature room, the Cliveden Suite, also has an antique four-poster bed
and whirlpool bath.

The English Room, which looks out onto a formal garden ablaze with
blossoms in spring and summer, offers wonderful gourmet dining, with several constantly changing specialties. Among my favorites is beef Wellington
(done in a puff pastry with bordelaise sauce) and tournedos Dijonais (medallions of beef topped with mustard brown sauce).

Sunday's champagne brunch is an institution in Lake Forest. It includes
choices like eggs Benedict, oysters Rockefeller, and ham with asparagus rolls
in Mornay sauce. Let's not forget the English trifles and profiteroles.

HOW TO GET THERE: From Chicago, take I-94 north to U.S. 41; continue
north and exit east on Deerpath Road; at Green Bay Road, turn south, go to
Illinois Road, and turn east to the inn.

Isle of View Bed and Breakfast
Metropolis, Illinois 62960

INNKEEPERS: Kim and Gerald Offenburger

ADDRESS/TELEPHONE: 205 Metropolis Street; (618) 524–5838

WEB SITE: www.bbonline.com/il/isleofview

ROOMS: 5, with 1 suite; all with private bath featuring claw-foot tub and shower, cable TV, telephones. EPB.

RATES: $65, single or double, weekdays; $75, single or double, weekends; suite, $95 weekdays, $125, weekends.

OPEN: Year-round

FACILITIES AND ACTIVITIES: One block to Players Riverboat Casino; short walk to antiques shops, restaurants, specialty shops, and Superman Square (Metropolis is the "hometown" of Superman). Short ride to Fort Massac State Park; Shawnee National Forest; Paducah, Kentucky; and The Land Between the Lakes.

*T*his 1889 Italianate Manor is one of the most impressive examples of a grand southern Illinois home overlooking the Ohio River and just a short walk to the Players Riverboat Casino. Built by a textile manufacturer who spared no expense for his family, the home's meticulous restoration allows you to revisit these luxuries.

My favorite is the Master Suite, with its king-sized canopy bed facing a coal-burning fireplace. Did I mention there's also a whirlpool for two? The Peach Room boasts Eastlake antiques; I especially like the chestnut armoire. And the Lilac Room—maybe this is my favorite after all, with its seven windows looking toward the Ohio River, Renaissance Revival antiques, and 100-year-old brass bed.

A gourmet breakfast is served in the formal dining room and might include homemade muffins, rolls and breads, fresh fruits and beverages, quiche lorraine, spinach soufflé, and eggs Benedict.

HOW TO GET THERE: Exit I–24 to downtown Metropolis; then turn left on Metropolis Street and continue 3 blocks to the inn, on your right.

Hillendale Bed & Breakfast Inn
Morrison, Illinois 61061

INNKEEPER: Mike and Barb Winandy

ADDRESS/TELEPHONE: 600 West Lincolnway; (815) 772–3454 or (800) 349–7702

WEB SITE:
www.hillend.com

E-MAIL:
hillend@clinton.net

ROOMS: 10; all with private bath. No smoking inn.

RATES: $60 to $160, single or double; EPB.

OPEN: Year-round

FACILITIES AND ACTIVITIES: Dining room, gathering room, billiard room, fitness room, outdoor koi pool, Japanese Teahouse. Nearby: Heritage Canyon (Fulton), Blackhawk Chocolate Trail, Whiteside County antiques, Morrison Rockwood State Park, Albany Indian Burial Mounds, riverboat gambling, Timber Lake Playhouse, Lock and Dam #13.

*E*xotic woods such as ebony, rosewood, and walnut are everywhere. Guest bedchambers are exquisite, and fireplaces abound. Huge whirlpool tubs beckon to romance. Breakfasts are delightful.

But it's the innkeepers, Mike and Barb Winandy, who transform Hillendale into one of the Midwest's most magical getaways. They've traveled the world looking for adventure: Kilimanjaro, Machu Picchu, New Guinea rain forests. They have photos and artifacts to prove it: roaming the African veldt, embracing tribal headhunters, scaling glaciers.

The Winandys share their world-travel bounties by displaying many of their artifacts and photographs in Hillendale's guest rooms. Each allows the visitor to "explore" a different part of the globe. The Jumbo Room recalls the earthy tones of Africa, and includes a zebra-drum nightstand. Another guest room, the Failte, has the feeling of the lush Irish countryside, offering photos from the Winandys' trip around the Ring of Kerry and visits to famous Irish castles. In the Outback Cottage, located behind the main house, Mike displays boomerangs he used to catch game in the desolate Outback regions of Australia.

Warm-weather visitors receive a bonus—a chance to relax at Hillendale's Japanese Teahouse, built by immigrant Sino artisans in the 1930s. The water garden in front of the teahouse contains the inn's Japanese koi collection—colorful Japanese "carp" as big as a muskie, and each potentially worth thousands of dollars.

HOW TO GET THERE: From Chicago, take I-88 west to exit 36 (Clinton—Route 30). Go 11½ miles on Illinois 30 (also known as Lincolnway in Morrison) to Olive Street in the town. Turn right; the semicircle driveway will be on your left.

High Adventure— B&B Style

It's the innkeepers themselves who transform the Hillendale from just another bed-and-breakfast into one of the Midwest's most magical getaways. They've traveled the world together searching for adventure—from the high peaks of Kilimanjaro and Machu Picchu to the lowland rain forests of New Guinea.

Get them to tell you some stories about their experiences—like the time Mike was presented with a 4-foot-tall woodcarving by headhunters in New Guinea. It would be impolite to turn down a gift from these fellows. The only problem was, he had to travel almost eight weeks to get to the nearest village in a small dugout canoe. Then he had a long tramp through the jungle ahead of him before arriving at his final destination.

"I just couldn't take it with me into the jungle," Mike said. "So I asked one of my guides if he'd eventually take the carving into another town and send it home to me in America."

Months passed upon Mike's return home without a hint about the woodcarving. "I never thought I'd see it again," he lamented. Imagine his surprise when the carving finally arrived at the doorstep of his house—two years later!

Living Legacy Homestead
Mt. Carmel, Illinois 62863

INNKEEPER: Edna Schmidt Anderson

ADDRESS/TELEPHONE: RRZ, P.O. Box 146A; (618) 298–2476

ROOMS: 4, 2 with private bath, 2 share bath. No smoking inn. EPB.

RATES: $50 to $70, single or double; senior citizen's discount.

OPEN: Year-round

FACILITIES AND ACTIVITIES: Gathering room with player piano; ten acres of gardens, meadows, lanes, wildlife areas, barnyard; explore outbuildings from historic farmstead. Near Shawnee National Forest.

*T*his historic ten-acre 1870s German homestead, originally a log house, offers you a chance to experience country living, period antiques, and good old relaxation. You can see some of the original timbers inside the home and in the loft, exposed here and there. Or wander outside among the homestead's many gardens, orchards, meadows, lanes, and more.

The farmstead belonged to innkeeper Edna Schmidt Anderson's grandparents, who added on the "modern" farmhouse in 1902. She has lovingly cared for this family treasure, and you can enjoy overnights in one of three guest rooms adorned with period furnishings.

Of course, you can't get away from a German farm without a homestyle country breakfast. It might include everything from fresh baked breads and goodies to eggs, breakfast meats, and pancakes.

HOW TO GET THERE: From St. Louis, take I-64 east to exit 130 at Grayville; then proceed about 10 miles northeast on Illinois Route 1 to the inn.

The Farm Bed and Breakfast
Mt. Carroll, Illinois 61053

INNKEEPERS: Herb and Betty Weinand

ADDRESS/TELEPHONE: 8239 Mill Road; (815) 244–9885

ROOMS: 3, all with private bath, whirlpool tub or hot tub, fireplaces. Continental breakfast.

RATES: $115, single or double, weekdays; $140, single or double, weekends. Two-night minimum on weekends.

OPEN: Year-round

FACILITIES AND ACTIVITIES: Hiking, biking, skiing. Few miles from the Mississippi River, Mt. Carroll's abundance of nineteenth-century architecture. Also a short drive to Timber Lake Playhouse, Clinton Riverboat Casino, eagle watching at Lock & Dam 13, skiing at Palisades State Park and Chestnut Mountain.

*D*on't let the name of this gracious, country B&B fool you—the only animal you're likely to see on The Farm is Ollie, the innkeepers' golden retriever.

This rehabbed 1850s farm is a treasure of country peace and quiet, as you'll see if you read testaments in the inn's guest book. In fact, one guest couple rates The Farm among the top five inns they've stayed in, and that's ranging from the Midwest and South to the East Coast.

You'll see why when you stay here. Try the Barn Spa Suite, in the remodeled 110-year-old red barn, which boasts its own private whirlpool room and fireplace. Another beauty is the Stable, which offers cozy comfort with another bubbling private whirlpool and sunroom. You can even stay in the old chicken coop, now simply called the Coop; today it boasts a cathedral ceiling, a TV/VCR, and a huge wooden hot tub.

Gracious country living as an escape from the city blues—you must be talking about The Farm!

HOW TO GET THERE: The Farm is located about 3 miles south from the Illinois 64 and 78 junction outside Mt. Carroll. Take Illinois 78 to the first gravel road after Timber Lake Playhouse Road, then turn right on Cut Off Road. Go to the gravel road intersection (½ mile) and turn left on Mill Road. The Farm is in sight—the yellow house and the red barn.

Pinehill Bed & Breakfast Inn
Oregon, Illinois 61061

INNKEEPER: Sharon Burdick

ADDRESS/TELEPHONE: 400 Mix Street; (815) 732–2061

ROOMS: 5, including 1 suite; all with private full or half bath and air-conditioning, 3 with fireplaces. No smoking inn.

RATES: $110 to $225, single or double; EPB.

OPEN: Year-round

FACILITIES AND ACTIVITIES: Year-round afternoon tea and tea parties; Sunday ice cream social; picnic basket lunches and dinners available. Sitting room, music room, screened and open porches. Croquet, bocce ball, badminton. Nearby: biking, cross-country skiing, golf, horseback riding, kids' playground, Rock River water activities—fishing, boating, water skiing, water slide. A short drive to three state parks, John Deere Historic Site, Sinissippi Christmas Tree Farm.

My pa couldn't resist innkeeper Sharon Burdick's banana nut muffins, whose mouth-watering aroma filled this mansion atop Jackson Hill. He ate two, then walked off his bounty on the inn's handsome three acres of manicured lawns. Later we explored the 1874 house, built by one of the first merchants in Oregon. I imagined how the home's tall tower once offered panoramic views of the lush Rock River Valley, a prime location for autumn colors.

Walking through the house's huge front doors is like traveling back into the nineteenth century. Floor-to-ceiling windows grace the sitting room; the music room boasts a grand piano engulfed by sheet music and art books covering ballet and modern dance. French silk wallcoverings provide another touch of elegance, and a staircase leading to the guest rooms is highlighted by ostentatious wheel windows with delicate blown glass.

The guest rooms are delightful. The Somerset Maugham Room is named for that man of letters, who often visited Pinehill in the 1930s; he probably enjoyed the wood-burning marble fireplace on chilly nights, though I doubt that the whirlpool tub was around back then. The Emma Lytle Room, named for a former owner, offers a marble fireplace and a Jenny Lind dressing table. It has an unusual cannonball four-poster bed that my girls, on a subsequent stay at this charming inn, found impossible not to bounce on. A family favorite is the two-room Lincoln Suite; kids love to sink into its European double feather bed.

Did I mention Sharon's delicious breakfasts, which might feature freshly baked muffins and crumpets, eggs, breakfast meats, juice, fresh fruits, and two Pinehill specialties—granola pancakes and hazelnut creme coffee?

This is a super inn for kids: Consider weeklong Easter egg hunts, teddy bear teas, ice cream socials, chocolate teas (for adults, too!), storytelling, and more. Adults will enjoy "Artistic Porch" events, featuring working craftspeople and artists demonstrating their talents.

HOW TO GET THERE: From Chicago, take Illinois 64 west into Oregon; then turn right on Mix Street and go up the hill to the house.

Fudge Facts

Sharon is the person most responsible for the development of the regions' "Chocolate Trail." Her Pinehill Gourmet Fudge Collection, an Illinois-homemade selection of exotic delights, featuring flavors like Seattle cappuccino (cinnamon, spices, and espresso) and Mississippi mud (white, milk, and dark chocolate with roasted peanuts), has delighted inn guests. Sharon organized other chocolate fanciers in the area, lobbied the state tourism and travel departments, and blitzed the media with a public relations campaign. Today you can receive a free map of the state's official "Chocolate Trail" highlighting all kinds of choco-treats that stretch through the middle of northern Illinois. And Sharon's fudge concoctions are still number one!

The Oaks
Petersburg, Illinois 62675

INNKEEPERS: Susan and Ken Rodger

ADDRESS/TELEPHONE: 510 West Sheridan; (217) 632–5444

ROOMS: 5, 3 with private bath; 3 share 1 bath. No smoking inn.

RATES: $70 to $130, single or double; EPB.

OPEN: Year-round

FACILITIES AND ACTIVITIES: Library, parlor, two dining rooms, front porch. Short drive to Lincoln's New Salem State Historic Site, Ann Rutledge Grave, Edgar Lee Masters home, canoeing on the Sangamon River. Drive to Springfield for Lincoln Home, Lincoln Tomb, Old State Capitol, Frank Lloyd Wright Dana Thomas House, Governor's Mansion, Washington Park Botanical Gardens, Illinois State Fairgrounds.

*T*he Oaks is nestled on a high bluff overlooking the Petersburg and Sangamon Rivers. If that spectacular view isn't enough, then consider that the elegant B&B is a romantic nineteenth-century Victorian mansion boasting three and a half acres of magnificent oak trees and beautiful gardens. If you need more enticing to come here, note that you can enjoy a candlelit seven-course dinner in the historic dining room.

Need I say more?

I'll let innkeepers Susan and Ken Rodger fill you in on other details. Let me get to the gracious bedchambers. I like the two-room Edward Laning Suite (named for the state senator who once owned this 1875 beauty), with its own fireplace and magnificent view of Petersburg. Another favorite is the period furnishings of the third-floor Olivia's Guest Suite; it's also a great family hideaway. The screened porch and private whirlpool in the Maid's Quarters, secreted away from the Main House, is another delight.

HOW TO GET THERE: From Springfield, follow Illinois 97 north to Petersburg. One block past the town square turn left on Sheridan. The Oaks appears atop the hill 4 blocks ahead. From the north or east, follow Illinois 123 to Petersburg. At the intersection of Illinois 123 and 97, turn left on Illinois 97 and follow for 1 block. Turn right on Sheridan. The Oaks is at the top of the hill, 4 blocks ahead.

The Potter House
Rock Island, Illinois 61201

INNKEEPERS: Frank and Maribeth Skradski

ADDRESS/TELEPHONE: 1906 Seventh Avenue; (800) 747–0339 or (309) 788–1906

ROOMS: 5, including 1 suite; all with private bath, air-conditioning, cable TV, phone. No smoking inn.

RATES: Weekdays, $65 to $85, single or double; weekends, $75 to $95; $100, cottage (for 1–3 days). Two-night minimum on certain weekends. EPB.

OPEN: Year-round

FACILITIES AND ACTIVITIES: Parlor, sitting room, solarium. Horse-drawn carriage rides from inn door. Antique trolley to downtown entertainment and arts district. Nearby: Circa 21 Dinner Theatre, Comedy Sportz club, murder mystery; 6 blocks to the Boatworks, on the Mississippi River, which includes river museum, restaurant on restored tug, and docks for Casino Rock Island high-stakes gambling boat. A short drive to quaint village of East Davenport; a few miles to Iowa low-stakes riverboat gambling ships.

*T*his exceptional inn is a real sleeper. Built in 1907 with elaborate Colonial Revival flourishes, its stucco exterior may appear somewhat ordinary at first glance. But don't be fooled. Inside is an elegant world of stained-glass windows, embossed leather wall covering, and Steuben glass shades; elaborate scrolls, scallops, and filigree; handsome mahogany hardwood; half a dozen fireplaces; even twenty-four-carat-gold "dots" that enhance the inn's huge beveled-glass entry doors.

Frank and Maribeth Skradski, who were innkeepers in historic Gettysburg, Pennsylvania, for seven years before coming here, have lovingly restored this home, which is on the National Register of Historic Places. Guest rooms are particularly beguiling. A huge fireplace is the focal point of Mrs. Potter's Room, the original master bedroom.

Debbie and I stayed in Marguerite's Room, charming quarters featuring unique hand-painted, rag-rolled walls done by Maribeth herself. We loved the huge antique brass bed. And we both were surprised to find an unusual "hat cupboard" inside the closet. Marguerite, who lived in this room for nearly fifty years, was very fond of her bonnet collection, we were told.

The innkeepers both lavish attention on guests at breakfast in the handsome dining room, a grand setting with its rich mahogany paneling. It might include an egg dish, breakfast meats, French toast, and pancakes. Be sure to take a peek at the former caretaker's house, now available for cozy overnights; the 1890s structure has handsome Mission-style furniture and its own living room, dining room, and full kitchen.

HOW TO GET THERE: From the east or west, take I–280 to Illinois 92; go northeast toward downtown Rock Island. (Note that the Mississippi River here runs east and west.) Take the Eighteenth Avenue exit; go east to a five-point intersection (Eighteenth, Seventeenth, and Twentieth Streets); turn left on the far side of the stone bell tower onto Twentieth Street; continue to Seventh Avenue, turn left, and continue to the inn.

The Hotel Baker 💙
St. Charles, Illinois 60174

INNKEEPER: Keith Sennstrom

ADDRESS/TELEPHONE: 100 West Main Street; (630) 584–2100, fax (630) 443–0795

WEBSITE: www.hotelbaker.com

ROOMS: 54; all with private bath, air-conditioning.

RATES: $179 to $199 rooms, single or double; $229 to $399, suites; $600 penthouse.

OPEN: Year-round

FACILITIES AND ACTIVITIES: Complimentary morning coffee, weekday newspapers; fitness area, lobby/lounge. Restaurant serves breakfast, lunch, and dinner. Located on the Fox River; lounge chairs, gardens, and riverwalk. Walk outside and shop at downtown boutiques, art galleries, and specialty stores.

*T*he Hotel Baker sits like a sentinel on the banks of the Fox River, a stunning Spanish Baroque piece of architecture that harks back to a time when St. Charles was a bustling town of commerce and a rising pleasure destination. The centerpiece was the hotel, built in 1928 by Col. Edward J. Baker, whose name today graces many places in this charming river town.

The colonel set out to build the "Gem of the Fox Valley" back in the 1920s. He succeeded mightily. Immediately upon opening, the hotel became so popular, especially among newlyweds, that it was known as the "Honeymoon Hotel." Celebrities like actress Mary Martin, politicians John F. Kennedy and Gerald Ford, even evangelist Billy Graham have stayed here.

And now you.

It's still a showcase, renovated in 1997 to its former splendor. Listed on the National Register of Historic Places, the hotel offers stunning, simply elegant guest rooms featuring stylish and expensive furnishings with all the ambience of a luxurious European-style hostelry. Suites boast whirlpool baths, balconies, and some with river views. For the ultimate in romance and luxury, treat yourself to the penthouse experience; you'll have to see it for yourself—I'm not spoiling it for you.

The hotel's Trophy Room restaurant boasts Mediterranean cuisine that's exotic and delicious. On our stay there, my wife, Debbie, enjoyed wild mushroom–stuffed ravioli, while I tried lemon-butter swordfish on a bed of couscous. There's riverside alfresco dining, too. After dinner, we browsed some of the boutiques that line downtown streets near the river.

All in all, it was a time of quiet elegance that was soothing to the soul.

The Wheaton Inn ♥
Wheaton, Illinois 60187

INNKEEPER: Dennis Stevens

ADDRESS/TELEPHONE: 301 West Roosevelt Road; (630) 690–2600 or (800) 447–4667.

WEB SITE: WheatonInn.com

ROOMS: 16; all with private bath and air-conditioning, some with Jacuzzi. Wheelchair accessible.

RATES: $145 to $225, single or double; EPB. Weekend packages.

OPEN: Year-round

FACILITIES AND ACTIVITIES: Patio, lawn area with croquet course and gardens, sitting room, dining area. Nearby: McCormick's Cantigny war museum, Prairie Path hike and bike trail; Herrick Lake paddle boating and fishing; Wheaton Water Park; Fox River and Geneva famous shopping districts; horseback riding; Morton Arboretum; Wheaton College's Billy Graham Center; golf courses; tennis courts; polo grounds. Also a short drive to Drury Lane Theatres.

BUSINESS TRAVEL: Located about 30 miles west of Chicago. Corporate rates, conference rooms, fax.

I enjoy The Wheaton Inn because it weaves so well today's sophistication with yesterday's elegance. The inn, completed in 1987, relies on opulence in the Colonial Williamsburg tradition for its distinctive flair.

Guest rooms are named after famous Wheaton citizens. Eleven have gas fireplaces, many boast Jacuzzi tubs, and each has an elegantly distinctive personality. All have European towel warmers in their bathrooms—another thoughtful touch, especially for travelers who venture out in Chicago winters.

Rooms have oversized styles often found in European concierge hotels. The Woodward Room is one of my favorites, with its Jacuzzi situated in front of a large bay window that overlooks the inn's gardens. The fireplace marble came from the face of Marshall Field's department store in downtown Chicago. (By the way, the room's namesake, Judge Alfred Woodward, is the father of newspaperman Bob Woodward, who broke the Watergate scandal for the *Washington Post* along with Carl Bernstein.)

Vaulted ceilings in the third-floor McCormick Room, along with its huge four-poster bed and windows overlooking the garden, make this another guest favorite. In fact, the mayor of Nairobi, Kenya, chose to stay in this room on a visit to the Chicago area. Another charmer is the Morton Room, with its alcoved ceiling, cozy fireplace, and 4½-foot-deep Jacuzzi, perfect for guests who yearn for a relaxing soak.

Especially romantic nights can be yours in the Rice Room, where a Jacuzzi sits almost in the middle of the room, in front of a fireplace, and two skylights let you gaze at the stars above.

Only the Ottoson Room, named after the inn's architect, departs from the Williamsburg theme. A brass-topped, black iron-rail bed is dwarfed by cathedral ceilings that harbor a skylight.

In a cheery, window-lit breakfast room, guests enjoy the innkeeper's

European-style buffet of imported coffee and teas, hot egg dishes, seasonal fruits, and delicious pastries and muffins. Personal service is a trademark here, so expect amenities like afternoon cheese and crackers, freshly baked cookies and milk, twenty-four-hour coffee, and bedtime turndown service with chocolate treats left on your pillow.

HOW TO GET THERE: From Chicago, take I–294 to Roosevelt Road, then go west to the inn.

Select List of Other Inns in Illinois

Westerfield House Bed & Breakfast
8059 Jefferson Road
Freeburg, IL 62243
(618) 539–5643

Eagle Ridge Inn & Resort
444 Eagle Ridge Drive
Galena, IL 61036
(815) 777–2444
(800) 892–2269

Eagle's Nest
410 South High Street
Galena, IL 61036
(815) 777–8400

Pere Marquette Lodge
Route 100
P.O. Box 429
Grafton, IL 62037
(618) 786–2331
fax (618) 786–3498

Forget-Me-Not Bed and Breakfast
1467 North Elizabeth Scale
Mound Road
Elizabeth, IL 61028
(815) 858–3744

White Lace Inn
204 West Poplar Street
Harrisburg, IL 62946
(618) 252–7599

The Homeridge
1470 North State Street
Jerseyville, IL 62052
(618) 498–3442

Standish House Bed & Breakfast
540 West Carroll Street
Lanark, IL 61046
(815) 493–2307

Corner George Inn
Mill and Main Streets
Maeystown, IL 62256
(618) 458-6660
(800) 458-6020

Old Squat Inn
14242 Liberty School Road
Marion, IL 62959
(618) 982-2916

The Poor Farm B&B
Poor Farm Road
Mount Carmel, IL 62863-9803
(613) 262-4663
(800) 646-3276

Hotel Nauvoo
1290 Mulholland
Nauvoo, IL 62354
(217) 453-2211

Mississippi Memories Bed & Breakfast
1 Riverview Terrace
Nauvoo, IL 62354
(217) 453-2771

Under the Ginkgo Tree Bed & Breakfast
300 North Kenilworth Avenue
Oak Park, IL 60302
(708) 524-2327

Wright's Cheney House Bed & Breakfast
520 North East Avenue
Oak Park, IL 60302
(708) 524-2067

Wildlife Prairie Park
3826 North Taylor Road
Peoria, IL 61615-9617
(309) 676-0998
Lodging; no meals.

Lithia Log Village
RR4, P.O. Box 109K
near Lake Shelbyville
Shelbyville, IL 62565
(217) 774-2701
Log cabins.

The Shelby Historic House & Inn
816 West Main Street
Shelbyville, IL 62565
(217) 774-3991
(800) 342-9978

The Little House on the Prairie B&B
RR2, Patterson Road
Sullivan, IL 61951
(217) 728-4727

Starved Rock Lodge
Routes 71 and 178
Utica, IL 61373
(815) 667-4211

Chateau des Fleurs
552 Ridge Road
Winnetka, IL 60093
(847) 256-7272

Indiana

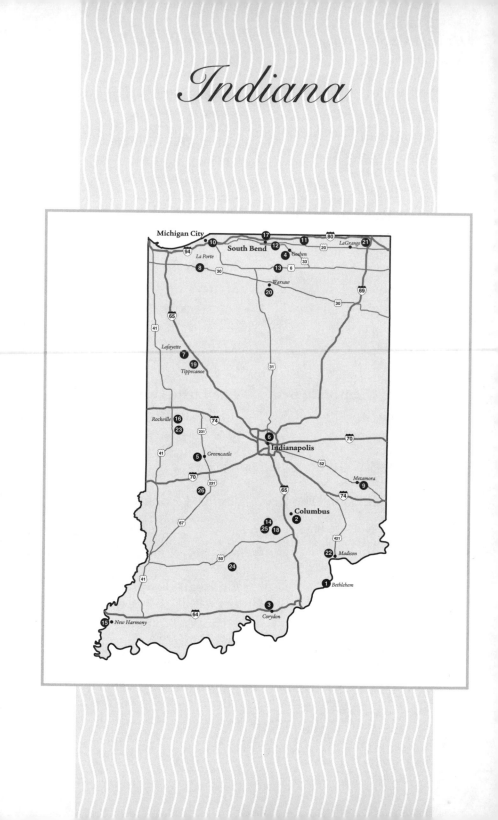

Indiana

Numbers on map refer to towns numbered below

*A Top Pick Inn

The Inn at Bethlehem
Bethlehem, Indiana 47104

INNKEEPER: Gloria Childers

ADDRESS/TELEPHONE: 101 Walnut Street; (812) 293–3975

ROOMS: 10, with 1 suite; all with private bath, air-conditioning.

RATES: $90 to $200. EPB.

OPEN: Year-round

FACILITIES AND ACTIVITIES: 26 acres to explore, bicycles on premises, antiquing along country roads.

Wandering twenty-six acres on a blufftop overlooking the Ohio River is a wonderful way to spend any weekend. It's even better when you can relax after your exploits at an historic inn that features gourmet-style meals.

That's all part of the experience at this 1830 Federal-style retreat that has seen a varied history that includes everything from a stint as a jail to a stop on the famed Underground Railroad.

Period antiques abound, but the real treat might be the gourmet meals provided by innkeeper. Imagine feasting on the likes of a saffron shrimp bisque, bourbon pecan chicken, beef tenderloin in Merlot sauce, and more.

Of course, after your meal, stake your claim to one of the inn's many rocking chairs for some after dinner conversation.

HOW TO GET THERE: From Indianapolis, take Interstate 65 South to the Scottsburg exit, then go east on Highway 56 to Highway 62; go west on 62 to New Washington. At New Washington–Bethlehem Road, proceed 6 to 8 miles—the road goes directly to the inn's driveway.

The Columbus Inn
Columbus, Indiana 47201

INNKEEPER: Paul Staublin

ADDRESS/TELEPHONE: 445 Fifth Street; (812) 378–4289

ROOMS: 34, including 5 suites; all with private bath, air-conditioning, TV, and phone. Wheelchair accessible.

RATES: $90, single; $100, double; $120 to $190, suites; EPB.

OPEN: Year-round

FACILITIES AND ACTIVITIES: Afternoon teas and sumptuous buffet breakfasts. Columbus is self-proclaimed "architectural showplace of America"—50 significant contemporary works in one of the richest, most concentrated collections anywhere. Horse-and-buggy tours of town stop at inn's front door. Historic district tour map provided upon arrival. City's Visitor Center across the street. Walk or drive to restaurants.

*D*on't fight city hall. Just sleep in it. This huge 1895 Romanesque brick building with its tall bell tower served as the city's seat of government for almost one hundred years. When it fell deserted, it seemed too august to simply demolish.

A Pittsburgh-based development company that specializes in historic preservation and restoration purchased the building in 1985, and the result is one of the most unusual and elegant inns around. In fact, *Time* magazine said that "a sense of quality has rubbed off all over Columbus."

Just stepping into the long entry hall is like entering an earlier era of elegance and gentility. Ornately embossed tin ceilings, hand-carved oak

Architectural Wonders

It's hard for some people to believe that this tiny town in south-central Indiana could be one of the architectural showplaces of the United States, but it's true. Wander the town (better yet, get a free pamphlet from the chamber of commerce) to see more than fifty significant contemporary works designed by some of the most notable architects in the country, including I. M. Pei, who is responsible for the pyramid addition to the Louvre in Paris.

In fact, Columbus's roster of world-class artisans reads like a "Who's Who" of contemporary architects, designers, and sculptors.

woodwork, and original Victorian terra-cotta floors are graced with Victorian and Gothic love seats, huge brass chandeliers, and mahogany claw-footed banquet tables.

Guest rooms are magnificently furnished, with handsome teal or peach wall coverings and American Empire antique reproductions fashioned in France. I especially like the cherrywood sleigh beds and second-floor rooms with floor-to-ceiling windows.

Most spectacular is the Charles Sparrell Suite (named for the architect of the old city hall), a stunning 1,200-square-foot chamber that you reach by ascending twenty-seven steps. It has 21-foot ceilings, 12-foot-tall windows, a sleeping loft (that's seventeen more steps), a second bedroom on the lower level hidden by mirrored French doors, and two and a half baths.

I forgot to mention the large Victorian parlor furnished in fine antiques.

Breakfast in the handsomely restored lower level means a stylized buffet that might include fresh fruits and juices, homemade pumpkin bread, English muffins, apple and cherry strudel, egg casseroles with meat and cheeses, fresh vegetables, and New Orleans–style bread pudding served piping hot.

The inn offers English-style afternoon tea daily from 11:00 A.M. to 6:00 P.M. But high tea, beginning at 4:00 P.M., is the most special treat with its authentic scones and other goodies.

If you still have an appetite for dinner, innkeeper Paul Staublin or his staff will recommend several good restaurants.

HOW TO GET THERE: From Indianapolis, follow U.S. 31 south into Columbus and turn south on Washington Street. At Fourth Street, turn west, then go north on Franklin Street to the inn.

Kinter House Inn
Corydon, Indiana 47112

INNKEEPER: Mary Jane Bridgewater

ADDRESS/TELEPHONE: 201 South Capitol Avenue; (812) 738-2020

ROOMS: 15, with 4 suites; all with private bath, air-conditioning, and phone. No smoking inn.

RATES: $59 to $99, single or double, Friday and Saturday; $49 to $79, Sunday through Thursday; EPB.

OPEN: Year-round

FACILITIES AND ACTIVITIES: Parlor, sitting room, porch. Nearby: Old Capitol building, Old Capitol Square antiques and crafts shops, art galleries, restaurants, Hayswood Theatre. Short drive to historic buildings, Battle of Corydon Civil War Site, historic Branham Tavern, Squire Boone Caverns and Village, Blue River canoeing, Marengo Cave Park, Wyandotte Caves, and Harrison-Crawford State Forest.

*I*n 1837 Jacob Kinter opened the doors of the Kinter House as Corydon's finest hotel. Today it remains the historic village's best hostelry and one of the most handsome inns in the Midwest. Old-fashioned hospitality is the hallmark of this carefully restored National Historic Landmark. From the rockers on the front porch to the fine period antiques gracing guest rooms named after historic Corydon figures, you're treated in first-class style.

Many guest room antiques are museum quality. The Josiah Lincoln Suite (named for Abe's uncle, who was a frequent guest here) boasts an 8-foot walnut headboard from circa 1800 and a marble-topped walnut dresser hand-carved in an elaborate grapevine design.

In the Governor's Room (named for Jonathan Jennings, the state's first chief

executive, who toiled for an annual salary of $1,000), an 1850 four-poster walnut-and-mahogany bed with intricate leaf hand carvings is magnificent.

Yet my two favorites remain the huge Squire Boone Room (Squire Boone was an early explorer and brother of Daniel), with its pencil-post cherry beds, plank floor, and exquisite inlaid star-pattern game table; and the President William Henry Harrison Room (Harrison, a onetime landowner here, was personally known by every citizen of early Corydon), with its 1880 hand-carved mahogany grapevine dresser that looks as though it belongs in the Smithsonian. (The claw-footed mahogany shaving stand would also be mighty handy for trimming mustaches like mine.)

Third-floor guest rooms reflect an Early American theme, with plank floors, brass beds, and antique quilts.

The inn's homemade breakfast treats are legion. The meal might include goodies like ham-and-egg puffs, sausage cheese grits, cocoa banana bread, and Sock-It-to-Me Cake (a house specialty).

HOW TO GET THERE: From Indianapolis, take I–65 south to I–64, go west to Indiana 135 (exit 105), then south to Indiana 62; turn east on Indiana 62, following that road to the inn at Capitol Avenue and Columbus Street.

The Checkerberry Inn ♥
Goshen, Indiana 46528

INNKEEPERS: John and Susan Graff, owners; Kelly Graff, general manager

ADDRESS/TELEPHONE: 62644 County Road 37; (219) 642-4445

WEB SITE: checkerberryinn.com

ROOMS: 14, including 3 suites; all with private bath and air-conditioning. Wheelchair access. No smoking.

RATES: Sunday through Thursday, $112 to $260; Friday and Saturday, $140 to $375; single or double; continental breakfast. Three-course dinner available.

OPEN: February through December.

FACILITIES AND ACTIVITIES: Full-service dining room, swimming pool, arbor, croquet course, tennis court, hiking trails, cross-country ski area. In the midst of Amish farmlands; offers horse-drawn buggy tours of Amish surroundings, sleigh rides in winter. Near Shipshewana auctions, Middlebury festivals.

" We wanted to create a European feel to the inn," owner Susan Graff said. "After all, being surrounded on all sides by Amish farmlands is more than enough country ambience." The fine appointments of this northern Indiana inn do remind me of intimate, elegant European hotels I've stayed at. In fact, the handsome photographs adorning the inn walls were taken by John, Susan's husband and the inn's co-owner, during his travels in the French Bordeaux region.

Amish straw hats hang over beds, lending a nice regional touch to luxurious guest rooms that boast fine art prints, furniture with a definite European flair, wide windows that allow views of the rolling countryside, and amenities like Swiss goat's milk soap in the baths. Rooms are named for

flowers; my favorite is Foxglove, with its whirlpool bath, sitting room fireplace, and six windows.

Queen Anne's Lace is another handsome room; its most interesting fea-

ture is a primitive secretary, made in the 1850s. It consists of 1,200 individual pieces, and it took three years to complete. Its geometric designs put that craftsman far ahead of his time.

The inn's restaurant leans toward country French and contemporary cuisine. Three-course meals begin with a fresh garden salad, followed by a fresh fruit sorbet, entree, and dessert. An inn specialty is double duck breast sautéed and served over sweet onions, topped with an orange and port wine sauce, accompanied by pommes Anna and a bouquet of fresh vegetables. The vegetables, herbs, and spices are grown specially for the inn. Other favorites include chicken basil, veal medallions, and rack of lamb served off the bone with herb cream-and-garlic cheese. Note that the menu changes frequently.

The inn sits on one hundred acres, so there's plenty of quiet and relaxation. It's just a walk through French doors to the swimming pool, and the woods offer numerous hiking trails. The inn provides Indiana's only professional croquet course, so now is the time to perfect your game.

HOW TO GET THERE: From Chicago, take the Indiana Toll Road (I–80/90) to the Middlebury exit (107). Go south on Indiana 13, turn west on Indiana 4, then go south on County Road 37 to the inn. It's 14 miles from the toll road exit to the inn.

European Flair in Amish Country

Debbie and I were quite taken with the Checkerberry Inn. After all, we had been driving for hours exploring the nooks and crannies of Indiana's Amish country before we stumbled upon this country inn delight. At first we thought it might be a mirage, so European was the ambience that we felt as we gazed at the structure. Then we felt as if we were dreaming as we walked inside, discovering how similar it was to some of the boutique hotels we frequented in both Paris and Zurich. But the Amish straw hats over the beds brought us back to the good old USA—and just in time for a great dinner at the inn's restaurant.

Seminary Place
Greencastle, Indiana 46135

INNKEEPER: Mary Tesmer

ADDRESS/TELEPHONE: 210 East Seminary Place; (765) 653-3177

ROOMS: 4, all with private bath. Continental breakfast. No smoking inn.

RATES: $75 to $115, single; $85 to $125, double. Two-night minimum on graduation weekends.

OPEN: Year-round

FACILITIES AND ACTIVITIES: Formal parlor, small kitchen area open to guests; also upstairs parlor area for guests. Complimentary coffee, tea, popcorn. Short drive to DePauw University campus.

his Victorian-style, 1887 Queen Anne inn is a pleasant surprise in this charming college town (home to DePauw University). In fact, the surprises start immediately in the greeting parlor, where innkeeper Mary Tesmer displays museum-quality antique musical instruments. My favorites were a Swiss music box, which reminded me of my frequent travels to that beautiful country, and a rare Cobb organ that plays old-fashioned musical cylinders (which resemble corn-on-the-cob; hence the name).

Guest quarters are another surprise, filled with all sorts of precious antiques. I, like many visitors, like the Gables best. This third-floor room boasts not only an 1880 Queen Victoria bed but also a two-person whirlpool done in marble and nestled beneath a dormer window.

Breakfast continues the string of surprises, with a selection of mouth-watering, homemade breads, delicious muffins, coffee cakes dripping with sweet icing, and seasonal fruit bowls.

HOW TO GET THERE: From Indianapolis, take I–70 west to Highway 23 north (the Green Castle/Cloverdale exit). Continue into Greencastle, past the town park, to Seminary Street. Turn left, and go 3 blocks to the grey, three-story Victorian inn.

Walden Inn of Greencastle
Greencastle, Indiana 46135

INNKEEPER: Matthew O'Neil

ADDRESS/TELEPHONE: 2 Seminary Square; (765) 653–2761

ROOMS: 55, with 3 suites; all with private bath, air-conditioning, phone, and TV. Wheelchair accessible.

RATES: $70 to $85, single; $80 to $95, double; $120 to $130, suites; EP. Two-night minimum on DePauw University parents' weekend, graduation weekend, and other special events weekends.

OPEN: Year-round except Christmas Day.

FACILITIES AND ACTIVITIES: Full-service restaurant, handsome sitting room and library, bar; short walk to DePauw University events, attractions.

From Dublin, Ireland, Matt O'Neil is a classically trained European chef who doubles as the innkeeper. The meals he now prepares have roots in indigenous American regional cooking but also reflect touches of his classical continental background.

He is especially proud of his Cape scallops, which he calls "absolutely the world's finest," served in cream and saffron sauce or sautéed with dill or raspberry butter. Another specialty is loin of lamb, wrapped in a puff pastry with duxelles of mushrooms and spinach. Then there's Chicken Pecan—a boneless chicken breast breaded with  Dijon mustard, coated with chopped pecans, and sautéed—served with della nonna sauce and a rainbow of vegetables.

Is it any wonder people drive hours to dine at Matt's gourmet table?

Guest rooms are bright and comfortable, featuring furnishings with simple Queen Anne lines built by Amish craftsmen of northern Ohio. Bedspreads are handmade by Wisconsin craftswomen. There's also a flower box outside almost every window. One of my favorite rooms is in the Cole Porter Suite, which has a fireplace and canopy bed.

HOW TO GET THERE: From Indianapolis, take I-70 west to U.S. 231. Go north into Greencastle. At Seminary Street (a green sign signals directions to DePauw University), turn left and go 4 blocks to the inn.

Dessert Delights

Did I mention Matt's dessert specialty? It's Fair Queen Chocolate Pie, made with brandied raisins and orange zest, or strawberries with caramel and bourbon sauce.

The Canterbury Hotel 📱
Indianapolis, Indiana 46225

INNKEEPER: Letitia Moscrip, manager

ADDRESS/TELEPHONE: 123 South Illinois; (800) 538-8186 or (765) 634-3000

ROOMS: 84, with 15 suites; all with private bath, some with whirlpools.

RATES: $125 to $175; $175 to $250, suites. EPB.

OPEN: Year-round

FACILITIES AND ACTIVITIES: All meals are available in hotel restaurant. Guests have access to two nearby fitness centers. Limousine, concierge, and 24-hour room service. Free newspaper with continental breakfast. Near all downtown attractions of Indianapolis, including Benjamin Harrison Home, Children's Museum of Indianapolis, Conner Prairie, Eagle Creek Park and Nature Preserve, Eiteljorg Museum of American Indian and Western Art, Hoosier Dome, Indianapolis Motor Speedway.

You probably guessed from the name that the Canterbury Hotel prides itself on English roots. Indeed, the historic hotel opened in 1928 as the Lockerbie, with the Duke of Canterbury, himself, attending the festivities.

Today the elegant hotel carries on its traditions in fine fashion. Guest rooms feature Chippendale furnishings, whirlpool baths, marble water closets, brass adornments—even English hunting prints on the walls.

You can always count on English high tea at the Canterbury, with scones, finger sandwiches, and European desserts part of the elegant ceremony.

HOW TO GET THERE: From the north, take I-65 south into Indianapolis; exit at Illinois. Proceed south to hotel.

Stone Soup Inn
Indianapolis, Indiana 46202

INNKEEPER: Jeneane Life

ADDRESS/TELEPHONE: 1304 North Central Avenue; (317) 639–9550

WEB SITE: www.stonesoupinn.com

ROOMS: 7, 5 with private bath, 2 rooms share one; all with TV/VCR. No smoking inn.

RATES: $85 to $135, single or double; EPB weekends only.

OPEN: Year-round

FACILITIES AND ACTIVITIES: Large gathering foyer includes baby grand piano; front garden with lily pond. Airport pick-up and drop-off available. Located within minutes of Circle Centre Mall, Indianapolis Convention Center, and other Indianapolis attractions.

I'm told that in the classic children's story "Stone Soup," three weary travelers come upon a small village whose inhabitants are wary of strangers and pretend to be in need themselves. So the travelers convince the townies that they can make soup out of stones. The townspeople are fascinated by this claim, and each slowly adds a hidden cache of food to the concoction, making a wonderful soup that the villagers and travelers enjoy together.

The Stone Soup Inn carries on this theme of hospitality to travelers. Located in the heart of the historic Old Northside, the 1901 Colonial Revival building boasts both Mission-style and Victorian antiques, as well as four charming guest rooms. The Craftsman Room is an Arts and Crafts delight, with a full-sized Mission-style bed, vanity, and dresser that'll take you back in time.

Other guest chambers include the Victorian Room, with its tiled fireplace; Lily's Room, overlooking the inn's lily pond and offering a two-person

Speaking in Tongues

Jeneane Life welcomes international travelers in a very special way. She speaks both German and Japanese, and she'll arrange assistance for guests who speak other non-English tongues.

Jacuzzi; and the Blue Room, featuring a 6-foot-high antique Victorian bed, tiled fireplace, and steam shower.

The inn's Butler's Pantry is stocked with all kinds of complimentary snacks and goodies.

HOW TO GET THERE: From the north, take I-65 south to the Meridian Street exit, which turns into Eleventh Street; continue to Delaware and turn left; go 2 blocks to Thirteenth Street, then turn right and go 3 blocks to the inn.

Loeb House Inn 🖤
Lafayette, Indiana 47901

INNKEEPER: Dick Nagel

ADDRESS/TELEPHONE: 708 Cincinnati Street; (317) 420-7737

WEB SITE: www.qklink.com/loebinn

ROOMS: 5; all with private bath. No smoking inn.

RATES: $85 to $175. EPB.

OPEN: Year-round

FACILITIES AND ACTIVITIES: Formal parlor, dining room, meeting room. Museums, theaters, and restaurants a short drive away, as are Columbian Park (swimming, rides, petting zoo), wolf park, historic Fort Ouiatenon, the Tippecanoe battlefield. Just across the river lies Purdue University, including the concert site of Elliot Hall of Music.

A grain dealer from New York City built the Loeb House in 1882; soon thereafter the Loeb family took possession. You can see the standards that family demanded in their residence: exquisite chandeliers, parquet floors, plaster ceiling medallions—and a grand staircase now leading up to second-floor rooms.

Carrie's Retreat is the inn's showcase bedchamber. It offers an elegant antique double bed, fireplace, bay window, original wallpaper—and a two-person whirlpool. The Pomegranate Room is pure Victorian with its rich reds, parquet floors; and then there's the fireplace and whirlpool tub to chase away all your stresses. And the East Room, sponge-painted in periwinkle blues, offers beautiful morning light—as well as a whirlpool and fireplace.

Breakfasts mean fresh fruits, homemade muffins, and breads and pastries, all made on the premises. And once you have indulged yourself, it's time to explore the town.

HOW TO GET THERE: Take I-65 to the Lafayette exit 172, State Road 26. Turn left and continue to 6th Street; turn left (north) and go to Cincinnati; turn right and proceed to the inn.

Arbor Hill Inn
La Porte, Indiana 46350

INNKEEPERS: Laura Kobat, Kris Demoret, Mark Wedow

ADDRESS/TELEPHONE: 263 Johnson Road; (219) 362–9200

ROOMS: 7, with 4 suites; also 1 cottage; all with private bath, telephone, cable TV, and central air-conditioning. EPB. No smoking inn.

RATES: $109 to $199, single or double. Special Midweek Shopping Getaway rates available.

OPEN: Year-round

FACILITIES AND ACTIVITIES: Parlor with fieldstone hearth; second-floor guest terrace. Short drive to La Porte Lakes for fishing, boating, cruises; specialty and antique shops; Lighthouse Outlet Mall; Lake Michigan; about a 30-minute drive to Notre Dame University.

BUSINESS FACILITIES: Meeting room, business support services, corporate rates.

*T*his handsome inn is located under a welcoming canopy of majestic trees, a harbinger that a time of peaceful relaxation is at hand. The 1910 Greek Revival structure boasts many special turn-of-the-century touches, including a second-story terrace perfect for savoring cooling summer breezes.

Another guest favorite is the Victory Garden bedchamber, a massive suite with its king-sized white iron bed, whirlpool bath, and see-through fireplace. I also like the Lady of the Lake, with its queen sleigh bed, cobblestone fireplace, and whirlpool. Or you might like the Jones Retreat, the house's premier suite, with a king brass bed, original fieldstone fireplace, cathedral ceilings, and oversized bath with whirlpool.

Evenings at the inn feature complimentary appetite teasers. You can bring along your own favorite wine. And there's a full breakfast of all kinds of down-home country goodies waiting for you in the morning.

HOW TO GET THERE: Exit either I–94 or I 80/90 at Indiana 35; proceed east to Johnson Road and turn west (right), continuing to the inn.

The Thorp House
Metamora, Indiana 47030

INNKEEPERS: Mike and Jean Owens

ADDRESS/TELEPHONE: Clayborne Street; (765) 647–5425 or (888) 427–7932

ROOMS: 5, including 1 suite; all with private bath.

RATES: $70, single or double; $125, suite; EPB.

OPEN: April through mid-December.

FACILITIES AND ACTIVITIES: Full-service restaurant and five craft shops on first floor. Nearby: more than 100 fine arts, crafts, and specialty stores; historic houses; old gristmill; canal boat rides, excursions on the Whitewater Valley Railroad.

he Thorp House is an original 1840 canal home transformed into a delightful inn by Mike and Jean Owens. (A unique treat: Arrive in Metamora via the scenic route aboard the steam-powered Whitewater Valley Railroad, and the innkeepers will pick you up in a horse and buggy for a ride back to the inn.)

Five guest rooms (all named for the innkeepers' first paternal Indiana settler ancestors) are country-cozy, dotted with crafts, dried flower bouquets, and antiques. My favorites: the William Rose Room, with stenciled walls, country quilt on the bed, and a window view of the canal; and Shedric Owens, boasting an antique pie-safe dresser. The inn's suite is very popular with

guests. Its two spacious rooms are graced with the heirloom furniture used by Jean's grandmother when she set up housekeeping more than seventy years ago.

Breakfast is an all-you-can-eat affair, with selections from the inn's regular menu. "We just fill up the plates, and if you want more, we'll fill 'em up again and again," Jean said. That's quite generous, considering that selections might include everything from homemade biscuits and sausage gravy and egg and cheese casseroles to French toast, Belgian waffles, black raspberry pie, and sourdough pecan rolls.

HOW TO GET THERE: From Indianapolis, take I-74 east to the Batesville exit, then proceed north on Indiana 229 to Metamora. Cross the canal footbridge to Clayborne and the inn.

Canal Capers

Whenever I come to the Thorp House and this history-laden town, which looks much like it did more than 150 years ago (clapboard-covered buildings, log cabins, and general stores lining the narrow Whitewater Canal, which originally stretched 76 miles between Hagerstown and Metamora to Lawrenceburg), I cannot resist a ride on the *Ben Franklin III*, the town's horse-drawn canal boat. It carries visitors over the only operating aqueduct in the country to an authentic canal lock.

I also can't resist giving the horses, Tony and Rex, a pat on their muzzles for a job well done.

Creekwood Inn
Michigan City, Indiana 46360

INNKEEPER: Mary Lou Linnen

ADDRESS/TELEPHONE: Route 20/35 at I-94; (219) 872-8357

WEB SITE: creekwoodinn.com

ROOMS: 13, including 1 suite; all with private bath and air-conditioning. Wheelchair accessible.

RATES: $130 to $155, single; $140 to $165, double. Rates increase during high season weekends and holidays; however, special midweek rates. Continental breakfast.

OPEN: Year-round except two weeks in mid-March and Christmas Day.

FACILITIES AND ACTIVITIES: Hearty breakfast and dinner on Friday and Saturday are available. A short drive to southeastern shore of Lake Michigan, Indiana Dunes State Park, Warren Dunes State Park in Michigan. Charter fishing, swimming, boating. Antiquing in nearby lakeside communities. Area winery tours. Old Lighthouse Museum. "Fruit Belt" for fruit and vegetable farms.

*T*he Creekwood Inn is nestled amid thirty-three acres of walnut, oak, and pine trees near a fork in tiny Walnut Creek. The winding, wooded roadway leading to the inn is breathtaking, especially in the fall, when nature paints the trees in glorious colors.

Done in English Cottage design, the inn is warm, cozy, and classically gracious. Massive hand-hewn wooden ceiling beams on the main floor were taken from an old area toll bridge by the original owner, who built the home in the 1930s. The parlor has a large fireplace, surrounded by comfortable sofas and chairs—a perfect setting for afternoon tea or intimate midnight conversation. Wood planking makes up the floors. You can gaze out a bay window that overlooks the estate's lovely grounds.

Innkeeper Mary Lou Linnen said she wanted to combine the ambience of a country inn with the modern amenities that people have come to expect. She has done better than that; she has established a first-class retreat. Twelve large guest rooms and a suite are tastefully decorated in a mixture of styles; some have fireplaces and terraces. All have huge beds, overstuffed chairs, and minirefrigerators.

The Conservatory, overlooking the inn's pond and

gardens, offers both a comfy spot to enjoy nature and a chance to luxuriate in the whirlpool or hit the exercise room.

Mary Lou visited Oxford, England, and was inspired to plant an English perennial garden on the east side of the inn. Things just keep getting better.

One winter my wife and I stayed here during an especially snowy stretch. We simply walked out the front door, slipped on our touring skis, and beat a path to the inn's private cross-country trails, which wind through deep woods and past Lake Spencer, the inn's private lake. Average skiers, we completed the loops in about twenty minutes, returning with a hearty breakfast appetite. Mary Lou serves a tasty continental breakfast of freshly baked breads, pastries, fruit, and coffee.

Late-afternoon tea in the parlor offers cookies and some delicious pastries. You may even have a cup of hot chocolate at bedtime on a blustery winter night, stretching before the fire and toasting your toes.

Every Friday and Saturday, Chef Cheryl Flynn of the inn's The Ferns restaurant will delight you with her special presentations. These might include New Zealand lamb loin with basil whipped potatoes and summer tomato salad, crispy soft-shell crab with citrus vinaigrette, portabello mushroom lasagna, and herb-roasted chicken with sweet corn and garlic polenta. Desserts might include anything from simple fruit tarts to "gooey chocolate" treats.

HOW TO GET THERE: Heading northeast to Michigan City on I-94, take exit 40B. Then take an immediate left turn onto 600W and turn into the first drive on the left. The inn is at Route 20/35, just off the interstate.

Hutchinson Mansion Inn
Michigan City, Indiana 46360

INNKEEPERS: Mary and Ben Duval

ADDRESS/TELEPHONE: 220 West 10th Street; (219) 879-1700

ROOMS: 10, with 5 suites; all with private bath, air-conditioning.

RATES: $85 to $140, single or double; EPB.

OPEN: Year-round

FACILITIES AND ACTIVITIES: Library, sunroom. Less than 1 mile to 18,000-acre Indiana Dunes National Lakeshore, city beaches. Short drive to Lighthouse Place outlet mall, Warren Dunes beach.

*T*here's nothing like breakfast by candlelight to start off the day right. And that's part of the charm of this stately inn, which covers almost an entire city block.

Built by lumber baron (and former mayor) William Hutchinson in 1876, the grand mansion is graced with all the turn-of-the-century amenities you'd expect a lumberman's home to have: fine architectural lines, stained-glass windows, polished wood paneling, tall beamed ceilings, shiny hardwood floors, and more. (Can you find the secret door hidden in the dining room's paneling?)

Guest quarters can be spectacular. The namesake Hutchinson Room boasts an 8-foot antique Renaissance Revival inlaid burl-wood bed fit for a millionaire. There's an 1820 Southern Plantation canopy bed in the Patterson Room that's of museum quality. And even the Servant's Quarters now boast a restored turn-of-the-century bath and a private balcony.

That redbrick coach house out back? No more horse-drawn carriages, here. Instead it has been fashioned into an ever more luxurious getaway with three grand suites, each with its own huge whirlpool.

HOW TO GET THERE: From Chicago, take I–90/94 southeast to Indiana; take exit 34B, U.S. 421 north to Michigan City; continue for about 4 miles, then turn left on Washington Street; finally turn right on West 10th to the inn.

Essenhaus Country Inn 🏨 ℂℂ
Middlebury, Indiana 46540

INNKEEPERS: Bob and Sue Miller, owners; Wilbur and Rosalie Bontrager, managers

ADDRESS/TELEPHONE: 240 U.S. 20; (219) 825–9447

ROOMS: 33, including 5 suites and the Dawdy House; all with private bath, air-conditioning, phone, and TV. Wheelchair accessible.

RATES: $72, single; $92, double; $130 to $150, suites; continental breakfast at the Dawdy House only. Children under 13 free; cribs and cots available.

OPEN: Year-round

FACILITIES AND ACTIVITIES: Large enclosed porch, game room, kids' playground. Renowned restaurant, Das Dutchman Essenhaus, also owned by the Millers, nearby. Villagelike setting; specialty and country stores a short walk away. Located in heart of Indiana Amish country. Amish quilt and crafts shops throughout Crystal Valley. Near Shipshewana, where numerous festivals are celebrated.

This handsome inn resembles a large Amish farmhouse—no coincidence, since it's located in the heart of Indiana's Amish country.

I saw black buggies pulled by horses clip-clopping down main highways, little girls with long black dresses and prayer bonnets, and boys wearing the familiar broad-brimmed hats.

Up and down side roads of the Crystal Valley, you're likely to find Amish quilt shops, bakeries, and crafts stores. Best bet for sightseers: a package deal that includes three-hour guided tours of Indiana's rich Amish heritage. You'll visit a cheese factory, buggy shop, Amish furniture factory, and hardware store and learn about the new Menno Hof Center in Shipshewana.

It's great to have the Essenhaus Country Inn as a base to explore Amish life. The inn has pure country styling, with handcrafted pine furniture specially made by craftsmen in nearby Nappanee, another heavily Amish settlement.

The main floor resembles a huge great room that's open to the rafters high above. It boasts all kinds of high-back sofas, rocking chairs, game tables, and sitting areas that truly have the feel of home. I also enjoy gazing about the fine country crafts and antiques that decorate the room. I especially like the silver-plated potbelly stove, a decorative gadget that my kids loved to snuggle next to.

The second floor resembles a country meadow. A white picket fence corrals the second-floor balcony, and a white clapboard, one-room country schoolhouse, complete with desks and strewn with handsome country crafts, adds to the charm. It's a great spot for kids.

Guest rooms are elegantly country, with their handcrafted pine furnishings. I'm always hooked by four-poster beds, as comfortable to lie in as to look at. Rosalie Bontrager, one of the inn's managers, made all the attractive

country drapes. Quilts and spreads were done by local artisans.

For a real treat, try the Heritage Country Suite, with its cathedral ceilings, antique lamps, and whirlpool tub.

As inn guests you may make dinner reservations at Das Dutchman Essenhaus, the popular Amish-style restaurant that normally seats on a first-come, first-served basis. (A wait in line often stretches toward thirty minutes.) Count on delicious family-style fare, with heartland meats, potatoes, dressing, heaping bowls of vegetables, and steaming loaves of homemade bread. Dessert includes tasty old-fashioned apple dumplings, my favorite.

HOW TO GET THERE: From South Bend, take U.S. 20 east to the inn in Middlebury.

The Beiger Mansion
Mishawaka, Indiana 46554

INNKEEPER: Ron Montandon

ADDRESS/TELEPHONE: 317 Lincoln Way East; (219) 256–0365, fax (219) 259–2622

WEB SITE: business.michiana.org/beiger

ROOMS: 7, with 1 suite; all with private bath and air-conditioning. No smoking inn.

RATES: $80 to $95, single or double; $205, suite; EPB. Corporate rates available.

OPEN: Year-round

FACILITIES AND ACTIVITIES: Dining room, gallery. Minutes from University of Notre Dame, St. Mary's College.

"Hey, Pa," shouted Dayne. "A gift shop." "Yesss!" chimed in Kate. My girls seem to have inherited a specific trait from wife Debbie: the ability, need, and craving to shop. That's okay. It's fun for me, too. And it keeps those folks happy at American Express.

Actually, The Beiger Mansion doesn't have a "shop." It boasts a gallery with scores of wonderful handcrafted pieces showcasing Indiana artists.

The inn is unique, too. The four-level neoclassical limestone home took six years to build. It was finally completed in 1909, all 22,000 square feet of it, for Martin V. Beiger, Mishawaka's first self-made millionaire. Guest rooms are fanciful. Room 1 offers a handsome sleigh bed and original stenciled tub. The Honeymoon Suite features its own "solarium." Room 2 boasts a wood-burning fireplace, and Room 7 registers a four-poster bed with lace canopy, wood-burning fireplace, and original chandelier.

Beiger is also known for its kitchen. Consider these delicious and eclectic choices on one Saturday evening: an appetizer of crab Rangoon (Dungeness crab meat with bok choy, yellow sweet peppers, and cheddar cheese) baked in a pastry shell; mushroom with hazelnut soup; and for an entree, rosemary lamb chops—the house specialty. Unless you'd rather have Mediterranean eggplant cassoulet.

HOW TO GET THERE: From South Bend, take U.S. 33 east to Mishawaka, which is Lincoln Way in town, and continue to the inn. Or exit the Indiana Toll Road at the Mishawaka exit.

The Victorian Guest House
Nappanee, Indiana 46550

INNKEEPER: Vickie Hunsberger

ADDRESS/TELEPHONE: 302 East Market Street; (219) 773-4383 or 773-7034

ROOMS: 6; all with private bath.

RATES: $59 to $119, single or double; $15 for extra person; EPB. Special rates for Notre Dame weekends.

OPEN: Year-round

FACILITIES AND ACTIVITIES: Formal tea monthly. In heart of Indiana Amish country. Nearby: restaurants, Amish Acres, Amish quilt shops, specialty stores, antiques, Borkholder Dutch Village. Near Shipshewana, famous for auctions of antiques and livestock and flea markets with more than 900 vendors. Numerous festivals throughout the year.

"When I saw a FOR SALE sign on this beautiful house, I had to think for a second," Vickie Hunsberger said. "After all, I'd worked in computers for fourteen years. Was this for me?

"Then I decided it might really be interesting to take a 'Victorian plunge' into innkeeping. And you know what! I love it!"

So do her guests.

Vickie has done quite a job on the old Coppes House, completed in 1893 after taking five years to build. That patience is evident in the craftsmanship used to turn the home into Nappanee's showplace. (It's also the only building in town listed on the National Register of Historic Places.) The Coppes Suite is the guests' favorite. Its most unusual attraction is a custom-made, freestanding bathtub, built for the 6′3″-tall original owner. It looks like a huge trough, but it's beautiful—and big. So big that it holds fifty gallons of water; so big that the innkeeper had to run a second set of pipes to fill it up in a reasonable amount of time.

The Wicker Room, with its brass bed and lots of white lace, boasts its own balcony. The Loft (old servants' quarters) features a tub that fills from the bottom up. The water comes out from where you'd expect the drain to be. It fascinates guests.

An elegant breakfast is served in the imposing dining room (look for the servant call button under the rug); count on treats like quiche, homemade

muffins, fresh fruit, tea, and juices. I suggest the Country Table, downtown, for good Amish-cooked dinners.

HOW TO GET THERE: From South Bend, take U.S. 31 south, then turn east on U.S. 6. Continue into Nappanee to the inn.

The Allison House Inn 💲💲
Nashville, Indiana 47448

INNKEEPERS: Bob and Tammy Galm

ADDRESS/TELEPHONE: 90 South Jefferson Street, P.O. Box 546; (812) 988–0814

ROOMS: 5; all with private bath. No smoking inn.

RATES: $95, single or double; EPB. Two-night minimum. No credit cards.

OPEN: Year-round

FACILITIES AND ACTIVITIES: Sitting room, porch. Walk to restaurants, specialty shops, craft stores, and boutiques. Summer theater. Brown County State Park a short drive away.

*J*found The Allison House Inn delightful. It was built in 1883, and the original owners had one of the first automobiles in Nashville. "Of course, no one in that family knew how to drive," innkeeper Tammy Galm said, "so they had to hire someone to tool them around town."

Guest rooms are named for the wildlife paintings that grace each of them. Some of my favorites: Eagle, with its iron-rail beds, quilt wall hanging, and Brown County crafts; Bluebird in Dogwood, with its sandpiper ceiling borders; Moor Hen, featuring an authentic, World War I military field desk; and Bluebird in Sumac, with a lovely, full-sized quilt wall hanging fashioned by Bob's great-grandmother in the 1800s.

You can take breakfast in the dining room and share some of your adventures with other guests, or you can sun on the large deck, where colorful flowers add to the country charm. Besides the usual fare, Tammy serves a caramel-nut roll that will make your mouth water. There are several restaurants that serve down-home family-style dinners; Tammy and husband Bob can recommend one that's right for you.

HOW TO GET THERE: From Indianapolis, take I-65 south to Indiana 46. Go west to Nashville. Turn north at Indiana 135 and proceed to Franklin Street. Turn left, go to Jefferson Street, and turn right to the inn.

The New Harmony Inn
New Harmony,
Indiana 47631

INNKEEPER:
Nancy McIntire

ADDRESS/TELEPHONE:
North Street; (812)
682–4491

ROOMS: 90; all with private bath and air-conditioning. Wheelchair accessible.

RATES: $75, single; $85, double; EP. Children under 12 free; 12 and over, $10. Special winter packages.

OPEN: Year-round

FACILITIES AND ACTIVITIES: Entry House, indoor swimming pool. Located in historic town renowned for early-nineteenth-century utopian society community. Modernistic visitor center distributes information on historic buildings that dot settlement and conducts audiovisual presentations and walking tours. Nearby: specialty shops, fine restaurants.

*A*mid historic structures that are a reminder of a long-ago utopian religious community stands The New Harmony Inn, blending harmoniously with its cultural surroundings. It's all dark brick, and its simple lines immediately call to mind Shaker stylings. Surrounded by tall trees, it looks unbelievably peaceful.

Like all guests, I walked into the Entry House, a welcoming area that features a large open sitting area, a high balcony, and a chapel intended for meditation. Rooms are located in buildings (referred to as "dormitories") across expansive lawns. My favorites are the rooms with a wood-burning fire-place and sleeping loft reached by a spiral staircase. Others have a kitchenette and exterior balcony overlooking the grounds.

The spartan furniture reflects the strong influence of Shaker design. Rocking chairs, simple oak tables, some sofa beds, and area rugs on hard-wood floors complete the decor.

HOW TO GET THERE: New Harmony is located at the point where Indiana 66 meets the Wabash River, 7 miles from I-64. In Indiana, take the Poseyville exit; in Illinois, take the Grayville exit.

Park Paradise

For a hint of the Ozarks' landscape, as well as some of the best rolling hills and hollows in this part of the country, be sure to visit Brown County State Park, just a short drive away. The panoramas in this handsome, tree-studded preserve are quite breathtaking. Fall color leafpeepers take note: This is some of the finest autumn color caravan country in the entire Midwest.

Billie Creek Inn
Rockville, Indiana 47872

INNKEEPERS: Carol Gum and Doug Weisheit

ADDRESS/TELEPHONE: RR 2, (mailing address: P.O. Box 27, Billie Creek Village); (765) 569-3430

ROOMS: 31, with 9 suites; all with private bath, air-conditioning, cable TV. Wheelchair accessible.

RATES: $49 to $99, single or double. EPB. Special canoeing and bike touring packages. EPB.

OPEN: May 1 through November 1.

FACILITIES AND ACTIVITIES: Player piano concerts nightly, heated pool crafts. Walk to Billie Creek Village; biking, canoeing, hiking.

esting on the outskirts of the historic Billie Creek Village, a turn-of-the-century living history museum, this handsome inn allows visitors easy access to more than thirty historic village buildings. Kids love the general store that sells old-time candy and snack treats; I like to explore the 1830s log cabin and imagine how an entire family lived in this cramped space for their entire lives.

You'll get more history when you come back home to the inn, where the innkeepers dress in period costumes and further explain how pioneers lived in the Indiana hill country in the late 1800s. But you won't rough it once you retire to your room. Built in 1996, this inn forsakes pioneer hardships for all the luxuries of the new millennium, including two-person Jacuzzis in the guest suites.

While you're in the area, explore Parke County's historic covered bridges, which dot backroads and jump across tiny creeks. There are more covered bridges here than in any other county in the United States.

HOW TO GET THERE: From Rockville, go 1 mile east on Highway 36, which leads directly to Billie Creek Village and the inn.

Queen Anne Inn ¢¢
South Bend, Indiana 46601

INNKEEPERS: Pauline and Bob Medhurst

ADDRESS/TELEPHONE: 420 West Washington; (219) 234–5959

ROOMS: 5, with 1 suite; all with private bath, air-conditioning, TV, and phone.

RATES: $65 to $104, single; $70 to $109, double; EPB. Two-night minimum on Notre Dame football and graduation weekends.

OPEN: Year-round

FACILITIES AND ACTIVITIES: Afternoon high tea available. Parlor, library, porch. Open House first Sunday in December. Located in West Washington Historic District. Nearby: Century Center, Tippecanoe Place, Covelski Stadium, Studebaker Auto Museum, Copshalom, Oliver House Museum. A short drive to restaurants and Notre Dame campus and its events and activities.

*I*t's hard to believe that the house, at one time called the best example of Queen Anne neoclassical architecture within 100 miles, was once traded for a single Commodore computer! Get owner Bob Medhurst to tell you that story. Or how the house was moved 7 blocks to save it from the wrecker's ball; it is the largest and heaviest house (350 tons) ever to be moved in the county.

Bob said that there are ten kinds of oak used throughout the house, and the dining room is done in solid mahogany. The crystal chandelier in the music room is original to the home. "Didn't know what we had until I went up there to polish it," Bob said. "Turned out to be solid sterling silver."

Guest rooms, named for common birds of the area, are attractive and filled with period antiques and reproductions. A few favorites: Scarlet Tanager Room, with its twin sleigh beds and bed quilt made by Pauline, Bob's wife and fellow innkeeper; Cardinal Suite, with a fireplace, cozy window seat, and queen-sized brass-and-pewter bed; and the Hummingbird Room, with its huge Jenny Lind bed graced with eyelet-lace covers.

Pauline is a great chef, and her baking fills the air with a scrumptious aroma. A full breakfast may include blueberry pancakes, Texas French toast, bran muffins, fruit, juice, beverages, and coffee cake.

And here's something more: afternoon high tea (also open to the public) featuring English scones, sweets, and tea breads.

HOW TO GET THERE: From Chicago, take I-94 east to U.S. 20, then continue east. At U.S. 31, exit north into South Bend. Go to Washington, turn left, and continue to the inn.

Story Inn
Story, Indiana
47448

INNKEEPERS: Bob
and Gretchen Haddix,
owners; Robin Smith and Suzanne Kelley, managers

ADDRESS/TELEPHONE: State Road 135 South, P.O. Box 64;
(812) 988–2273

ROOMS: 12, including 4 cottages with suites; all with private bath and
air-conditioning, some with TV. No smoking inn.

RATES: $108, single or double; $185, cottages; EPB.

OPEN: Year-round

FACILITIES AND ACTIVITIES: Gourmet restaurant serves breakfast to
public every day except Monday; dinner, Tuesday through Sunday. Tea
time (including homemade desserts) 2:00 to 5:00 P.M. daily. Nearby:
Edges Brown County State Park for hiking, biking, relaxing. Nashville,
with scores of specialty stores, antiques shops, and art galleries, is 14 miles
north.

*N*ow I'm gonna tell you the story about Story. My wife and I had driven from Nashville, down twisting backroads and through dense
forest, in search of the Story Inn. We finally came to a T in the
road, and there was Story, Indiana—a tumbledown old mill, a few cottages,
and a tin-sided general store that looked like something straight out of *The
Beverly Hillbillies.*

That general store was the Story Inn. It even had two old American Oil
gas pumps on its front porch, their red-and-gold glass crowns lighted and
shining, along with a collection of broken stoves and other geegaws.

We fought the urge to flee and walked inside. Fresh flowers graced tables
in an expansive dining room, whose ceilings, walls, and timbers were
crammed with antiques, kerosene lamps, patent medicine bottles that
promised cures for the grippe, and all kinds of gadgets. A big wood-burning
stove sat in the center of the room. And the menu read like a gourmet's wish
list.

There's been a general store here since the 1850s, although this building went up in 1916. During the 1920s Studebaker chassis were assembled on the second floor. Upstairs, workers used to slide them out from the loft to the ground below.

Food. That's the real story. Gustatory delights change weekly. Maybe you'd enjoy steak au poivre (an eleven-ounce rib eye marinated in wine, garlic, and pepper, and deglazed in brandy); poulet printemps (chicken breast breaded in pecan meal, sautéed and finished in rhubarb, rosé wine, and savory sauce); or medallions of baked pork stuffed with apricots, currants, pine nuts, herb bread crumbs, and marinated mustard seed, glazed with maple syrup and honey mustard and topped with orange sauce.

Many vegetables and herbs come from the inn's garden. The restaurant offers a selection of California, French, and Australian wines. The house dessert is Turtle Cheese Cake, tinged with coffee liqueur and topped with toffee, crushed pecans, and chocolate.

I don't think I ever want to leave here.

HOW TO GET THERE: From Nashville, take Indiana 46 east, then Indiana 135 south into Story. You can't miss the inn.

Bessinger's Hillfarm Wildlife Refuge
Tippecanoe, Indiana 46570

INNKEEPERS: Wayne and Betty Bessinger

ADDRESS/TELEPHONE: 4588 State Road 110; (219) 223-3288

ROOMS: 3, with shared baths. No smoking inn.

RATES: $55 to $65, single; $60 to $70, double; EPB.

OPEN: Year-round

FACILITIES AND ACTIVITIES: Miles of hiking trails and panoramic overlooks. Canoeing available; skiing and sledding in winter

If you want a day of total relaxation, this is the place. Bessinger's Hillfarm is an Eden, nestled on a lake stretching for nearly 5 miles, with more than thirty small islands strewn about in helter-skelter fashion. All kinds of waterfowl are the main attractions, including Canada geese, ducks, and blue heron.

Another great wildlife-spotting site is Goose Marsh and Woodchuck

Pond. And if it's sunsets you're after, try the aptly named Sunset-Sunrise Overlook.

Guest rooms in this new log home are homey and comfortable. A full breakfast of homemade goodies might include French toast, eggs, breakfast meats, and seasonal fruits.

Did I mention you can really relax in nature's beauty here at Bessinger's?

HOW TO GET THERE: From the intersection U.S. 31 and Indiana 110, travel 5 miles east on Indiana 110. Bessinger's is on the left.

White Hill Manor
Warsaw, Indiana 46580

INNKEEPER: Melissa Cunningham

ADDRESS/TELEPHONE: 2513 East Center Street; (219) 269–6933

ROOMS: 8, including 1 suite; all with private bath, air-conditioning, TV, and phone. Wheelchair accessible.

RATES: $89 to $129, single or double; EPB.

OPEN: Year-round

FACILITIES AND ACTIVITIES: Afternoon tea and evening snacks. Lunch and dinner can be arranged for inn guests. Porch, common room. Next door to Wagon Wheel Dinner Theatre and Restaurant. Nearby: exercise spa and racquet club; a short drive to nearly 100 lakes for all kinds of water sports, golf, skiing, camping, summer festivals, bike trails, quaint shopping, and sights in northeastern Indiana's Amish country.

BUSINESS TRAVEL: Located about 40 miles southeast of South Bend, 40 miles northwest of Fort Wayne. Corporate rates, meeting room, fax.

*T*his elegant English Tudor mansion, built in 1934, has been called "the finest hotel I have ever had the pleasure of staying in" by guests from all around the world.

It's a testament to a time when $7,000 of mortgage money could buy crown moldings, hand-hewn oak beams, arched entryways, mullioned windows, and a slate roof.

Situated on the highest land in Warsaw and surrounded by whispering trees, the inn is a retreat into the elegance of yesteryear. In the singularly English common room, I literally sank into one of the twin burgundy leather sofas that front a roaring fire, sorely needing therapy after a punishing day on snowy roads. Soon afternoon tea was served in a garden room sprinkled with white wicker chairs and glass-topped tables.

Then it was time for guests to retreat to their handsome rooms. A favorite is the Windsor Suite, with its thoroughly English decor, sitting room windows overlooking the courtyard, and a luxurious spa bath (two-person whirlpool) that has provided plenty of adventurous nights for honeymooners and romantics alike.

I also like the Buttery, formerly part of the home's original kitchen. It boasts specially designed stained-glass windows and an antique claw-footed tub.

Don't pass up a chance to overnight in the Library. The arched door to this room looks like something out of an English manor house. Step inside and you'll see hand-hewn oak ceiling beams that add to the British ambience, along with a king-sized brass bed.

Breakfasts on the porch, itself a handsome room that has more hand-hewn beams and the original slate floor. The meal might include fresh fruits, stuffed eggs, cinnamon-spiked French toast, and hot coffee.

And here's one for you trivia buffs: Did you know that more ducks are raised here in Kosciusko County than anywhere else in the world?

HOW TO GET THERE: From the west, take U.S. 30 into Warsaw; turn south on Parker Street, then east on Center Street to the inn. From the east, take U.S. 30 into Warsaw; turn west on Center Street to the inn.

Indiana State Park Inns
Statewide in Indiana

I've discovered that Indiana state park inns are some of the most enjoyable places for families in all of Hoosier-land. You get panoramic vistas, dense forests, rolling hills, outstanding recreation opportunities, naturalist-led trekking and lectures, and a varied cultural arts program of music, dance, and theater.

All of the inns are open year-round, offering winter fun, too. Guest room accommodations vary from inn to inn; some are a bit more luxurious than others, but all are terrific getaways, especially for families with kids. Also, most inns boasts full-service restaurants with some mighty tasty fare.

Room rates vary, generally ranging from $50 to $100 per night. Reservations are always recommended, as the parks fill up rather quickly—especially for the summer season. For more specific information (including directions), contact the individual inns directly or call the state's travel information number, (800) 800–9939.

Here are your choices.

Potawatomi Inn
Angola, Indiana 46703

Pokagon State Park's pride and joy is an English-style lodge with especially fine wintertime activities: a long toboggan slide and groomed cross-country ski trails. There are also an indoor pool and sauna. And let's not forget home-cooked meals. Call (219) 833–1077.

Clifty Inn
Madison, Indiana 47250

Private balconies in the inn's Riverview Section overlook the grand Ohio River and the historic river town of Madison (another must-see for vacationers). There's a cherry-paneled dining room specializing in baked chicken and homemade desserts. Located in Clifty Falls State Park. Call (812) 265–4135.

Turkey Run Inn
Marshall, Indiana 47859

This inn, at Turkey Run State Park, draws lots of attention due to its location in the heart of the state's historic covered bridge country. Come during October to help celebrate the heritage of these bridges during nearby Rockville's annual festival, which draws thousands. Accommodations here include inn rooms and cabins. Enjoy an Olympic-sized swimming pool, tennis courts, hiking trails, and more. Call (765) 597-2211.

Spring Mill Inn
Mitchell, Indiana 47446

This inn, located in Spring Mill State Park, offers a little bit of everything: a reconstructed pioneer village, hiking trails, caves, even the Virgil "Gus" Grissom Memorial. The inn boasts a heated indoor/outdoor swimming pool. Call (812) 849-4081.

Abe Martin Lodge
Nashville, Indiana 47448

Brown County State Park is one of my Midwest favorites, with incredible scenic vistas, undulating hills and hollows, and a charming rustic lodge and cabins. There's even a luxurious retreat for more private couples up on Skunk Ridge. The dining room features homemade cobbler and pies. It's just a short ride from the quaint town of Nashville, filled with specialty shops and summer playhouse theater. Call (812) 988-4418.

Canyon Inn
Spencer, Indiana 47460

Located in McCormick's Creek State Park, Indiana's first state park, the Canyon Inn is an active families' favorite, with a large recreation center and swimming pool. There's a dining room here, too. Check out special weekend getaway packages offered during the winter season. Call (812) 829-4881.

Select List of Other Inns in Indiana

Colonial Rose Inn
8230 South Green Street
Grand Detour, IN 61021
(815) 652-4422

Crown Plaza at Union Station
123 West Louisiana Street
Indianapolis, IN 46225
(317) 631-2221

The Patchwork Quilt Country Inn
11748 County Road 2
Middlebury, IN 46540
(219) 825-2417

Brown Country Inn
51 East State Road 46
Nashville, IN 47448
(812) 988-2291

The Jelley House Country Inn
222 South Walnut Street
Rising Sun, IN 47040
(812) 438-2319

The Rockport Inn
130 South Third Street
Rockport, IN 47635
(812) 649-2664

Old Davis Hotel
228 West Main Street
Shipshewana, IN 46565
(219) 768-7300

The Book Inn
508 West Washington Street
South Bend, IN 46601
(219) 288-1990

Oliver Inn
630 West Washington Street
South Bend, IN 46601
(219) 232-4545

Iowa

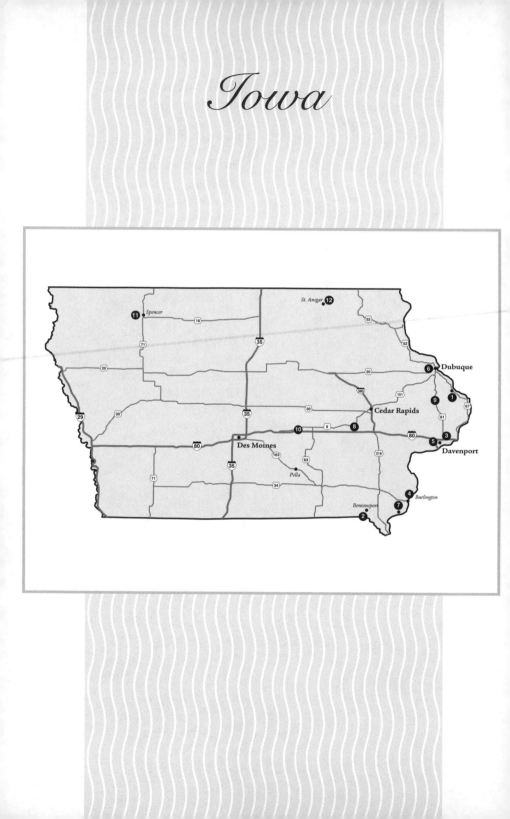

St. Ansgar 12

11 Spencer

18

52

71

35

52

20

20

6 Dubuque

380

151

9 1

30

35

30

Cedar Rapids

61

67

29

30

10 6 8

80

5 3

80

Des Moines

163

218

Davenport

35

63

71

34

Pella

4 Burlington

Bentonsport 7

2

Iowa

Numbers on map refer to towns numbered below.

A Top Pick Inn

Mont Rest Victorian House of Bellevue
Bellevue, Iowa 52031

INNKEEPERS: Christine Zraick

ADDRESS/TELEPHONE: 300 Spring Street; (319) 872–4220 or (877) 872–4220

WEB SITE: www.montrest.com

ROOMS: 11; all with private baths, air-conditioning. No smoking inn.

RATES: $105 to $175, single or double; EPB.

OPEN: Year-round except Christmas Eve and Day.

FACILITIES AND ACTIVITIES: Sitting room with fireplace, gourmet meals, therapeutic massage, panoramic views of Mississippi River due to inn's bluff-top location. Situated in one of the most picturesque river towns in Iowa. Nearby: nine parks (several with great bluff-top river views), trout streams, nine-hole golf course, Young Museum, tours of Lock and Dam No. 12, butterfly garden, antiques shops, hiking, biking, cave. Festivals include Fourth of July Heritage Days and Tom Sawyer Days in August.

Getting Back to Nature

The Baker Room, located in the building's tall tower, offers one of the Midwest's best river vistas. But Christine said, "It's not for the faint of heart." Wicker antiques, hooked rugs, and a roof garden boasting a gingerbread deck are some additional perks.

Eagle's Nest, a charming room with hand-stenciled hardwood floors and an iron-rail bed, is a guest favorite. But it's not just the ambience that makes it a winner. Sometimes, right outside your windows, you can see eagles making their nests in the trees.

Now, that's what I call getting back to nature—without sacrificing any luxury.

"This house was once lost in a poker game," innkeeper Christine Zraick said. That was in 1896, just three years after Seth Baker built Mont Rest, a nine-acre estate nestled halfway up a wooded bluff affording one of Iowa's most panoramic views of the Mississippi River.

Locals nicknamed the imposing white house, with its round white tower protruding like a periscope from the home's belly, Baker's Castle—a moniker that has stuck into the 1990s. Today Mont Rest stands as the river town's most notable "Painted Lady."

The Bellevue Room has a great view of both the river and the quaint town. It's high Victorian style includes a 9-foot headboard on the bed and matching furniture with pink marble tops. The room's a favorite for honeymoon and anniversary couples. Another favorite is the Great River Room, all done in delicate blues with print ceiling borders, a pinwheel-style bed quilt, and an Eastlake marble-topped dresser; it's a terrific spot from which to gaze out endlessly over the mighty "Miss'sip."

And the Angelic Tower room, at the top of the castle, is where that high-stakes poker game took place. Today the room features a queen-size iron-rail bed, huge double shower, (a favorite among honeymooners) and a private observation deck with five-person Jacuzzi.

A full country breakfast awaits overnight guests. Imagine country-style eggs with green peppers and cheese, smoked sausage, homemade banana nut bread and coffee cake, fresh fruit, orange juice, and beverages.

HOW TO GET THERE: From Dubuque, take U.S. 52 south into Belle-vue. Turn right on Spring Street and continue to the inn.

Mason House Inn
Bentonsport, Iowa 52565

INNKEEPERS: Dr. William and Sheral McDermet

ADDRESS/TELEPHONE: RR 2 (mailing address: P.O. Box 237, Benton-sport/Keosauqua, Iowa 52565); (319) 592-3133

ROOMS: 8; 5 with private bath. No smoking inn.

RATES: $64 to $84; EPB. No credit cards.

OPEN: Year-round

FACILITIES AND ACTIVITIES: Located in village declared National Historic District in 1972. Walk to shops (open April through November, daily) that include native crafts, antiques, blacksmith, weaver, and potter. Nearby: bike, hike, canoe on Des Moines River. A short drive to restaurants, Shimek State Forest, cross-country skiing.

*I*f you look upstream from the 1882 bridge in this historic riverfront village, you'll see ripples on the water marking the site of the old dam. It's a reminder of the days when the Des Moines River teemed with riverboat traffic, mills lined the winding banks, and nearly 1,500 people lived in the town. Today the year-round population numbers 31.

The Mason House Inn was built in 1846 by Mormon craftsmen who stayed in Bentonsport for one year while making their famous trek to Utah. It mainly served steamboat passengers traveling from St. Louis to Des Moines.

No wonder the inn still stands sturdy, its cozy Georgian stylings providing a warm welcome for big-city visitors who want to experience a quiet and restful stay.

Many of the rooms appear as they did in their heyday, with several original furnishings. Especially interesting is a memorial hair wreath measuring 3 feet by 4 feet that hangs in the parlor. Here you can also pump and play tunes on an 1882 Estey organ.

Dr. William McDermet (a former pastor for the Christian Church) and his wife, Sheral (who holds a degree in hotel and restaurant management), did extensive remodeling in 1990, connecting the inn with the old railroad station. Now it boasts two extra rooms: the Wash House and Old Country Store, each with period furnishings.

Other guest quarters include the Wild Rose Room, with its 9-foot-high

walnut headboard, and the Mason Room, with matching bedroom set, 9-foot French mirror, fainting couch, and wood-burning stove—all original to the inn.

I especially like the Steamboat Room, with its burl walnut bedroom set and windows offering a good view of the river. Don't miss the copper-lined "Murphy" bathtub, which unfolds from the Keeping Room wall cabinet. The innkeepers claim that it's the only one of its kind in Iowa.

The country breakfast, served in the Keeping Room next to the 1803 cookstove, is a special event. How do eggs and sausage, blueberry waffles, peach crisp, and Mason House sticky pecan rolls sound? Sheral serves dinner, including such dishes as smoked brisket of beef, orange roughy filet, and roasted chicken breast, with advance reservations.

There's now an antiques shop out back, called the Outback Antique Shop—what else? Get the innkeepers to tell you how the Mason House was saved from the tragic "flood of the century" a few years back. Hint: lots of help and love from neighbors—and 31,000 sandbags!

HOW TO GET THERE: Bentonsport is in the southeast corner of Iowa's Van Buren County between Keosauqua and Bonaparte on J40, a paved county road. Take Iowa 1 south through Keosauqua, cross the river, and go uphill to J40. Then go east to Bentonsport. Turn right on any village road toward the river. The inn is along the bank.

The Abbey Hotel
Bettendorf, Iowa 52722

INNKEEPERS: Joseph and Joan Lemon and Joseph Lemon Jr., owners; Theresa Lemon, manager

ADDRESS/TELEPHONE: 1401 Central Avenue; (319) 355-0291 or

(800) 438–7535, fax (319) 355–7647

ROOMS: 19, with 1 suite; all with private bath. No smoking inn.

RATES: $99 to $119, single or double; $149, suite; continental breakfast.

OPEN: Year-round

FACILITIES AND ACTIVITIES: Dinner, room service available. Breakfast room, banquet rooms, verandas with Mississippi River views, courtyard, Gothic chapel, outdoor swimming pool. Nearby: a short drive to President Riverboat Casino, Adler Theater and River Center, Casino Rock Island Riverboat, Rock Island Arsenal, Quad City Downs Harness Race Track, PGA championship golf course.

BUSINESS TRAVEL: Located 5 minutes from downtown Bettendorf, 8 minutes from downtown Davenport. Corporate rates, meeting rooms, fax.

*I*t wouldn't be any exaggeration to describe a night at the Abbey Hotel as "heavenly." That's because this landmark Bettendorf building was originally opened in 1917 as a convent for the Sisters of Our Lady of Mount Carmel. It continues to display many trappings of its former life. There's a statue of an angel blowing a trumpet perched on one of the roofs, and stained-glass windows have prayers scribed in Latin.

Even a spectacular Gothic chapel remains, still used for masses and weddings by the Anglican church. Its domed exterior replicates the grand cathedrals of Europe; inside, you'll find a turn-of-the-century altar imported from Belgium and beautiful stained-glass windows depicting Christ, Mary, saints, and nuns.

Since its conversion to a hotel in 1982, the Abbey has achieved all kinds of awards. As many as five of the original nuns' "cells" have been combined for a spacious and luxurious guest room. Ours featured an imported marble bath, a mahogany armoire with cable television, a sitting area with two overstuffed chairs and couch, and several tall windows offering spectacular views of the Mississippi and the Quad Cities.

The room also had a second entry door, which opened onto a long veranda overlooking a lovely courtyard. This is where the sisters often walked for contemplation; today a corner of the courtyard is filled by the hotel's in-ground swimming pool. (Incidentally, the pool was added by the Franciscan Brothers, who took over the building as a monastery in 1978 after the nuns moved to a smaller outpost in Eldridge, about 10 miles north of here.)

For a peek at how the monastery appeared before its luxurious makeover, head to the third-floor museum. One cell has been maintained in its original size and configuration. Note the nun's habit, sandals, and Bible; these were among the few possessions that sisters were allowed to keep during their lifetime of sacrifice and prayer here. The simple bed is just a board covered with straw.

HOW TO GET THERE: From Rock Island, take I-74 across the Mississippi River into Iowa; get off at the first exit past the river, Highway 67 (signs may say STATE STREET, GRANT STREET, RIVERFRONT EXIT). Follow that exit road, which turns into Fourteenth Street. Then continue on Fourteenth Street, up the hill, to the hotel.

Jumer's Castle Lodge
Bettendorf, Iowa 52722

INNKEEPER: Dan Conners, general manager

ADDRESS/TELEPHONE: I-74 at Spruce Hills Drive; (319) 359-7141 or (800) 285-8637

ROOMS: 210 rooms, lofts, and suites; all with private bath and air-conditioning, some with fireplace, whirlpool bath, wet bar, and other amenities. Wheelchair accessible.

RATES: $81 to $137; EP. Special seasonal packages available.

OPEN: Year-round.

FACILITIES AND ACTIVITIES: Full-service restaurant, Bavarian dining room, room service, Schwarzer Bar lounge and Library Bar, indoor and outdoor swimming pools, sauna, exercise room, game court, putting green, limousine service, antiques shop, gift shop. Nearby: riverboat casinos.

BUSINESS TRAVEL: Located about 5 minutes from downtown Bettendorf and downtown Davenport. Corporate rates, meeting and conference rooms, fax.

Bookworm's Delight

If there is a hotel library more elegant than the one here at Jumer's, I'd like to see it. Bookshelves soar to incredible heights as a giant hearth roars with a warming blaze, surrounded by two high-back hand-carved walnut chairs and other luxurious appointments.

Makes you want to settle down in a comfy chair with a good long book (maybe *War and Peace* or *Gone with the Wind*) and not come out for a day or two.

If you'd like to experience a bigger-than-life European getaway, walk into this eastern Iowa hostelry that's earned national recognition. Centuries-old traditions of European innkeeping are evident everywhere as you step through heavy beveled-glass doors into a grand lobby. Like the other common rooms, the lobby has magnificent tapestries hanging on walls, regal statuary, sleek bronzes, and what the hotel likes to call "a veritable pageant of precious artwork."

One of my favorite guest room styles is the loft, with an iron spiral staircase leading to upstairs bedchambers. Perhaps you'd prefer a spacious suite, complete with its own four-poster canopy bed, fireplace, and antique oil paintings.

Dining is another Jumer's experience not to be missed. It's award-winning kitchen serves up authentic German house specialties like wursts, sausages, spaetzle, and sauerkraut. Savor the flavors of the restaurant's fresh-baked rolls and breads. Desserts, ranging from tortes and strudels to creamy cheesecakes, are heavenly.

HOW TO GET THERE: From the (Quad Cities) Moline Airport, exit at Spruce Hills Drive and continue to the hotel.

Schramm House B&B
Burlington, Iowa 52601

INNKEEPERS: Sandy and Bruce Morrison

ADDRESS/TELEPHONE: 616 Columbia Street; phone/fax
(319) 754–0373 or phone toll-free (800) 683–7117

WEB SITE: www.visitschramm.com

ROOMS: 4; all with private bath.

RATES: $85 to $125. EPB.

OPEN: Year-round.

FACILITIES AND ACTIVITIES: Library, turndown service, guest robes.
Six-block walk to the Mississippi River. Short walk to Snake Alley,
America's crookedest street. Antiquing, biking, shopping nearby.

*L*ocated in Burlington's Historic District, the Schramm House is an 1866
beauty that has been restored to all her nineteenth-century charm. Perhaps the inn's crowning architectural gem is the third-story tower, but
that's just a harbinger for the lavish restoration guests will experience inside.

Parquet floors, tin ceilings, exposed brick walls are all part of the effort,
which leans toward the Victorian in keeping with the house's 1880s additions.

You'll also savor breakfasts at this beauty, with the likes of baked pears
smothered with toasted almonds, fresh baked muffins, French toast, and
more, all served on fine china and crystal. You can work off your bounty by
walking down to the Mississippi, just 6 blocks away. Or stroll through the rest
of this delightful little town's historic district to discover other hidden gems.

HOW TO GET THERE: From the Quad Cities, U.S. 61 south to Burlington;
take Route 61 north to Route 34 east, then take the Main Street exit to
Columbia Street. The inn is located at 616 Columbia.

Bishop's House Inn

Davenport, Iowa
52803

INNKEEPER:
Sandy Krueger

ADDRESS/TELEPHONE:
1527 Brady Street; (319)
322-8303

ROOMS: 6, including 1
suite; all with private bath, air-conditioning, and ceiling fan.

RATES: $65 to $115, single or double; $140, suite; EPB. $10 room-rate
discount Monday through Thursday.

OPEN: Year-round

FACILITIES AND ACTIVITIES: Formal parlor, sitting room, dining
room, second-floor guest parlor. Nearby: a short drive to riverboat casinos, The Children's Museum, Wildcat Den State Park, Buffalo Bill's
family homestead in LeClaire, Rock Island Arsenal and Museum.

"It sure beats a room at the parish rectory," I told my brother,
Mark, as we walked into the Bishop's House Inn, an 1871 land-
mark Italianate mansion that was once the personal residence of
Roman Catholic Bishop John L. Davis.

Oak woodworks, six marble fireplaces, parquet floors, stained glass, ceiling medallions, and hand-painted and -stenciled walls are just some of the
many spectacular features of this nineteenth-century architectural gem,
which is as impressive today as it was when the bishop roamed the house.
Innkeeper Sandy Krueger presides over a Victorian showplace. Take my word
that the common rooms are elegant; let's get right to guest rooms.

Most opulent is the Davis Suite, a huge Victorian bedchamber that
includes hand-printed Bradbury and Bradbury wall coverings, a massive oak
bedroom set adorned with a huge featherbed, and a wood-burning fireplace
(circa 1890) whose mantel shows off unusual spindles, tiles, and beveled
mirrors. I especially like the suite's bath, clad in Vermont marble and featuring an oval whirlpool tub.

Another spectacular room is the Rohlman Chamber, named for Bishop
Henry P. Rohlman, the second Catholic clergyman to occupy the home. The

bedchamber was originally part of the bishop's sitting room; now it has an Eastlake walnut bedroom set, wood burning fireplace, featherbed, and an unusual marble shower stall.

Other guest rooms are equally gracious, including the Housekeeper's Chamber, which features the house's original bathroom (yep, that's the bishop's claw-footed tub).

Take if from me; you're going to like it here.

HOW TO GET THERE: From I-80, exit at U.S. 61 (which turns into Brady Street in Davenport); go south and continue to the inn, located at the intersection of Brady and Kirkwood Boulevard.

The Hancock House
Dubuque, Iowa 52001-4644

INNKEEPERS: Chuck and Susan Huntley

ADDRESS/TELEPHONE: 1105 Grove Terrace; (319) 557-8989

ROOMS: 9, including 4 suites, 1 cottage; all with private bath and air-conditioning, 4 with whirlpool tubs; TV and phone on request. No smoking inn.

RATES: $80 to $175, single or double; EPB and complimentary beverages.

OPEN: Year-round

FACILITIES AND ACTIVITIES: Sitting rooms, porch. Located in the heart of historic Mississippi River town, with magnificent river views.

Nearby: restaurants, cable-car elevator, riverboat rides, Woodward River-boat Museum, Ham House Museum. Brilliant fall colors, hiking, biking, cross-country and downhill skiing.

BUSINESS TRAVEL: Located a few minutes from downtown Dubuque. Corporate rates, conference room, fax.

*H*ere's a triple treat: a magnificent bluff-top setting, an exquisite Queen Anne mansion, and spectacular views of the Mississippi River.

I know those are many superlatives, but it would take a thesaurusful of adjectives to do justice to The Hancock House, listed on the National Register of Historic Places.

"You can see sixteen church steeples from any guest room," innkeepers Chuck and Susan Huntley told me. I challenge guests to find them all. Of course, I think you have to be a native Dubuquer to get the tough one.

Chuck and Susan have continued to meticulously restore this twenty-seven-room mansion built in 1891 by Charles Hancock, owner of the largest wholesale grocery in the Midwest at that time. Everything is larger than life. You really must experience the 28-by-18-foot dining room—completely done in quarter-sawn oak, with a coffered and beamed ceiling and an elegant fireplace—to appreciate it.

Speaking of fireplaces, the one in the sitting room, with its elaborate gingerbread detailing, took first place in design competition at the 1893 Columbian Exposition in Chicago.

Guest rooms are fabulous. I like the North Bedroom, with its magnificent half-tester bed, original marble bath with handsome mosaic floor, marble coal-burning fireplace (which includes a coal-powered footwarmer), and Bradley & Howard–signed table lamp.

Maybe you'd rather try the East Bedroom. It has a white iron-rail bed, marble sink, claw-footed tub, and four huge windows.

You get spectacular views of the Mississippi. At night you can see the yellow running lights of double-decked river paddleboats. In the summer you see scores of sailboats.

Chuck and Susan said: "Then there are the church bells that ring on Sunday mornings. The sound is heavenly. But one day a guest asked which church played 'Blue Moon.' Those are the bank chimes."

Newer rooms include the original servant's bedroom, with great river vistas, and the Doll Room, a third-floor aerie that claims both the house's turret and a whirlpool tub. For a real touch of elegance, sample the inn's huge suite. Its 900 square feet include a large living/sitting room brightened by the light from seven windows, a wet bar located in the old nursemaid's pantry, an inviting whirlpool bath for two, and a bedroom with a white iron-rail bed and handsome stained-glass window.

In one of the inn's spectacular sitting rooms, with its incredible views, you can see three states at once—Iowa, Illinois, and Wisconsin.

Or perhaps you'd like to enjoy complete privacy in the restored cottage across the street from the main inn. More good times for The Hancock House.

HOW TO GET THERE: From Illinois, take the Julien Dubuque Bridge to Locust Street, turn north on Locust, and continue. At Twelfth Street, turn left, then take another left on Grove Terrace to the inn.

The Mandolin 💟
Dubuque, Iowa 52001

INNKEEPER: Amy Boynton

ADDRESS/TELEPHONE: 199 Loras; (319) 556-0069, fax (319) 556-0587

WEB SITE: www.mandolininn.com

ROOMS: 8; 4 with private bath, all with air-conditioning. No smoking inn.

RATES: $75 to $135, single or double; EPB.

OPEN: Year-round.

FACILITIES AND ACTIVITIES: Sitting room, music room. Wraparound veranda. Nearby: restaurants, riverboat rides on the Mississippi, museums, Cable Car Square, Fenelon Place Elevator, Sundown ski area, hiking, dog racing.

*O*ne glance inside and I saw that the home had been built for someone special—and incredibly wealthy. Imagine stained-glass windows, parquet floors, and hand-painted canvas wall coverings. In fact, this 1908 Queen Anne mansion was the home of Nicholas Schrup, Dubuque's leading financial figure in the early part of the twentieth century. Apparently he spared no expense, and luckily most of his special touches have survived through the years.

The foyer is massive, graced with tall oak columns and an inlaid wood parquet floor. I immediately noticed the stained-glass window on a stairway landing, featuring the likeness of St. Cecilia, patron saint of musicians. She's clutching a mandolin; hence the name of the inn. The parlor is dressed with cypress woodwork, probably brought up the Mississippi in a riverboat. The usual sheen of the wood changes with movement. It has almost an iridescence to it.

The Music Room boasts original hand-painted murals on the north wall. And the dining room! It's engulfed by oak paneling, a floor-to-ceiling beveled-glass china cupboard, and an Italian fireplace. My favorite touch: the original hand-painted wall mural that makes it appear as if you're in the middle of a dark Victorian forest.

Rooms are equally impressive. Holly Marie boasts a seven-piece French walnut furniture set, complete with huge armoire, marble-topped dresser, and full-length dressing mirror. I especially like Grand Tour, graced with American walnut pieces and an Irish rose lace bedspread, as well as an antique Irish pitcher and bowl brought back from Ireland. In fact, the touches of "auld sod" would sit quite well with my Irish mom, whose ancestral relatives hail from County Armagh.

Breakfasts are three-course gourmet affairs that include everything from stuffed French toast to tropical-fruit breads and hazelnut coffee. You'll need to walk around historic Dubuque to work off the goodies.

HOW TO GET THERE: From Galena, take U.S. 20 west across the bridge into Dubuque, turn right on Locust Street, proceed to Loras Street (Fourteenth Street); turn right and continue 1 block to Main Street, then turn left and continue to the inn.

The Redstone Inn 📱 💟
Dubuque, Iowa 52001

INNKEEPER: Jerry Lazore, manager

ADDRESS/TELEPHONE: 504 Bluff Street; (319) 582–1894, fax (319) 582–1893

ROOMS: 15, with 6 suites; all with private bath, air-conditioning, phone, and TV.

RATES: rooms: weekends: $85 to $108, single or double; weekdays: $70 to $85, single or double; $125 to $195, suites; continental breakfast.

OPEN: Year-round

FACILITIES AND ACTIVITIES: Afternoon teas (Tuesday through Sunday, 2:00 to 6:00 P.M.). Walk to restaurants. Dubuque attractions include Sundown downhill ski area, Mississippi riverboat cruises, riverboat museum, Cable Car Square (specialty shops in a historic location), scenic railcar climbing 189-foot bluff with view of three states.

BUSINESS TRAVEL: Located in the heart of downtown Dubuque. Corporate rates, meeting rooms, fax.

*I*registered in a rich, oak-paneled hallway on a first floor that retains much of the home's original ambience. The mauve, deep blue, green, and burgundy colors are used to complement the Redstone's many original stained-glass windows.

Because no two guest rooms are alike, you can select your favorite from a color-photo portfolio kept at the reception area. My room was like many offered at the inn—antique furnishings with walnut beds, balloon curtains, period lighting fixtures, muted floral wallpapers, and bed quilts. Mine also had a whirlpool bath, which I headed for immediately; some also have fireplaces, with free logs.

Breakfast is served in your room or downstairs in the small dining room. Starched white table linens and fresh flowers adorn the tables. I munched on chewy homemade caramel rolls, croissants, and bagels. Afternoon teas feature a variety of English teas, dainty finger sandwiches, tarts, biscuits—and maybe gingerbread cherry pie, an inn specialty. Count on English truffles, too. I recommend the 225 restaurant and its nouvelle cuisine delights for romantic dinners; it's just a short drive away.

HOW TO GET THERE: Whether entering Dubuque from the west via U.S. 151 or east on U.S. 20, pick up Locust Street at the bridge and proceed to University. Turn left and drive to Bluff, then turn left again. The inn is on the street's left side.

Kingsley Inn
Fort Madison, Iowa 52627

INNKEEPER: Alida Willis, manager

ADDRESS/TELEPHONE: 707 Avenue H; (800) 441–2327 or
(319) 372–7074.

ROOMS: 14; all with private bath, 3 with whirlpools. No smoking inn.

RATES: $75 to $135, single or double; two-night minimum on holiday
weekends and first weekend after Labor Day. Continental breakfast.

OPEN: Year-round

FACILITIES AND ACTIVITIES: Parlor with overstuffed chairs, Morning
Room. Short drive to Catfish Bend Casino paddlewheel riverboat; Old
Fort Madison; Sante Fe Bridge; eagle-watching along the Mississippi River.

This handsome and historic inn, perched on the banks of the Mississippi River, was built in 1859 and served as a newspaper office
for many years. Well, here's an "Extra! Extra! Read All About It!"
for you—don't miss a chance to stay at this wonderful hotel.

Inside, the inn more resembles a modern hostelry, complete with an
atrium. But once you get to the rooms, Victorian elegance returns, with vintage cherrywood furnishings—none made later than 1870. Two rooms even
have matching period cherry furniture sets; they remain a favorite with
antique lovers.

Enjoy your breakfast in the Morning Room: pastries, fresh fruit, and granola are part of the fare. Then stroll outside and enjoy some of the town's
rich history.

HOW TO GET THERE: Enter Fort Madison from Highway 61; continue to the
downtown area. Downtown, Highway 61 changes to Avenue H. So just proceed to the inn.

Die Heimat Country Inn
Homestead, Iowa 52236

INNKEEPERS: Warren and Jacki Lock

ADDRESS/TELEPHONE: Main Street; (319) 622–3937

ROOMS: 19, including 8 deluxe; all with private bath, air-conditioning, and TV. Well-behaved pets okay. No smoking inn.

RATES: $64.95 to $74.95, single or double; EPB. Special weekday winter rates.

OPEN: Year-round

FACILITIES AND ACTIVITIES: Sitting room. Shaded yard with Amana wooden gliders. Walk to restaurant, nature trail. Short drive to historic Amana Colonies villages, with antiques, crafts, and specialty stores; museums; bakeries; Amana furniture shops. Also nearby: winery, summer theater, golf, biking, cross-country skiing in Lake Macbride State Park, Palisades Kepler State Park.

*H*omestead is a peaceful little village off a busy interstate in the historic Amana Colonies, settled in the 1840s by German immigrants seeking religious freedom and a communal lifestyle. As soon as I turned off the highway to reach Die Heimat Country Inn, I became absorbed in the quiet of this century-and-a-half-old agricultural community.

Jacki Lock greeted me at the desk, full of good cheer and chatter. The charming lobby is generously decorated with nationally famous Amana furniture (the sofas are original to the 1854 inn) and a large walnut Amana grandfather's clock ticking softly in the corner of the room. Soothing German zither music wafted through the inn, and I immediately began to feel at home. (*Die Heimat* is German for "the homestead" or "the home place.") On the way to my room, Jacki pointed out the cross-stitched hangings on the walls; they're German house blessings, many brought from the old country.

My room was small and cozy, with sturdy Amana furniture, an electric kerosene lamp, writing desk, rocking chair, and brass-lantern ceiling lamp. It's so quiet that you'll probably wake up in the morning to the sound of chirping birds, as I did.

Other rooms feature handsome Amana four-poster walnut beds graced with lace canopies, handmade Amana quilts, handmade Colonies crafts, and rocking chairs.

Breakfast includes French toast, eggs, fruit soup, and home-baked goodies. Afterward, I explored the thrumming communities of the seven Amana Colonies villages, with all kinds of historical and commercial attractions, including fabulous bakery goods and meat shops. Jacki and husband Warren can point out the "can't miss" stops.

Bill Zuber's restaurant, just down the street from the inn, was one of their recommendations. Zuber was a pitcher for the New York Yankees, a hometown boy discovered by scouts when he was seen tossing cabbages during a local harvest. I liked the menus in the shapes of baseballs, and the homestyle cooking, from historic recipes used by the Amana Colonies' old communal kitchens, was delicious. My baked chicken with fried potatoes, veggies, and green peas in thick gravy would be hard to beat. Also served are Amana ham, pork, and baked steaks.

HOW TO GET THERE: Take I–80 to exit 225 (151 north), and go about 5 miles. At the intersection of Highways 6 and 49, turn left past Bill Zuber's restaurant to the inn just down the block.

Squiers Manor
Maquoketa, Iowa 52060

INNKEEPERS: Cathy and Virl Banowetz

ADDRESS/TELEPHONE: 418 West Pleasant Street; (319) 652–6961

WEB SITE: www.squiersmanor.com

ROOMS: 8, including 3 suites; all with private bath and air-conditioning.

RATES: $80 to $110, single or double; $160 to $195, suites; EPB.

OPEN: Year-round

FACILITIES AND ACTIVITIES: Library, parlor, porch. A short drive to Mississippi River towns; Dubuque, site of low-stakes riverboat casino gambling; and Galena, Illinois, a Civil War–era architectural wonderland.

*N*othing prepares you for the splendor of this 1882 house, listed on the National Register of Historic Places. The handsome Queen Anne home boasts fine wood everywhere. There's a walnut parlor, a cherry dining room, and butternut throughout the rest of the house.

Fine antiques are everywhere, too; some, like the 1820s Federal four-poster mahogany bed in the Harriet Squiers Room, are of museum quality. That's not surprising, since innkeepers Cathy and Virl Banowetz also own a nationally renowned antiques store just a few miles out of town.

I especially liked the Jeannie Mitchel Bridal Suite. Its canopied brass bed stands more than 7 feet tall. (Note the mother-of-pearl on the footboard.) The Victorian Renaissance dresser with its marble top is another treasure.

Did I mention that the suite has a double whirlpool bath?

So does the J. E. Squiers Room; there a green marble floor creates a path leading to a cozy corner whirlpool for two.

Opal's Parlor (named after a longtime resident of the manor when its rooms were rented as apartments) features not only 1860s antiques and hand-crocheted bedspreads but also a Swiss shower that acts "like a human car wash," said Cathy.

Every common room bespeaks luxury and splendor. The parlor's fireplace, with tiles depicting characters in Roman mythology, is unusual. Look at the fabulous hand-carved cherry buffet in the dining room. The dining room's 10-foot-tall, hand-carved jeweler's clock is another conversation starter. The library, an enclave done entirely in butternut paneling and graced with its original fireplace, is flat-out gorgeous.

Great atmosphere isn't the only treat you get; Cathy's breakfasts are terrific, too. Consider pumpkin pecan muffins, black-walnut bread, eggs Katrina, pecan-stuffed French toast, seafood quiches, and apple pudding.

Another delight is "candle-light evening desserts." Imagine nibbling on Cathy's chocolate bourbon pecan pie, delicious tortes, or Grandma Annie's bread pudding, a guest favorite.

There are two fantastic suites reclaimed from the home's grand ballroom. The Loft boasts a gas log fireplace for instant romance, a 6-by-4-foot whirlpool tub, a wicker sitting room—and breakfast delivered to your bedchamber.

The Ballroom (that's the other suite's name) is an incredible 1,100 square feet of luxury, with a whirlpool tub nestled in a "garden" setting, king-sized bed, cathedral ceiling, massive sitting room, reading nook, and lots more surprises.

HOW TO GET THERE: From Dubuque, take U.S. 61 south to U.S. 64, then turn east into town. One block past the second stoplight, turn right, then go 1 block to the inn.

La Corsette Maison Inn 🖤
Newton, Iowa 50208

INNKEEPER: Kay Owen

ADDRESS/TELEPHONE: 629 First Avenue; (641) 792-6833

WEB SITE: www.innbook.com/inn/lacor

ROOMS: 5, including 2 suites; all with private bath and air-conditioning. No smoking inn.

RATES: $75 to $110, single or double; $160 to $180, suites; Sister Inn, 2 bedchambers, $145 and $180; EPB. Multinight minimum during Pella, Iowa, Tulip Festival and some other special events. Pets allowed by prearrangement.

OPEN: Year-round

FACILITIES AND ACTIVITIES: Gourmet five-course dinners. Two sitting rooms with fireplace; porch. Nearby: Maytag Company tours, tennis courts, golf courses, horseback riding, cross-country skiing. A short drive to Trainland, U.S.A.; Prairie Meadows Horse Track; Krumm Nature Preserve.

*M*y wife, Debbie, and I sat in front of a roaring fire in an elegant parlor, enjoying a romantic gourmet-style breakfast. First innkeeper Kay Owen brought us a delightful fresh fruit compote of pink grapefruit, mandarin orange slices, grapes, and kiwi. Her home-baked apple muffins with strudel were next. (We could have eaten four apiece, they were so delicious.)

We sipped on raspberry and orange juice, which washed down authentic English scones, another of Kay's specialties. Then came a wonderful frittata with two cheeses—and some special La Corsette French bread.

It was one of the ultimate bed-and-breakfast breakfast experiences.

No wonder food at Kay's inn has received a 4½-star rating from the *Des Moines Register* and has been hailed as a "gleaming jewel in the crown of fine restaurants."

The mansion itself is a 1909 Mission-style masterpiece built by an early Iowa state senator. Not much has changed in the intervening years. Gleaming Mission oak woodwork, art nouveau stained-glass windows, and other turn-of-the-century architectural flourishes make La Corsette a special place.

We overnighted in the Windsor Hunt Suite; the massive bedchamber has a huge four-poster bed (you use a stepstool to reach the high mattress), and the sitting room boasts its own fireplace—which we used for a romantic end to the day—as well as a two-person whirlpool bath. Other rooms are imbued with their own particular charms. The Penthouse bedchambers, for instance, are located in the tower and surrounded by beveled-glass windows.

Kay gives house tours before dinner each evening. One of her anecdotes reveals that Fred Maytag, of washing machine fame, got his seed money from La Corsette's owner to start his company. Another tells that Fred personally used a "one-minute brand" washer made by another company in town. His own Maytag "chewed up" his clothes.

Kay's five-course, gourmet-style dinners, prepared by both herself and her chef, are renowned. The first person to make reservations for the evening sets the night's menu. Choices include French veal in cream, broccoli-stuffed game hen with Mornay sauce, and roast loin of pork with prune chutney. Maybe you'd rather have a basket dinner delivered to your door during week-day visits. This three-course treat might include stuffed pork chops, fancy veggies, and home-baked breads.

Or choose to stay at the 100-year-old Sister Inn next door. Here Kay offers rooms with double whirlpools and antique soaking tubs. Looks like fun.

HOW TO GET THERE: From the Quad Cities, take I-80 to Newton (exit 164), and go north until the second light (Highway 6); then turn right and continue 7 blocks to the inn.

Hannah Marie Country Inn
Spencer, Iowa 51301

INNKEEPER: Mary Nichols

ADDRESS/TELEPHONE: U.S. 71, R R 1; (712) 262–1286

WEB SITE: www.nwiowabb.com/hannah.htm

ROOMS: 5; all with private bath, whirlpools, and air-conditioning. No smoking inn.

RATES: $79 to $115, single or double; $15 extra person; EPB and afternoon hors d'oeuvres. Special packages.

OPEN: April through December.

FACILITIES AND ACTIVITIES: Lunch, afternoon high tea, and evening hors d'oeuvres available. Located on 200-acre corn and soybean farm; hammock, rocking chairs, and country swing on porch; rope swing on old farm tree; croquet. Nearby: a short drive to restaurants. Boating, fishing, and swimming in Iowa's great lakes 20 miles away. Lots of antiques shops, arts and crafts nearby.

*M*ary Nichols may be the most cheerful innkeeper I've ever met. "I want you to feel right at home, so it's okay to open the door and shout, 'I'm here, Mom,' " she said.

Mary's historic farmhouse was built in 1910. "It took talented craftsmen two years to restore the building," she said. A San Francisco expert on Victorian paints was called in to custom-mix turn-of-the-century colors for the inn. "That accounts for our special glow," Mary added.

Everything is special about the Hannah Marie, named for Mary's mother. Consider the guest rooms. Beda, named for her aunt, is the "tomboy" room. It has walnut furniture, soft apricot and forest green colors, a queen bed, and a whirlpool bath. "It's delightfully cuddly," Mary said. "You get a great feeling of being wrapped in a cocoon."

Elisabeth, the "genteel woman" room, boasts lots of bird's-eye maple and has an antique white iron tub. "I tell people to relax here," Mary said. "That's why all baths come with yellow rubber duckies. We also have the best bubbles around. So many guests just soak in their tub immersed in their bubble baths. Even lots of the men."

Louella, the inn's smallest room, features a red acrylic claw-foot tub. "When the sun shines through the lace curtains and falls on the tub, it's really beautiful," Mary said.

Elegant breakfasts include fresh fruit and juice, strata, homemade scones and muffins, strudel, and tortes. Afternoon tea luncheons (also served to the public) can be three-course affairs. The special "Tea with the Mad Hatter" takes its theme from Alice in Wonderland, with guidelines provided by the Alice Shops of Oxford, England, and the Lewis Carroll Society. "Near the afternoon's end, everyone gets to celebrate their un-birthday," Mary said, "complete with un-birthday candles."

Her top-hat scones are also special, receiving rave reviews from veteran England vacationers. Hors d'oeuvres are served daily between 5:00 and 7:00 P.M.

"I also provide parasols and walking sticks for farm strolls," Mary said. She can't wait for a croquet course to be constructed on her "farm lawns." In the meantime, Mary moved a country Victorian-vintage home 6 miles from the middle of town to her property. The Carl Gustav dining room hosts afternoon tea luncheons, gourmet cooking classes, evening

dinner, and more. Upstairs are two luxury rooms with double whirlpool baths.

HOW TO GET THERE: From Minnesota, take U.S. 71 south to Spencer (in northwest Iowa), then continue south 4 miles; the inn is on the east side of the road.

Blue Belle Inn B&B
St. Ansgar, Iowa 50472

INNKEEPERS: Sherrie Hansen

ADDRESS/TELEPHONE: 513 West 4th Street, P.O. Box 205; (515) 736-2225.

WEB SITE: www.deskmedia.com/~bluebelle

ROOMS: 5, with 2 suites; all with private bath, Jacuzzis and air-conditioning.

RATES: $65 to $140; EPB.

OPEN: Year-round

FACILITIES AND ACTIVITIES: Library, video library with VCR, piano.

*Y*ou would never guess by looking at this magnificent Queen Anne that it was built from a mail-order catalog! Put together in 1896, the handsome home features extensive wraparound porches, stained-glass windows, delicate woodwork, and more.

Rooms are named for some of the innkeepers favorite books. For example, Plum Creek might be the namesake of the Laura Ingalls Wilder classic; but you can be sure that none of the Little House characters ever imagined a place as grand as this bedchamber, with its Jacuzzi, claw-footed tub for two, and private fireplace.

You can almost see heaven through the skylights in Heaven to Betsy. And I'll wager that Never-Never Land never boasted a French shower.

HOW TO GET THERE: Take U.S. 218 to 4th Street, then turn west for 0.4 mile to the inn.

Select List of Other Inns in Iowa

Spring Side Inn
300 Ensign Road
Bellevue, IA 52031
(319) 872-5452

Hallock House B&B
3265 Jay Avenue, P.O. Box 19
Brayton, IA 50042
(712) 549-2449

The Mississippi Manor
809 North Fourth Street
Burlington, IA 52601
(319) 753-2218

Fulton's Landing Guest House
1206 East River Drive
Davenport, IA 52803
(800) 397-4068

Another World Paradise Valley Inn
Dubuque, IA 52039
(319) 552-1034
(800) 388-0942

Haverkamp's Linn Street Homestay
619 North Linn Street
Iowa City, IA 52245
(319) 337-4363

The Captain's House
160 North Third Street
Lansing, IA 52151
(319) 538-4872

English Valley Bed and Breakfast
4459 135th Street
Montezuma, IA 50171
(515) 623-3663

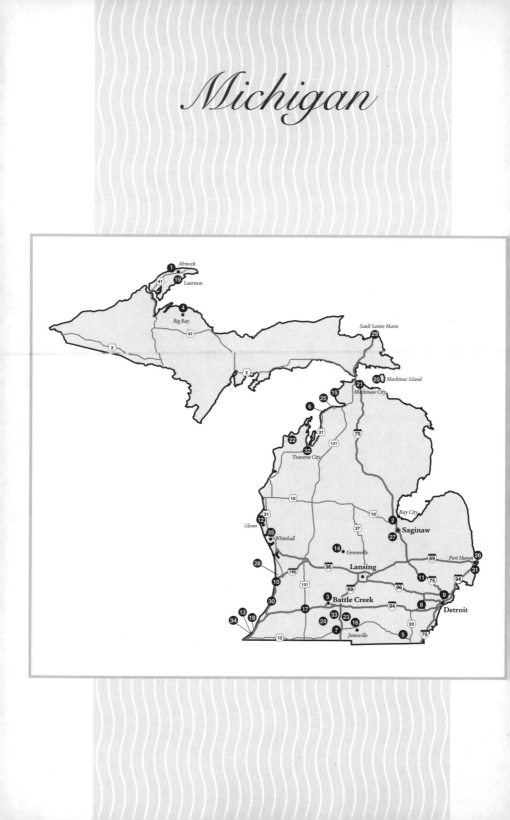

Michigan

Ahmeek
1
19 Laurium

4
Big Bay

Sault Sainte Marie
29

2

Mackinac Island
20
21
Mackinaw City
15
25
6
2 Bay City
22
32
Traverse City

10
10
12
31
27
Glenn
35
27 Saginaw
Whitehall
14 Greenville
69 Port Huron 26
28
196
96 Lansing
11 31
10
75
131
69
96 94
30
3 Battle Creek 94
17
8
9
13
33
Detroit
34 18
24 23 16
23
7 Jonesville
5
12
75

Michigan

Numbers on map refer to towns numbered below.

*A Top Pick Inn

*A Top Pick Inn

Sand Hills Lighthouse Inn
Ahmeek, Michigan 49901

INNKEEPERS: Bill and Eve Frabotta

ADDRESS/TELEPHONE: Five Mile Point Road, P.O. Box 414;
(906) 337–1744

ROOMS: 8; all with private bath, air-conditioning

RATES: $125 to $185, single or double; EPB.

OPEN: Year-round

FACILITIES AND ACTIVITIES: Spectacular sunrises from breakfast dining room, half-mile of private shoreline. Nearby: short drive to Brockway Mountain Drive, perhaps the most incredible views of autumn foliage in the Midwest; antiquing in small towns along the shore.

*N*estled on Five Mile Point, the Sand Hills Lighthouse was the last named lighthouse, specially built in 1917, to house *three* lightkeepers and their families. So it's huge and has been restored to Victorian splendor by Bill and Eve Frabotta.

In fact, they bought the lighthouse thirty-five years ago with the intention of someday transforming this bit of maritime history into a retreat for travelers. "It was in a shambles from years of neglect," Bill said. "So we started from the ground up." What you now see is the result of five years' restoration work—much of it done by Bill and Eve themselves.

Look at their handicraft—ornate crown moldings, hand-tooled walls, a spectacular staircase balustrade that's original to the house, rich hardwoods (I love the English paneling in the Gathering Room)—it's a Victorian paradise with many updated luxuries, too.

Sand Hills boasts eight guest rooms, all offering private baths, several with whirlpool. My favorites might be

the balcony rooms, whose private aeries open onto Lake Superior for vistas of spectacular sunrises and sunsets. Especially inviting is the King Room, with its ninty-six yards of purple velvet in a crown canopy around the bed, along with its own fireplace and romantic lake views.

Bill encourages guests to climb up the lighthouse tower for more panoramic views of the shoreline and surrounding wilderness. (He calls it a 100-step lighthouse—there are 100 steps from entering the front door to reaching the tower room, which housed the lens that signaled ships and led them away from a dangerous, rocky shore.)

There's also a half-mile of lakeshore to explore and thirty-five acres of woods and trails, which explode with spring wildflowers. Let's face it—this is a serious and special get-away-from-it-all place.

A final note: I mentioned that sunrises and sunsets over Lake Superior are incredible. But did I tell you about nature's other sky show—the northern lights dancing under nighttime's canopy of stars!

HOW TO GET THERE: Located about 25 miles northeast of Houghton. Follow U.S. 41 along the Keweenaw Peninsula's shoreline to the tiny village of Ahmeek; turn left at the first street. Immediately upon turning, you'll see signs directing you to Five Mile Point Road, where you'll continue 8 miles to the lighthouse.

Clements Inn
Bay City, Michigan 48708

INNKEEPERS: David and Shirley Roberts

ADDRESS/TELEPHONE: 1712 Center Avenue (Michigan 25); (517) 894–4600 or (800) 442–4605

ROOMS: 6, all with private bath, 1 with whirlpool. No smoking inn.

RATES: $70 to $175, single or double; midweek rates available. Continental breakfast.

OPEN: Year-round

FACILITIES AND ACTIVITIES: Exercise room and pool table. Tour historic Central Avenue homes, Bay City Historical Museum, Bay City Player's (community theater); summer concerts at Friendship Music Shell on Saginaw River; hiking and biking in Bay City State Park. Two-mile-long Riverwalk. About 20 minutes to Frankenmuth; 30 minutes to Dow Gardens.

*T*his 1886 Queen Anne Victorian mansion, with twenty-four original rooms that included six fireplaces, has been transformed into a pampering palace that caters to your getaway pleasures.

Perhaps the inn's most romantic retreat is the Elizabeth Barrett Browning Suite, with its own whirlpool, gas fireplace, king-sized bed, and sitting area with love seat. The Emily Bronte Suite is another charmer, with wicker, lace, and ivy decor; light the candles and whisper sweet nothings to each other in this snuggable room.

The Alfred Lord Tennyson Suite (the manse's former ballroom) is perfect for families—all 1,200 square feet of it.

There are lots of surprises here, too. Guests find gift bags on their pillow

Clements Inn "Top Ten"

Clements Inn once had its own "Top Ten" list—reasons for couples to stay here.

10. Experience the life of luxury in your large whirlpool suite complete with a crackling fire.
9. Feed the ducks and share a ride on the swings at Carroll Park.
8. Share a sunset of passing ships on the Riverwalk.
7. Awake to the sounds of Mozart and the candlelit breakfast that awaits you.
6. Enjoy a glass of lemonade and a quiet moment on a wicker settee.
5. Snuggle under the stars on a blanket for two at a waterfront concert.
4. Walk hand-in-hand among Victorian homes of yesteryear.
3. Light the candles and soak in a bubble bath for two.
2. Dive under a handmade quilt for an afternoon nap.
1. Sneak a kiss on our winding staircase.

with treats inside. Breakfast brings classical music and a candlelit continental breakfast of homemade breads, muffins, fruit and juices, breakfast meats, and cheeses. And the hospitality can't be beat.

HOW TO GET THERE: Bay City is located off I–75, north of Saginaw and Frankenmuth, and east of Midland. The inn is located directly on Michigan 25 (which is called Central Avenue in town), just about ¼-mile west of Michigan 15.

The Old Lamp-Lighter's Homestay
Battle Creek, Michigan 49017

INNKEEPERS: Tracy Greenman and Cheryl Pearce

ADDRESS/TELEPHONE: 276 Capital Avenue, Northeast; (616) 963–2603

ROOMS: 7; all with private bath, air-conditioning, and TV. No smoking inn.

RATES: $95 to $145; EPB. Cross-country skiing and golf packages available.

OPEN: Year-round

FACILITIES AND ACTIVITIES: Sitting room, parlor, dining room, library, antiques shop. Nearby: fitness center, parks, McCamly Place (Saturday night concerts), Civic Theater, shops, restaurants, jogging, biking.

*A*local architect once called this 1912 mansion "flagrantly medieval." It has also been cited by a national architectural association as "one of the purest Arts and Crafts–style houses" existing today.

Let me list a few of the home's outstanding features: The dining room is a showplace. You enter by walking through intricate stained-glass French doors that depict a Victorian forest, and you are confronted by four hand-painted, original canvas wall murals portraying another forested landscape—an almost mythological scene that quickly grabs your attention. That's not all. Over a long dining room table where guests eat breakfast hangs a massive Steuben chandelier so breathtaking that it looks as if it belongs in the Metropolitan Museum of Art. In the living room a large stone fireplace is flanked by two of the thirteen stained-glass windows that grace the home. Add a French Aubusson rug and fine Victorian furnishings to the tally. Honduran mahogany and oak woodwork are everywhere.

For overnighters, consider the Kellogg Room, with its 1912 Circassian walnut bedroom set; the Rich Room, with its heirloom hand-hooked rug; and the McCamly Room, which is great for families—it sleeps six and offers period tables and chairs for fun and games.

The atmosphere remains very Gothic here. The inn is private and quiet, and even on sunny days it can be quite dark, due to its stylings. But the opportunity to enjoy these one-of-a-kind surroundings makes it a sunny day for travelers.

HOW TO GET THERE: From east or west, take I-94 to Battle Creek; exit north on Michigan 66. Follow Michigan 66, which turns into Division and then Capital Avenue Northeast, to the inn.

Big Bay Point Lighthouse
Big Bay, Michigan 49808

INNKEEPERS: John Gale, Jeff and Linda Gamble

ADDRESS/TELEPHONE: 3 Lighthouse Road; (906) 345–9957

WEB SITE: lighthousebandb.com

ROOMS: 7; all with private bath. No smoking inn.

RATES: May through October: $123 to $183, single or double; November through April: $99 to $160; EPB. Two-night minimum on weekends. July 1–Oct. 31.

OPEN: Year-round

FACILITIES AND ACTIVITIES: Great Room, sauna in tower, ½-mile of shoreline. Nearby: half-day treks to waterfalls and mountaintops by Huron Mountain Outfitters; North Country Outfitters for boats, hunting, fishing equipment, and ski rentals; North Shores Treasures features works of local artists; Lumberjack Inn, used in film *Anatomy of a Murder.* Thirty minutes to Marquette, Presque Isle Park, the Ore Docks, Superior Dome stadium, Marquette Golf Club.

Visited here in the waning months of winter. But winter dies slowly in Michigan's Upper Peninsula. There was still nearly a foot of snow on the ground around the lighthouse, and snow caves on Lake Superior soared more than 14 feet into the air.

The lighthouse sits atop a high cliff jutting out into the deep waters of Lake Superior. It's one of the few surviving lighthouses in the country that offer visitors a chance to relive the days of the keepers by staying overnight in its historic quarters.

Built in 1896 on a ½-mile of shoreline and surrounded by fifty pristine acres filled with deer, foxes, wild turkey, and other creatures that feed near the lighthouse's meadow at daybreak, the inn still sends out a warning beam of light to sailors on the lake; however, an automated signal replaced the original light in 1941.

You can see the 1,500-pound, third-order Fresnel lens (second largest ever used on the Great Lakes); make sure you hike stairs to the top of the lighthouse lantern—its tower rises more than 120 feet above the water's surface.

Guest rooms are very comfortable, decorated in Victorian style. One of my favorites, the Lake View Suite, might be the inn's best spot to watch sunrises over the water. The Tower Room, formerly the head keeper's office, also boasts a nice view of the lake.

For those of you who love sunsets, the Sunset Suite offers that view over both the lake and Huron Mountains.

Did I mention the inn's resident ghost? Nooooo? Well, get Linda Gamble to tell you about this apparition, thought to be a former lighthouse keeper—who was found mysteriously hanging from a tree less than a mile from the lighthouse. Sweet dreams!

HOW TO GET THERE: From Marquette, take Highway 550 north into the town of Bog Bay (about 30 miles north of Marquette); follow the lighthouse signs for 3½ miles to the point and the inn. Roads remain clear throughout the year.

Hiram D. Ellis Inn
Blissfield, Michigan 49228

INNKEEPERS: Christine Webster and Frank Seely

ADDRESS/TELEPHONE: 415 West Adrian Street; (517) 486-3155

ROOMS: 4; all with private bath, air-conditioning, TV, and phone.

RATES: $81 to $102.20, single or double; EPB.

OPEN: Year-round

FACILITIES AND ACTIVITIES: Two sitting rooms. Part of the Hathaway House "village" of restaurants and specialty shops. Nearby: Main Street Stable and Tavern, Crosswell Opera House, Lenawee Historical Museum, Michigan International Speedway. Seventy minutes southwest of Detroit, 20 minutes northwest of Toledo.

*O*ne of the first things I noticed was a sign hanging in the bathroom. It read simply ENJOY THE SOFT WATER. A typically quaint touch in this comfortable inn.

The fine redbrick home was built in 1883 by its namesake, a Scotch-Irish harness-and-hardware store operator. Walk around the northwest side of the home and you'll see the cornerstone confirming that date.

All rooms are tastefully furnished with period antiques and reproductions. I especially liked the Hervey Bliss Room, named after the village's founder. The Hiram D. Ellis room boasts a Victorian headboard at least 6 feet high. Soft wildflower-print wallpaper adds a soothing touch, as do Dutch lace curtains that hang on the room's three tall windows.

HOW TO GET THERE: From Detroit, take I-75 South to U.S. 223. Then go west into Blissfield. Note: U.S. 223 is called Adrian Street in Blissfield.

The Bridge Street Inn
Charlevoix, Michigan 49720

INNKEEPERS: John and Vera McKown

ADDRESS/TELEPHONE: 113 Michigan Avenue; (616) 547–6606

ROOMS: 7; 6 with private bath. No smoking inn.

RATES: $85 to $145, single or double; EPB. Two-night minimum on holiday and summer weekends. Off-season rates available.

OPEN: Year-round

FACILITIES AND ACTIVITIES: Charlevoix is a colorful harbor town on Lake Michigan. Nearby: huge marina, fleet, pleasure boating, and charter fishing; restaurants, specialty and antiques shops. Swimming and picnicking on Lake Michigan and Lake Charlevoix beaches. Ferry boats to Beaver Island. July Venetian Festival; August Art Fair; Fall Color Cruises.

*I*nnkeepers John and Vera McKown have created a whimsical world of antique attractions inside this magnificent building with its spiky gables, leaded- and stained-glass windows, and long wrap-around porch. The decor reflects a gentle English cottage look, with original maple floors covered with Oriental area rugs, Waverly print fabrics on love seats, and blue-checked wing chairs.

Both living and dining rooms are graced with English, German, and Chinese antiques, and a baby grand piano invites guests to play some of the old tunes charted on scores of sheet music. Seven guest rooms are warm and friendly, with hardwood plank floors dashed with antique floral rugs. Vera adds a special touch with fresh flowers in each of the rooms, which are individually decorated with more antiques.

In the Autumn Leaves Room are a quarter-sized cigar-store Indian and a genuine humpback steamer trunk. The Harbor Rose Room has oak and cherry furnishings and a view of the lake. But I'll take Evening Glow, where I had a spectacular view of Charlevoix's great sunsets.

Breakfast is served in the dining room, with its handsome woodwork and rose-colored Victorian print carpeting; or you might

open the French doors and take your meal to a cozy sitting area. Vera's choices include homemade Belgian waffles with fresh fruit, home-baked scones with fresh marmalade, strawberry bread with cream cheese, plum and apple tarts, and sour cream coffee cake.

HOW TO GET THERE: From Chicago, take I–94 north to I–196 and continue north. At U.S. 131, go north; at Michigan 66, turn northwest. At U.S. 31, go north into downtown Charlevoix. Here the road is also called Michigan Avenue. Take U.S. 31 1 block north of the drawbridge to Dixon and the inn.

Chicago Pike Inn
Coldwater, Michigan 49036

INNKEEPER: Rebecca A. Schultz

ADDRESS/TELEPHONE: 215 East Chicago Street; (517) 279–8744 or (800) 471–0501

ROOMS: 8, including 2 suites; all with private bath; TV and phone on request.

RATES: $100 to $195, single or double; EPB.

OPEN: Year-round

FACILITIES AND ACTIVITIES: Parlor, library, dining room, wraparound front porch, gardens, gazebo. Walk to downtown shops. Nearby: antiquing; golf; boating, fishing, and swimming at Morrison, Randall, Marble, and Coldwater Lakes; cross-country skiing; orchards; nature trails. Turkeyville Dinner Theatre, museums, wineries; historic architecture.

*O*ne glance at the Chicago Pike Inn, and my pa and I realized we were about to experience something special. This spectacular house was built in 1903 by Morris Clarke. Owners Jane and Harold Schultz, along with daughters Becky and Jody, have carefully restored it to reflect early 1900s grandeur. I admired the stately reception room, with its double-manteled cherrywood fireplace adorned by Staffordshire dogs, and with a sweeping cherry staircase that leads to upstairs guest rooms.

"Local legend says that the wood came from Morris Clarke's own cherry orchard," my tour guide, Jane, said.

The rest of the inn reflects Jane's impeccable taste in antiques and fine fabrics. Treasures include leaded Bradley & Howard lamps, Schumacher and Waverly wall coverings, fluted cherrywood columns, hand-carved antique furniture, stained-glass windows, parquet floors—the list is seemingly endless.

What results from all this attention to the smallest details (guests are supplied with thick terrycloth robes, and Jane's Victorian candy stand in the library is always stocked with fine goodies) is a feeling of luxury and comfort that's difficult to match.

We headed to the library, with its unusual whitewood woodwork. My pa settled in a wing chair next to a roaring fire and immersed himself in his reading. I complimented Jane on a spectacular restoration. "It's such a grand old house," she said. "Restoring it is kind of our legacy to the community."

Guest quarters are exquisite. I stayed in Ned's Room, its bold red-and-paisley wall coverings, huge brass bed, and green leather wing chair giving it the feel of an exclusive gentlemen's club. My pa opted for Charles's Room, reflecting the Victorians' fascination with period Chinese and boasting a handsome sleigh bed framed by a wall canopy.

My daughters would love the Grandchildren's Room, all pink with two twin iron-and-brass beds, white Victorian wicker, and eleven antique portraits of darling little girls.

Then there's Miss Sophia's Suite, two rooms fairly bursting with a hand-carved antique bed, an oak-manteled fireplace, a velvet-covered period sofa, a Martha Washington chair—and even its own private balcony.

Another addition is the Carriage House, a two-room beauty whose rooms feature such amenities as whirlpool baths, balconies, and canopy beds. Add Becky's mouth-watering breakfasts and her delightful hospitality, and you have all the ingredients for one of the best Midwest inns.

HOW TO GET THERE: The inn is located on U.S. 12 (the old Chicago Pike), midway between Detroit and Chicago, just minutes south of I-94.

The Dearborn Inn 📱
Dearborn, Michigan 48124

INNKEEPER: Yves Robin, general manager

ADDRESS/TELEPHONE: 20301 Oakwood Boulevard; (313) 271–2700 or (800) 228–9290, fax (313) 271–7464

ROOMS: 222, including 20 suites, plus 5 reproduced historic homes; all with private bath, air-conditioning, TV, radio, and phone.

RATES: $119 to $129, weekends; $159 to $209, weekdays, single or double; EP. Special weekend and B&B packages available.

OPEN: Year-round

FACILITIES AND ACTIVITIES: Two full-service restaurants, lounge, sitting room, concierge, room service, gift shop, newsstand; baby-sitting service on request. Also gardens, patio, outdoor swimming pool, tennis courts, fitness center. Nearby: Henry Ford Museum, Greenfield Village, professional sports, Fairlane Town Shopping Center, Dearborn Historical Museum, Henry Ford Estate, Northville Downs, golf, and Windsor, Ontario.

BUSINESS TRAVEL: Located about 30 minutes from downtown Detroit. Corporate rates, meeting rooms, fax.

*M*y wife, Debbie, and I drove up the sweeping circular driveway that leads to the graceful porticoed entrance of The Dearborn Inn. It reminded me of a grand mansion of a wealthy Colonial landowner.

Listed on the National Trust (recognized for its stately Georgian architecture), the hotel was built in 1931 by Henry Ford. It served as the nation's first "airport hotel" (a small landing field was located across the street) and housed visitors to the Henry Ford Museum and Greenfield Village just down the road.

It has become an elegant showplace, showered with opulent appointments. I easily recognized Ford's love for early America carried out in the hotel's decor. Our suite in the main building exhibited handsome Colonial fashions, with four-poster beds, wing and Windsor chairs, polished wooden chests, and brass lamps. We easily surrendered to this kind of luxury.

Particularly fun is a small Colonial "village on the green," with five historic-home replicas of famous Americans; you'll feel like a houseguest of Edgar Allan Poe, Patrick Henry, Barbara Fritchie, Walt Whitman, or Revolutionary War hero Oliver Wolcott.

My favorite remains the Poe Cottage, a little white clapboard house that often serves as a honeymoon suite. A delightfully devilish touch: the black iron raven hovering above the doorway.

Dining here is a gustatory delight. The Early American Room, romantic with glittering chandeliers, crisp white linen, and fresh flowers on tables, pampers food lovers. We dined on rock Cornish game hen Madeira and country pork loin applejack while a tuxedo-clad, three-piece combo provided music for evening dancing.

After a delightful meal we headed to the Snug, a lounge where liquor bottles are still kept out of sight, underneath the copper-topped bar, in deference to Ford's lifelong opposition to alcohol.

HOW TO GET THERE: From Detroit Metro Airport, go north on Merriman Road to I–94 East. Follow I–94 about 5 miles to Southfield Freeway, then go north 3 miles to Oakwood Boulevard. Finally, go west 2 miles to the inn.

The Blanche House
Detroit, Michigan 48214

INNKEEPERS: Lesa Bucceri

ADDRESS/TELEPHONE: 506 Parkview; (313) 822–7090

ROOMS: 11, including 3 suites; all with private bath. No smoking inn.

RATES: $65 to $115, single or double; $125, suites; EPB.

OPEN: Year-round

FACILITIES AND ACTIV-
ITIES: Sitting room, din-
ing room. Nearby:
minutes to downtown
Detroit and its attrac-
tions: Renaissance Cen-
ter, Greektown, Detroit
Institute of Arts, Comer-
ica Park, Detroit Historical Museum, Museum of
African American History, Children's Museum, Detroit Science Center. A
short drive to Henry Ford Museum, Greenfield Village, Cranbrook Institute of Science, auto barons' homes, Belle Isle.

"Wow!" my pa said. "This place looks like a mini–White House."
We laughed upon discovering that, historically speaking,
this 1905 Colonial Revival home is known as the "Little
White House." It also keeps good company, nestled in the historic Berry sub-
division of Detroit, just a block from the Detroit River and close to the
mayor's residence. Just pull up to the curb and you'll realize how this house
got its nickname: 20-foot-tall Corinthian porch pillars support a portico
entrance that will have you straining to see the President and First Lady
walking around inside. Ten-foot entrance doors adorned with etched glass
herald the elegance about to greet visitors within.

Inside, classically handcrafted plasterwork includes ornate moldings,
medallions, and rosettes. Restored oak woodwork sparkles throughout the
house. There's even a smattering of Pewabic tiling, which is native to Michigan.

A Little R&R

Here's a note especially for women travelers: The
Blanche House offers a unique service for its female
guests, one that you just don't regularly find at small-
ish bed-and-breakfasts: spa service. A special overnight
rate includes everything from a massage and facial to a
manicure and pedicure.

Guest rooms are lovely snapshots of period charm, filled as they are with antique furnishings, like four-poster beds, embroidered coverlets, and handmade quilts. Among my favorites are those bedchambers near the back of the manse, which provide vistas of the Detroit River and the Stanton Canal.

Other favorites are the inn's three suites, spacious bedchambers offering a welcoming whirlpool bath for romantics. The finest might be the Lee Stanton Canal Suite, with its art deco antique fireplace, queen-sized sleigh bed, whirlpool, and private balcony complete with porch swing—all overlooking its namesake canal.

HOW TO GET THERE: From the south, take I-75 north into Detroit; exit at I-375 and go south. Proceed about 1 mile to East Jefferson Avenue, then turn east (left) and continue to Parkview. There you'll see a sign directing you to the inn.

The Kirby House
Douglas, Michigan 49453

INNKEEPERS: Ray Riker and Jim Gowran

ADDRESS/TELEPHONE: Center Street and Blue Star Highway (mailing address: P.O. Box 1174, Saugatuck, Michigan 49453); (616) 857-2904 or (800) 521-6473

WEB SITE: kirbyhouse.com

ROOMS: 8; all with private bath, 5 with fireplaces.

RATES: $90 to $155; EPB. Special weekday package.

OPEN: Year-round

FACILITIES AND ACTIVITIES: BYOB. Common room, swimming pool, hot tub. Walk to Lake Michigan beach. Nearby: restaurants; art colony in Saugatuck; Allegan Forest; Grand Rapids antiques markets; Holland's ethnic Dutch villages, museums, specialty shops. Cross-country skiing close by.

*T*he grand Kirby House is an irresistible Victorian pleasure. It just jumped out at me with its turrets, gables, leaded- and stained-glass windows, and a quaint peach-colored picket fence surrounding the grounds.

The innkeepers have preserved elegant Victorian interiors that really

impressed me. Especially fetching are leaded-prism windows that fling shards of sunlight on original hardwood floors. I was particularly taken with the parlor fireplace (one of four in the house). It is of an unusual cast-iron design.

The home was built in 1890 by Sarah Kirby, who made her considerable fortune from farming ginseng. She wanted to be rid of troublesome pitchers and wash basins, so she replaced them with corner sinks in the bedrooms; some remain to this day.

Breakfast means croissants, cheese Danish, old-fashioned sticky buns, fresh fruit, sausage, bacon, eggs, quiches, and juices, all served buffet-style. By early morning many of the guests were already enjoying the inn's back-yard deck, where lounge chairs, a hot tub, and a swimming pool await.

HOW TO GET THERE: From Chicago, take I–94 north to I–196 north and go to exit 36. Go north on Blue Star Highway into Douglas. Turn left at the only traffic light and you're there.

The Rosemont Inn 💙 ₵₵
Douglas, Michigan 49406

INNKEEPERS: Joseph and Marilyn Sajdak

ADDRESS/TELEPHONE: 83 Lakeshore Drive (mailing address: P.O. Box 214, Saugatuck, 49453); (616) 857–2637 or (888) 767–3666

WEB SITE: rosemontinn.com

ROOMS: 14, with 3 Jacuzzi suites; all with private bath and air-conditioning, 10 with gas fireplace. Wheelchair accessible. No smoking inn.

RATES: Mid-June through mid-September, $155 to $285, single or double. Three-night minimums on weekends in July, August, and holidays; two-night minimums other weekends. Continental breakfast. Off-season rates available.

OPEN: Year-round

FACILITIES AND ACTIVITIES: Garden room, swimming pool, screened porch, Victorian gazebo. Across the road from Lake Michigan. Nearby: charter fishing, boating, scenic supper cruises; golf, hiking the Lake Michigan dunes, dune rides; summer theater; cross-country skiing in winter. Fine restaurants, art galleries, antiques shops, boutiques.

*T*he last time I spoke to Joe and Marilyn Sajdak, they'd just completed their newest addition to the inn—a Victorian gazebo on the front lawn facing Lake Michigan. "We've already had our first gazebo wedding, too," noted Marilyn.

It's certainly the perfect spot for any kind of celebration or weekend getaway. Winds rustle tall trees, which shade the inn's landscaped grounds from a bright sun. Waves crash on the lakeshore, just across the tiny road and down a steep bluff. And an expansive wraparound porch invites peace and relaxation.

In fact, the Rosemont Inn stands like an inviting friend, a turn-of-the-century Queen Anne Victorian that got its start as an 1886 tourist hotel. Enter through French doors opening onto a formal sitting room; the handsome antique hardwood fireplace signals the elegance you will find throughout the inn.

Joe and Marilyn continue to improve this already wonderful place. Relax on the enclosed front porch, overlooking the lake. I love the Garden Room, perhaps my favorite spot out back. It's bright and sunny, with cathedral ceilings and a ceiling-to-floor glass wall that

looks out over the gardens and swimming pool. There are also a sauna and whirlpool in the back, overlooking the pool.

Check out the fireplace here, great for warming up guests on cool spring and autumn nights, to say nothing of Michigan winters. Of course, the inn is perfect headquarters for cross-country ski adventurers. The deck, with its colorful umbrella tables, is another addition that's become a favorite guest hangout.

The Garden Room serves as the location of the buffet-style continental breakfasts. Count on juices, croissants, muffins, delicious quiches, bagels, cereals, and more. Marilyn and Joe can also suggest some fine dinner spots in nearby Saugatuck.

Country Victorian antiques and reproductions fill the delightful guest rooms, each unique in design; ten have gas fireplaces, which add a cozy touch. I especially liked our room, with its brass bed adorned with a charming crazy quilt, a pinch of colorful pizzazz. Some rooms have a view of the lake through the tall maples that ring the grounds.

Two of three common areas also feature wet bars.

One summer Debbie, Kate, and I, along with some relatives, spent a glorious long weekend at the inn. Especially inviting was the swimming pool, where the kids splashed and played endlessly. It made for good memories—especially when we were blessed with Dayne about nine months after our stay here!

HOW TO GET THERE: From Chicago, take I-94 north to I-196 north. At exit 36, near Douglas, take Ferry Street north to Center Street. Turn west on Center Street and go to Lakeshore Drive, then turn north to the inn.

Pine Ridge Inn 🧡
Fenton, Michigan 48430

INNKEEPERS: Jim and Val Soldan

ADDRESS/TELEPHONE: N-10345 Old U.S. 23; (810) 629-8911 or (800) 353-8911

ROOMS: 4; all with private bath, whirlpool tub, and fireplace.

RATES: $125, single or double, Monday through Thursday; $175, single or double, Friday through Sunday and holidays; continental breakfast.

OPEN: Year-round

FACILITIES AND ACTIVITIES: Walking paths through forest and by pond. Less than an hour's drive to Pontiac Silverdome, Henry Ford Museum and Greenfield Village, and metro Detroit.

f ever there was a setting for privacy and romance, this is it. Secluded in a very private forty acres amid swaying pine trees and rolling hills, the Pine Ridge Inn is an exclusive hideaway. No phones. No pets. Just you and your honey for a luxurious and romantic interlude.

Guest rooms are elegant and huge, with lovey-dovey relaxation kept in mind. Those king-sized beds are actually firm waterbeds. Whirlpools are massive, measuring 7 by 7 feet. A romantic fire in the hearth is only a fingertip away, thanks to gas fireplaces that light up the room with a very romantic glow.

They say you never have to leave your room at the Pine Ridge. Sure enough. A gourmet snack tray is delivered to your bedchamber each evening, and a delicious continental breakfast tray will be found at your door come morning.

For those who do venture outside, walk along a cozy forest path marked with red hearts. Or gaze longingly at the inn's pond. Winter visitors might cross-country ski on a blanket of newly fallen snow.

But when your guest room has all of the above, plus stereo and remote-control television, why bother ever leaving until it's time to go?

HOW TO GET THERE: From east or west, take I–96 to U.S. 23. Turn north and continue to White Lake Road exit; turn left, then turn left immediately onto Old U.S. 23, and continue to inn.

Will O' Glen Irish Bed and Breakfast
Glenn, Michigan 49416

INNKEEPERS: Shelly and Ward Gahan

ADDRESS/TELEPHONE: 1286 64th Street, P.O. Box 288; (616) 227–3045

WEB SITE: www.irish-inn.com

ROOMS: 4; all with private bath. No smoking inn.

RATES: $79 to $165; EPB.

OPEN: Year-round

FACILITIES AND ACTIVITIES: Afternoon tea in the sunroom, great room with fireplace; six horse stables, expansive grounds. Minutes from Lake Michigan beaches and parks. Near Allegan National Forest, Kal-Haven Bike Trail. Drive to Holland, Saugatuck, and South Haven. Wineries, orchards, and farmers' markets throughout the area.

*M*e Irish mother would love the Will O' Glen, a farmhouse resting on seventeen acres near the shore of Lake Michigan. Ward, himself, is from Ireland, or as me ma calls it, the Holy Land. So he and wife, Shelly, have transformed this 1920 farmhouse into a little bit of country elegance of the kind you might find in County Mayo.

A full Irish breakfast can be delivered up to your room, to be sure, which includes bangers (morning meats and sausages), Irish soda bread, and Irish coffee. Guest rooms boast more Irish finery, including Irish down comforters, not that you'll need them with the fireplace in your room.

Aye, now, me ma would say that this authentic Irish country inn comes with everything you need to imagine you're in Auld Sod, itself. Saints be praised!

HOW TO GET THERE: From South Haven, take U.S. 31/I–196 north to exit 26 and go east on 109th Avenue; turn left (north) on 64th Street and proceed to the inn.

Tall Oaks Inn
Grand Beach,
Michigan 49117

INNKEEPER: Julia Mead

ADDRESS/TELEPHONE:
Station and Crescent Roads;
(616) 469–0097 or (800)
936–0034

WEB SITE:

harborcountry.com/guide/talloaks

ROOMS: 12, including 10 suites; all with private bath and air-conditioning. Wheelchair accessible.

RATES: $65 to $230, single or double; EPB. Reduced rates on off-season weekdays. Two-night minimum on weekends June through October.

OPEN: Year-round

FACILITIES AND ACTIVITIES: Living room, garden room. BYOB. Five acres of heavily wooded grounds. Private beach, cross-country ski trails. Inn has twelve pairs of cross-country skis for guest use, also eight bicycles. A short drive to restaurants, New Buffalo's antiques and specialty shops; Lake Michigan dunes, Warren Dunes State Park, orchards, wineries.

*T*he inn was built in 1914 as a summer retreat for employees of a Midwest box-making company. Later it became part of a complex that included the largest frame hotel ever seen in these parts; yes, bigger than the Grand Hotel on Mackinac Island. That hotel, with its own 70-meter ski jump, cross-country trails, huge pier, and twenty-seven-hole golf course (which still is part of Grand Beach), burned down during the winter of 1939.

Enough history. Tall Oaks is the story today, and it is fabulous. Guest rooms are named for North American wildflowers and are so attractive that you'll have a hard time deciding on a favorite. Suites are huge. Typical is the Prairie Clover, which I like very much. Its spindle bed, tall Victorian dresser, 8-foot armoire, and wood-burning fireplace would seem to be enough to entice any traveler. But there are also a sitting room, a two-person whirlpool bath, and a private deck looking out over the handsome grounds, which were blooming in trillium and dogwood during my visit.

I'll bet you never saw a single room as gracious as the Wild Rose. It boasts a full-sized German antique bed that's split in the middle so that it might be divided if the occupants are not married, a traditional Old World touch. It also has its own whirlpool bath, solid-pine plank floors, and a private deck.

HOW TO GET THERE: From Chicago, take I–94 to U.S. 12 (second New Buffalo exit). Go south to the Grand Beach sign, cross the railroad tracks, turn left through arches, and continue to the Y in the road. Bear left (on Station Road) and continue to Crescent Road and the inn.

Winter Inn ⓒⓒⓒ
Greenville, Michigan 48838

INNKEEPERS: Wade and Becky Thornton

ADDRESS/TELEPHONE: 100 North Lafayette Street; (616) 754–3132 or 754–7108

ROOMS: 14; all with private bath, air-conditioning, phone, and TV.

RATES: $49, single; $54, double; continental breakfast.

OPEN: Year-round

FACILITIES AND ACTIVITIES: Full-service restaurant and bar. A short drive to several ski areas, Grand Rapids historical district, and Gerald R. Ford Presidential Museum.

he Winter Inn is an unusual find, tucked on a busy commercial street of this small town. It seems that lumbermen who worked the Big Woods would come to the "city" for some rest and relaxation. They'd take stagecoaches from the city train station to the hotel on "Main Street."

The 1902 inn was one of Greenville's two first-class hotels. I could see lots of evidence for that claim. For example, the lounge contains one of my favorite inn antiques: an immense Brunswick oak-and-mahogany bar made in the 1880s, complete with a long brass footrail. With the lounge's pressed-tin ceiling, oak floor, and a collection of antique prints, oil lamps, and memorabilia, it made me feel as though I had just stepped into an authentic Victorian pub.

The dining room boasts more handsome surroundings. Tables are cast with the warm glow of light filtered through stained-glass windows, and there's lots of greenery. A light breakfast of fresh fruit, Danish, and coffee comes with your stay. Dinner fare is all-American small-town good, featuring seafood, home-baked chicken, and tasty steaks.

The lobby is filled with more antiques. Handsome nineteenth-century Victorian couches and chairs, cut and stained glass, magnificent tapestries, and ceiling-high hallway mirrors celebrate the inn's heritage. There's a pub, with dancing, in the base-

ment. It's also fun to browse among the inn's historic photos (located on the second floor), which depict a long-ago era.

Guest rooms are furnished in contemporary style and remain comfortable and cozy. All have extra-long beds, especially attractive to someone like me who stands 6'2".

HOW TO GET THERE: From Chicago, take I–94 north to I–196 and continue north to U.S. 131. Go north to Michigan 57 and turn east, continuing to Greenville. The road turns into Lafayette Street in the city.

Kimberly Country Estate 💚
Harbor Springs, Michigan 49740

INNKEEPERS: Ronn and Billie Serba

ADDRESS/TELEPHONE: 2287 Bester Road; (231) 526–7646 or 526–9502

ROOMS: 6, including 3 suites; all with private bath. Wheelchair accessible.

RATES: $150 to $250, single or double; EPB and afternoon tea. Two-night minimum on weekends. Special packages. No smoking inn.

OPEN: Year-round

FACILITIES AND ACTIVITIES: Living room, library, lower-level entertainment room, terrace, swimming pool. Nearby: golf, biking, hiking; sailing and other water activities on Little Traverse Bay. A short drive to chic shops in Harbor Springs, downhill skiing at Boyne Highlands and Nubs Nob.

onn and Billie Serba's inn could be a showcase for *House Beautiful.* That's not surprising, I guess; Ronn, an interior designer, has transformed this Southern plantation-style home into an elegant

retreat that offers some of the most extraordinarily luxurious inn surroundings possible.

My brother, Mark, and I got the red-carpet treatment (literally) as we
mounted the steps to the house, set atop a gentle hill and surrounded by
fields and farms. Inside, Chippendale and Queen Anne furniture, Battenburg linens, Laura Ashley fabrics, and exquisite antiques collected by the
innkeepers for over forty years add to the elegance.

The Lexington Suite is the epitome of romance, with its four-poster bed
and Battenburg linens lending touches of sophistication. This room also has
its own sitting area, wood-burning fireplace, and Jacuzzi.

Le Soleil is another of my favorites, with its walls of windows, sunny yellow
color, and hand stenciling. Four of the rooms open onto a shaded veranda
overlooking the inn's 22-by-40-foot swimming pool.

The library is a most stunning common room. It's entirely paneled with
North Carolina black walnut—milled on the spot as the house was built, Billie told me.

Pampering is an art form here. Guests find a decanter of sherry in their
rooms on arrival, with an invitation to join Ronn and Billie for afternoon tea
and hors d'oeuvres—sometimes at poolside in good weather. At night guests
return to their rooms to discover beds turned down and chocolate truffles
on the pillows.

Weekend breakfasts are another Southern-tinged plantation treat. Billie
might serve fresh fruit compote, scrambled eggs, smoked turkey sausage,
and home-baked muffins.

If you want to experience the "estate of the art" in country inn living,
make your reservations now.

HOW TO GET THERE: From Petoskey, take U.S. 31 north to Michigan 119,
continue north toward Harbor Springs; turn right at Emmet Heights Road,
then left on Bester Road, and continue to the inn.

Munro House B&B
Jonesville, Michigan 49250

INNKEEPER: Mike and Lori Venturini
ADDRESS/TELEPHONE: 202 Maumee Street; (517) 849–9292
ROOMS: 7; all with private bath, 3 with fireplace.

RATES: $89 to $179, single or double; EPB. Lower rates on weekdays.

OPEN: Year-round

FACILITIES AND ACTIVITIES: Evening coffee with homemade dessert. Gift shop, sitting parlor, gardens. Nearby: walk to Grosvenor House Museum. Mill Race golf course, restaurants, two arboretums, biking, canoeing, and cross-country skiing. More than fifty antiques shops located minutes away in Allen, antiques capital of the state. Professional summer theater in Coldwater.

This handsome pre–Civil War home, started in 1832, was the first brick house built in Hillsdale Coun-ty. In fact, it took seven years to complete, and the bricks were hauled here by ox and cart from 10 miles away.

The Munro House also was part of the Underground Railroad. The innkeeper showed me the hidden room that housed runaway slaves, located above the ceiling of what is now one of the guest baths. Slaves were moved at night, along a route through Detroit to Windsor, Ontario, in Canada—to freedom.

This is a gracious house, with ten Italian marble fireplaces, 12-foot ceilings, and guest rooms furnished with fine period antiques. The Munro Room, named after the Civil War general whose family occupied the home

A Jeffersonian Touch

The Venturinis are only the seventh owners of the home since 1832. Get Mike or Lori to show you the original shutters that fold up, hidden in the window frames. They are of the type invented by Thomas Jefferson. Or maybe you'd rather see the two Jacuzzi rooms. Now, Thomas Jefferson did not invent those whirlpool jets, that's for sure.

for more than one hundred years, has original poplar plank floors, a handsome American Empire–style sleigh bed, fireplace, crystal chandelier, and its own porch. There are also vintage period linens on the bed, double-stack pillows, and a cozy down comforter.

If you stay in the Sauk Trail Room, you'll be living history. That's because Wild Bill Hickok, who was from Ohio, slept in these antique four-poster cannonball beds. I also like the Shaker Room, resplendent in its simplicity. The room features plank floors, a trundle bed, ladderback chairs, and utilitarian wooden peg rack in true Shaker style. There's also a Shaker "hired man's bed" made especially for this room.

Breakfast is a treat. The orange-vanilla French toast is a specialty, and you may also be served morning meats, fresh fruit, juices, freshly baked sweets, and beverages. Lori'll be happy to recommend a nearby restaurant to suit your dinner tastes, whatever they may be.

HOW TO GET THERE: From Detroit, take I–94 west to U.S. 127. Go south to U.S. 12, then turn west and continue into Jonesville. The inn is at the corner of that highway and Maumee Street.

Hall House
Kalamazoo, Michigan 49007

INNKEEPERS: Jerry and Joanne Hofferth

ADDRESS/TELEPHONE: 106 Thompson Street; (616) 343–2500 or (800) 761–2525

WEB SITE: www.hallhouse.com

ROOMS: 6, with 2 suites; all with private bath, air-conditioning, and TV. No smoking inn.

RATES: $75 to $140; EPB. Two-night minimum on selected weekends.

OPEN: Year-round

FACILITIES AND ACTIVITIES: Kalamazoo is a city of festivals, with some event scheduled virtually every weekend. Nearby: parks, Kalamazoo

Museum, Institute of Arts, Air Zoo, Timber Ridge downhill-ski area, tours of General Motors plant, year-round theater, two universities with music, sports, and other events. Also antiques stores, winery tours, restaurants, dinner train.

*A*s I walked through the dining room on one visit here, the innkeeper pulled me to a window. "There's one of our guests you haven't met yet," he said, pointing to a woman walking out front, wearing a down-to-the-ankles English day dress. "That's Lady Wedgwood. She and her secretary are staying here while she's taking part in the Western Michigan Medieval Festival."

While I didn't expect to meet lords and ladies at the Hall House, I wasn't really surprised. This Georgian Revival redbrick home, built in 1923, is fit for a king. The foyer is graced with Pewabic tile, and common rooms boast handsome ceiling moldings and mahogany woodwork. It is beautiful.

The guest rooms are named for previous owners of the house. The Vander Horst Room, a bow to the home's builder, has a tile fireplace, four-poster canopy bed, custom cedar closets, and a large bath (including a Swiss shower) done in tile made at Detroit's own Pewabic pottery site. Every piece of tile is still handmade and glazed. (By the way, *Pewabic* is an Indian word meaning "clay with a copper color." Pewabic's founders used copper ore in many of their glazes, giving them a characteristic verdigris color. The Hall House is the only identified residential building in southwestern Michigan with original Pewabic tile installations.)

Lady Wedgwood stayed in the Borgman Room, with its queen-sized brass bed. One guest remembers sitting with her at breakfast one morning while Lady Wedgwood instructed her in the fine art of mating parakeets.

The Rutherford Room has an elegant shower that features seven shower heads. The two newest rooms are the Finn Library and Costello Penthouse. The Penthouse is an apartment-sized suite complete with a "workout loft" outfitted with an exercise bike so you can work off your breakfast.

And I challenge you to find two secret hiding places that apparently held the family jewels in earlier times.

HOW TO GET THERE: From Detroit or Chicago, take I–94 to U.S. 131 north (exit 74). Go north to Michigan 43 east (West Main Street, exit 38). Turn east and continue for about 3 miles. As you start down a hill, look for the inn almost at the bottom, on the southwest corner of Thompson Street.

Stuart Avenue Inn

Kalamazoo, Michigan 49007

INNKEEPERS: Thomas and Mary Lou Baker

ADDRESS/TELEPHONE:
229 Stuart Avenue; (616) 342–0230 or
(800) 461–0621, fax (616) 385–3442

WEB SITE: www.stuartaveinn.com

ROOMS: 7 in the Bartlett-Upjohn House, 8 in the Chapell House, 2 in the Carriage House; all with private bath, air-conditioning, phone, and TV. No smoking inn.

RATES: $85 to $175; EPB.

OPEN: Year-round

FACILITIES AND ACTIVITIES: Dinner available; two parlors, music room, and dining room. Located in the Stuart Avenue Historic District. Nearby: Western Michigan University, Kalamazoo College, and the schools' many sports facilities, and downtown. Many citywide festivals, antiques stores. Less than an hour's drive to Lake Michigan beaches and water activities.

*A*t this collection of historic houses loosely identified as the Stuart Avenue Inn, I stayed at the Bartlett-Upjohn House, a magnificent example of 1886 Victorian, Queen Anne, and Eastlake architecture, with several pointy gables and lots of exterior gingerbread. (Look up and you can see the unusual gold roof ornament high on the home's imposing tower.)

Walk into the house and you're overwhelmed by Victorian excess. There's even a fireplace located in the handsome foyer, which opens onto two parlors, a music room, and the dining room. Those rooms are paneled in oak and cherry, and the hand-painted wall coverings are authentic restorations. The main staircase leading to second-floor guest rooms is itself an elegant touch, with unusual straight spindles.

Then there's a massive stained-glass window on the staircase landing that often washes the foyer in jagged slashes of color.

My guest room had a great view of the historic neighborhood, with floor-to-ceiling windows, Belgian lace curtains, elaborate woodwork, a Chippendale sofa, and one of the most comfortable beds I've ever slept in. "We've been restoring old homes for many years," Tom said. "And one thing we've learned is that a good bed is most appreciated by guests."

Breakfast is served in the handsome dining room, which overlooks woods and the McDuffee Gardens—an acre of trees, greenery, and flowers where guests may stroll, picnic (in the gazebo), or watch goldfish frolic in the lily-graced pond. "This type of garden is common in England but rare in the United States," Tom said.

HOW TO GET THERE: From Chicago, take I-94 east to northbound U.S. 131 exit. Go north to Michigan 43 (exit 38A), turn east, and continue for 3 miles to Stuart Avenue. Then turn left to the inn.

The Pebble House
Lakeside, Michigan 49116

INNKEEPERS: Tom Ward and Judy Lichtenstein

ADDRESS/TELEPHONE: 15093 Lakeshore Road; (616) 469–1416

ROOMS: 4, plus 3 suites and 1 house; all with deck or balcony, private bath, and air-conditioning. Wheelchair accessible.

RATES: $115 to $190; Mid-June through mid-September, weekly rentals only. EPB.

OPEN: Year-round

FACILITIES AND ACTIVITIES: Screen house with hammocks. Access to beach across road. Nearby: hiking, boating, fishing, charter fishing for chinook salmon and coho, sailing, golf, biking, horseback riding, downhill and cross-country skiing, snowmobiling, tobogganing. Warren Dunes State Park nearby. A short drive to restaurants, antiques shops, art galleries, winery tours, pick-your-own fruit farms. Hang gliding in Warren Dunes.

*I*like this inn for its peaceful, laid-back ambience. It's as comfortable as your favorite easy chair, a good place to wind down and relax. And it's located in the heart of Michigan's dune-swept Harbor Country, with Lake Michigan just across the road.

"We call it a European-style inn," the innkeeper said, "because of our Scandinavian breakfast." That's a special treat, with European breads, imported cheeses, smoked sausages, herring, and fresh muffins and home-baked pastries.

There's a daily hot dish, too; it might include anything from Swedish pancakes to Danish brunch eggs.

The main building, constructed in 1912, is located in a tranquil village with rolling countryside noted for its farms, orchards, and vineyards. I could see the lake from the porch and from some of the guest room windows and decks.

One of my favorite spots is an enclosed porch with a large fireplace, perfect for nighttime reading by a crackling fire. The inn also has a large collection of oversized Mission-style furniture, giving it one of the most distinctive looks around.

Guest rooms have self-descriptive names. The Rose Room boasts lace curtains, rose borders, and an art nouveau rocker in front of a floor-to-ceiling etched-glass window that overlooks Lake Michigan.

Trek through the grounds on boardwalks that pass among wildflower gardens and manicured lawns to reach the Coach House and Blueberry House, whose suites make guests feel like owners of this lakeside estate. I especially enjoy the Coach House's Garden Room, done in Arts and Crafts style and graced by a leaded-glass window and a deck facing the lake.

Try Miller's for formal nouvelle cuisine dining that draws many media types from Chicago; Hannah's offers fine dining, too. Escape to Beyond the Sea Crab House or Red Arrow Road House for less glitzy surroundings but great food. For gourmet cuisine, head to Jenny's.

I also suggest the Harbert Swedish Bakery, in Harbert on Red Arrow Highway. The freshly baked Danish butter-pecan sweet rolls, pineapple bran muffins, pecan brownies, and elephant ears are a delight to anyone with a sweet tooth.

HOW TO GET THERE: Take I–94 to the Union Pier (exit 6). At the bottom of the ramp, turn left if coming from Chicago, or right if coming from Detroit or the west, to Lakeside Road. Continue on Lakeside Road, crossing Red

Arrow Highway, until you reach the stop sign at Lakeshore Road. Turn left and continue for ½ mile. The Pebble House is on the left.

Laurium Manor Inn
Laurium, Michigan 49913

INNKEEPERS: Julie and Dave Sprenger

ADDRESS/TELEPHONE: 320 Tamarack Street; (906) 337–2549

WEB SITE: lauriummanorinn.com

ROOMS: 18; all with private bath. No smoking inn.

RATES: $79 to $149, single or double; winter rates available; EPB.

OPEN: Year-round

FACILITIES AND ACTIVITIES: Parlor, music room, library, den, dining room, kitchen, gift shop, ballroom. Expansive front porch. One mile to Swedetown Trail for winter cross-country skiing, 4 blocks to snow-mobiling trails. Short drive to Michigan Tech University campus and sports, scuba diving, cycling, antiques shopping, Calumet Theater, fishing, ghost towns. Five miles from Lake Superior.

*I*magine silver leaf–covered ceilings in the music parlor. Embossed and gilded elephant hide wall coverings in the grand dining room. A hand-carved oak triple staircase. A panoramic landscape mural and

Breakfast Bonanza

A hot breakfast is part of the Laurium experience at this elegant inn. Consider fresh fruits and home-baked breads, locally made jams and jellies, and granola. The main dish might be walnut pancakes with orange sauce, French toast with fresh ground nutmeg and sausage, Salsa Eggs with cheese, biscuits and sausage gravy, or Finnish pancakes with fruit sauce.

Maybe you need to stay here long enough to sample all these goodies.

gilded fireplace in the den. Hand-painted murals in most of the guest rooms. Even a 100-foot wraparound front porch with tile floor.

If this sounds like one of those magnificent turn-of-the-century mansions built by copper kings in this part of Michigan's Upper Peninsula, you're right.

In fact, this 1908 mansion, built for the owner of the Calumet & Arizona Mining Company, might be the most opulent one of them all. The forty-five-room, 13,000-square-foot manse was constructed at a time when miners earned 25 cents an hour for their dangerous job. The home cost $50,000 to build, with another $35,000 worth of furnishings added.

Guest rooms are magnificent, filled with period antiques. Ask innkeeper Julie Sprenger about the goldplated seven-foot bathtub that used to greet visitors in the guest bath when the house saw such visitors as Grover Cleveland.

HOW TO GET THERE: The inn is located off Michigan 26, which turns into Third Street once in Laurium. Follow M-26 (Third Street) southeast to Tamarack Street, then turn right. Continue on Tamarack to the inn.

Grand Hotel 💙 📷
Mackinac Island, Michigan 49757

INNKEEPER: R. D. Musser III, corporation president

ADDRESS/TELEPHONE: Mackinac Island; (906) 847-3331 or (800) 334-7263 (reservations)

WEB SITE: grandhotel.com

ROOMS: 366; all with private bath.

RATES: $175 to $515, per person, May through mid-June; $195 to $555 mid-June through early September. Children in same room with two persons, $25 to $99 per child; MAP. Special packages available.

OPEN: Mid-May to late October.

FACILITIES AND ACTIVITIES: Main dining room, Geranium Bar, Grand Stand (food and drink), Audubon Bar, Carleton's Tea Store, pool grill. Swimming pool, private golf course, bike rentals, saddle horses, tennis courts, exercise trail. Carriage tours, dancing, movies. Expansive grounds, spectacular veranda with wonderful lake vistas.

Nearby: museums, historic Fort Mackinac, Mackinac Island State Park; guided tours; specialty shops. There are no motor vehicles allowed on historic Mackinac Island; visitors walk or rent horses, horse-drawn carriages and taxis, and bicycles.

The Grand Hotel, built in 1887, has been called one of the great hotels of the railroad and Great Lakes steamer era. Its location high on an island bluff provides magnificent vistas over the Straits of Mackinac waters.

Its incredible, many-columned veranda is 660 feet long (it claims to be the longest in the world) and is decorated with huge American flags snapping in the wind, bright yellow awnings that catch the color of the sun, and colorful red geraniums everywhere. Many guests simply sit in generous rockers, sip on a drink, relax, and enjoy cooling lake breezes. I also like to admire the hotel's acres of woodland and lawns, finely manicured with exquisite flower gardens and greenery arrangements.

At the Grand Hotel, I feel immersed in a long-ago era of luxury and elegance. Even the attire of hotel attendants is impressive; they're dressed in long red coats and black bow ties. Once I rode the hotel's elegant horse-drawn carriage (the driver wore a black top hat and formal "pink" hunting jacket) from the ferry docks, up the long hill, to the grand portico.

Inside, the hotel is all greens, yellows, and whites, with balloon draperies on the windows, high-back chairs and sofas everywhere in numerous public rooms, and a healthy dash of yesteryear memorabilia hanging on hallway walls. One 1889 breakfast menu especially caught my eye, listing an extraordinary selection of foods, including lamb chops, lake fish, stewed potatoes in cream, and sweetbreads.

Special services include complimentary morning coffee, concerts during afternoon tea, horse-drawn-carriage island tours, and dinner dances. It seems as if the pampering never stops.

Many of the guest rooms have spectacular lake views. Rates include breakfast and dinner, with Lake Superior whitefish an evening specialty. A dessert treat—the Grand Pecan Ball with hot fudge sauce—almost made me melt.

HOW TO GET THERE: From either Mackinaw City from the Lower Peninsula or St. Ignace on the Upper Peninsula, a thirty-minute ferry ride brings you to Mackinac Island. Dock porters will greet your boat. There's an island airstrip for chartered flights and private planes.

Haan's 1830 Inn
Mackinac Island, Michigan 49757

INNKEEPERS: Nicholas and Nancy Haan

ADDRESS/TELEPHONE: P.O. Box 123; (906) 847-6244 (winter number: 847-526-2662)

WEB SITE: haansinn.com

ROOMS: 7, with 1 suite; 5 with private bath.

RATES: $80 to $160, single or double; $130 to $145, suite; continental breakfast. Most of May through early June and September, 20 percent discount; October, 25 percent discount. No credit cards.

OPEN: Mid-May to mid-October.

FACILITIES AND ACTIVITIES: Located off Front Street, main street of Mackinac Island, one of the Midwest's most famous summer resort communities. Short walk or drive to historic sites, specialty shops, restaurants, golf course, ferryboats, other attractions.

*H*aan's 1830 Inn is easily one of my favorite Mackinac Island hide-aways. A stately Greek Revival design with tall white columns, it dates all the way back to... surprise—1830. That's when the island was still operating as a fur-trading center.

The home, listed on the National Register of Historic Places as one of the oldest examples of Greek Revival architecture in the old Northwest Territory, was once owned by Colonel William Preston, the last physician at the historic English settlement of Fort Mackinac and the first mayor of the island. I never pass up a chance to tour this fort, which stands sentinel atop the island overlooking the straits.

The exterior is a gem. Once a frontier log cabin (it's actually built on the foundations of a trader cabin brought over from the mainland during the American Revolution), the main house's Greek Revival features date back to 1830, and the west wing was added in 1847. I could see original tongue-and-groove walls and the wavy paned leaded windows made in the early 1800s.

Guest rooms are furnished in striking authentic period antiques, beautiful pieces that call to mind the island's rich legacy. Such historic items as Colonel Preston's original desk and bed grace the premises.

Rooms are named after significant island figures. The Lafayette Davis Room has a cherry four-poster bed with a hand-tied canopy. It also has fine English prints. Old newspapers, dating from March and April 1847, were found inside the walls during restoration. They were used as a crude insulation against the frigid winter wind.

The John Jacob Astor Room has a handcrafted antique burled-walnut double bed with English bedspreads and a rare butternut chest; a screened-in porch offers a view of the garden of neighboring St. Anne's Church. (The church, whose congregation began worship here in 1695, was the first one dedicated in this part of the country.)

Haan's has added a private suite with post-and-beam construction, 1790 cannonball beds, sunroom, and whirlpool bath. Try it!

Breakfast is taken in the dining room on a handsome 12-foot-long farm harvest table. It includes home-baked spice breads, muffins, coffee cakes, juice, and other beverages. The innkeepers will recommend one of the island's many restaurants for dinner fare.

Did I mention that no cars are allowed on the island? You must walk, or you can rent a horse or horse-drawn carriage, hansom (horse-drawn taxi), or bicycle. There are miles of rugged lakeshore to explore.

HOW TO GET THERE: Catch a ferryboat from the Upper or Lower Peninsula, off I–75, at St. Ignace or Mackinaw City. Once on the island, walk a few blocks east down Huron (Main) Street, around Hennepin Harbor, to the inn.

Metivier Inn
Mackinac Island, Michigan 49757

INNKEEPERS: George and Angela Leonard

ADDRESS/TELEPHONE: Market Street, P.O. Box 285; (906) 847-6234 or
(888) 695-6562

ROOMS: 22; all with private bath.

RATES: $115 to $275, single or double; continental breakfast. Spring
and fall discount packages and off-season rates available. Cribs and cots
available.

OPEN: May through October.

FACILITIES AND ACTIVITIES: Short walk from Main Street on Mackinac Island. No motor vehicles allowed—only horses, carriages, bicycles.
Nearby: restaurants, many specialty shops, historic island sites, horseback riding, swimming, golf, tennis.

*T*his handsome 1877 building, situated on one of the most history-
laden streets of historic Mackinac Island, borrows heavily from
the Colonial English and French influences that saturated the
region in the 1700s and 1800s.

Most of the furniture is from the Ethan Allen English pine collection. It's
perfectly suited to the inn's styling. There also are a number of original
antiques gracing both common and guest rooms.

The guest rooms are enchanting, especially if you want to enjoy country-
inn ambience without sacrificing modern conveniences. Each room is named
for a historic island figure. The John Jacob Astor Room (a building used as
one of his historic fur-trading offices is located just down Market Street;
it's now a preserved historic home) has a four-poster bed, wicker chairs,
and soothing rose-colored wallpaper. A special touch: I could see the bay
waters from a romantic turret alcove.

Other rooms have
antique headboards and
iron-rail beds, marble-
topped dressers, tulip lamps,
and padded rockers. Four
rooms and an entire tower
have been added more
recently. The owners have

decorated in more of a "Victorian, Mackinac Island style," with antique wicker dominating the rooms warmed by light peach and yellow floral colors.

HOW TO GET THERE: Take a ferryboat to Mackinac Island. Ferries run from both the Upper and Lower peninsulas, off I-75. From the Sheppler ferry dock, follow the road leading up the hill; turn right on Market Street to the inn.

Routraville
A Round-Up of Mackinac Island Inns

his wonderful island retreat may have more inns, elegant cottages, and historic hotels per square mile (and the island is only 8 miles in circumference) than any place else in the world. And while the above three Mackinac Island inns are among my favorites, I would do you readers a great injustice if I didn't at least mention some of the additional recommended accommodations I've discovered on this rock. Hope you find the place that's just right for your getaway.

• **Bay View Bed and Breakfast,** $95 to $195; EPB; (906) 847-3295. Built in 1891, grand Victorian style; each room has spectacular seascape of Straits of Mackinac.

• **Chippewa Hotel,** $175 to $425; (906) 847-3341 or (800) 241-3341. This large Victorian charmer is on the water's edge, on Main Street, in the heart of downtown Mackinac.

• **Cloghaun Bed & Breakfast,** $100 to $165; continental breakfast; (906) 847-3885 or (888) 442-5929. Pronounced "claw han" ("land of little stones" in Gaelic), this home of Irish immigrants to the island was built in 1884. Filled with antiques.

• **Harbor View Inn,** $125 to $325; continental breakfast; (906) 847-0101. Built in 1820, this was the residence of Madame La Framboise, a Great Lakes fur trader and great-granddaughter of Returning Cloud, a chief of the Ottawa Nation. Incredibly elegant and gracious accommodations, with history luxuriously restored.

• **Hotel Iroquois,** $125 to $390; (906) 847-3321. Turn-of-the-century charm, cool evening breezes, breakfast room service, but I like my meal on the sun-filled veranda on the waterfront.

• **Lilac House,** $80 to $100; continental breakfast; (906) 847-3708. Charmer located between downtown area and Huron Street.

- **Lilac Tree Hotel,** $155 to $305; (906) 847-6575. Luxury suites with whirlpool baths, antique reproductions, marble baths, water vistas.
- **Market Street Inn,** $100 to $195; (906) 847-3811. Uniquely decorated bedrooms in prime location.
- **Murray Hotel,** $79 to $250; continental breakfast; (906) 847-3360 or (800) 462-2546. Has been offering hospitality to island visitors for more than one hundred years. Located on Main Street.
- **The Inn on Mackinac,** $89 to $275; continental breakfast; (906) 847-3360 or (800) 462-2546. Sprawling "Painted Lady" (thirteen colors on exterior) Victorian mansion, built in 1867; on the waterfront.
- **Small Point Bed and Breakfast,** $75; (906) 847-3758. The 1882 Sheeley House offers a quiet retreat just across the road from the shore, and about ¾ of a mile from the hustle and bustle of town center.
- **Windemere Hotel,** $175 to $195; (906) 847-3301 or (800) 847-3125. Venerable 1887 hotel with incredible straits views, picnic and sunbathing beach, and more.

Brigadoon Bed & Breakfast
Mackinaw City, Michigan 49701

INNKEEPERS: Doug and Lydia Yoder

ADDRESS/TELEPHONE: 207 Langlade Street, P.O. Box 810; (231) 436-8882

Brigadoon Magic

Doug and Lydia write that "Brigadoon's residents could not leave the magical village without breaking the spell. Visitors to Brigadoon B&B will find it equally difficult to say farewell to the rare combination of casual elegance, accommodating staff, and outstanding service. Come to Brigadoon, and let the magic capture your heart."

I couldn't have said it any better.

ROOMS: 8; all suites with whirlpool, fireplace, balcony, wet bar, canopy bed. No smoking inn.

RATES: $95 to $125, single or double; EPB.

OPEN: Year-round

FACILITIES AND ACTIVITIES: Tiffany dining room, veranda. Short stroll to Mackinac Island ferry boats, unique shops, restaurants, sand beaches.

f you remember the Broadway musical of the same name, only once every one hundred years did the mythical seaside village of Brigadoon appear in the mist of the Scottish Highlands. Well, the misty shores of Lake Huron might well substitute for the land of tartans, and this handsome bed-and-breakfast might be a good representation of the village of Brigadoon.

This gracious inn offers old-world enchantment as well as new-world elegance. Each of the eight guest suites features all kinds of luxuries—from heated marble floors and fireplaces to whirlpool baths and king-sized canopy beds.

In the morning, take your breakfast in the sunlit Tiffany dining room, or enjoy breezes on the veranda—with its views of the Straits of Mackinac. Then stroll this vibrant summer resort town, filled with both wonderful shops and natural lakeshore beauty.

HOW TO GET THERE: Take the Jane Street exit off I–75, and continue through four stop signs until you reach Langlade Street. Turn right, and the huge yellow inn is the second house on the right.

Leelanau Country Inn
Maple City, Michigan 49664

INNKEEPERS: John and Linda Sisson

ADDRESS/TELEPHONE: 149 East Harbor Highway; (231) 228–5060 or (877) 2–THE INN

WEB SITE: leelanaucountryinn.com

ROOMS: 6 share 2 baths.

RATES: $50 to $60, single or double; continental breakfast.

OPEN: Year-round

FACILITIES AND ACTIVITIES: Full-service dining room with wheelchair access; sitting area, porch. Area winery tours. Nearby: Sleeping Bear Dunes National Lakeshore; Glen Lake; Lake Michigan; historic Leland "Fishtown" with crafts, art, and specialty shops.

he house is an old farmstead that was built in 1891. Pictures of the then newly built structure hang on the walls. Linda Sisson pointed out photos of all the families that have lived here and said that the granddaughter of the original owners now lives right across the street.

The inn began serving traveling families from Chicago. Linda has an early-1900s guest register. "Some deal," she laughed. "Guests paid $1 per day for a room and three meals."

Although there are three dining rooms, my favorite one is on the long enclosed porch; it's done in lively colors and offers a view of the flowers and grounds out front. The inn specializes in seafood, which Linda's husband, John, has flown in fresh from Boston. Another inn specialty is homemade pasta. Favorites like blackfish Provençal and chicken with pecan sauce are served regularly. So is the delicious prime rib. And don't pass up desserts like the inn specialty—Peanut Butter Pie drenched in fudge topping.

Linda has fashioned guest rooms that are simple, quaint, and charming.

Prize-winning Cuisine

One final note: Maybe I didn't emphasize strongly enough how wonderful the food at Leelanau Country Inn is. Well, in a local newspaper poll, the inn has been voted the best restaurant in Leelanau County, with the best Sunday brunch, the best country setting, and the best service; it was also voted the best place to go for a drive and have a meal. I get hungry just writing about it.

The plank floors made me feel as though I were back at my aunt's Wisconsin farm. Fancy bedspreads and wall wreaths add attractive splashes of color, and the old-fashioned rocking chairs are fun.

Breakfast includes fresh fruit, freshly made croissants, rolls, coffee, and tea.

HOW TO GET THERE: From Chicago, take I-94 north to I-196 north. Continue to U.S. 31 north. Turn north on Michigan 22 and continue north just past County Road 667. Turn right into the inn's driveway.

The National House Inn
Marshall, Michigan 49068

INNKEEPER: Barbara Bradley, manager

ADDRESS/TELEPHONE: 102 South Parkview; (616) 781-7374

WEB SITE: nationalhouseinn.com

ROOMS: 16, including 2 suites; all with private bath and air-conditioning. Wheelchair accessible.

RATES: $66 to $145; EPB. Business rates available.

OPEN: Year-round except Christmas Eve and Christmas Day.

FACILITIES AND ACTIVITIES: Sitting room, dining room, The Tin Whistle Gift Shoppe. Nearby: many fine examples of historic Victorian homes throughout town, with twelve national historic sites and thirty-five state historic sites. Museums, including the Honolulu House. Antiques stores. Stage productions at local theaters. Boating, fishing, swimming at nearby lakes. Winter cross-country skiing. Monthly town events and annual celebrations.

BUSINESS TRAVEL: Located about 10 miles east of Battle Creek. Corporate rates, meeting rooms, fax.

*S*tepping into The National House Inn is like entering a way station on frontier back roads of the nineteenth century: Rough plank wood floors, hand-hewn timbers, and a massive brick open-hearth fireplace with a 13-foot single-timber mantelpiece bring back visions of the frontier.

And why not? The house was built in 1835 as a stagecoach stop. It's the oldest operating inn in Michigan.

More history? Manager Barbara Bradley told me that the inn is reputed to have been part of the Underground Railroad and once also functioned as a wagon factory. Now it provides a glimpse into the past for travelers and is furnished with antiques and Victorian finery.

The rooms are named after local historical figures. "Color schemes are authentic to the early 1800s," Barbara said. So you'll see muted salmons, blues, and greens—all copied "from original milk-paint colors that were made from wild berries to achieve their hue."

The elegant Ketchum Suite is formal Victorian, with a high bedstead and a tall dresser with a marble top. Other rooms reveal iron- and brass-rail beds, elaborate rockers, and balloon period curtains.

I was overwhelmed by the huge armoire in the Charles Gorham Room; it must stand 9 feet high. Still more rooms evoke pure country charm, with bright quilts that complement pine, maple, and oak furniture, and folk art portraits that grace the walls.

Breakfast in the nineteenth century–styled dining room features five different home-baked pastries (including bran muffins, bundt cake, and nut breads), boiled eggs, fruit, cereal, applesauce, juice, and other beverages.

Ask Barbara to suggest an area restaurant; there are several good ones nearby. I love touring the town, which is teeming with all sorts of Victorian-era homes, histories, and legends.

HOW TO GET THERE: From Detroit, take I-94 west to Marshall (exit 110). At the Fountain Circle, jog right and follow the road around to the inn.

The Mendon Country Inn
Mendon, Michigan 49072

INNKEEPERS: Geoff and Cheryl Clarke

ADDRESS/TELEPHONE: 440 West Main Street; (616) 496–8132 or (800) 304–3366, fax (616) 496–8403

WEB SITE: www.rivercountry.com/mci

ROOMS: 18, including 9 suites with Jacuzzi and fireplace; all with private bath, air-conditioning. Wheelchair accessible.

RATES: $69 to $159; continental breakfast.

OPEN: Year-round

FACILITIES AND ACTIVITIES: Rooftop garden with view of creek, special inn weekend events like Country Fair, featuring the work of more than thirty craftspeople; Halloween night, with spooky magic, ghost stories, and goblin's brew; Saturday night summer concerts; winter dinners; Valentine's Day special; Thanksgiving in the Country; and family Christmas weekends, an old-fashioned celebration. Tandem bikes and canoes available for guests. Nearby: antiques market and Shipshewana, Indiana, Auction and Flea Market; local Amish settlement. Restaurants, golf, tennis, fishing, boating, museums, winery tours.

*T*he Mendon Country Inn is everything I imagine a country inn should be. Others must feel the same way: It's been featured in *Country Living, Country Home,* and *Country* magazines—the accolades just keep coming.

Built as a frontier hotel in the 1840s, the inn was rebuilt with locally kilned St. Joseph River clay bricks in 1873. It was called The Wakeman House, a name the locals still use for the inn today. Guest rooms are decorated thematically, though several exhibit interiors done in the grand style so popular after the Civil War. The Amish Room has a beautiful antique Amish quilt. The Nautical Room features country-pine furnishings, with a swag of fishermen's netting used for the bed canopy; it also has a creekside porch. But my favorite is the Wakeman Room, of elegant post–Civil War design, including 8-

More Inn-viting News

The inn's Creekside Lodge is fashioned in Native American stylings; but I doubt if early Indian inhabitants of the area enjoyed whirlpool suites with fireplaces, full cedar saunas, and covered decks overlooking water and wildlife areas.

There's lots more to enjoy. The innkeepers' Sanctuary at Wildwood, about 20 miles west of the inn (near Jones), is a ninety-five-acre private retreat with five Jacuzzi and fireplace suites, two deer herds, and almost 5 miles of cross-country ski trails. The stained-glass window in the gathering room is a real knockout. What a beautiful and very private getaway!

foot-tall windows, a 12-foot-high ceiling, and fine oversized country Empire furnishings.

The best bargain is the Hired Man Room, a small space in country-style decor with a three-quarter bed and a shower across the hall, for only $50. That includes a breakfast of juice, rolls, and coffee.

HOW TO GET THERE: From Chicago, take the Dan Ryan Expressway south to the Indiana toll road (I–80/90), and go west past Elkhart to U.S. 131. Then go north to Michigan 60/66. Head east into Mendon. M–60/66 is called Main Street once in town; follow it to the inn.

Stafford's Bay View Inn
Petoskey, Michigan 49770

INNKEEPERS: Stafford and Janice Smith; Reg Smith, manager

ADDRESS/TELEPHONE: U.S. 31, P.O. Box 3; (616) 347–2771 or (800) 737–1899

WEB SITE: staffords.com

ROOMS: 31, with 10 suites; all with private bath and air-conditioning. Wheelchair accessible.

RATES: $155 to $225, single or double. Special packages available. Non-peak-season rates available.

OPEN: Year-round

FACILITIES AND ACTIVITIES: Full-service restaurant, sitting rooms, sun porch. Nearby: Bay View, a city whose Victorian architecture qualifies it as a National Historic Site; Petoskey's Gaslight Shopping District and ritzy Harbor Springs boutiques. Bay View Chautauqua programs feature concerts and lectures throughout summer. Biking in summer; cross-country skiing at Boyne Mountain, Nubs Nob, ice boating, snowmobiling in winter. Sailboat charters on Lake Michigan; golf.

*S*tafford's Bay View Inn, overlooking Little Traverse Bay, calls itself a "Grand Old Dame of the Victorian resort era." It's certainly steeped in rich Victorian traditions; in fact, it sits next to a village whose treasure of Victorian gingerbread architecture may be unmatched anywhere.

Built in 1886, this elegant white clapboard inn has served North Country hospitality to four generations of discerning travelers. It's a classic summer house, in the sense that it offers cool breezes due to its bayside location, all kinds of outdoor activities, and an ambitious community program of music, drama, and art. There's great shopping nearby, too. Chic boutiques in nearby Harbor Springs are just a short drive away.

A long sunporch, furnished with oversized wicker pieces, overlooks the bay. Guest rooms filled with antiques and reproductions from several famous Michigan furniture makers reflect the styles of the Victorian era. Room 3 has a four-poster bed so high that even I had to use a stepstool to climb atop it— and I'm 6'2".

Several dining rooms serve food with a fine reputation, including fresh Great Lakes whitefish and local specialties, such as honey mustard shrimp and Veal Louisiana in creole mustard sauce, which have been featured in *Gourmet* magazine.

A full breakfast ordered from the regular menu is included in the price of the rooms. That means choices like malted waffles or

Hemingway's Hangout

Would you rather overnight in a hotel that Ernest Hemingway slept in? Then head to Stafford's other inn, the Perry Hotel, where the famed writer stayed in 1916 during a trout-fishing expedition; records show he paid 75¢ for a room.

The hotel retains its turn-of-the-century ambience, with tin-pressed ceilings, Victorian furnishings, elegant guestrooms—even wicker chairs on the long veranda. Get a bayside room for views of the water from your private balcony. The hotel's pub serves breakfast, lunch, and dinner, with entertainment on weekends.

whole-wheat pancakes with Michigan maple syrup, biscuits with sausage gravy, even eggs Benedict and red-flannel hash.

HOW TO GET THERE: From any direction, the inn is right on U.S. 31, just outside Bay View.

The Victorian Inn

Port Huron, Michigan 48060

INNKEEPERS: Marv and Sue Burke

ADDRESS/TELEPHONE: 1229 Seventh Street; (810) 984–1437

ROOMS: 4; 2 with private bath

RATES: $85 to $135, single or double; EPB

OPEN: Year-round

FACILITIES AND ACTIVITIES: Dining room. Short drive to Bluewater Bridge (to Canada), Pine Grove Park, St. Clair River, Edison Depot, Fort Gratiot Lighthouse, Military Street Historic Home District. An hour's drive to metro Detroit.

I heard about the Victorian Inn because of its food. In fact, it's probably safe to say that the establishment is far more famous for its superb kitchen than for its bed-and-breakfast offerings.

Consider this dinner menu, from which I chose during my visit in April. First there is filet mignon with béarnaise sauce; accompany this with a 1993 Haywood Cabernet, and you've got a winning dinner combination.

Not in the mood for steak? How about grilled swordfish with Dijon lime-ginger sauce? Or pecan chicken, dipped in a honey-mustard glaze, pressed into chopped pecans, and roasted?

Or maybe barbecue-spiced sea scallops with roasted tomato butter is more your mood today? The sauce is concocted from roasted plum tomatoes, chilies, chicken stock, fresh cilantro, and lime juice.

And wait until you see the dessert tray.

The green-clapboard building was constructed in 1896 for Scottish immigrant John Davidson, who became a successful local dry-goods dealer. When the innkeepers restored the house in 1983, they used the original plans and drawing supplied by the home's architect, Issac Erb. Because of this good fortune (and lots of long hours and hard work), preservation and restoration took place within six months.

The four guest rooms are charming. The Victorian Room boasts a bird's-eye maple headboard. Another favorite appointment: A handsome four-poster bed graces the Edward Room, along with a marble-topped dresser and original brass-and-blown-glass chandelier.

Oh, and I need some advice. Is it polite to eat dinner twice in one day?

HOW TO GET THERE: From Flint, take 69 west into Port Huron; turn on Seventh Street and proceed to the intersection of Seventh and Union and the inn.

Montague Inn
Saginaw, Michigan 48601

INNKEEPERS: Willy Schipper

ADDRESS/TELEPHONE: 1581 South Washington Avenue; (517) 752-3939

WEB SITE: www.montagueinn.com

ROOMS: 15, including 1 suite; all with private bath, all with air-conditioning, TV, and phone.

RATES: $75 to $195; continental breakfast. Add $10 for third person or child in room; kids under 10 free.

OPEN: Year-round

FACILITIES AND ACTIVITIES: Full-service restaurant (lunch, dinner Tuesday through Saturday by reservation). Nestled on eight beautifully landscaped acres, formal flower gardens, herb garden; cooking classes in summer, elegant picnic lunches provided guests for afternoons spent at Lake Linton, just behind inn. Nearby: Japanese Garden and Teahouse, children's zoo, Hoyt Park, Old West Side business district. Health club, summer and winter sports activities available to guests.

*A*fter driving nearly sixteen hours with my wife and daughter Dayne, then six months old, I made an evening call to the Montague Inn, searching for a room. It was answered by one of the owners who told me he had had a cancellation, so he'd be expecting us. Turns out we got the last room.

We were lucky in several ways, since the Montague Inn quickly became one of our favorite stopovers. It's an elegant Georgian mansion, built in 1929 by its namesake, a prosperous businessman who made products from Saginaw's sugar beet crop. The inn has the ambience of a fine, intimate European hotel, with elegant classical Georgian antiques, Oriental and Persian rugs, formal flower and herb gardens, private park, and lakeside location all adding to its clublike atmosphere.

It also boasts six fireplaces, a dining room overlooking Lake Linton, and a library that contains a swinging shelf to reveal a small hidden room.

Our quarters, the third-floor Goodridge Room, was a cozy bedchamber tucked beneath a gable, with three alcove windows overlooking the grounds, two twin beds, and a cedar-lined bath. Most inn rooms are far more spacious; some offer marble fireplaces, art deco–tiled baths, pegged oak floors, and views of the lake or park.

Dining is also a treat. Formal servers wear what closely resemble butlers' uniforms. Entrees include shrimp sautéed in hazelnut oil and finished with strawberry puree and ground hazelnuts; Norwegian salmon served with brie in a puff pastry; and grilled medallions of tenderloin sauced with Dijon and demiglace. Even lunch offers selections like grilled tenderloin tips and smoked turkey salad.

HOW TO GET THERE: From Detroit, take I-75 north into Saginaw. Exit on Michigan 46 and go west to Remington. Follow Remington northwest to Washington and turn left. Continue to the inn.

Kemah Guest House
Bed and Breakfast on the Hill
Saugatuck, Michigan 49453

INNKEEPERS: Phil and Carolyn Caponigro

ADDRESS/TELEPHONE: 633 Allegan Street; (616) 857-2919 or (800) 445-3624

WEB SITE: www.bbonline.com/mi/kemah

ROOMS: 6; 2 with private whirlpool bath, 2 with private bath down the hall.

RATES: May through October, $95 to $175, single or double; continental breakfast. Off-season rates available.

OPEN: Year-round

FACILITIES AND ACTIVITIES: Rathskeller (for guests only). Located on a quiet hill, high above the bustle of this lakeside Midwest art colony village. Nearby: a short drive to restaurants, antiques and specialty shops, art galleries, beaches, swimming, boating, dunes exploring, and more.

*T*he Kemah Guest House is one of the most intriguing residences in the lakeside village of Saugatuck. It reminds me of traditional European homes and combines an old-world German flair with touches of art deco—and Frank Lloyd Wright.

Built by a German sea captain, the home is named for its site on a breezy hill. (*Kemah* is a Potawatomi Indian word meaning "teeth of the wind.") The captain, ever a superstitious seaman, wanted to ensure that his sails would always billow with the winds, so he graced his home with a good luck moniker.

The building was remodeled in 1926 by William Springer, a Chicago Board of Trade member. You can see his initials carved everywhere—from wood panels in the rathskeller to the massive wrought-iron arched doorway.

There are so many highlights:

Stained- and leaded-glass windows depict sailing scenes.

Hand-carved wooden landscapes on the solarium paneling recount the house's various appearances through the decades.

A bricked, semicircular solarium with a running fountain was designed by T. E. Tallmadge, a disciple of Frank Lloyd Wright, and captures the master's Prairie School architectural style.

Beamed ceilings, cornice boards, and a fireplace (of Pewabic tile) recall the art deco era.

Have a drink in a genuine rathskeller, displaying the home's original wine casks, wall stencils, and leather-strap and wood-frame chairs hand-carved in Colorado in the 1930s.

Can you find the secret panel that hid whiskey and spirits during Prohibition days? A hint: Look at the windows near the arched door and kitchen.

There's a cave on the grounds and a Native American grave on the side of the hill.

Charming guest rooms are furnished in rich individual styles. One is done in fine imported Dutch lace; another recalls a gentleman's room, with its oak furniture and a 6-foot-tall Victorian headboard on the bed. My favorite room features an eleven-piece bedroom set made in 1918, one of only two like it ever made. It's all walnut, of gorgeous craftsmanship. Look for the secret jewelry drawer in the dresser.

There are rolls, Danish, fresh fruit, juices, and coffee for breakfast; sometimes you'll also be treated to French toast, quiche, and more. If you wish, the innkeepers will recommend one of many good area restaurants, too.

HOW TO GET THERE: From Chicago, take I-94 north to I-196. Take exit 36 just south of Douglas, merge onto Blue Star Highway, and go north to Lake Street. Turn left (west), go ½ mile, and turn right on Allegan; proceed to the top of the hill (Allegan and Pleasant).

The Park House
Saugatuck, Michigan 49453

INNKEEPERS: Lynda and Joe Petty

ADDRESS/TELEPHONE:
888 Holland;
(616) 857–4535 or (800) 321–4535

WEB SITE: www.bbonline.com/mi/parkhouse

ROOMS: 9, including 2 suites, plus 6 cottages; all with private bath and air-conditioning. Wheelchair accessible.

RATES: $95 to $165, rooms; $150, suites; $125 to $225, cottages; EPB. Three-night minimum stay in July.

OPEN: Year-round

FACILITIES AND ACTIVITIES: Gathering room, screened porch. Nearby: a short drive to restaurants, Lake Michigan beaches, swimming, boating, charter fishing, cross-country skiing, specialty stores, antiques shops, art galleries, sand dune schooner rides, golf, hiking, biking, lake cruises.

*T*he Park House is a treasure. Built in 1857 by a local lumberman, the two-story clapboard home is Saugatuck's oldest historic residence. Innkeepers Lynda and Joe Petty recently restored the historic wing of this handsome inn, which had been removed in the 1940s. Now the porch wraps around the house, is screened in, and overlooks pretty gardens.

Lynda told me a great story of how the inn got its name. Seems that a former owner fenced the home's almost eight acres and stocked the pasture with deer. Their grazing cropped the grass, giving the grounds a manicured look. People started calling it the "park" house.

Want more history? Susan B. Anthony stayed here for two weeks in the 1870s and helped form the county's first temperance society. In fact, Joe laughingly said, Anthony was responsible for closing down half the bars in Allegan County.

The house is built from original timbers that once stood on the property. Some special touches include the original wide-plank pine floors, pretty wall stencils done by Lynda, a wide fireplace, and antique furnishings throughout the home. French doors in the parlor open onto an herb garden. All in all, it's a real country charmer. Each cozy guest room is distinctively decorated, and all have a queen-sized iron-rail bed and warm oak furniture. Six rooms also feature a fireplace.

For more elegant surroundings, repair to a Park House suite; each comes with a fireplace, two-person whirlpool bath, and a private balcony. Lynda will even serve you breakfast in bed.

Or rent one of the inn's cottages. The Rose Garden sits just west of the main inn house and has its own outdoor hot tub. The Mill House, complete with a Franklin stove, offers spectacular vistas from floor-to-ceiling windows that overlook the harbor. Indian Point features lots of cedar with a wall of glass overlooking the Kalamazoo River. And there are two more in nearby Douglas.

HOW TO GET THERE: From Chicago, take I–94 north to I–196 and continue north to exit 41 (Blue Star Highway). Turn west and continue on Washington (where Blue Star turns left) to the inn. (Washington changes to Holland at the city limits.)

Twin Gables Country Inn
Saugatuck, Michigan 49453

INNKEEPERS: Bob Lawrence and Susan Schwadener

ADDRESS/TELEPHONE: 900 Lake Street, P.O. Box 881; (616) 857–4346

WEB SITE: twingablesinn.com

ROOMS: 14, with 1 suite; all with private bath and air-conditioning, some with wheelchair access; 3 cottages, 1 with fireplace.

RATES: May 1 through September, $75 to $150; EPB. Two- to seven-day rates for cottages. Off-season rates available. Two-night minimum on weekends during summer season; three-night minimum on holiday weekends.

OPEN: Year-round

FACILITIES AND ACTIVITIES: Sitting and dining rooms, great room with wood-burning fireplace. Heated swimming pool, indoor hot tub, garden terrace with pond. Short walk or drive to art galleries, specialty shops, antiques stores, beaches; swimming, boating, and more.

This inn originally stood on a hill across the Kalamazoo River. One winter it was moved across the frozen waters by mule team and log sled to Saugatuck. After all that trouble, the owners thought they'd put it too close to a road, so they moved it again to its present location.

The inn is all that's left of a genuine Midwest ghost town. The old logging town of Singapore hugged a spot on the dune-filled eastern shores of Lake Michigan that is now occupied by Saugatuck. But when the trees had been cut down, lumber interests left and the town was abandoned. Eventually the crumbling buildings were buried under tons of ever-shifting sand dunes. Now the old town is just a historical footnote.

The 1865 inn is built from timbers cut in the old Singapore sawmill. It was designed by the same architect who built the magnificent Grand Hotel on Mackinac Island.

The guest rooms are lovingly furnished, each distinctive and warm. The Bright Oak Room, of course, has lots of light oak furnishings and is brightly decorated in shades of yellow—quite a sight on a sun-drenched morning—while the Cape Cod Room features beautifully crafted pine furniture. But my favorite is the Dutch Room, all tulips and royal blue colors, with 1914 furniture made in Gettysburg, Pennsylvania.

The inn's heated outdoor pool is a great haven, or you can take a dip in the large indoor hot tub.

HOW TO GET THERE: From Chicago, take I-94 north to I-196. Continue north to exit 36 and go north on Blue Star Highway. Turn left on Lake Street and continue to the inn.

Wickwood Inn 🧡
Saugatuck, Michigan 49453

INNKEEPERS: Julie Rosso-Miller and Bill Miller, owners; Corinne Roberts, manager

ADDRESS/TELEPHONE: 510 Butler Street; (616) 857–1097 or (800) 385–1174

WEB SITE: www.wickwoodinn.com

ROOMS: 11, with 2 suites; all with private bath and air-conditioning. Wheelchair accessible.

RATES: $150 to $180, weekdays; $165 to $225, weekends; EPB and evening hors d'oeuvres. Off-season rates available.

OPEN: Year-round except December 24 and 25.

FACILITIES AND ACTIVITIES: Weekend buffet brunch available. Sunken garden room, library/bar. Nearby: beaches of Lake Michigan, Saugatuck specialty stores, antiques shops, restaurants, golf, boating, fishing, cross-country skiing.

BUSINESS TRAVEL: Located about 45 miles west of Grand Rapids/Kent County Airport. Corporate rates, meeting room, fax.

*S*taying at the Wickwood Inn is almost like taking a mini–European vacation. That's because it was inspired by a visit to the Duke's Hotel in London.

The result is outstanding. All linens, wallpapers, and fabrics are from British designer Laura Ashley's collections. There are elegant pieces from Baker Furniture's "Historic Charleston" line. Complimentary soaps and shampoos by Crabtree & Evelyn of London are provided in every bathroom.

These are some of the finest guest rooms I have ever seen. Exquisite walnut, pine, and cherry antique furnishings are outstanding. The Carrie Wicks Suite, features a four-poster Rice bed. In the Master Suite, I found a cherrywood canopy bed with an antique hand-crocheted canopy. Its sitting room contains an Empire-style couch, with finely carved swan heads gracing the arms. For a more casual feel, try Sydney Alexander. This room, with its country French red-and-white Souleiado print, overlooks the inn courtyard; it feels like a bit of Provence.

Morning pampering begins upon awakening, with coffee and your favorite newspaper waiting at your door.

Then make your way down to the sun-dappled Garden Room, where breakfast awaits; it's fit for royalty, with the likes of country ham, cheese and herb strata, blueberry French toast, fresh-baked croissants, homemade scones and coffee cake, fruit salads, granola, and juices and coffee. It's an ever-changing menu—all prepared from the best-selling *Silver Palate* cookbook of author/innkeeper Julee Rosso-Miller.

After breakfast head for refreshing breezes at the inn's screened gazebo, which demands nothing of you except to relax in oversized California redwood furniture.

HOW TO GET THERE: From Chicago, take I-94 north to I-196. Continue north to exit 41; turn southwest on Blue Star Highway, just outside Saugatuck. At the fork in the road, take Holland Street (to the right) into town. Turn right at Lucy, then left at Butler to the inn.

Ojibway Hotel
Sault Sainte Marie, Michigan 49783

INNKEEPER: Todd Medert, general manager

ADDRESS/TELEPHONE: 240 West Portage Avenue; (906) 632–4100 or (800) 654–2929, Canada; (705) 945–8583, fax (906) 632–6050

WEB SITE: ojibwayhotel.com

ROOMS: 71, all with private bath, some with whirlpools.

RATES: $125 to $185, single or double. Summer, winter rates available. Corporate rates and facilities available.

OPEN: Year-round

FACILITIES AND ACTIVITIES: Lobby with fireplace, leather wing chairs, and sliding rockers. Full-service restaurant, lounge. Indoor swimming pool, sauna, spa. Walk to Soo Locks, shops along Portage Avenue. Short drive to Soo Locks Boat Tours, Tower of History, Valley Camp ship museum, bridge to Canada, Searchmont Resort, Agawa Canyon Train Ride.

*T*his little gem of a hotel, located just across the street from the Soo Locks, is perhaps one of my finest personal discoveries in a long time of inn-hopping. I was really swept away by this elegant retreat, which has been capturing the hearts of Upper Peninsula visitors since 1928.

Just walking inside was a pleasure; I knew immediately that this would be a welcome respite from being on the road. The hotel is warm and charming; the staff is friendly and helpful. Guest rooms are elegant yet homey. What a rare combination.

You might want to treat yourself to a suite here, especially if you're on a romantic getaway. The sitting area is a wonderful mixture of timeless woods and original artwork. And the adjoining bedroom boasts its own double whirlpool just a few steps from the bed— and a wet bar to boot!

Soo Locks, the inn restaurant, has been recognized as one of the top 500 in the country, and rightly so for its combination of steak, Great Lakes seafood, and other mouth-watering creations.

My daughters and I rejuvenated ourselves after a long road trip with a long soak in the indoor pool and spa. Of course, I also had to sample the sauna, a passion of mine.

As I'd mentioned, the Ojibway is located across the street from the Locks. The girls discovered that the Great Lakes' longest ship (more than 1,000 feet, longer than three football fields end to end) would be passing through the locks around midnight. So we left our rooms a little past eleven, walked to the dock and viewing balcony, and waited for this behemoth to arrive. It did, and it was quite spectacular.

But you know, spending that time with my girls, waiting for the ship to come, was my biggest reward.

HOW TO GET THERE: From I-75, take the exit 394 ramp, then turn left on Easterday Avenue; continue to Portage Avenue, then turn right. The Ojibway Hotel is on the corner of Portage Avenue and Osborn Boulevard, next to the Soo Locks.

Old Harbor Inn
South Haven, Michigan 49090

INNKEEPER: Frank York

ADDRESS/TELEPHONE: 515 Williams Street; (616) 637-8480 or (800) 433-9210

WEB SITE: oldharborinn.com

ROOMS: 44, including 6 suites; all with private bath and air-conditioning, some with whirlpool bath and kitchenette. Wheelchair accessible.

RATES: $110 to $295; EP. Two-night minimum on weekends. Off-season rates available.

OPEN: Year-round

FACILITIES AND ACTIVITIES: Indoor pool, hot tub; quaint shops and eateries in village. Nearby: beaches, sailing, sailboarding, spectacular sunsets, U-pick farms, windswept sand dunes, biking, hiking, horseback riding, cross-country skiing, boutiques, art galleries.

*T*he Old Harbor Inn sits on the banks of the Black River, in what resembles a re-created New England fishing village. I strolled along cobblestoned walkways, on boardwalks that skirt the water, and through quaint shops that had names like Bahama Mama's and

Flying Colors (both specializing in splashy beachwear).

By far my favorite room is Number 6. It's huge, with a handsome sitting area, a fine mix of antique reproductions and contemporary furnishings, a queen-sized bed, a white wicker settee, and a minikitchen. It also has magnificent views of the Black River from a long bank of windows on two walls; you can soak up river views while relaxing in a massive indoor hot tub that seems to assure romance. There's even more: A blue-and-white ceramic-tile fireplace sits in the corner of the room, and French doors open to a walkout balcony facing the river.

Visit during Labor Day weekend and you'll be treated to the Venetian Festival's lighted-boat parade, with miles of brightly illuminated boats floating down the Black River.

HOW TO GET THERE: Exit I-196 at Phoenix Street. Continue for three stoplights, then turn right to the inn.

Yelton Manor
South Haven, Michigan 49090

INNKEEPERS: Elaine Herbert and Robert Kripaitis

ADDRESS/TELEPHONE: 140 North Shore Drive; (616) 637-5220

WEB SITE: www.yeltonmanor.com

ROOMS: 17, including 2 suites and a guest house; all with private bath and air-conditioning.

RATES: $95 to $240, single or double; EPB and hors d'oeuvres. Two-night minimum on weekends in high season. Special rates and packages and off-season rates available.

OPEN: Year-round

FACILITIES AND ACTIVITIES: Sitting rooms, enclosed porch dining area. Nearby: beach, specialty shops; Lake Michigan water activities, including salmon and trout charters; restaurants. U-pick fruit farms, winery tours, cider mills, golf, nature trails, biking, hiking, cross-country skiing, Todd Farm Goose Sanctuary.

My wife, Debbie, and I consider South Haven's North Beach among the finest in the Midwest. In fact, a summer never passes without our bringing our daughters, Kate and Dayne, up to South Haven for a little sand castle construction and a dip in the water.

Now that the inn has been lavishly restored to its historic *chalet de la mer* ("house of the sea") style, we may have to invent even more excuses for trips up this way. Originally built in 1873 for two Chicago sisters, the handsome home is a delightful mix of country Victorian and luxury. Many of the furnishings were handcrafted—the pencil-post beds found in many guest rooms were fashioned by Amish craftsmen.

We stayed in the elegant Rose Room—a special treat—with slanted walls tucked under the house's gables, Dutch lace curtains, and window views of the lake. Snuggling is easy in the huge king-sized bed adorned with eight pillows and a down comforter, and a large Jacuzzi can be adventurous—without the kids. There's also a sitting room with television, but I've got the feeling it's not often used.

A cozy common sitting room warmed by a fireplace is a good spot for conversation during winter months. In summer I especially like to breakfast on the enclosed porch. The meal might include ham soufflés with salsa, stuffed French toast with cream cheese, apple tortes with cheese filling, or homemade poppyseed cake.

HOW TO GET THERE: From the north or south, take I–196 to I–196 Business Loop (Phoenix Street), then turn right on Broadway. At the drawbridge, Broadway turns onto Dyckman; take Dyckman to the stop sign. The inn is located on the left corner of Dyckman and North Shore Drive.

St. Clair Inn
St. Clair, Michigan 48079

INNKEEPER: Ves Calvert

ADDRESS/TELEPHONE: 500 North Riverside; (313) 963–5735

WEB SITE: stclairinn.com

ROOMS: 79, with 20 suites; all with private bath.

RATES: $100 to $160, single or double; $140 to $165, suites; $240, Jacuzzi suites; $400, Captain's House. EP. Wheelchair accessible.

OPEN: Year-round

FACILITIES AND ACTIVITIES: Breakfast, lunch, and dinner available in six dining rooms. River lounge, indoor swimming pool and whirlpool, riverfront boardwalk. Nearby: winter cross-country skiing; summer water sports, charter fishing, hiking, golf, and tennis. Antiques and specialty stores across the street.

BUSINESS TRAVEL: Meeting rooms, fax, conference calling, electronic copy boards, corporate rates.

The St. Clair Inn hugs fast to the shore of its namesake river overlooking Canada, just across the channel. Built on the site of a historic sawmill in 1926, the inn luxuriates in its English Tudor architecture while providing a comfortable vantage point for viewing a constant parade of merchant ships and tankers that ply these waters leading to Great Lakes ports.

Inside heavy oak doors, note massive pillars supporting a rough-hewn beamed ceiling, calling to mind the spine of a sailing ship. Two massive stone hearths flank windows looking out over the river; each has high-back chairs nearby for cozy conversations or serious reading.

On my last stay here, I ran to the inn's dock (sometimes referred to as "the world's longest freshwater boardwalk") on hearing the blast of a foghorn. A massive freighter, seemingly an arm's length away, almost scraped both shorelines as it moved through the mist-shrouded channel. I waved to a sailor standing on the high aft deck. He tipped his cap and waved back.

I like all the guest chambers, especially the north wing's river-view rooms, with their own private balcony looking out over the water. Then there's the Captain's House, with its sunken lounge, fireplace, sunporch, Jacuzzi, and wet bar. The Annex rooms have their own riverfront docks.

Even the indoor swimming pool boasts more spectacular river views.

The inn menu owes much to its proximity to Lake Huron. It includes northern Canadian walleye and lake perch. The pork chops are an inn specialty, and a fresh strawberry pie is served in a sea of whipped cream.

HOW TO GET THERE: Follow I-94 east to exit 257. Turn right (east) onto Fred Moore Highway and follow it to Clinton Avenue. Then turn right to North Riverside. Turn left and proceed to the inn.

Grand Traverse Resort 📇 📱
Traverse City, Michigan 49610

INNKEEPER: Irving Kass, general manager

ADDRESS/TELEPHONE: 100 Grand Traverse Boulevard, P.O. Box 404; (231) 938-2100 or (800) 748-0303

ROOMS: 666; all with private bath, many with whirlpool, fireplace, wet bar, more.

RATES: $105 to $435; single or double, depending on the room (Tower, main resort, Valleyview, Shores, condos) and season. Two-night Carefree and Family Escape packages available.

OPEN: Year-round

FACILITIES AND ACTIVITIES: Two golf courses, indoor and outdoor swimming pools, lap pool, indoor tennis courts, exercise and fitness room (and classes), running/biking/hiking trails, three elegant restaurants with lounges, sprawling grounds. Winter: cross-country skiing, ice skating, horse-drawn sleigh rides. Short drive to shops in Traverse City, beach, cruising, swimming.

*O*kay, so I lied. This sprawling resort doesn't even faintly resemble an inn. And it's not located in Traverse City, but in Acme—6 miles northeast of Traverse City. I can explain the fibbing. First of all, you need to know that even though Grand Traverse is not an inn, it is one of the region's finest resorts and a very romantic getaway.

Second, nobody, even people living in Michigan, seems to know where Acme is, but everyone knows Traverse City. Besides, when I think of Acme, I think of those contraptions Wile E. Coyote uses to try to capture the Roadrunner.

So there.

There's so much to do here. The resort features a Jack Nicklaus–designed golf course and offers tennis, golf, and swimming (indoor and outdoor pools), as well as hiking, running, and biking trails. There are elegant shops in the lobby, a great Christmas season festival of lights, cross-country skiing on groomed trails in winter . . . the list is endless.

During our last stay here, we overnighted in the Tower, the resort's seventeen-story glass "skyscraper" that can be seen for miles—literally. (When my daughters and I were on the beach in Traverse City, we could point across Lake Michigan and see the Tower rising majestically on the horizon.) We enjoyed breathtaking views of the surrounded wooded countryside while luxuriating in our room, complete with refrigerator, whirlpool tub, and wet bar.

"There's even television and phones in the bathroom," the girls excitedly reported. So you know it was almost impossible to get them out of the bubble bath that evening.

The Trillum Restaurant is probably best left for romantics, with food served from the top o' the Tower. We pigged out on pizza in a lower-level eatery and had a ball.

But then, there is nothing but good times at the Grand Traverse Resort.

HOW TO GET THERE: The resort is located 6 miles east of Traverse City. From that town, take U.S. 31 east to the inn, located just past the intersection of U.S. 31 and Michigan 72.

The Victorian Villa Inn 🍂
Union City, Michigan 49094

INNKEEPERS: Ronald Gibson, owner; Cynthia Shattuck, manager

ADDRESS/TELEPHONE: 601 North Broadway Street; (517) 741-7383 or (800) 34-VILLA

WEB SITE: avictorianvilla.com

ROOMS: 10, including 4 suites; all with private bath, 5 with air-conditioning. No smoking inn.

RATES: $95 to $170; EPB and afternoon tea/refreshments;

Sunday through Thursday discount rates.

OPEN: Year-round

FACILITIES AND ACTIVITIES: Seven-course nineteenth-century champagne and wine dinners available Friday and Saturday by reservation; five-course picnic basket lunches available by reservation; luncheons and afternoon tea, too. Sitting room, parlor, Christmas & Sherlock Holmes gift shop. Gazebo is the site for classical music concerts. Specialty weekends include Victorian Summer Days, murder mysteries, Sherlock Holmes Days, Victorian dinner theater, and more. Nearby: about 500 quality antiques dealers within 25 miles. Six Victorian homes/museums, nineteenth-century historical walking tours, three summer stock theaters, country auctions, fishing, summer festivals, golf, cross-country skiing, biking (free tandems to guests).

*S*teady yourself before entering The Victorian Villa for the first time. The grandeur of its elegant Victorian appointments is overwhelming. I could manage only a silly "Wow!"

This Italianate mansion, built in 1876 at the then-whopping cost of $12,000, is nestled in the quaint river village of Union City. Its formal Victorian decor makes it an absolutely perfect romantic hideaway.

The formal entrance hallway, with a winding staircase, is all dark woodwork, highlighted with hurricane lamps, red velvet curtains, and gingerbread transoms. The "informal" parlor is absolutely elegant. Heavy red velvet highback chairs are placed around a marble fireplace. Tall hurricane lamps and tulip-shaped chandeliers cast a warm glow over the room. One of my favorite touches is a massive gingerbread arch over the doorway.

Guest rooms are equally impressive. The 1890s Edwardian Bedchamber has a headboard almost 8 feet high, with antique quilts and pillows, dark rose wallpaper, and a marble-topped dresser. The 1860s Rococo Bedchamber has a working fireplace, Tiffany-style lamps, an antique armoire, and a tall Victorian rocker.

Tower suites are decorated in country Victorian and separated by a small sitting room. I like the rough-hewn country feel, with iron-rail beds, exposed brick walls, and round tower windows. The inn's Carriage House bedchambers are equally impressive. Try the Sherlock Holmes Bedchamber, very English with its grand library. (The inn is becoming renowned for its Holmes and Dr. Watson weekends.)

Breakfast in the formal dining room includes special treats: breakfast meats; concoctions that offer heaping helpings of sausage, cheddar cheese, eggs, and onions; muffins; homemade preserves; Amish pastries; fresh fruits; imported teas; and more. Afternoon English tea also is part of Villa tradition, with scones, tea cookies, fresh pastries, and lots of other extras. You'll find fancy chocolates on your bed pillows at turndown time.

HOW TO GET THERE: From east or west, take I–94 to I–69 and go south. Turn west on Michigan 60 (exit 25) and continue 7 miles to Union City. There Broadway Street is the town's main street.

The Inn at Union Pier
Union Pier, Michigan 49129

INNKEEPERS: Mark and Joyce Pitts

ADDRESS/TELEPHONE: 9708 Berrien, P.O. Box 222; (616) 469–4700

WEB SITE: innatunionpier.com

ROOMS: 16; all with private bath and air-conditioning, 12 with Swedish wood-burning stove. Wheelchair accessible.

RATES: $135 to $205, single or double; EPB. Off-season rates and packages available.

OPEN: Year-round

FACILITIES AND ACTIVITIES: Sitting rooms, enclosed porch, deck and dining area; desktop hot tub, dry sauna. Located in southwestern Michigan's Harbor Country, where lakeshore communities hug Lake Michigan. Walk to breathtaking beaches, drive to antiques shops or U-pick fruit farms. Inn will arrange sailboarding, bicycling, fishing, canoeing, horseback riding, winery tours, cross-country skiing in winter.

I cannot put out of my mind those cylindrical, ceiling-high, wood-burning Swedish stoves that grace most guest rooms. These colorful tile masterpieces are so difficult to assemble that the inn "imported" experts from Sweden to ensure that they were installed correctly.

But that's only one of the highlights of this elegant inn, located on the eastern shore of Lake Michigan. Just a walk from the sand castles and sweeps of the lake's beaches—only 200 steps from the front door—I enjoyed refined hospitality with all the comforts of a well-appointed country home.

Guest rooms, located in the Great House (the main building), Four Seasons quarters, and Pier House, are pictures of country elegance. From the polished hardwood floors and comfy country furnishings to those wonderful Swedish stoves and lacy window curtains, I felt like a country squire. A long wood deck connects the main house with the Four Seasons; just between them is an outdoor hot tub, a favorite gathering spot for guests.

Breakfast is served in a dining room whose many windows make the meal a bright and happy affair. Tables are adorned with white linen napkins and fresh flowers, some of the innkeepers' attentive touches. There are two courses: first comes fresh fruit, juices, and home-baked breads; then hearty entrees like blueberry pancakes, cinnamon bread—maybe even a Finnish eggs Florentine, a blend of eggs with spinach, cheeses, and sausage. In winter you might enjoy some old-fashioned baked apples, or "egg bakes," with fried tomatoes and all the trimmings, including homemade biscuits and muffins. Especially mouth-watering are cinnamon butter and blueberry streusel muffins.

HOW TO GET THERE: From Chicago, take I–94 north to exit 6. Go north on Townline Road less than a mile to Red Arrow Highway. Turn right; then go a little more than ½ mile and turn left on Berrien. The inn is about 2 blocks ahead on the left side of the road.

Pine Garth Inn 💟
Union Pier, Michigan 49129

INNKEEPERS: Russ and Paula Bulin

ADDRESS/TELEPHONE: 15790 Lakeshore Road, P.O. Box 347; (616) 469–1642

WEB SITE: www.pinegarth.com

ROOMS: 7; all with private bath. No smoking inn.

RATES: $135 to $185, single or double; EPB.

OPEN: Year-round

FACILITIES AND ACTIVITIES: Gathering room, screened porch, five decks overlooking Lake Michigan, 200 feet of private white-sand beach, beach chairs. Short drive to New Buffalo arts and antiques stores, skiing, water sports, restaurants.

When I first came to this stretch of shifting sands in southwestern Michigan almost twenty years ago, all I found was an empty Lake Michigan shoreline, sleepy towns, and small cottages. How times have changed.

Now there's a huge marina crammed with massive cabin cruisers, luxury townhouses stacked one atop the other, and a small-town "Main Street" that's increasingly filled with tony shops to lure big-city spendthrifts.

And those small cottages—they're more likely to have four-bedroom summer mansions as next door neighbors than somebody's clapboard cabin.

Yet Harbor Country, a 50-mile swath of white-sand beaches stretching from Michigan City, Indiana, to Harbert, Michigan (and beyond), somehow manages to retain its small-town charm and be a big attraction (especially for stressed-out Chicago folks) at the same time.

In fact, Harbor Country is now the cool weekend place to be, with a wave of lodgings, stores, and restaurants hitting the beaches and environs.

One of the best ways to enjoy the region is by staying at the Pine Garth Inn—the only bed-and-breakfast in Harbor Country nestled on the lakeshore. Located on a high bluff, six of the seven rooms in the 1905 inn offer breathtaking vistas of Lake Michigan and the hostelry's private white-sand beach below.

Rachel's Room, a favorite of my daughters Kate and Dayne, boasts flamingos perching on the headboard and an entire wall of windows overlooking Lake Michigan and opening out to a private terrace.

Or go upstairs to Melissa's Room, done in Laura Ashley blues and yellows. Another favorite of the girls, because "it's so romantic," it features a canopied bed and deck overlooking the lake. Even the bathroom boasts a lake view.

Of course, the girls love the private beach, reached by walking down a terrace of stairs clinging to the bluff. We looked for shells and ran around in the sand. Spending time with those girls—life can't get much better than that.

HOW TO GET THERE: Take I-94 to Michigan exit 6, which is the Union Pier exit. Turn right (on Towline Road) and proceed west toward the lake and go to the flashing red light, which is Red Arrow Highway. *Do not turn.* Continue on Townline Road to the next stop sign, which is Lakeshore Road. Turn right and proceed about ¼ mile to the inn (it'll be on your left).

Michillinda Beach Lodge 🏨
Whitehall, Michigan 49461

INNKEEPERS: Don and Sue Eilers

ADDRESS/TELEPHONE: 5207 Scenic Drive; (231) 893-1895

WEB SITE: michillinda.com

ROOMS: 50; all with private bath, 32 with lake views, 30 with balcony or deck.

RATES: $145 to $195 per couple; MAP. Weekly rates available. Also children's, extra person's rates.

OPEN: Mid-May through Labor Day.

FACILITIES AND ACTIVITIES: Full-service dining room, private beach, swimming pool, wading pool, miniature golf, tennis, volleyball court, shuffleboard, basketball, kids' playground. Also bingo, Western campfire

Dune Thrills

While in the area, you cannot pass up the chance to roam the dunes on Mac Woods' dune rides, in nearby Mears. The souped-up four-wheelers dash passengers over tall sand dunes and past windblown landscapes that look more like the moon than Michigan. It's also a thrill when your kamikaze driver skims the surf at about 50 miles an hour, resulting in splashy thrills for all involved.

program, children's morning games, Friday evening staff variety show, daily coffee hours, Sunday morning meditations. Nearby: a short drive to Lake Michigan dune rides, golf, horseback riding, Michigan's largest water park.

*O*riginally a turn-of-the-century country estate built by a Michigan lumber baron, the twenty-two-acre lodge combines spectacular lake vistas with hearty homemade meals. On first glance, it seemed like a perfect location for a relaxing getaway.

We were not disappointed. Our deluxe surfside cottage unit included three rooms (plenty of roaming space for daughters Kate and Dayne). An entire wall of windows and balcony overlooked the water; we spent lots of time here watching passing sailboats and cargo ships and the crashing surf.

But scenic Lake Michigan vistas aside, the test of a beachside resort is the beach. Michillinda boasts a great kiddie beach; the sandy-bottomed shallow extends nearly 50 feet into the water without passing over an adult's waist. It's perfect for kid water adventures that won't have parents stressed out with worries about possible dangers. It's also great sand castle-building and sun-bathing territory, as we soon found out.

Kate and Dayne never wanted to leave this place.

HOW TO GET THERE: From Muskegon, take U.S. 31 north and exit at White Lake Drive (White-hall); go west to White-hall Road and turn south (left). Continue to Michillinda Road, then turn west (right) to the lodge on Lake Michigan's shoreline.

Select List of Other Inns in Michigan

Saravilla
633 North State Street
Alma, MI 48801
(517) 463-4078

Michigamme Lake Lodge Resort
U.S. Highway 41
Champion, MI 49814
(906) 339-4400

MacDougall House Bed & Breakfast
109 Petoskey Avenue
Charlevoix, MI 49720
(616) 547-5788
(800) 753-5788

Dusty's English Inn
728 South Michigan Road
Eaton Rapids, MI 48827
(517) 663-2500

House on the Hill
9661 Lake Street
Ellsworth, MI 49729
(616) 588-6304

The Crane House
6051 124th Avenue
Fennville, MI 49408
(616) 561-6931

The Homestead Resort
Wood Ridge Road
Glen Arbor, MI 49636
(616) 334-5000
fax (616) 334-5120

Harbor House Inn
114 South Harbor Drive
Grand Haven, MI 49417
(616) 846-0610
(800) 841-0610
fax (616) 846-0530

Holly Crossing B&B
304 South Saginaw Street
Holly, MI 48442
(248) 634-7075

Garland Resort
County Road 489
Lewiston, MI 49756
(517) 786-2211
(800) 968-0042
fax (517) 786-2254

Snyder's Shoreline Inn
903 West Ludington Avenue
Ludington, MI 49431
(616) 845-1261
fax (616) 843-4441

Blueberry Ridge B&B
18 Oakridge Road
Marquette, MI 49855
(906) 249-9246 phone/fax

Landmark Inn
230 North Front Street
Marquette, MI 49855
(906) 228-2580
(888) 526-6275

Sans Souci Bed & Breakfast
19265 South Lakeside Road

New Buffalo, MI 49117
(616) 756-3141
fax (616) 756-5511

Bay Winds Inn
909 Spring Street
Petoskey, MI 49770
(616) 347-4193
fax (616) 347-5927

Terrace Inn
1549 Glendale
Petoskey, MI 49770
(231) 347-2410

Raymond House Inn
111 South Ridge Street
Port Sanilac, MI 48469
(810) 622-8800
(800) 622-7229

Victorian Inn
447 Butler Street
Saugatuck, MI 49453
(616) 857-3325
(888) 240-7957

The Seymour House
1248 Blue Star Highway
South Haven, MI 49090
(616) 227-3918

Sweethaven Resort
9517 Union Pier Road
Union Pier, MI 49129
(616) 469-0332

Minnesota

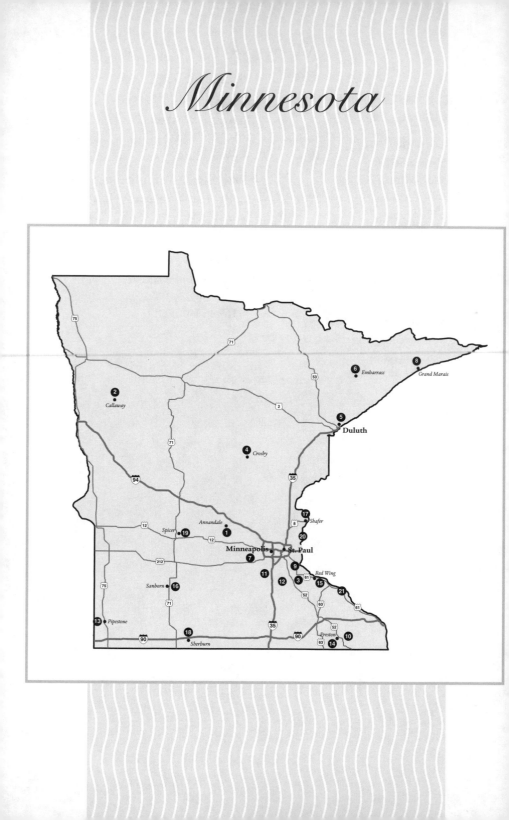

75

71

75

Callaway ②

71

94

6 Embarrass
● Grand Marais ⑧
53

8

2

5 ●
Duluth

4 ● Crosby

35

17 Shafer
8
20

Annandale
Spicer ● 19 ●
1 ●
12
12

Minneapolis ● ● St. Paul
7

9 ●
61 Red Wing
11
3 ● 15
52
21
61

Sanborn ● 16

212

75

71

13 ● Pipestone

18 ●
90
Sherburn ●

35
90
Preston ● 52
63 14 10

Minnesota

Numbers on map refer to towns numbered below.

*A Top Pick Inn

Thayer's Historic Bed n' Breakfast
Annandale, Minnesota 55302

INNKEEPER: Sharon Gammell

ADDRESS/TELEPHONE: Downtown on Highway 55; P.O. Box 246; (320) 274–8222 or (800) 944–6595

WEB SITE: www.thayers.net

ROOMS: 11; all with private bath and air-conditioning, some with TV.

RATES: $125 to $245, single or double; EPB. Special picnic, theater, golf, and cross-country ski package rates.

OPEN: Year-round

FACILITIES AND ACTIVITIES: Full-service restaurant, lounge, sauna. Very good antiquing area. Nearby: 25 lakes within 5 miles. Snowmobiling and skiing.

*T*his 1888 structure was built to accommodate overnight passengers and crew of the Soo Line railroad at this turn-of-the-century resort town. (There are scores of lakes within an hour's drive of the hotel.) Now I know why all the handsome glass transoms above the guest room doors are etched with Soo Line themes—everything from massive locomotives to the line's attractive logo.

Guest rooms are charming, decorated to convey a turn-of-the-century feel. Some have canopy, four-poster, or iron-rail beds. Others have fancy Dutch lace curtains on windows that stretch almost from ceiling to floor.

Getting to Know You

One of the most interesting features of the hotel is the innkeeper herself. Sharon Gammell is a psychic, and she'll do readings for guests at their request. In fact, she even offers "psychic weekend" packages; you can spend a few days getting to know yourself better (Sharon already knows you!), maybe even peek into your own future.

Some highlights: The Hunter's Room offers a big brass bed and masculine colors. Kitty's Room features, New Orleans-style decor, with a double walnut bed and a seascape whirlpool perfect for relaxation. Or try the opulent Angels and Lace Room, complete with fireplace, hand-carved double oak bed, and huge 5-foot by 6-foot whirlpool. An-

other bow to the present: There's a sauna on the third floor.

Of course, there's always Gus's Room—as in "Gus the Ghost," the hotel's very own doppelganger.

Sample the hotel's interactive mystery dinners, where everyone's a suspect. Sharon's four-course breakfast is another treat. Imagine a fruit compote with juices, home-baked bread, eggs Ostrich, cheese blintzes, and, for sweet tooths, chocolate-covered strawberries.

HOW TO GET THERE: From Minneapolis, take Minnesota 55 northwest to Annandale. The hotel is located on 55, in the heart of the downtown area.

Maplelag
Callaway, Minnesota 56521

INNKEEPERS: Jim and Mary Richards, Jay and Jonell Richards

ADDRESS/TELEPHONE: Route 1, 30501 Maplelage Road; (218) 375-4466, (800) 654-7711

WEB SITE: www.maplelag.com

ROOMS: 20 buildings can hold about 175 people. No smoking inn.

RATES: $185 to $230 per person, two nights; $250 to $305, three nights; EPB. Midweek and weekend one-day rates available.

OPEN: Labor Day to Memorial Day

FACILITIES AND ACTIVITIES: Main lodge, gathering room, cabins, skiing and hiking trails, hot tub.

ost of these historic farmstead buildings have been brought here from Finnish settlers' homesteads. The Richards continue that Scandinavian theme with a Sunday smorgasbord, which features all kinds of ethnic treats like egg soufflé, pickled herring, imported cheeses, and lefse.

This upper Midwest retreat always ranks among the finest for cross-country skiing. There are more than 35 miles of groomed trails on 660 acres. Old Sap Runs, trails used to haul male sugar in springtime, are great ways for beginners to experience the beauty of Maplelag. The 6-mile Roy's Run is another matter, appealing to those with far greater skills as it skims through very remote and dense forests north of the resort.

When skiing is finished, and before you head to your lodge guest room, take a dip in the ten-person hot tub, called the "Rolls Royce of models" by the innkeepers.

HOW TO GET THERE: From the Twin Cities, take I–94 to the Clearwater exit; travel 3 miles to Highway 10. Take Highway 10 about 150 miles to Detroit Lakes. At the first stoplight in Detroit Lakes, take a right onto Route 21 and go 12 miles north to the town of Richwood. Turn right onto County Road 34, then take County Road 110 (Goat Ranch Road) 1¼ miles west. Turn at the MAPLELAG sign and continue 1 mile to the inn.

Quill and Quilt
Cannon Falls, Minnesota 55009

INNKEEPER: Stacy Smith

ADDRESS/TELEPHONE: 615 West Hoffman Street; (507) 263–5507 or (800) 488–3849

ROOMS: 4, with 1 suite; all with private bath and air-conditioning.

RATES: $60 to $130, single or double; EPB. Midweek and holiday packages available.

OPEN: Year-round

FACILITIES AND ACTIVITIES: Social hour, sitting room, library, dining room, recreation room, coffeepots in all rooms, porches. Nearby: Cannon Valley trail (biking, hiking, cross-country skiing); antiques shops, boutiques, historic river towns; golfing, tennis, swimming, boating, canoeing, tubing, downhill skiing.

This 1897 house, a delicate Colonial Revival, is country elegant. From its gracious daily social hour to dainty chocolates set on your pillow during evening's turndown time, you'll discover that innkeeper Stacy Smith has lots of pampering in mind.

Guest rooms are charming. The first-floor Quilter's Room has a classic gingerbread panel overhanging the pocket-door transom. Inside you'll enjoy a brass bed, a handmade sampler quilt and a wall hanging that closely matches it, and wood-planked floors. You'll also discover fluffy, color-coordinated bathrobes in your private bath down the hall.

The Covill Suite is bright and dramatic, with seven windows; a lace-canopied, four-poster king-sized bed; and a double whirlpool bath. Relax on the private porch, and you may catch action on the baseball field out back.

Breakfast treats include French toast, quiches, and breakfast meats; the specialty is a crab and asparagus quiche that's a guest favorite. And since Stacy is also an antiques collector and dealer, here's your chance to get your questions answered about restoring and collecting historic furniture.

HOW TO GET THERE: From the Twin Cities or Rochester, take U.S. 52 to the Cannon Falls exit (Minnesota 19). Turn east on Minnesota 19 to Seventh Street (about ½ mile), turn north on Seventh to Hoffman, and go east a half block to the inn.

Nordic Inn Medieval Bed and Breakfast
Crosby, Minnesota 56441

INNKEEPER: Rick Schmidhuber

ADDRESS/TELEPHONE: 210 First Avenue NW; (218) 546–8229

ROOMS: 5, 4 with private bath.

RATES: $45 to $115; EPB. Viking Dinner Feast can be arranged with at least one week's notice.

OPEN: Year-round

FACILITIES AND ACTIVITIES: Viking feast, Valhalla recreation room with rock waterfall, darts, indoor grill, Ansgard Room offers bar and game table, the Hoard Room serves all food and doubles as a nightly movie theater. Crosby is the antique capital of the Brainerd area. Short walk to Paul Bunyan paved biking trail and the Cuyuna Mine Pits. Cuyuna Country Club (golf) nearby. Famous Cuyuna Mine Pit Lakes offers startling clear water and good fishing. •

"*S*teinarr Elmerson" and "Blade Richardson" might greet you at the door of this Nordic castle (really a former church). And when these folks are dressed in their Viking best (horned helmets, animal skins, large sword and shield), it can be quite an impressive welcome.

You might want to overnight in the castle's Odin's Loft, which has a bed built into a dragon-headed Viking longship, though I don't think any real Viking ever got to enjoy a large Jacuzzi like the one tucked into these quarters.

Freya's Room is named for the goodness of love, so it's not surprising that there's another Jacuzzi in this bedchamber. But those other Vikings, Minnesota's entry in the NFL, are feted in the Locker Room, which includes artificial turf with yard markers and two double beds with goal posts.

Viking breakfasts are another treat. Imagine a 14-foot-long medieval table groaning with the likes of heavy meat pies, parsnips, glazed carrots, and oatmeal apple tarts. After a meal like that, you'll be ready to go out and tangle with more barbarian hordes.

HOW TO GET THERE: Crosby is located about 14 miles north of Brainerd. Drive through Crosby on County 210 and turn north on First Avenue at the gas station (Citgo at last notice). Then proceed 3 blocks until you arrive at the castle.

The Ellery House
Duluth, Minnesota 55812

INNKEEPERS: Jim and Joan Halquist

ADDRESS/TELEPHONE: 28 South Twenty-first Avenue East;

(218) 724–7639 or (800) 355–3794

ROOMS: 4, with 2 suites. No smoking inn.

RATES: $64 to $125, single or double; EPB.

OPEN: Year-round

FACILITIES AND ACTIVITIES: Dining room, veranda, short trek to lake walk along Lake Superior. Nearby: boat excursions, charter fishing, Lake Superior Zoological Gardens.

I met Jim Halquist a few years ago, when he and his wife, Joan, had just opened this charming inn. It's gotten better over the years. This 1890 Queen Anne offers a respite to stressed out visitors who just want to sit back and relax.

The Ellery Suite is a favorite, with its private balcony. The Sunporch, which boasts (of course) an airy, sunny porch, is another charmer. But the guest favorite might be the Thomas Wahl Room, particularly for its bay window that boasts lake views—though its double marble shower must figure into the appeal equation somewhere.

Joan is a concert violinist for the Duluth-Superior Symphony Orchestra. She might regale you with a beautiful piece of music on some evenings. After listening to such beauty, grab the hand of that special someone and stroll romantically down the popular lake walk, less than 3 blocks away.

HOW TO GET THERE: From I–35 west, take the Twenty-first Avenue-East exit. Take a left at the end of the ramp onto Twenty-first. Cross London Road and the Jefferson Street. The inn is located at the first driveway on the right ½ block up from Jefferson.

Fitger's Inn
Duluth, Minnesota 55802

INNKEEPER: Donald James, general manager

ADDRESS/TELEPHONE: 600 East Superior Street; (218) 722–8826 or Minnesota toll-free (800) 726–2982

ROOMS: 60, including 18 suites; all with private bath, air-conditioning, TV, and phone. Wheelchair accessible.

RATES: $90 to $125, single or double; $150 to $250, suites; rates mid-May through November; continental breakfast in lobby.

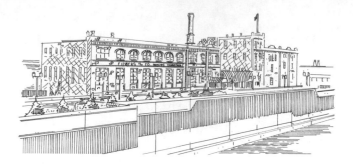

Off-season rates available.

OPEN: Year-round

FACILITIES AND ACTIVITIES: Three restaurants, two lounges, and a nightclub. Expansive patio courtyard facing Lake Superior. Nearby: boat excursions, charter fishing, Lake Superior Zoological Gardens, Glensheen historic estate, sailboat rentals, The Depot (art museum).

BUSINESS TRAVEL: Located a few minutes from downtown Duluth. Corporate rates, meeting rooms, fax.

I sat on a chair in the courtyard on a sweltering summer day and toasted my good fortune. Lake Superior was throwing some cooling breezes over its cold waters. Colorful sailing boats crisscrossed choppy waves. In the distance a large tanker slowly passed across the horizon. Fitger's Inn surely comes in handy during the dog days of August.

The inn is located in a brick complex of ten buildings that overlook Lake Superior. The complex housed the Fitger Brewing Company for 115 years until it closed its doors in 1972. The elegantly crafted, hand-wrought-iron registration desk is original to the inn. This 1884 masterpiece used to be the brewery's cashier's cage.

Notice all the original oak woodwork, the oak stairway, and the charcoal drawing of Gambrinus (mythical Flemish king and inventor of beer, naturally) done by a member of the Fitger family in Bremen, Germany. That shiny copper planter used to be a tasting pot for the brewmaster.

There's a lot more brew lore, but let's head to the guest rooms. They're handsome and tasteful, with antique and reproduction furnishings, elegant wallpaper, and brass lamps. My favorites are those with floor-to-ceiling windows overlooking the lake, which afford great views of the sunrise.

HOW TO GET THERE: From Minneapolis, take I–35 north to Duluth and follow the Superior Street exit to the inn.

The Mansion
Duluth, Minnesota 55804

INNKEEPERS: Warren and Susan Monson

ADDRESS/TELEPHONE:
3600 London Road; (218)
724–0739

ROOMS: 10, with 2 suites; 7
with private bath. Wheel-
chair accessible.

RATES: $105 to $195, sin-
gle or double; $205, suite;
EPB. Off-season rates available.

OPEN: Memorial Day
through mid-October; most weekends at other times of the year by special arrangement.

FACILITIES AND ACTIVITIES: Sitting and dining rooms, library,
screened porch. Six acres of grounds with 525 feet of Lake Superior
shoreline; lawns, woods, and gardens. An hour's drive from Apostle
Islands National Lakeshore.

"It's kind of like a medieval castle," innkeeper Susan Monson
said. Sure is. The entryway Gallery is all massive plaster-cast
walls sand-finished to resemble blocks in a great baronial hall,
with heavy exposed beams adding to the Middle Ages styling. With its spiky
iron wall sconces and floor-to-ceiling torchlights, I expected Sir Lancelot to
clank down the hall in his shiny suit of armor.

Urge to Splurge?

Would you like to have an entire floor of the fabulous
mansion to yourself? The master suite at The Mansion offers windows overlooking the lake, including a
big bay that's the setting for a king-sized bed, two
dressing rooms, and an 18-foot-long black-and-white
marble bath with a crystal chandelier.

Warren Monson said that the majestic 1932 Tudor home took four years to build; it has twenty-five rooms, with ten guest rooms. This house made me feel special. An exquisite touch is the library, crafted in English hand-hewn white pine, with a 5-foot-wide fireplace and a tremendous selection of classic books. A cozy spot is a Swedish pine-paneled living room, with another fireplace, brass chandeliers, and leaded-glass windows. Just down the hallway is a large screened porch with arched windows.

Seven guest rooms have a view of Lake Superior. One of my favorites is the South Room, with its high walnut Victorian headboard and matching furnishings, which are at least 150 years old. There's also a working fireplace. Even from here I could hear the sound of crashing waves pounding the beach.

Nobody goes hungry here. Susan whips up a handsome country breakfast of French toast, bacon, eggs, and sausage—and her special home-baked caramel rolls. Best bets for a Duluth dinner are at the Pickwick and Fitger's.

HOW TO GET THERE: In Duluth, follow U.S. 61 (also called North Shore Drive and London Road). Follow this north and turn into the driveway leading to the mansion.

Finnish Heritage Homestead
Embarrass, Minnesota 55732

INNKEEPERS: Buzz Schultz and Elaine Braginton

ADDRESS/TELEPHONE: 4776 Waisanen Road; (218) 984-3318 or (800) 863-6545

ROOMS: 5 rooms, 2 with private bath.

RATES: $78.50 to $105; EPB. Special seven-night packages available.

OPEN: Year-round

FACILITIES AND ACTIVITIES: Finnish wood-fired sauna, parlor, library, gardens with gazebo, barn, farm animals, farm tasks. Picnic lunches can be prepared for guests who wander the farm. Short drive to Boundary Waters Canoe Area, Giants Ridge (ski and golf), three thousand miles of snowmobile trails start from the farm's doorstep; Sisu Tori, Heritage Pioneer Homestead, mine tours.

*T*his Finnish log homestead home, started by John Kangas more than a century ago, originally served as a *poikatalo* (boarding house) for area loggers and railroad workers. Now everybody gets to enjoy the homestead in country comfort.

I especially like to wander the homestead, feast on wild berries in season, and just putter around in the beauty of this far north country. Of course, that's summer fun; in winter, it's time to hop on a snowmobile, wax up the cross-country skis, or maybe take a sleigh ride that'll have you thinking *Doctor Zhivago* in no time.

Which makes the inviting Finnish sauna at this wonderful retreat an even bigger treat. You did know that there is about one sauna for every three people in Finland even today?

HOW TO GET THERE: The homestead is located about 80 miles north of Duluth. From Duluth take U.S. 53 north past the town of Virginia; proceed on State 169 north/northwest to County 135 and go south; at County 21 turn left; proceed to Country 362 and go south ½ mile to the homestead.

James H. Clark House Bed & Breakfast
Excelsior, Minnesota 55331

INNKEEPERS: Skip and Betty Welke

ADDRESS/TELEPHONE: 371 Water Street; (952) 474-0196

ROOMS: 4, all with private bath, 2 with whirlpool. No smoking inn.

RATES: $109 to $159; EPB. Two-night minimum on weekends.

OPEN: Year-round

FACILITIES AND ACTIVITIES: Fireplaces in gathering room, library, huge wraparound open porch. Four blocks from Lake Minnetonka, boat cruises, restaurants. Nearby: Old Log Theater, Chanhassen Dinner Theater, Minnesota Arboretum, Farmers Market. Easy access to downtown Minneapolis and Mall of America.

This handsome Italianate home dates to 1858. It is awash in Victorian finery, such as stained-glass windows and period antiques, and is listed on Excelsior's register of historic buildings.

Skip and Betty Welke offer four wonderful guest bedchambers. One of my favorites is the Garden Room, with its trompe l'oeil painting on the walls, stained glass, and classical arched windows, not to mention the freestanding fireplace that warms your romantic quarters on chilly autumn or winter nights. Effies Room is cozy and romantic, boasting a queen-sized Victorian walnut bed and whirlpool. The Brent Suite is a two-room getaway with its own sitting area and access to the home's veranda.

But Teri Anne might be the favorite guest quarters. This spacious romantic retreat offers a canopy bed, double whirlpool, and lots of privacy.

HOW TO GET THERE: Take I–494 south to exit 7 west. Continue until exiting at the Excelsior ramp; then follow the road until reaching Water Street and turn left. Continue north to the inn, just north of George Street.

Naniboujou Lodge
Grand Marais, Minnesota 55604

INNKEEPERS: Tim and Nancy Ramey

ADDRESS/TELEPHONE: U.S. 61, 20 Naniboujou Trail, P.O. Box 505; (218) 387–2688; same number for fax.

WEB SITE: naniboujou.com

ROOMS: 24, all with private bath, 12 with lake views, 5 with fireplaces. No smoking inn.

RATES: $65 to $95, single or double.

OPEN: Mid-May through mid-October.

FACILITIES AND ACTIVITIES: Great hall, grounds include shoreline on Lake Superior. All three meals available. Basketball and volleyball courts. Hiking and fishing along Brule River. Gunfling Trail begins in Grand Marais, only 15 miles away.

*M*y dad especially liked the tranquillity of this historic lodge on the banks of Lake Superior, once a private club that hosted the likes of Babe Ruth, Jack Dempsey, and Ring Lardner. And we were both overwhelmed by the Great Hall, easily the highlight of Naniboujou and one of the greatest architectural stairs in the state. The hall's decor is inspired by Cree Indian mythology; its plank walls are decorated in brilliant oranges, yellows, reds, greens, and at the other end of the hall sits what is called the largest native rock fireplace in Minnesota. Weighing in at more than 200 tons, it might very well be the biggest anywhere in the Midwest.

Our room was like many at the lodge: some reproduction antiques, print wallpaper, and down-home comforters. Some rooms have wood-burning fireplaces, others have lake views, and a few have Murphy beds. But the room wasn't important to my dad. He simply wanted to walk the grounds, relax in a comfy Adirondack chair and look out over the water, and stargaze at night. Believe me, this is a perfect place for that.

HOW TO GET THERE: From Duluth, head north on U.S. 61, one of the most breathtaking drives in the Midwest. Continue toward Grand Marais. Watch for signs and the inn off the highway.

Rosewood Inn 💟
Hastings, Minnesota 55033

INNKEEPERS: Pam and Dick Thorsen

ADDRESS/TELEPHONE: Seventh and Ramsey; (615) 437-3297 or (888) 846-7966

ROOMS: 8, with 4 suites; all with private bath and air-conditioning; TV and phone upon request. No smoking inn.

RATES: $97 to $277, single or double; EPB. Two-night minimum on weekends. Special packages available.

OPEN: Year-round

FACILITIES AND ACTIVITIES: Dinner by reservation. Sitting room, parlor, library, porch. Nearby: historic river-town architecture, arts and crafts, stores, antiques shops, specialty boutiques, Mississippi River water activities, bluff touring on bikes and hikes, St. Croix Valley Nature Center, Alexis Bailly vineyard winery, downhill and cross-country skiing, snowshoeing, golf.

This handsome Queen Anne, built in 1878, now houses one of the most romantic getaways imaginable. That's not really surprising, since Pam and Dick Thorsen's other Hastings hideaway (the Thorwood Inn) features similar pampering-inspired luxuries.

As soon as you see Rebecca's Room, you'll get the idea. This is a stirring romantic retreat, with a marvelous all-marble bathroom highlighted by a double whirlpool bath resting in front of its own fireplace. There's a second fireplace opposite an inviting four-poster antique bed. A four-season porch offers views of the inn's rose garden.

Or consider the Vermillion Room, with a see-through fireplace that warms both an ornate brass bed and a sunken double whirlpool bath.

If you want shameful opulence, try the Mississippi Room. As large as an apartment, it offers skylights over a sleigh bed, its own fireplace, a baby grand piano, a bathroom with both a copper tub and a double whirlpool, and a meditation room where "people can either relax or be creative," said the innkeepers. "We've even had several guests do paintings here." A collection of some of those works are hanging about the room.

The breakfasts are added treats, and the mealtime flexibility is unusual: They'll serve whenever guests are hungry, between 6:00 and 11:00 A.M. Eat in one of the dining areas, on the porch, in your room, or in bed—the choice is yours.

The feast might include homemade breads and blueberry muffins, cheese strata, wild-rice gratiné, cherry strudel, raspberry coffee cake. . . . Aren't you hungry just thinking about all this food? Another chance to feast: The inn offers gourmet dinners in the formal parlor or in your own room. The meal might feature delights such as beef Wellington and a raspberry strudel with chocolate and vanilla sauce. The cost is $44.70 to $56.70 per couple.

The innkeepers are also happy to arrange an in-room "hat box" supper, or to package a delightful evening with dinner at one of the town's fine restaurants, including limousine service. They occasionally arrange dinner at the inn featuring Minnesota-accented recipes accompanied by live chamber music.

HOW TO GET THERE: From the Twin Cities, take U.S. 61 south into Hastings and exit at Seventh Street; then turn left and proceed 1½ blocks to the inn.

Thorwood Inn
Hastings, Minnesota
55033

INNKEEPERS: Pam and Dick
Thorsen

ADDRESS/TELEPHONE: Fourth and
Pine; (651) 437–3297 or (888)
846–7966

ROOMS: 7; all with private bath and
air-conditioning. Wheelchair accessible. No smoking inn.

RATES: $97 to $277, single or double; EPB. Can arrange for pet-sitters.
Special package rates available.

OPEN: Year-round

FACILITIES AND ACTIVITIES: "Hat box" dinners in your room. Nearby:
walking tour of historical area just blocks away. Quaint Mississippi
River town with specialty and antiques shops, several good restaurants.
Parks and nature trails; also river, streams, lakes, and all sorts of summer and winter sports.

"*P*eople seem to enjoy the morning breakfast baskets more than
anything else," Pam Thorsen told me as we sat in the parlor of
her gracious inn. "It has grown into quite a tradition." Once
when she mentioned to a repeat couple that she'd been thinking of changing
that practice, "They immediately spun around, with dismayed looks on their
faces, and said, 'You wouldn't.' I knew right then we could never change."

Lucky for us. The breakfast basket, delivered to the door of your room,
is stuffed with platters of fresh fruits, omelettes or quiches, pull-apart
pastries and rolls, home-baked breads, coffee, juice, and more. As Dick
Thorsen says, "Pace yourself."

It's all part of the pampering the innkeepers lavish on guests.

A complimentary bottle of wine from the local Alexis Bailly vineyards
and snacks of fruits and pastries continue the Thorwood notion of caring
for guests.

The home, fashioned in ornate Second Empire style and completed in 1880, is a testament to the innkeepers' restoration prowess. When I saw the marble fireplaces, ornate rosettes and plaster moldings on the ceilings, and elegant antiques and surroundings, it was difficult to imagine that the house had once been cut up into several apartments.

For fine detail, just look to the music room. Pam said that maple instead of oak was used for flooring because it provided better resonance for live piano concerts, popular with society crowds at the turn of the century.

One of my favorite guest rooms is Captain Anthony's, named for the original owner's son-in-law, who operated a line of steamboats on the Mississippi. It has a canopied four-poster brass bed and Victorian rose, teal, and blue Laura Ashley fabrics. The Lullaby Room (the house's historic nursery) has a double whirlpool bath. "Guests in this room feel like they're in the treetops," Pam said, as she looked out a tall window.

Maureen's Room is another popular choice, with its unusual rag-rug headboard, fireplace, country-quilted bed, and double whirlpool bath.

Or try Sarah's Room, with its bedroom-sized loft, window views of the Mississippi River Valley, and skylight over a queen-sized brass bed.

But perhaps the ultimate retreat is the Steeple Room, with its see-through fireplace and double whirlpool—set in the house's steeple. The steeple rises 23 feet above the tub and boasts a ball chandelier hanging from the pinnacle.

HOW TO GET THERE: From LaCrosse, take U.S. 61 north to Hastings, then turn left on Fourth Street and proceed to inn.

Mrs. B's Historic
Lanesboro Inn and Restaurant ¢¢
Lanesboro, Minnesota 55949

INNKEEPERS: Bill Sermeus and Mimi Abell

ADDRESS/TELEPHONE: 101 Parkway; (507) 467-2154

ROOMS: 10; all with private bath and air-conditioning. Wheelchair accessible. TV and phone on request.

RATES: $58 to $78, single or double, weekdays; $85 to $95, single or double, weekends; EPB. Lodging, MAP package available Wednesday through Sunday (five-course, three-hour gourmet dinner, $22.95). No credit cards.

FACILITIES AND ACTIVITIES: Gourmet dinners; Friday tea time. Sitting room, porches. Nearby: bike and cross-country ski trails, antiques shops, bluffs, golf, tennis, fishing. In heart of state hardwood forest.

*I*magine a five-course nouvelle meal featuring the likes of a delicious homemade soup made with parsnips, potato, and olive oil; salad with sun-dried tomatoes, fresh artichokes, and leafy greens; spaetzle (German dumplings); boneless turkey stuffed with wild rice and fresh vegetables; and triple chocolate cake with dark chocolate, coffee, and caramel garnish.

That's the kind of gustatory delights that Chef Allen Schleusener, who is classically trained in heartland cuisine, has planned for visitors to this charming destination.

The guest rooms are comfortable and cozy, with pine headboards and canopy beds, quilts, rose-floral-print wallpaper, writing desks, and other antique pine reproductions. One room has a headboard with two hand-carved dragon's heads on its posts. Some of them have outside balconies, and it's fun to sit out on a ladder-back rocking chair and look out over the Root River behind the inn to the high bluffs beyond. New terraces have been added onto the back of the historic building.

Also try the weekend dinner package, a gastronomic treat. Imagine filet of beef tenderloin with Yorkshire pudding, baked trout pilaf, and more.

Bluffs for Breakfast

I recommend a walk along a hiking trail that crosses the old bridge and faces the bluff. Then you'll really get a feel for the bluff country. It's probably also a good way to work off Allen's breakfasts, which include treats like blueberry buttermilk pancakes, Canadian shoulder bacon, and fresh fruits.

Historic Lanesboro is surrounded by high bluffs covered with tall hardwood trees. In fact, a 500-foot bluff, looming just beyond the inn, almost blocks the town's main street.

HOW TO GET THERE: Take Minnesota 16 to Lanesboro. In town, turn north on Parkway and proceed to the inn.

Schumacher's Historic European Hotel
New Prague, Minnesota 56071

INNKEEPERS: John and Kathleen Schumacher

ADDRESS/TELEPHONE: 212 West Main Street; (651) 758-2133 or (800) 283-2049

ROOMS: 11; all with private bath, air-conditioning, and phone, some with gas fireplace and hair dryer.

RATES: $112 to $175, single or double; EPB. Special packages and senior citizens' rates available. Personal checks from Minnesota only.

OPEN: Year-round except Christmas Eve and Christmas Day.

A Czech Fest

Guess who's the chef? John is a classically trained cooking school graduate who specializes in excellent old-world cuisine with a Czech flair. His extensive menu features more than fifty-five dinner entrees.

"What's your pleasure? I'll cook you a feast!" he said. A typical Central European meal includes *romacka* (cream of bean soup with dill) and Czech roast duck served with red cabbage, potato dumplings, and dressing, with apple strudel for dessert. Then you're ready to browse in the hotel's gift shop, which offers handmade gifts and glassware from Central Europe.

FACILITIES AND ACTIVITIES: Full-service restaurant with wheelchair access. Bavarian bar, European gift shop, travel agency. Nearby: drive to cross-country and downhill skiing, swimming, golf, boating, fishing, biking, hiking, orchard, museums, racetrack, amusement park.

I stepped into Schumacher's Historic European Hotel through a hand-stenciled door and thought I'd somehow been caught in a time warp, ending up in old-time Bavaria.

John and Kathleen Schumacher are very proud of their beautiful inn, and rightly so. It looks similar to many European country hotels I've stayed at. A peaceful air of rich handiwork, fine craftsmanship, wonderful imported old-world antiques, and a deep commitment to dining excellence are what make Schumacher's one of the best there is.

Built in 1898, the hotel has an ornate European-style lobby, with pressed-tin ceilings, rich floral wallpaper, fine European antiques, and Oriental rugs that cover original maple hardwood floors. A wonderful front desk is original, too.

John commissioned renowned Bavarian folk artist Pipka to design the graceful stenciled scenes that enliven guest, lobby, and restaurant rooms.

Upstairs are eleven individually decorated guest rooms, named in German for the months of the year, and furnished with trunks, chairs, beds, and wardrobes. Several have fireplaces, and all boast double whirlpool baths. More authentic touches include eiderdown-filled pillows and comforters, and 100 percent cotton bedding and tablecloths, which were purchased in Austria, the former Czechoslovakia, and Germany.

August is my favorite, with its king-sized bed, primitive Bavarian folk art, and a red wildflower theme carried out in stenciled hearts on the pine floor and on an ornately decorated wardrobe. You'll feel as if you've been transported to southern Germany.

Mai has a high-canopied double bed, reached by a small ladder; the design inside the canopy features storybook-style figures from newlyweds to senior couples. John places a complimentary bottle of German wine and two glasses in each room, just one of the many thoughtful touches.

HOW TO GET THERE: From Minneapolis, take 35 W south; exit on County Road 2. Continue to Minnesota 13 and turn south. Proceed directly into New Prague; the hotel is on the left.

The Archer House
Northfield, Minnesota 55057

INNKEEPER: Bob Carel

ADDRESS/TELEPHONE: 212 Division Street; (507) 645–5661 or (800) 247–2235

WEB SITE: www.archerhouse.com

ROOMS: 36, with 19 whirlpool suites; all with private bath, air-conditioning, TV, and phone.

RATES: $45 to $140, single or double; EP.

OPEN: Year-round

FACILITIES AND ACTIVITIES: Tavern restaurant, deli, ice cream and coffee shop, book store, specialty stores. Nearby: Carleton and St. Olaf colleges and Northfield Arts Guild offer programs of theater, art, concerts, films, and lectures. Hiking, biking, canoeing on Cannon River, tennis, swimming, cross-country skiing, ice skating (in season).

irst let me tell you that The Archer House is just a short walk from the local bank that the Jesse James gang attempted to rob in 1876. Yep, the Great Northfield Raid was a desperado disaster that virtually ended Jesse's reign of terror on the frontier.

This is a terrific restoration job. Doors are left open to unoccupied rooms

Jesse's Downfall

Come during September for some real Wild West ambience. That's when Jesse's gang "robs" the local bank in a colorful festival celebrating "The Town That Defeated Jesse James."

so that browsers can appreciate the rooms' turn-of-the-century charm. Each room reflects a personality of its own, with ruggedly elegant country warmth. I loved the hand-crafted pine furniture, some with rosemaling, and the brass beds, handmade quilts done by local artisans, and embroidered samplers.

I stayed in the Manawa Room, done in a Dutch-country style, with blue floors, stencils on walls, a pine bed with blue-and-white-point star quilt, and a needlepoint sampler. I'm sure my room's Dutch hex sign has brought me good luck. New suites all feature inviting whirlpool baths, and some have a lovely view of the Cannon River, which is sporting a new riverwalk.

HOW TO GET THERE: From the Twin Cities, take I–35 south to the Northfield exit. Follow Highway 19 east to the first stoplight. Go east for 2 blocks. Turn left onto Division Street and go 2 blocks. The Archer House is on the left. From Rochester, take Highway 52 north to Cannon Falls. Then take Highway 19 west 11 miles to Northfield. Go straight onto Division Street. The Archer House is on the right.

Historic Calumet Inn
Pipestone, Minnesota 56164

INNKEEPER: Cheryl Kruse

ADDRESS/TELEPHONE: Corner of Main and Hiawatha; (507) 825–5871 or (800) 535–7610

ROOMS: 38, 15 antique, 23 modern; all with private bath and air-conditioning. Wheelchair accessible.

RATES: $50 to $75, single; $60 to $75, double; continental breakfast.

OPEN: Year-round

FACILITIES AND ACTIVITIES: Full-service dining room, lounge, pub, gift shop featuring Native American crafts. In Pipestone historic district; walk to other historic structures. Nearby: a short drive to Pipestone National Monument, Upper Midwest Indian Cultural Center, Pipestone County Museum, health club, Hole-in-the-Wall ski area.

he Historic Calumet Inn is located in the historic district of tiny Pipestone, a wisp of a town located in the heart of traditional lands of the Dakota Yankton–Sioux nation. I drove just outside of town and stood gazing over the "grass prairies," still a massively empty, windy landscape—the beginning of the Great Plains.

Native Americans mined pipestone at ancient quarries nearby. The soft stone, considered sacred, still is used for ceremonial pipes. Visitors can view the quarries and local tribal members mining the stone as their ancestors did before them.

This pioneer legacy continues at the inn, a massive pink-and-red quartzite building made of hand-chiseled, locally quarried stone, completed in 1888. Easily its most outstanding feature is a four-story exposed red-stone wall that dominates the lobby.

Everything here seems larger than life. I walked up a magnificent four-story staircase of oak and maple to reach my room. A high skylight washed the stairs in warm sunlight. (I counted ninety-two steps. Don't worry, there's an elevator, too.)

My room was classically restored to Victorian elegance, with marble-topped dressers, a velvet-covered rocking chair, and two walnut beds sporting high headboards. Later I found out that antiques brokers were commissioned to seek out the nineteenth-century pieces. They searched old British estates, Colorado gold-rush mansions, Carolina plantations, and historic New England homes to uncover the splendid period pieces.

The rooms have names like Paradise Regained and Abigail's Dream. My favorite is the Choctaw Indian Walk, with a wall of exposed brick and Native American artifacts and designs.

Throughout the restored rooms I found fainting couches, chairs of golden oak built extra wide to accommodate ladies' Victorian-era bustles, claw-foot dressers, and antique prints and photos. The hotel quickly became one of my favorites. A photo album at the front desk helps you choose what style room most appeals to you.

The inn is enjoying a highly rated renaissance through its restoration efforts. Its restaurant was named one of the top fifty dining establishments in

Minnesota. Be sure to wander on the edge of the Great Plains, where the nearby Pipestone National Monument (ancient Indian pipestone quarries a short drive away) is fascinating. I stayed there for hours.

HOW TO GET THERE: I–75 and Minnesota 30 and 23 lead into Pipestone, located in extreme southwestern Minnesota. Once in town, make your way to East Main Street and continue to the corner of Hiawatha and the inn.

The Jail House
Preston, Minnesota 55965

INNKEEPERS: Marc and Jeanne Sather

ADDRESS/TELEPHONE: 109 Houston Street, P.O. Box 422; (507) 765–2181

ROOMS: 12, with 3 suites; all with private bath and air-conditioning; TV and phone on request.

RATES: Weekdays: $42 to $115, single or double; weekends: $69 to $149; EPB weekends, continental breakfast weekdays.

FACILITIES AND ACTIVITIES: Two common areas with stone fireplaces, parlor, basement dining room. Nearby: state parks, biking, hiking, cross-

country skiing, Amish country tours, trout fishing, antiques and Amish crafts stores, cave tours, golf, historic sites, museums, canoeing, tubing, bird-watching, local summer theater.

"*S*lumber in Our Slammer." That's how "wardens" Marc and Jeanne Sather invite guests to enjoy their handsome inn, complete with a fully restored exterior and lavish surroundings inside.

This was once the Fillmore County Jail, built in 1869 and housing unwilling guests until 1971. Get the innkeepers to tell you the story about prisoners who chiseled their way to freedom by using dinner spoons.

Once modern-day guests step inside, they won't want to leave. The innkeepers have done a magnificent job of transforming this historic building into one of the more ornate Minnesota inns, complete with authentic period antiques dating from 1860 to 1890.

Of course, Marc and Jeanne couldn't resist keeping one guest room looking much as it might have during its jail heyday. The Cell Block is all steel doors and iron bars—you even sleep behind bars. One big difference—you have the keys. And I doubt that prisoners had a walk-through shower leading to a double whirlpool tub, fluffy quilted beds, rocking chairs, and other decidedly unconvict niceties.

What's ironic is that this room looks like the innkeepers have done the least to it, but it caused the most backbreaking work.

Guest rooms are named for former sheriffs who served at the jail. Among my favorites: the original courtroom now fashioned into a huge suite with a sitting room and double whirlpool; and the Drunk Tank, boasting Eastlake antiques and original wide-plank pine flooring.

Back to the inn's antiques: Consider an old china tub weighing nearly 1,000 pounds; an 1880s, spoon-carved, three-piece bedroom set; and an antique copper bath made in Chicago.

Breakfast is served in the skylit basement and might include baked egg casseroles, home-baked breads and muffins, and more—the "Cook's Choice" doesn't allow any "convict" to go away hungry.

One problem with this "jail house": As soon as "prisoners" are paroled and sent home, they begin to plot another caper that will land them back in the slammer!

HOW TO GET THERE: From the north, take Minnesota 52 south into Preston. Turn right on County Road 12 and continue to Houston Street, then turn right to the inn.

St. James Hotel
Red Wing, Minnesota 55066

INNKEEPER: E. F. Foster

ADDRESS/TELEPHONE: 406 Main Street; (612) 388–2846

ROOMS: 60; all with private bath, air-conditioning, TV, and phone, 10 with whirlpool bath. Wheelchair accessible.

RATES: $105 to $245, single or double; EP.

OPEN: Year-round

FACILITIES AND ACTIVITIES: Two dining areas, thirteen specialty shops, two lounges. Nearby: walking and driving tours of historic river-front town; antiques and specialty shops; Mississippi River water sports and activities.

BUSINESS TRAVEL: Located 44 miles south of downtown St. Paul, 55 miles south of downtown Minneapolis. Corporate rates, meeting rooms, fax.

E. F. told me that the St. James Hotel was one of the first fine Victorian hotels in the Midwest. It was built in 1875, and its elegance reflected Red Wing's prosperity as the world's largest wheat market at the time. Now Red Wing is just a historic Mississippi River town, but the St. James's tradition of refined Victorian tastes continues.

"Quiet elegance" is the phrase that best describes the guest rooms. Each is uniquely decorated; I especially like the fancily scrolled wall borders, so popular back in the hotel's heyday. In fact, they set the color tones for coordinated wallpapers and handmade quilts.

Authentic antiques and fine reproductions re-create a long-ago era of luxury. E. F. has a great collection of beds—massive four-poster beds, Jenny Lind spindles, shiny brass beds, and more. Unique gingerbread window treatments splash spiky shafts of sunlight into rooms. In some rooms a view of the Mississippi River and surrounding high bluffs is a big treat.

You'll be spoiled after just one day at the St. James. A complimentary chilled bottle of wine welcomes you to your room, and there'll be a steaming pot of coffee and morning paper delivered to your door.

(*Note:* Ask for a historic room if that is your preference; there are several with modern decor.)

HOW TO GET THERE: Take U.S. 61 into Red Wing, where it becomes Main Street; the hotel's address is 406 Main Street.

Sod House on the Prairie
Sanborn, Minnesota 56083

INNKEEPERS: Virginia and Stan McCone

ADDRESS/TELEPHONE: 12598 Magnolia Avenue; (507) 723–5138

ROOMS: 1 sod house with 2 double beds and outhouse

RATES: $90 to $150; EPB

OPEN: Year-round

FACILITIES AND ACTIVITIES: Prairielands to wander. Tranquillity. Relaxation. Star-gazing.

For a chance to live like the original settlers on the Great Plains, come to Virginia and Stan McCone's wonderful historic re-creation—a sod house. Stan McCone, a former cattle buyer, cut great blocks of sod from the earth and constructed two buildings in the midst of the tall grasses.

One is a "poor man's dugout," the other a "rich man's soddy." While both are museums and open to the public, you can overnight in the large soddy to get the feel of a true pioneer lifestyle.

How true to life (and history) is it? The sod house indeed has turf walls, a potbellied stove for heat, and air-conditioning from open windows. Oil lamps are used for light. An outhouse (a two-seater!) is only steps away from the soddy's front door.

You can cook your own breakfast on the wood-burning stove, or the innkeepers will provide one for you that'll stick to your ribs. This is an incredible experience, staying at the Sod House. You are living history.

HOW TO GET THERE: At the junction of Routes 14 and 71, travel 1 mile east on Route 14. At the SOD HOUSE sign, turn right onto a gravel road and continue ⅓ mile to the inn.

Country Bed & Breakfast 💷
Shafer, Minnesota 55074

INNKEEPERS: Lois and Budd Barott

ADDRESS/TELEPHONE: 32030 Ranch Trail Road; (651) 257–4773

ROOMS: 3; 2 with private bath, all with air-conditioning. No smoking inn.

RATES: $65 to $95; EPB. No credit cards.

OPEN: Year-round

FACILITIES AND ACTIVITIES: Porch. Spacious tree-shaded lawn. Maple groves. Walking in surrounding fields. Nearby: restaurants; Ki-Chi-Saga Lake; the Sunrise and St. Croix Rivers with riverboat cruises, tubing, canoeing, swimming, fishing; two downhill ski resorts. Cross-country ski and nature trails at Wild River State Park. Also antiques, pottery shops in area. Five miles west of historic Taylors Falls.

"*I*'m so tired from collecting sap, and I still have to boil it down today. Then I'll just go to sleep." Poor Budd Barott. I'd stopped by his thirty-five-acre country spread and caught him in the middle of his busy chores. But that didn't stop him or his wife, Lois, from showcasing their overwhelming country hospitality. After a few minutes with them, I felt as if I'd returned home after a long journey away from this pretty farmstead.

Both Lois and Budd showed me around the place. Lois pointed to the chicken coop. "I'm so proud of my chickens," she said. "I got to have lots of them. You know, fresh eggs for breakfast."

Budd and I laughed. "Yeah, we give you an $18 breakfast here for nothing," he said, "and you can eat as much as you want."

This is no mere boast. Country breakfast features Swedish egg-coffee; omelettes with ham, sausage, or bacon (Budd's specialty); Lois's buttermilk pancakes with homemade maple syrup from their groves out back; and rasp-

berries and strawberries from Budd's organic garden. "If you leave here hungry, it's your own fault," he joked. In the evening they suggest that guests take a short drive to Marine on St. Croix for delicious homemade dinners at Crabtree's Kitchen.

The farmhouse is a quaint 1881 redbrick Victorian. Lois, who grew up here, pointed out original plank floors and a big wood-burning stove in a country kitchen. A comfortable sitting room has a sofa, chair, and television.

Guest rooms upstairs are pictures of farm-country charm. Lois has covered plank floors with scatter rugs; she also uses some white wicker chairs and other country antiques, sheer white curtains on tall windows that flood rooms with sunlight, and pretty print wallpapers. The Country Estates Room is especially inviting, with its antique double bed, jade green and rose colors, and a claw-foot tub.

HOW TO GET THERE: Enter Shafer on County Road 21. Go through town 1 mile. Then turn left on Ranch Trail and proceed to the second farm on the left (the redbrick house).

Four Columns Inn
Sherburn, Minnesota 56171

INNKEEPERS: Norman and Pennie Kittleson

ADDRESS/TELEPHONE: Route 2, P.O. Box 75; (507) 764-8861

ROOMS: 4, 3 with shared bath. No smoking inn.

RATES: $75 to $80, single or double; EPB.

OPEN: Year-round

FACILITIES AND ACTIVITIES: Located on 350-acre working farm. Inn nestled atop hill with scenic view, ten acres of trees, gardens. Den with fireplace is guest room gathering place; great room; gazebo, solarium.

This handsome 1884 inn sits atop a knoll overlooking the historic Winnebago-Jackson Stage Road, where it served many of the stagecoach passengers who came to the area for its prime fishing and hunting. Today its a Greek Revival charmer with four tall white columns framing the inn entrance—hence its name.

Perhaps the inn's most striking feature is the handcrafted winding staircase that leads to second- and third-floor guest rooms. The All Antique Room boasts an iron-rail bed and 1842 immigrant trunk, along with its fireplace and views of the lawn and garden; the Canopy Room has a huge four-poster lace canopy bed; and the Masters Room also boasts a fireplace, along with a balcony overlooking the grounds.

Guests can take breakfast at the round oak table in front of a brick fireplace that's part of the Great Room. Or innkeepers Norman and Pennie Kittleson will serve your down-home treats in the nineteenth-century-style Victorian gazebo on the lawn.

HOW TO GET THERE: The inn is located 2 miles north of Sherburn. To get there, take I–90 and exit at the Sherburn (Highway 4) ramp. Go north on Highway 4 for 2 miles until reaching County Road 132, then turn left and continue west for about a quarter mile to the inn.

Bridal Beauty

For complete privacy, the Bridal Suite is your best bet. This rustic charmer is located on the third floor, away from other guest rooms. It has a claw-foot tub, perfect for bubble baths and other lovey-dovey luxuries. It also boasts a pull-down stairway to the roof and the widow's walk, where romantics are graced with breathtaking starry-night vistas. (During the day, you can even see traces of the old stagecoach trail from up here.)

Spicer Castle
Spicer, Minnesota 56288

INNKEEPERS: Allen and Marti Latham

ADDRESS/TELEPHONE: Off Minnesota 23 on Green Lake, P.O. Box 307; (320) 796–5870

ROOMS: 10, plus 1 cottage and 1 cabin; all with private bath.

RATES: $80 to $170; EPB.

OPEN: Year-round, but weekends only mid-September through mid-May.

FACILITIES AND ACTIVITIES: Afternoon tea, sitting room. Located on beautiful Green Lake. Spacious porch and grounds. Nearby: restaurants, sandy beach, fishing, hiking, golf, cross-country skiing.

*T*he house was built in 1893 by the grandfather of Allen and Marti. It was part of the Medayto Farm, where he experimented with new agricultural techniques.

What a gorgeous piece of country, too. Hugging the shore of huge Green Lake, Spicer Castle stands sentinel on a craggy bluff overlooking the blue water. I gazed out at the lake from the inn's back porch, watching a storm brew far out over the waves.

I asked how the inn got its name. "Fishermen used the house as a landmark to locate good fishing spots," I was told. "Before long, references to 'Spicer's Castle' began appearing on fishing maps of the area. The name just stuck."

That's not surprising. It's an imposing house, sitting on five acres with a proud, Tudor-style profile that includes a tall tower resembling those found at ancient castles.

Guest rooms, comfortable and cozy, have the same warm family feel to them. Mason's Room has a four-poster mahogany bed graced with a paisley

quilt, the likes of which I hadn't seen before. Frances's Room boasts an iron-rail bed, triple French windows, and a Victorian dresser. Jessie's sports a walnut Jenny Lind spindle bed. But the most spectacular room (one of the most popular with guests, anyway) is Eunice's Room.

It's bright and sunny, with fourteen windows, natural woodwork, a turn-of-the-century swinging bed, and a two-person whirlpool tub. Ooh-la-la!

HOW TO GET THERE: From Minneapolis, take U.S. 12 west to Minnesota 23 and turn north into Spicer. Turn right on County 95 (Indian Beach Road, which is the lake road) and follow to the sign that tells you where to turn onto the access road reaching the castle.

Food for Thought

Mornings are great fun because they mean breakfast on the dining porch overlooking the lake. You may enjoy Belgian waffles, eggs Benedict, homemade muffins, juice, and coffee. The innkeeper said that guests sometimes receive morning salutes from captains passing in their boats.

The Lowell Inn
Stillwater, Minnesota 55082

INNKEEPERS: Arthur and Maureen Palmer

ADDRESS/TELEPHONE: 102 North Street; (651) 439–1100 or (888) 569–3554

ROOMS: 21, including 2 suites; all with private bath, air-conditioning, and phone.

RATES: Weekdays: $79 to $169, single or double; EP. Weekends: $269 to $329, single or double; AP.

OPEN: Year-round

FACILITIES AND ACTIVITIES: Full-service restaurant with wheelchair access. Nearby: many quality antiques, gift, and specialty shops; good town bakeries; cave tours. Not far from the Mississippi River. The inn can arrange River Run excursions May to September. Winter cross-country skiing at O'Brien State Park. Downhill skiing at three resorts.

*I*remember The Lowell Inn for its china cats. That's right. I walked into my enormous French Provincial–style room only to find a little "kitty" curled up at the foot of my bed. Cats and kittens are in every guest room; innkeepers Arthur and Maureen Palmer believe they add homey warmth to the elegant rooms.

It's not something I expected to find here. The inn, which opened on Christmas Day 1930, is built in a formal Colonial Williamsburg style. The huge veranda is supported by thirteen tall white pillars that represent the original thirteen colonies, and each bears a pole flying the respective state flag.

Stepping inside, I saw an exquisite mixture of Colonial and French Provincial antiques. Many of the inn's gorgeous collectibles are part of the private collection of Nelle Palmer, wife of the original owner.

The dining rooms are handsome, dotted with Dresden china, Capodimonte porcelain, and Sheffield silver. They also exhibit a bit of a classy atmosphere. The George Washington Room is adorned with hand-crested Irish linen, authentic Williamsburg ladder-back chairs, and portraits of George and Martha. Still another surprise is an indoor trout pool in the Garden Room. You can select your dinner by pointing to the fish of your choice. Huge polished agate tables accentuate the earthy quality of the room.

Easily my favorite is the Matterhorn Room, all done in deep, rich woods and authentic Swiss wood carvings. The inn's showpiece, as far as I'm concerned, is a life-sized eagle, hand-carved by a seventy-eight-year-old Swiss master wood-carver.

Dinners here might begin with Swiss escargots (pure-white snails picked from vineyards in France and Switzerland), followed by a large chilled green salad with pickled relishes. For an entree, try fondue Bourguignonne (beef or shrimp individually seasoned with six different sauces).

Guest rooms are individually decorated in a combination of Colonial and French Provincial styles, with soft colors, frills, mirrors, antiques, and goose-down comforters; four have inviting Jacuzzis. A complimentary

bottle of wine in my room was a welcome surprise, another pampering touch that pleases guests.

HOW TO GET THERE: From Minneapolis–St. Paul, take State Road 36 east. It changes into Stillwater's Main Street. Turn left on Myrtle and go about a block to Second Street.

The Rivertown Inn
Stillwater, Minnesota 55082

INNKEEPERS: Jeff and Julie Anderson

ADDRESS/TELEPHONE: 306 West Olive; (651) 430–2955 or (800) 562–3632

WEB SITE: www.rivertowninn.com

E-MAIL: rivertn@aol.com

ROOMS: 8, including 4 suites; all with private bath, air-conditioning, whirlpool bath, and fireplace. No smoking inn.

RATES: $175 to $250, single or double; EPB. Off-season rates.

OPEN: Year-round

FACILITIES AND ACTIVITIES: Lunch by arrangement, afternoon tea, hors d'oeuvres, dinner. Sitting room. Gazebo on grounds. Nearby: a short drive to scenic St. Croix River way, riverboat rides; art galleries, specialty shops, antiques stores; golf courses; apple orchards; biking, hiking, cross-country and downhill skiing, canoeing, swimming; tours of historic homes; restaurants.

*I*ntricate gingerbread fretwork adorns many inn rooms. It's all original to the house. It was found stored in rows out back in the carriage house. It was quite a discovery.

As I walked through the inn, lovely violin music played. It was a perfect accompaniment for exploring the guest rooms, each named for romantic nineteenth-century poets. A favorite is the John O'Brien bedchamber, with its huge oak-mantled tile fireplace, tall walnut Victorian headboard and dresser, parquet floors, and splash of gingerbread. It has the feel of a room in an exclusive English men's club.

I also love its double whirlpool bath.

Lord Byron's Suite, with its hand-carved British Colonial bed and Jacuzzi whirlpool boasting underwater lights and its own waterfall is spectacular.

More highlights: The two-room Lord Tennyson Suite offers a pillow-filled French daybed with an enclosed, canopied two-person Jacuzzi. And the Browning Suite features a rococo half-tester bed, fireplace, and views of the inn's gazebo.

The inn's Cover Park Manor is an 1890s country Victorian home with four guest suites, all with whirlpool bath and gas fireplace.

Breakfast is served in the dining room, prepared by resident chef Donna Taras. It could include fresh berries and cream, basil and Brie scrambled eggs, sun-dried tomato baked French toast, apple-cranberry sausage and hickory-smoked bacon—and a peach-blueberry tart!

HOW TO GET THERE: From Minneapolis, take Minnesota 36 east to Stillwater. Turn left on Olive Street; go up the hill to Fifth Street and the inn.

The Anderson House
Wabasha, Minnesota 55981

INNKEEPER: John Hall

ADDRESS/TELEPHONE: 333 North Main Street; (612) 565–4524 or (800) 535–5467

WEB SITE: theandersonhouse.com

ROOMS: 31, including 6 suites; all with private bath, all with air-conditioning, some with TV. Pets OK in certain rooms.

RATES: $53 to $149; EP. Midweek and other packages available.

OPEN: Year-round; restaurant closed in January.

FACILITIES AND ACTIVITIES: Full-service dining room with wheelchair access, ice cream parlor. In winter, ice fishing, skating, boating. Nearby: about 30 miles from three ski resorts. Across the street from Mississippi River fishing, boating. Drive to antiques shops.

The Anderson House has the most unusual selection of special inn services I've ever run across.
• Hot bricks wrapped in cotton warm your feet after a long day's journey.

 • Shoes will be shined free of charge if you leave them outside your door before retiring for the evening.

 • Mustard plasters will be conjured up to treat stuffy congestion and chest colds.

 • Eleven cats are on daily call: You can rent one to help purr you to sleep and make you feel more at home. Aloysius and Morris are guest favorites.

 • Pennsylvania Dutch specialties such as scrapple and fastnachts, a meat dish with tasty doughnuts, are served for breakfast.

 Now have I got your attention?

 It's the oldest operating hotel in Minnesota, never having closed its doors since its opening day in 1856. The rambling redbrick inn, which takes up a block of the town's Main Street, traces its roots back to Pennsylvania Dutch country. In fact, Grandma Ida Anderson, who ran the hotel at the turn of the century, earned her reputation for tasty meals conjured up in the hotel's kitchen. The tradition continues under her great-grandson, John Hall.

 John has delightfully renovated the guest rooms. Some have floral-print wallpaper; antique maple, oak, and walnut beds and dressers; and handmade quilts and bedspreads. John said that the latter were made by two talented ladies from a nearby nursing home. Some rooms boast huge whirlpool tubs; others afford you a glimpse of the Mississippi River, just across the street. Note that there are standard rooms, whirlpool suites, and European rooms.

 A favorite of mine is a room with an enchanting Dutch sleigh bed and matching chest; both are hand-stenciled with flowery patterns and fine handiwork. A few rooms now have a whirlpool bath.

 Get ready for a real dining treat. Unique inn offerings include cheese soup, chicken with Dutch dumplings, bacon-corn chowder, kugelhopf, limpa, pork tenderloin medallions cooked in sauerkraut, and Dutch beer—and, if you're very lucky, sometimes sticky-sweet shoo-fly pie for dessert.

John's family marks the fourth generation of Anderson House ownership. That means a long-standing tradition of warm hospitality that's hard to beat. HOW TO GET THERE: U.S. 61 and Minnesota 60 go right through town. The inn is located on North Main Street.

Select List of Other Inns in Minnesota

Cedar Rose Inn
422 7th Avenue West
Alexandria, MN 56308
(320) 762-8430

Bluff Creek Inn
1161 Bluff Creek Drive
Chaska, MN 55318
(612) 445-2735

The Olcott House
2316 East First Street
Duluth, MN 55812
(218) 728-1339
(800) 715-1339

Bearskin Lodge
124 East Bearskin Road
Grand Marais, MN 55604
(218) 388-2292
(800) 338-4170
fax (218) 388-4410

Pincushion Mountain Bed & Breakfast
968 Gunflint Trail
Grand Marais, MN 55604
(218) 387-1276
(800) 542 1226

Lindgren's B&B on Lake Superior
5552 County Road 35
P.O. Box 56
Lutsen, MN 55612
(218) 663-7450

Asa Park House
17500 St. Croix Trail North
Marine-on-St. Croix, MN 55407
(651) 433-5248
(888) 857-9969

Nicollet Island Inn

95 Merriam Street
Minneapolis, MN 55401
(612) 331–1800
fax (612) 331–6528

Whistle Stop Inn

Route 1, Box 85
New York Mills, MN 56567
(218) 385–2223
(800) 328–6315

Covington Inn

Pier 1
Harriet Island
St. Paul, MN 55107
(612) 292–1411

William Sauntry Mansion

626 North Fourth Street
Stillwater, MN 55082
(612) 430–2653
(800) 828–2653

The Log House & Homestead on Spirit Lake

P.O. Box 130
Vergas, MN 56587
(218) 342–2318
(800) 342–2318

Hospital Bay B&B

620 Northeast Lake Sreet
Warroad, MN 56763
(218) 386–2627
(800) 568–6028

Hungry Point Inn

One Olde Deerfield Road
Welch MN 55089
(612) 437–366

Missouri

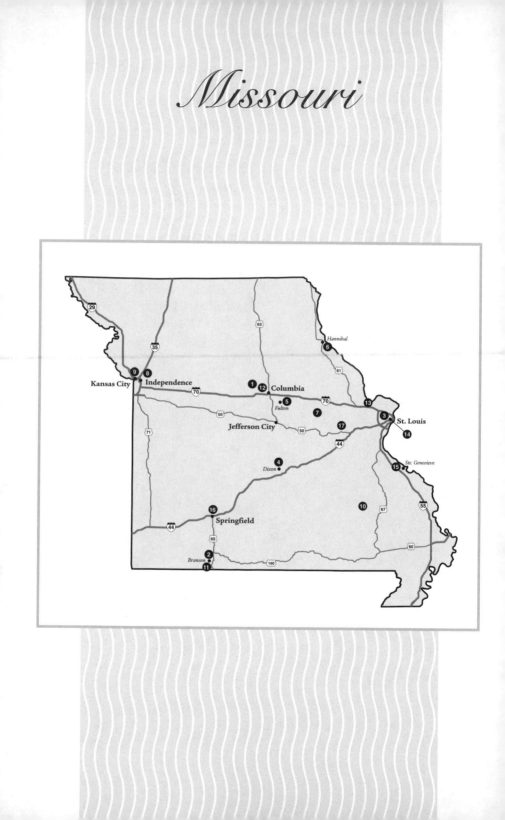

Kansas City Independence Columbia Hannibal Fulton Jefferson City St. Louis Ste. Genevieve Dixon Springfield Branson

29 35 63 61 70 50 71 44 65 160 60 55 67 70

Missouri

Numbers on map refer to towns numbered below.

*A Top Pick Inn

Borgman's Bed and Breakfast
Arrow Rock, Missouri 65320

INNKEEPERS: Kathy and Helen Borgman

ADDRESS/TELEPHONE: Van Buren Street; (660) 837–3350

ROOMS: 4 share 3 baths; all with air-conditioning. No smoking inn.

RATES: $55, single; $65 to $70, double; continental breakfast.
No credit cards.

OPEN: Year-round

FACILITIES AND ACTIVITIES: Sitting room. Porch with rockers.
Nearby: walk to restaurants, state historical buildings and sites,
archaeological digs, antiques and specialty shops, and The Lyceum
Theatre, one of Missouri's oldest repertory companies. Guided walking
tours of town also offered.

*B*orgman's Bed and Breakfast has been called "one of the most
enjoyable inns in the state." After my visit to this charming
white clapboard home, I heartily agree. Helen Borgman greeted
me at the door of her little farmhouse, built between 1855 and 1865 in this
tiny historic town. It's filled with country-style antiques and furnishings
that put even the most harried guests at ease.

Helen's daughter, Kathy, designed the stenciled wall borders that adorn
each of the guest room ceilings. The beautiful country quilts that add
splashes of colors to the beds were handmade by Helen, of course.

Relaxation is the key here. I just sat on the porch, in the shade of tall trees,
feeling the cool summer breeze. Helen wound up the old Victrola for a song.
It's also fun to stop by the kitchen to visit with Helen when she's making her
famous cinnamon buns fresh each morning for breakfast.

"It's gotten to the point where guests kind of expect me to serve them," Helen said. "I guess they feel it's a real treat." She also offers homemade breads, cereal, fruits, and beverages.

As Helen and I walked to the upstairs guest rooms, I could feel the country comfort soaking into my city bones. I saw tall Victorian headboards, exposed chimney brick, hurricane-style lamps, lacy window curtains, and rocking chairs in the handsome rooms. The only first-floor guest room has the original plank floor, a four-poster bed adorned with one of Helen's bright quilts, and another antique rocker. All the rooms are bright, cheery, and peaceful.

HOW TO GET THERE: From Kansas City or St. Louis, take I–70 to Route 41. Go north to Arrow Rock and turn right on Van Buren (the first road into Arrow Rock) to the inn about 2 blocks up the street.

Lewis and Clark Were Here!

Area history is fascinating. Lewis and Clark noted the region during their historic explorations. Native Americans used local outcroppings of flint to point their arrows; hence the town name. Three forts were once located in the area; one was used during the War of 1812. A portion of the town was burned down during the Civil War.

In town, I toured a wonderful "pioneer" Main Street, lined with historic buildings that still have wooden-board sidewalks and rough-hewn stones forming crude street gutters. A guided historic walking tour is offered from April through October (sometimes on weekends only, so check ahead).

The Branson House
Bed & Breakfast Inn
Branson, Missouri 65616

INNKEEPER: Sylvia Voyce

ADDRESS/TELEPHONE: 120 Fourth Street; (417) 334–0959

ROOMS: 7, including 1 suite; all with private bath and air-conditioning.

RATES: $75 to $105, single or double; EPB. No smoking inn.

OPEN: April 1 through December 15.

FACILITIES AND ACTIVITIES: Parlor, front porch. Nearby: walk to Lake Taneycomo, historic downtown Branson. A short drive to more than thirty live country music theaters, Silver Dollar City, Shepherd of the Hills outdoor drama, lakes, water sports, fishing, antiques shops, and boutiques.

*T*iny Branson has become the live country-music capital of the world, boasting more than thirty music theaters featuring the likes of Glen Campbell, Willie Nelson, Jim Stafford, Johnny Cash, Mel Tillis, The Statler Brothers—even Andy Williams, who built his own Moon River Theatre in this down-home hamlet.

"I ran into Mel Tillis the other day at the grocery store," one Branson resident told me. "He was pushing a cart just like everyone else."

Nestled in Ozark Mountain hill country, with its Southern-style friendliness and great weather, Branson is a great place for a B&B—such as The Branson House, located near the heart of historic downtown. Done in 1920s Arts and Crafts stylings, the inn features beautiful stone and boulder masonry.

Owner Opal Kelly treats guests like treasured country cousins. She serves specially prepared breakfasts of egg and meat casseroles, homemade coffee cake, fresh fruit, and beverages; in warm weather you can eat on the veranda overlooking downtown Branson and Lake Taneycomo.

Guests enjoy complimentary sherry or port from the buffet in the living room. And late-night snackers might weather a milk-and-cookie attack in the country kitchen.

The seven guest rooms are individually decorated with antiques and collectibles from all over the country. The Honeymoon Suite features an 1830s four-poster spool bed found in California; its massive armoire, which Opal discovered in Arkansas, dates to the 1830s. I also like the French Balcony room, with its fine French linens and private perch—perfect for Ozark summer days.

HOW TO GET THERE: From Springfield, Missouri, or Harrison, Arkansas, take I-65 to Branson. Exit on Missouri 76 (its name changes to Main Street close to town); go west to Fourth Street, turn left, and proceed to the inn at the intersection of Fourth and Atlantic.

Chateau on the Lake 👪
Branson, Missouri 65616

INNKEEPER: John Q. Hammons, chairman

ADDRESS/TELEPHONE: 415 North State Highway 265; (417) 334–1161 or (888) 333–5253

ROOMS: 302, with 57 suites. Wheelchair accessible.

RATES: $179 to $229, single or double; $269 to $499, suites.

OPEN: Year-round

FACILITIES AND ACTIVITIES: All-inclusive resort. Ten-story atrium, courtyard; restaurants (Chateau Grille—fine dining); library where you can take espresso, coffees, afternoon teas; Sweet Shoppe; Steeple's Lite Deli. Family activities include Crawdaddies Kid's Club. Full-service marina, rental of pleasure boats, excursion cruises. Scuba diving, parasailing, waterskiing lessons, fishing, hiking trails, indoor and outdoor pools, sauna, fitness center, tennis courts, salon, and spa. Three golf courses nearby.

" A castle rises in our midst," one newspaper story headline screamed not long ago. It was heralding the building of Chateau on the Lake, a 302-room luxury hotel modeled after European castles. It even has a two-story indoor waterfall.

The theme continues throughout this luxurious $45 million palace. For example, the grand hall of the Chateau boasts twenty-two massive chandeliers that measure 9 feet across and 12-foot-high murals of famous European castles. The ballroom, at 132 feet wide and 256 feet long, is the largest in the Southeast.

Many of the guest rooms, which more resemble elegant sitting rooms, nestle around a scenic centerpiece of meandering streams, towering trees, and lush foliage. Third- through tenth-floor rooms each have a private balcony and panoramic vistas of either the Ozark Mountains or Table Rock Lake.

There's so much to do here, it's pointless to take the space to tell you. Just know that your dreams can come true at the Chateau, and isn't that what the magic of a castle is all about?

HOW TO GET THERE: The Chateau is located on the shore of Table Rock Lake at the junction of Highways 265 and 165 and the Ozark Highroad (U.S. 765)—just five minutes from downtown Branson.

Seven Gables Inn 🗓 📱
Clayton, Missouri 63105

INNKEEPER: Dennis Fennedy

ADDRESS/TELEPHONE: 26 North Meramec; (314) 863–8400

ROOMS: 32, including 4 suites; all with private bath, air-conditioning, TV, and phone. Wheelchair accessible.

RATES: $139, weekends, $162, weekdays, single or double; $185 to $300, suites; EP.

OPEN: Year-round

FACILITIES AND ACTIVITIES: Two restaurants, bistro, garden court. A short drive to all St. Louis attractions: Busch Stadium, Union Station,

Relais et Château

The Seven Gables Inn has been included in the exclusive Relais et Châteaux, an organization listing some of the finest hotels in the world. (Only a few U.S. hotels are so honored. To give you an idea of their standards, the list includes the renowned Crillon in Paris.) Also included is the Canoe Bay in Chetek, Wisconsin, an elegant inn written up in the Badger State section of this book.

the Arch, historic river district, and more.

BUSINESS TRAVEL: Located about 15 miles west of downtown St. Louis. Corporate rates, meeting rooms, fax.

*S*even Gables is a masterpiece of sorts. It was built in 1918, and the architect based his design on Hawthorne's House of Seven Gables, which stands in Salem, Massachusetts.

This romantic continental getaway also provides great European-style dining experiences. Chez Louis—intimate, elegant, and serving classic continental gourmet cuisine—has received awards and rave reviews from the likes of the *New York Times* and the *St. Louis Post-Dispatch*. Chef Bernard is reluctant to reveal much of the menu, since it changes weekly and sometimes daily. Seafood prepared in classical French style is always a good choice.

The restaurant also boasts a 320-item wine list featuring French, Italian, and Californian varieties.

Guest rooms are uniquely European, done in handsome country French antiques and reproductions, some with brass and white iron-rail beds, writing desks, and comfortable chairs. Fresh flowers give rooms a sweet scent. Fluffy terrycloth robes are part of a luxurious bath. Even the soap is hand-milled in France.

Of course, there's turndown service, with chocolates left on your pillow. You had to wonder?

HOW TO GET THERE: From the airport, take I–170 south to the Ladue exit and go west into Clayton. This road will take you directly to the hotel.

Rock Eddy Bluff 🄒🄒
Dixon, Missouri 65459

INNKEEPERS: Kathy and Tom Corey

ADDRESS/TELEPHONE: HCR 62, 10245 Maries Road #511, P.O. Box 241; (573) 759–6081 or (800) 335–5921

ROOMS: 1 room, 1 three-bedroom cottage, and Line Camp cabin.

RATES: $95 to $130; EPB.

OPEN: Year-round

FACILITIES AND ACTIVITIES: Heated spa, large deck. Located near Gasconade River. Horse-drawn carriage rides into Amish country, hiking trails to river, canoeing, fishing, birdwatching, mushrooming, mountain biking; antiquing nearby.

"We are truly blessed to live in such a place," say Kathy and Tom, who returned here to the Missouri hills of their youth after years of "town living." Lucky for them—and us.

This remote retreat in south-central Missouri sits atop the scenic Gasconade River valley, awash in natural splendor. Views are spectacular; wildlife abounds; hills, hollows, and streams await your trekking discoveries. Relax in an Adirondack chair with your favorite book. Help harness the buggy horse for a clip-clop down country lanes in Amish fashion. Take a canoe and meander through Ozark streams.

Guest rooms are comfortable, too. Turkey Ridge Cottage is secluded in the trees overlooking the valley; it comes complete with fireplace, library, outfitted kitchen, three bedrooms, and a great room. Bluffhouse guest rooms boast antiques, homemade quilts, and paddle fans. The Line Camp cabin is a fanciful step back in time, containing all the modern conveniences of one hundred years ago. It's all a short walk to the Gasconade River.

HOW TO GET THERE: From I-70, follow Highway 63 south to Vienna. Two miles south of Vienna, take Highway 28 (toward Dixon). Follow Highway 28 for 11 miles to left; turn on Route E. Then take Route E for 7 miles to "pavement ends." Turn right on country road 511 for less than 1 mile. Follow signs to the inn.

Loganberry Inn ¢¢
Fulton, Missouri 65251

INNKEEPERS: Carl and Kathy McGeorge

ADDRESS/TELEPHONE: 310 West Seventh Street; (573) 642–9229

ROOMS: 4; 2 with private bath; EPB.

RATES: $75 to $150, single or double. Special packages available.

OPEN: Year-round

FACILITIES AND ACTIVITIES: Victorian parlor with fireplace, dining room. Walking distance to Westminister College, Winston Churchill Memorial, William Woods University, Undercroft Museum. Also wander brick-lined streets to see historic homes, visit shops and boutiques.

*F*ulton is the home of Westminister College. Winston Churchill gave his famous "Iron Curtain" speech there, and Lady Margaret Thatcher came to the school in 1996 to commemorate the fiftieth anniversary of the event.

While they were in town, Lady Margaret and her husband, Sir Dennis, stayed at the Loganberry Inn. I guess guests that overnight here are in pretty good company. At least you know that you'll be treated like royalty.

Innkeepers Carl and Kathy McGeorge's enthusiasm is gracious and contagious. I love their 1899 Victorian inn, with guest rooms that boast decorator wall coverings, antique furnishings like sleigh beds and walnut eye tables, and more. Breakfasts in the spacious dining room might include homemade cinnamon rolls, banana nut muffins, peach French toast, sausage and egg casseroles, flavored coffees, tea, and fresh fruit—all served on fine china.

HOW TO GET THERE: From I–70, exit 148, which is Route 54 west, then exit left on Route I; continue to Wesminister Avenue and turn left. Go to Seventh Street and turn right, continuing to the inn.

Romancing the Past Victorian B&B
Fulton, Missouri 65251

INNKEEPERS: Jim and ReNee Yeager

ADDRESS/TELEPHONE: 830 Court Street; (573) 592–1996

ROOMS: 3; all with private bath and fireplace.

RATES: $100 to $170; EPB.

OPEN: Year-round

FACILITIES AND ACTIVITIES: Afternoon tea, snacks/refreshments at night. Wraparound porch. Hot tub in garden. Drive to Winston Churchill Memorial and Library, Tanglewood Golf Course, Katy Trail, Earthquake Hollow, Mark Twain Forest, Westminster College, Burney L. Fishback Museum.

*T*his 1886 Queen Anne is a real beauty, with its handsome wraparound porch a perfect respite for sunny summer days. You can wander the beautiful grounds, filled with rose gardens and ancients trees. Or perhaps a screened porch is more your style—that's out back. Along with a hot tub.

Inside is a Victorian picture postcard: a walnut archway in the grand hall that opens to polished parquet floors, handsome woodworks, grand staircases, and period antiques.

Bedchambers are Victorian elegant, too. The Renaissance Suite offers a massive antique walnut canopy bed, as well as a sitting room and large bath. The Victorian Rose Room boasts a private balcony. And Miss Jaime's Study is the ultimate in inn luxury, with its feather mattress, fireplace, and solarium ultraspa for two.

HOW TO GET THERE: From I-70, exit 148 onto Highway 54 south (this is the exit at Kingdom City, 22 miles east of Columbia, MO; 3 miles east of Kansas City; or 90 minutes west of St. Louis). Three miles south of I-70 on U.S. 54, take the first Fulton exit, marked Bus. 54 and William Woods University. The exit ramp is on the left side. Follow Bus. 54 1 mile to the first light, and ½ mile more to the second light, then ½ mile more to the third light at 10th Street. Turn right, go 3 short blocks to Court Street (one way street to the left). Continue 1 block to cross 9th, and the inn's the fourth house on the left. There is off-street parking by the house.

Garth Woodside Mansion
Hannibal, Missouri 63401

INNKEEPERS: John and Julie Rolsen

ADDRESS/TELEPHONE: RR 3, P.O. Box 578; (573) 221–2789

WEB SITE: www.garthmansion.com

ROOMS: 8; all with private bath and central ai- conditioning, phone on request.

RATES: $95 to $195, single or double; EPB.

OPEN: Year-round

FACILITIES AND ACTIVITIES: BYOB. Sitting rooms, parlors, wrap-around porch. Acres of gardens, meadows, woodlands. Tours of the mansion given 11:30 A.M. to 3:00 P.M. daily. A short drive to restaurants, Mark Twain's boyhood house, Huckleberry Finn landmarks, Mississippi River paddle-wheel rides, caves, sightseeing tours, Mark Twain Outdoor Theater, specialty shops, and Great River Road that follows the Mississippi.

This is a historic country estate at its finest, a handsome Victorian home on thirty-nine acres of meadows and woodland, graced with noble old trees and a private fishing pond. (Guests can angle for bass and perch.) Built in 1871 as a summer home for prominent Hannibal businessman John Garth, the mansion was the focal point for notables passing through Hannibal.

Hometown boy Samuel Clemens (Mark Twain) spent several nights here in his lifelong friend's home in 1882 and also during his last visit to Hannibal in 1902.

Amazingly, the mansion contains mostly original furnishings; they are exquisite. The library, with its 9-foot-tall doors, is done in elegant walnut, with 1840 Empire furniture, a marble fireplace with gold inlay, and a red-velvet Victorian reclining chair.

The dining room is graced with the original table and twelve chairs. The hostess chair was made extra wide to accommodate the full petticoats that were the style of the day. There's also an original painting done by Garth's wife in the family parlor.

We walked up the magnificent flying staircase that vaults three stories high with no visible means of support. It appears even more spectacular, hanging high in the air, because of the mansion's 14-foot-high ceiling.

Guest rooms are decorated in Victorian splendor. On the second floor, the John Garth Room, occupying the old master bedroom, has a beautiful black walnut Victorian bed, with a 10-foot-tall headboard in grand Renaissance Revival style. The three-piece matching bedroom set is original to the home. Even the dresser stands nearly 10 feet high.

The Rosewood Room has become one of the inn's most popular lodgings. It's bright and airy, with long windows, great views of the grounds, lively "grapevine" Victorian print wallpaper, and a hand-decorated claw-footed bathtub.

It also boasts the "most expensive bed in Missouri," a walnut half-tester bed from the 1850s that's museum quality.

Also check out the Samuel Clemens Room, with its 12-foot-tall half-tester bed, a hand-carved rosewood beauty, to say the least.

Third-floor rooms are country beautiful, with wicker themes and great views of the grounds.

Breakfasts might feature goodies like ham-and-cheese quiche, marmalade-filled muffins, rolls, and more. Iced tea is served on the spacious veranda during summer between 4:00 and 6:00 P.M. Hot mulled apple cider is the winter treat inside.

HOW TO GET THERE: From St. Louis, take I–70 west to Missouri 79 and go north into Hannibal. Turn west on Broadway, then south on U.S. 61. Turn east at Warren Barrett Drive (the first road south of the Holiday Inn) and follow signs to the inn.

Captain Wohlt Inn ¢¢¢
Hermann, Missouri 65041

INNKEEPERS: Matt and Kent Wilkins

ADDRESS/TELEPHONE: 123 East Third Street; (573) 486-3357

WEB SITE: www.bbonline.com/mo/bbim/ or www.innsite.com/bbim

ROOMS: 8, including 3 suites; all with private bath and air-conditioning, 1 with wheelchair access.

RATES: $70 to $80, single or double; $120 to $150, suites; EPB. Two-night minimum during festival weekends (Maifest and Oktoberfest). Children under 12 free. Stay third night for half price.

OPEN: Year-round

FACILITIES AND ACTIVITIES: Short walk from restaurants, shops, and historic buildings of Hermann and the Missouri River. Short drive to area wineries and vineyards.

*T*his quaint inn sits high on a hill overlooking Third Street in the middle of ethnic Hermann's historic district, which is listed on the National Register of Historic Places for its architectural and historical significance. I immediately liked it, feeling as though I were visiting a favorite aunt's house; it had a comfortable, welcome-home kind of atmosphere.

The home was built in 1886 by its namesake, a German riverboat captain who founded the Hermann ferry boat company. The building was renovated and restored in 1986. A first-floor room (one of the very few inn rooms in

Oom Paa Paa

For dinner, try Taylor's Landing, which features hearty German ethnic foods like sauerbraten, bratwurst, and schnitzel. Vintage 1847 at Stone Hill Winery offers its own schnitzel, rainbow trout, and steak fillets in a romantic setting.

Then wander along Third Street, between Schiller and Market, which has remained largely as it appeared in the 1800s. Lots sold in 1839 for $50. The street was cut through a high knoll; hence the inn's "hillside" site.

Hermann equipped for the handicapped) has bright country stylings and a four-poster bed.

As I walked up the staircase, I ran my hands over a walnut handrail that's original to the home. I found second-floor rooms equally appealing: pink-and-blue-bouquet country wallpapers, country ceiling borders, and handsome furnishings, including ceiling fans and a beechnut Jenny Lind bed. It's also one of the prettiest I've seen in a long time.

Third-floor dormer rooms feature more pastel country prints, dormer windows, and, as in most rooms, lovely country quilts made by local artisans.

Breakfasts may include filling egg casseroles, morning sausage, ham loaf and bacon, fresh fruit and juice, and delicious home-baked goodies. Her specialty is spinach–zucchini casserole, seasoned with cheese and onions. Yum!

A restored 1840 building next to the inn houses two additional guest suites. Country furnishings, wooden decks, a garden with tables and benches, and a whirlpool make this house a comfortable retreat.

HOW TO GET THERE: From St. Louis, take I–70 west to Missouri 19, then go south into Hermann. Turn east on Third Street to the inn. Private parking is between Second and Third Streets, down an alley named Hollyhock Lane.

Woodstock Inn B&B
Independence, Missouri 64050

INNKEEPERS: Todd and Patricia Justice

ADDRESS/TELEPHONE: 1212 West Lexington Avenue; (816) 833–2233 or (800) 276–5202

ROOMS: 11, with 2 suites; all with private bath. Wheelchair accessible.

RATES: $72 to $189; EPB.

OPEN: Year-round

FACILITIES AND ACTIVITIES: Turndown service. Near the Harry S. Truman Library and Museum, Old Jail Museum. Short drive to Kansas City's Country Club Plaza.

*I*f you're lucky enough to stay at the Woodstock, consider one of their Romantic Retreat packages.

Perhaps the Oriental Suite will be to your tastes. Of course, there's black lacquer and mother-of-pearl furnishings. And a museum-quality antique wedding bed imported from China.

But the real attraction of this bedchamber is the Roman columned spa, with fifty-six-jet thermo massage whirlpool for two.

Breakfasts are out of the ordinary, too. You might try the inn's famous gourmet malt Belgian waffles with specialty syrups and fresh fruit sauces. But then there's always ham-and-cheese-stuffed French toast, apple crisps, and garden frittatas.

Nobody goes away hungry—or dissatisfied—here.

HOW TO GET THERE: From Kansas City, take Independence Avenue east (it eventually becomes U.S. 24); continue until North River Boulevard and turn right; at Lexington Avenue, again turn right and proceed to the inn.

Southmoreland on-the-Plaza
Kansas City, Missouri 64112

INNKEEPERS: Penni
Johnson and Susan Moehl

ADDRESS/TELEPHONE: 116
East Forty-sixth Street; (816)
531–7979, fax (816) 531–2407

ROOMS: 12, 1 carriage house;
all with private bath and air-
conditioning. Wheelchair
accessible. Free local phone
calls.

RATES: $110 to $170, single; $130 to $190, double; EPB.

OPEN: Year-round

FACILITIES AND ACTIVITIES: Special dinners available in dining room.
Library sitting room, wicker solarium, open-air balconies, courtyard,
gardens, croquet lawn, off-street parking. Guests get free passes to Rock-
hill Tennis Club, a private facility. Nearby: walk to 300 specialty shops
and restaurants of famed Country Club Plaza. Short drive to Nelson-
Atkins Museum of Art, Henry Moore Sculpture Garden, Missouri
Repertory Theater, Mill Run Creek, Crown Center, Harry Truman
Sports Complex (home to Kansas City Chiefs and Royals).

BUSINESS TRAVEL: Located about 5 minutes from Crown Center and
downtown. Corporate rates, meeting rooms, fax.

The minute we arrived, this elegant, sophisticated inn became one
of my pa's top five places to stay. I couldn't agree more. The
superb 1913 Colonial Revival mansion boasts centuries-old
shade trees, gracious lawns, rock walls, and formal gardens not often seen in
the heart of the city. Inside, it has undergone a million-dollar restoration and
renovation that includes some of the finest guest rooms in the Midwest.

Rooms are named for Kansas City notables. I stayed in Number 10—
George Caleb Bingham (a mid-nineteenth-century painter whose works
hang in the nearby Nelson-Atkins Museum of Art). It's graced with museum-
quality prints of Bingham's portraits featuring Col. Napoleon Geddings,

grandfather of the house's previous owner, and his wife. Other room treasures include a four-poster mahogany bed, a Chinese rosewood gossip bench, and bold wall coverings done in yellow, navy, and brick.

Pa drew number 4—Thomas Hart Benton—complete with Mission-style furnishings, an oak and copper four-poster bed, and a Tiffany-style lamp.

Each of our rooms had a private balcony, mine with a great view of the plaza.

Attention baseball fans: Choose the Leroy "Satchell" Paige room during baseball season when the Royals are in town, and you will receive complimentary tickets to the ball game.

Or if you crave complete privacy, try the Carriage House, complete with fireplace and Jacuzzi.

Innkeepers Susan Moehl and Penni Johnson were looking for a Maine coast inn when they stumbled across this treasure. "Welcome to Camden in Kansas City," Susan quipped.

They're also proud that the inn showcases the efforts of determined women to restore one of Kansas City's famed residences. "Since 1948 the house has had only women owners," Susan said.

The innkeepers want you to know that it's a business travelers' paradise, too. CEO-style perks include made-to-order breakfasts, round-the-clock reception and checkout, free local calls and fax, modem connections, and membership privileges (sports and dining) at a nearby historic private club.

All guests enjoy Penni's breakfasts on an 1860s harvest table in the informal dining room. Pa and I savored banana-apricot frappés, home-baked banana nut bread, and French toast stuffed with Lorraine Swiss cheese and dusted with powdered sugar and almonds.

If you're in a movie mood, repair to the living room. Inside an 1860s Austrian armoire, there's a television, VCR, and movie library with a hundred titles.

"All with happy endings," Penni said.

HOW TO GET THERE: From I-70, I-35, and I-29 in downtown Kansas City, take the Main Street exit. Go south to East Forty-sixth Street, turn east (left), and go about 1½ blocks to the inn, on the left side of the street.

Wilderness Lodge
Lesterville, Missouri 63654

INNKEEPER: Bob Schall

ADDRESS/TELEPHONE: P.O. Box 90; (573) 637–2295 or toll-free from St. Louis (800) 296-2011

ROOMS: 26 units; all with private bath and air-conditioning.

RATES: $79 per person, rooms and cottages; $85 per person, suites; MAP. Children's rates available. Two-night minimum required. Special package rates.

OPEN: Year-round

FACILITIES AND ACTIVITIES: Dining room, bar. Archery, shuffleboard, volleyball, horseshoes, Frisbee-golf course, walking trails, tennis courts, platform tennis. Also children's playground, swimming pool, hot tub (cold weather only), hayrides, canoeing, tube floats. Horseback riding.

drove deep into the beautiful Ozark Mountain foothills to find this woodsy retreat. Located on 1,200 rolling acres near the bank of the crystal-clear Black River, the Wilderness Lodge offers some of the best country-style fun imaginable.

A group of young canoers were excitedly telling their parents about the afternoon's adventures as I entered the Main Lodge, the oldest and largest building on the property. The heavy log-beam construction and tan pitch made me feel like a pioneer in the wilderness.

The lodge's rough-hewn furniture is just what you'd expect. Especially interesting are Native American–style rugs displayed on the walls, animal trophies, and the obligatory rifle hanging above a manteled hearth.

Later I sat in an open dining room with a giant picture window looking out over the grounds, watching more kids frolic in the pool. A game room, just off to the side, has card and game tables for all kinds of family fun. For romantics the lodge has a large fireplace room for snuggling on chilly evenings.

Family-style breakfasts and dinners are lodge specialties. Morning menus include eggs, pancakes, and beverages; dinner platters are heaped high with good country cooking such as fried chicken, fresh bread, and sweet pastries. After dinner you might sidle up to the bar for a nightcap.

HOW TO GET THERE: From St. Louis, take I–270 south to Route 21 and continue south to Glover. Head west on Route 21/49/72. Near Arcadia, take Route 21 south, then west for about 22 miles to Peola Road. Turn left and continue down the dirt and gravel path, following the signs to the lodge.

City Slickers

I've rarely seen guest cabins so complement the beautiful Ozark countryside. Especially attractive is the use of native rock, peeled logs, pine siding, and porches built right into the landscape. Country-antique furniture and Native American artifacts add to the woodsy ambience; many rooms feature large fireplaces and high loft ceilings.

Try one of the most popular lodge treats: "City Slickers" trail rides. These weeklong horsey treks for up to 200 riders follow local trails through the woods, along rivers, and over meadows. Held in April, June, July, September, and November, they cost $153 per person and include three meals daily and camping fees. Livery horses are $30 per day.

Big Cedar Lodge
Ridgedale, Missouri 65739

INNKEEPER: John Morris, owner

ADDRESS/TELEPHONE:
612 Devil's Pool Road;
(417) 335–2777,
fax (417) 334–3956

ROOMS: 200; all with private bath. Wheelchair accessible.

RATES: $99 to $399, depending on season; Governor's Suite, $599 to $899. Packages available, including bed and breakfast.

OPEN: Year-round

FACILITIES AND ACTIVITIES: Where to start? Big Cedar Lodge has everything, but here are only a few highlights. Top of the Rock, a Jack Nicklaus–designed par 3, nine-hole golf course; carriage rides; evening campfire wagon tours; horse trail rides; swimming pool and hot tub; tennis courts; nature trail; kids' playground; running trail; basketball; horseshoes; guided chuckwagon tours; guided trophy trout fishing and streamside lunch tours; boat rentals; professional fishing guide service; waterskiing lessons.

*T*he beauty of this place simply overwhelms me. Built to resemble the grand wilderness architecture of the Adirondacks, Big Cedar Lodge has quickly become one of my favorite retreats. It's like traveling back to a grand and more extravagant time, and the notion sends goosebumps down my spine. See if you get 'em, too, when you see the lodge for the first time, nestled majestically high on a ridge overlooking the valley below.

By the time you open the door to your room or cabin, settled in a thick forest ridge, you'll already be Big Cedar believers. But note the handcrafted metal chandeliers, hand-carved log beds, handwoven rugs, Jacuzzi bath, and private deck with incredible views of the Big Cedar wonderland that stretches out for miles on end.

If you're really decadent, overnight in the Governor's Suite—all 2,500 square feet of it.

This resort is mesmerizing and unforgettable. When can I come back here?

HOW TO GET THERE: Big Cedar Lodge is located about 10 miles south of Branson. Turn off U.S. 65 to State 86 and follow the signs to the lodge.

School House Bed and Breakfast
Rocheport, Missouri 65279

INNKEEPERS: John and Vicki Ott, owners; Penny Province, manager

ADDRESS/TELEPHONE: Third and Clark Streets; (573) 698–2022

ROOMS: 10; all with private bath and air-conditioning, 1 with wheelchair access. No smoking inn.

RATES: $85 to $215, single or double; EPB.

OPEN: Year-round except Christmas Day.

FACILITIES AND ACTIVITIES: BYOB. Sitting rooms, outdoor garden, courtyard. Town on National Register of Historic Places, filled with nineteenth-century homes. Nearby: antiques stores and craft and pottery shops. Short drive to restaurants, local winery (Les Bourgeois) overlooking Missouri River and Boone Cave. Hiking and biking on renowned Missouri River State Trail.

*T*walked into this 1914 three-story brick schoolhouse just as Vicki Ott, the co-owner was beginning a tour of the inn and quickly discovered that it is a magnificent example of what restoration and renovation with a visionary eye can accomplish.

Guest rooms are very spacious, almost imperial, with their 13-foot-high ceilings, cheery ceiling and wall borders, schoolhouse-sized windows, shiny oak floors, and antique furnishings. I complimented

Vicki on her handsome curtains; her talented hands made all the window treatments throughout the inn.

One guest room has a white iron-rail bed and cane-backed chairs; another is fashioned with a brass four-poster bed that's 7 feet tall. I also found delicately carved Victorian dressers, high-back chairs, pastel wall coverings, and even a trundle bed that adds a down-home feel.

I love the second floor's executive suite, with its mahogany four-poster bed, arched doorway, and three huge windows that spill light into this happy room. It boasts the schoolhouse's original fir floors, handsomely restored by Vicki and husband John. Oops! I forgot to mention the two-person whirlpool, too.

For newlyweds and incurable romantics, the Bridal Suite is a must. Imagine a heart-shaped whirlpool tub, upholstered wall coverings, and more.

Vicki does all the breakfast cooking in an expansive second-floor kitchen that opens onto the inn's main common room. "Just seems like everyone follows me up here, and we end up talking as I prepare the food," Vicki said. Prepare yourself for her famous egg casserole, fresh fruit and juices, and homemade bran and cinnamon muffins.

Then browse among the hallway display case's historic town and school photos and memorabilia.

HOW TO GET THERE: From Columbia, take I–70 west to Rocheport exit, then follow Highway BB 2 miles northwest into town. The inn is at Third and Clark Streets (right on Highway BB).

Historic Haven

Rocheport itself is a "very Southern town," Vicki said. Its history stretches back to Native American times, as early journals noted primitive red-keel paintings on limestone bluffs that edge out over the Missouri River near here. In fact, members of the Lewis and Clark expedition passed by in 1804, citing "uncouth paintings of animals."

At the height of ferryboat traffic, the town grew to more than 800 people. Today about 300 residents keep Rocheport's legacy alive; several historic structures still dot the landscape. You can pick up a walking-tour booklet at the inn.

Boone's Lick Trail Inn
St. Charles, Missouri 63301

INNKEEPER: V'Anne Mydler

ADDRESS/TELEPHONE: 1000 South Main Street; (636) 947-7000 or (888) 940-0002

WEB SITE: www.booneslick.com

ROOMS: 6, including 1 suite; all with private bath. No smoking inn.

RATES: Sunday through Thursday: $115 to $135, single or double; Friday and Saturday: $135 to $165, single or double; EPB. Slightly higher during festivals and holidays.

OPEN: Year-round except Christmas Eve and Day.

FACILITIES AND ACTIVITIES: In the heart of Frenchtown, with restaurants, specialty shops, boutiques, and antiques stores. Overlooks Frontier Park, the Missouri River State Trail, and Lewis and Clark Trail. National Historic District, Golden Rod Showboat, Ameristar Casino.

I was intrigued by the numerous doors leading to rooms overlooking the gallery porch of the historic 1840 Carter-Rice building, now known as the Boone's Lick Trail Inn. It reminded me of a boarding house—but that wasn't quite it.

"Madame Duquette had her girls entertain patrons in those little rooms," innkeeper V'Anne Mydler told me. "See, folklore tells us that in the 1820s, Duquette ran a brothel here. When I restored the building, those four doors still led to tiny, little cubbyhole stalls, big enough for only a cot and washstand."

The Boone's Lick Trail Inn, one of the oldest homes in town, is intertwined with all kinds of interesting history. Frenchtown is the site of many

firsts, including the Lewis and Clark Rendezvous, the start of the Zebulon Pike expedition, and the beginnings of Daniel Boone's salt-lick trail. It's also where the Sante Fe Trail was planned and drafted.

The 1840 inn hosted hundreds of early adventurers and settlers passing through the town on their way west. V'Anne has restored second-floor guest rooms into country-charmed quarters. Some rooms have original plank floors, antique iron-rail beds, German lace curtains, and family antique heirlooms.

The newest room is the third-floor suite, with its hand-carved maple bed, antique slave's bed (daybed), and a private widow's walk overlooking the Missouri River.

I found the inn quiet and private, a welcome respite just a stone's throw from the hubbub that engulfed me on Main Street during this summer holiday weekend.

V'Anne prides herself on her never-ending breakfasts; no one will leave here hungry. Eggs Olé is a treat; so are her French crepes and special home-baked breads, homemade jams, yummy cinnamon rolls, and lemon biscuits. Following breakfast, take a walking tour that showcases the town's historic architecture (self-guided tour pamphlets can be obtained at the tourism department on Main Street).

If you work up a good appetite, I'd recommend the Mother-in-Law House on South Main for lunch, where I enjoyed their turkey-and-salad plate with a glass of white wine. Lewis and Clark's (also on South Main) arguably offers the town's finest evening dining. You'll also find restaurants specializing in local-flavored specialties like Crab Rangoon, beignets, catfish, and down-home barbecue.

This historic city is alive with festivals year-round, including May's Lewis and Clark Rendezvous, August's Fête des Petites Côtes (Festival of the Hills), and Oktoberfest.

HOW TO GET THERE: From St. Louis, take I–70 west to First Capitol Drive, exit, and continue to Main Street. Turn right; the inn is at Main and Boone's Lick Road.

The Lafayette House
St. Louis, Missouri 63104

INNKEEPERS: Bill Duffield, Nancy Buhr, Annalise Millet

ADDRESS/TELEPHONE: 2156 Lafayette Avenue; (314) 772–4429 or (800) 641–8965, fax (314) 664–2156

ROOMS: 5, with 1 suite; 2 with private bath, 3 share one large bath; EPB

RATES: $75 to $145; two-night minimums on weekends.

OPEN: Year-round

FACILITIES AND ACTIVITIES: Large dining room, sunny porch. Stroll through surrounding Lafayette Square Park, enjoy shops and restaurants along Park Avenue. Only 5 minutes from downtown St. Louis and Union Station, St. Louis Center, St. Louis Cathedral, Gateway Arch, Busch Stadium.

*T*his 1876 Queen Anne, fourteen-room brick mansion was built as a wedding gift for the daughter of a rich construction magnate. Located in the historic Lafayette Square District, it boasts the finest materials—walnut woodwork, 14-foot-high ceilings, rooms with fireplaces, and a wonderfully hand-carved walnut staircase.

Guests are greeted with fresh flowers throughout the main floor and bedchambers. Another standout is the breakfast here, prepared by Annalise Millet, one of the innkeepers who is also a pastry chef. It might include everything from homemade muffins and breads or Belgian waffles smothered in blueberry compote to crab-stuffed quiche.

The Lafayette Room's large four-poster bed, brass fixtures, antiques, and huge space make it one of the inn's most popular guest quarters. On the third floor, there's a contemporary suite with all kinds of nooks and crannies.

HOW TO GET THERE: From the west, including the airport, take I–70 east through downtown St. Louis to I–44 west. Take the first exit, Jefferson Avenue, turning right (north) and right again at the first light, onto Lafayette Avenue. It's 1 block to the inn.

The Inn St. Gemme Beauvais
Ste. Genevieve, Missouri 63670

INNKEEPER:
Mike Emerson, owner

ADDRESS/TELEPHONE: 78
North Main Street, P.O. Box
231; (573) 883–5744

ROOMS: 14, with 1 carriage
house and 1 guest house
across the street; all with
private bath. No smoking
inn.

RATES: $89 to $185, single or double; $15 extra person in room, $6 for
child; EPB and afternoon tea; wine and cheese.

OPEN: Year-round

FACILITIES AND ACTIVITIES: Private dinners for six or more people by
reservation. Dining and common rooms. Nearby: walk to antiques
shops, galleries, and museums (many specializing in pre–Civil War
pieces). Historical town architecture includes some of the best examples
of French Colonial homes in the United States, including vertical-log
homes. Annual Jour de Fête second full weekend of August.

This 1847 three-story, redbrick building is located in a town that's
been called "the finest surviving example of French Colonial
architecture in the country," with more than fifty historic buildings dating from the 1700s, when the fur traders settled here.

Walls here are pioneer-tough—18 inches thick—and they're only one of the
inn's unique features. In the foyer, I walked under a historic chandelier, dating from the early 1800s, that casts an amber glow over the hallway. Just to the
right of the door is the inn desk, an old rolltop.

I enjoyed a French feast for breakfast, with hand-filled ham and cheese
crepes, an inn specialty. There are also tasty quiches, delicious homemade
orange-pecan nut breads, fresh fruit cups, and other delicious treats.

For dinner, innkeeper Mike Emerson will suggest a spot to match your
tastes. I like the Hotel Ste. Genevieve, just a short walk down the street, for

scrumptious steaks, fish, and chops.

Eating in the inn's historic dining room is a treat in itself. It's cozy and quaint, with white walls, a white marble fireplace, and antique tables and chairs. I also felt a bit larger than life as I walked around this room. That's because its scaled-down dimensions are typical of the town's historic French-style homes. After all, this is the state's oldest inn.

There is also a common room in the cellar that at one time served as a "moonshine" tavern. It's a favorite gathering place for guests, offering books, magazines, games, and a continuously in-the-works jigsaw puzzle.

Mike spent ten years operating a Florida inn. He's completely renovated and restored the inn, crafting five two-room suites (two with Jacuzzi tubs), all with comfy king beds. He also put a hot tub in the backyard for outdoor relaxation. Also, out back is a carriage house with whirlpool tub. And across the street at the inn's guest house are five more deluxe accommodations.

Just a short walk away are all the town's fabulous architectural attractions. Especially interesting is the 1770 Bolduc House, a vertical-log "fort" regarded as the most authentically restored Colonial Creole house in the country.

This is also a great town for antique hunting. My favorite place is Le Souvenir, housed in the oldest brick building west of the Mississippi River.

HOW TO GET THERE: From St. Louis, take I–55 south to Route 32. Turn east and continue into Ste. Genevieve. Turn right on Market Street and continue for about 3 blocks to Main Street. Turn left on Main Street and continue to the inn.

The Southern Hotel 🄌
Ste. Genevieve, Missouri 63670

INNKEEPERS: Michael and Barbara Hankins

ADDRESS/TELEPHONE: 146 South Third Street; (573) 883–3493 or (800) 275–1412

ROOMS: 8; all with private bath and air-conditioning.

RATES: $93 to $125; EPB.

OPEN: Year-round

FACILITIES AND ACTIVITIES: Billiard room, gracious common rooms, off-street parking. Located in heart of historic town, one of the oldest settlements west of the Mississippi River. Walking tours of French Colonial architecture, other historic buildings, quaint shops, boutiques, restaurants.

"Beginning in the 1820s, The Southern Hotel was known for the finest accommodations between St. Louis and Natchez, Tennessee," innkeeper Barbara Hankins said as we walked through swinging doors into the hotel's old saloon, which now acts as a guest parlor. "The Mississippi was then about 4 blocks away, and the hotel employed a young slave to sit in the belvedere atop the house and watch for steamboats arriving at Ste. Genevieve's dock. Then he'd run across the street to the stables and get a wagon to meet hotel guests."

I never suspected that this grand old dame, built in Federal style with a graceful front porch around 1800, had become a deserted eyesore in the mid-1980s, "a dumping ground for everything people no longer wanted," Barbara said. It is a testament to Barbara and Michael Hankinses' magnificent restoration work that The Southern once again exudes warmth, hospitality, and classical graciousness.

Guest rooms are charmers; much of the credit goes to Barbara, whose whimsical, artistic touches are evident everywhere. If you're one of the first guests, Barbara will let you wander among the eight rooms to choose your

Breakfast Bonus

Barbara cooks up some fabulous breakfasts in her kitchen, which she decorated with handsome rosemaling, a Scandinavian folk art. I am fascinated by the unusual gourmet breakfast, which might include strawberry soup, banana bisque, mushroom quiche, freshly baked croissants, juices, and chocolate-tinged coffee. Six fine restaurants are within walking distance; Barbara will match one to your particular tastes for evening meals.

The innkeepers have restored the "summer kitchen" behind the hotel; it's now a gracious craft boutique featuring works of local artisans. Blossom-filled gardens surround the building and encourage visitors to stroll, sit, and enjoy.

favorite. But let me warn you: The combination of country Victorian furnishings and fabulous folk art makes the selection a difficult task.

The Japonisme Room is tinged with Oriental influence, reflecting the Victorian fascination with the Far East, and includes Chinese silk prints in the bathroom as well as a claw-foot tub painted to match the room's decor.

The River Room features a headboard of "Old Man River" carved out of Missouri cedar logs by a local artist. Buttons and Bows boasts a linen-draped canopy bed. Cabbage Rose is quite romantic, with its carved Victorian headboard, white lace, and elegant wall coverings. But one of my favorites is Wysocki's Room, named for folk artist Charles Wysocki. With its three-dimensional folk-art headboard depicting a charming village, it's one of the most unusual beds I've ever seen.

HOW TO GET THERE: From St. Louis, take I–55 south to the Ste. Genevieve exit (Route 32). Continue into town and turn right at Market Street; go 1 block to Third Street; turn right to the hotel.

Walnut Street Inn
Springfield, Missouri 65806

INNKEEPERS: Karol, Gary, and Nancy Brown

ADDRESS/TELEPHONE: 900 East Walnut; (800) 593–6346 or (417) 864–6346

WEB SITE: www.walnutstreetinn.com

ROOMS: 14, including 5 suites; all with private bath and air-conditioning. Wheelchair accessible.

RATES: $99 to $169, single or double; EPB.

OPEN: Year-round

FACILITIES AND ACTIVITIES: Two sitting rooms, front porch, rear enclosed porch, deck, garden, goldfish pond. Nearby: Southwest Missouri State University campus, University Art Exhibition Center, Hammons Sports Center, Center for Performing Arts. A short drive to Springfield Art Museum, Landers Theatre, Bass Pro, Wilson's Creek National (Civil War) Battlefield.

BUSINESS TRAVEL: Located 5 minutes from Federal Building, Springfield City Hall, downtown. Corporate rates, meeting room, fax.

"*I*s this a room or an apartment?" my pa kidded as we settled in at this gracious inn just a block from Southwest Missouri State University. Our third-floor quarters, called The Loft, were spacious. *Huge* is probably a better word. The former attic sprawled along three rooms, graced with beautifully chosen furnishings that included two double beds, reading chair, sofa, writing desk, antique tables, chairs, and chests.

I also liked the interesting nooks and crannies, sun-filled skylights, and sounds of scurrying squirrels who often run over the rooftops in pursuit of falling pecans.

It's all part of the captivating atmosphere at this Victorian showplace, built in 1894 and now a designated State Historic Site.

Karol Brown told us that the inn was Springfield's Designer Showcase house when it opened in 1988. "Noted artists designed each room," she said. It's easy to see why it was a winner—the results are imbued with nineteenth-century grace but possess all the comforts of home.

Imagine oak floors, leaded-glass windows, Victorian sofas, and soft lighting. In the Jewell Sitting Room, there's even a square grand piano that predates the Civil War. But be forewarned—it looks better than it sounds.

Morning chimes summoned us to breakfast in the dining room, and Karol served up a mouthwatering feast of black walnut waffles, fresh fruit, and homemade breads. A nice touch: Nonguests can join you here for breakfast for $7.00 per person.

Of course, romantics might choose the breakfast-in-bed option.

After our meal Pa grabbed a cushy chair by the fireplace while I browsed through pictures of the inn's restoration in a scrapbook in the second-floor Gathering Room.

I also lined up dinner possibilities. The winner: Le Mirbelle. Entree choices include filet de boeuf Wellington with shallots and mushrooms; Scotch-cured salmon; and boule de neige—a snowball of vanilla ice cream smothered in chocolate sauce and topped with coconut shavings.

Don't you love the Carriage House master suites with fireplace and whirlpool bath? Things just keep getting better here.

HOW TO GET THERE: From St. Louis, take I–44 west to Glenstone Road, then go south to Walnut. Turn right and proceed to Hammons Parkway and the inn.

The Schwegmann House
Washington, Missouri 63090

INNKEEPERS: Bill and Cathy Nagel

ADDRESS/TELEPHONE: 438 West Front Street; (636) 239–5025

ROOMS: 10; 8 with private bath, all with air-conditioning.

RATES: Sunday through Thursday: $95 to $140, single or double; Friday and Saturday: $110 to $150; EPB. Off-season rates available.

OPEN: Year-round

FACILITIES AND ACTIVITIES: Guest parlors, formal gardens. Across the street from Missouri River. Nearby: historic riverfront district and preserved 1800s architecture; restaurants; antiques and specialty shops. In the heart of Missouri's Wine Country; a short drive to winery tours.

*I*nnkeepers Bill and Cathy Nagel have captured all the warmth and old world hospitality of this historic German-influenced Missouri river town in this charming inn. I found it exciting to look out my window and see the waters of the Big Muddy and listen to the distant bellow of boat traffic on the river.

This stately pre–Civil War Georgian-style home was buzzing with activity upon my arrival. A family with three tow-headed kids was in the parlor looking over the dinner menus from area restaurants that are provided for guests. They couldn't decide if they wanted to "dude up" for supper or grab a hamburger and picnic next to the river.

Another young couple had bicycled to area wineries (this is the heart of Missouri Wine Country) and were showing off some of the bottles they'd purchased. They promised me samples later that evening. That's just typical of the inn's friendly atmosphere.

Most of the guest rooms are furnished with fine antiques and fun country accents. Some have river views; all have cute names. My favorites:

The Country Room, with its local handcrafts, high-back rocking chair, marble-topped lamp stand, tall armoire, and calico curtains on the window. I especially liked the hand-stitched star quilt on the bed.

The Eyelet Room, generously decorated with shockingly white lace. White eyelet curtains brighten three tall windows and sprinkle sunlight in all directions. A padded rocking chair is absolutely required for gazing out at the river. There's also a marble-topped dresser, a writing desk, and a colorful hand-stitched quilt on the bed.

Breakfasts are a treat. There are plates of imported and domestic cheeses, sausages, and croissants. But save some room for homemade bread, muffins, thick fruity jams, and some fresh fruit to satisfy a morning sweet tooth.

Especially interesting are the historic town's many antiques shops and fine restaurants. The Basket Case Delicatessen (a big-city deli in a tiny town) serves terrific sandwiches. At the East End Tavern, you can grab a tasty burger while listening to colorful talk about "Mizzou's" college football teams. The Landing is an informal dinner spot for families, with pizza and great burgers that are favorites. Then there's Lehmann's and Creamery Hill for fine dining.

HOW TO GET THERE: From St. Louis, take I–44 southwest to Route 100 and go west until you reach Washington. Turn north on Jefferson, then west on Front Street (along the river). The inn is at the corner of Front and Olive.

Select List of Other Inns in Missouri

Bellevue B&B
312 Bellevue Street
Cape Girardeau, MO 63701
(573) 335-3302
(800) 768-6822

The Inn on Crescent Lake
1261 Street Louis Avenue
Excelsior Springs, MO 64024
(816) 630-6745

Angels in the Attic Bed and Breakfast
108 East Second Street
Hermann, MO 65041
(573) 486-5930

Pelze Nichol Haus
179 State Highway 100 East
Hermann, MO 65041
(573) 486-3886

The Doanleigh Inn
217 East 37th Street
Kansas City, MO 64111
(816) 753-2667

The Raphael
325 Ward Parkway
Kansas City, MO 64112
(816) 756-3800
(800) 821-5343

The Dickey House B&B
331 South Clay Street
Marshfield, MO 65706
(417) 468-3000

The Mansion at Elfindale
1701 South Fort
Springfield, MO 65807
(417) 831-5400

Shakespeare Chateau B&B
809 Hall Steet
Saint Joseph, MO 64501
(816) 232-2667

Frisco Street B&B
305 Frisco Street,
P.O. Box 1219
Steelville, MO 65565
(573) 775-4247

Nebraska

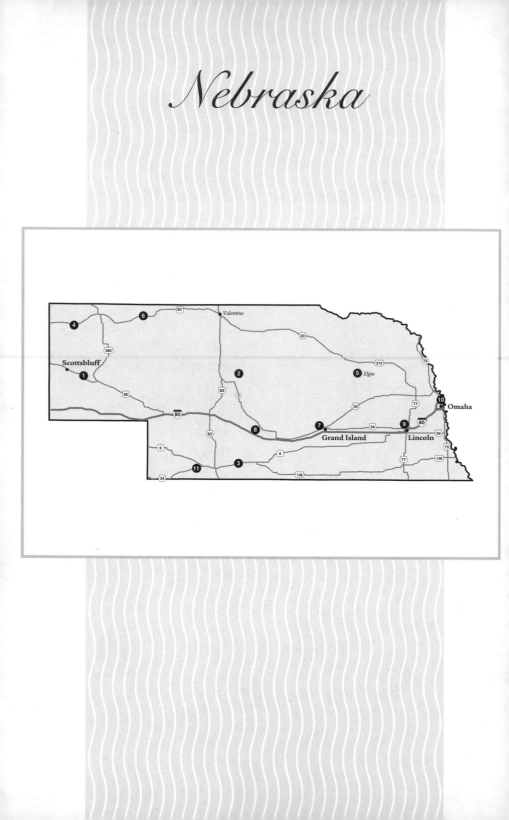

Nebraska

Numbers on map refer to towns numbered below.

*A Top Pick Inn

Oregon Trail Wagon Train
Bayard, Nebraska 69334

INNKEEPERS: Kevin and Connie Howard

ADDRESS/TELEPHONE: Route 2, Box 502; (308) 586–1850

ROOMS: 13 covered wagons; plus 3 log cabins, 2 with bath and shower, 1 primitive.

RATES: 24-hour wagon-train treks: $175 per adult, $150 each child under 12. Log cabins: $50 per night; discounts on 2 or more nights. Wagon trains, EPB; cabins, EP.

OPEN: April to November.

FACILITIES AND ACTIVITIES: Ranch, picnic, and shelter areas. Chuck wagon cookouts, Old West tours, Sunday campfire breakfasts, canoe rentals. Nearby: Jail Rock and "Courthouse," Chimney Rock, Ash Hollow, Scotts Bluff National Monument.

*I*t's the quintessential Nebraska experience—riding a covered wagon through Little Monument Valley over the Oregon Trail. That's right, the same Oregon Trail that brought more than 350,000 pioneers to the West between 1841 and 1869 on wagon trains that rallied at jumping-off points along the Missouri River. So before we talk about Kevin and Connie Howard's efforts to re-create that westward trek in some small, exciting way, let's brush up on more history.

By the time immigrants reached Little Monument Valley (Scotts Bluff, or Chimney Rock, which is located about 35 miles east of here), they'd already been on the trail for nearly two months. These landmarks signaled that almost one-third of the trail leading to Oregon had been traversed. The immense sandstone-and-clay formations, about 14 million years old and nearly 5,000 feet high, were a startling change from the oceans of prairie grasses and monotonous flatlands that wagons had crossed for weeks. These High Plains remnants still startle visitors to the region. And it's through these very landforms, along the same pioneer trail, that Kevin and Connie's wagon trains move.

"We've had visitors from Russia, Israel, Australia, Japan, people from just about everywhere, on the wagon train," the "wagonmasters" said. "They all crave a little bit of the Old West, and that's what we give them."

Their covered wagons rumble over the Oregon Trail, past Scotts Bluff, Chimney Rock, and through the High Plains prairie. One- to six-day treks recreate the life of an 1850s' outfit. That means learning how to camp pioneer style, grease wagon wheels, pack trail bags and wagons, even fashion sunbonnets. Meals are taken at the wagon-train mess, and campfire history stories are shared after dinner—before you hit the hay by camping out under the stars.

HOW TO GET THERE: From Ogallala, take U.S. 26 west. About 2 miles past Bayard, turn right on Oregon Trail Road; continue about 1½ miles to the Wagon Train Camp.

Wagons, Ho!

If you'd rather take a morning tour of the trail and see where some of the old trail ruts cut into the prairie, sign up for the daily Old West trek, which leaves the ranch's base camp at 8:30 A.M. and returns before noon. Later you can go on a chuck wagon steak-dinner cookout and overnight in one of the ranch's three log cabins.

Let's face it. If you've ever wondered what it'd be like to pioneer across the Old West, this is your last best chance.

Sandhills Country Cabin
Brewster, Nebraska 68821

INNKEEPERS: Lee and Beverly DeGroff

ADDRESS/TELEPHONE: HC 63, P.O. Box 13; (308) 547–2460

ROOMS: 1 rustic cabin and 1 large cabin; each with private bath.

RATES: Rustic cabin: $65, single; $75, double; $12, each child under 12; large cabin: $200 per night; EPB. Horse and pet day charges available.

OPEN: Year-round

FACILITIES AND ACTIVITIES: Views of rivers, cattle ranch; horse barn available for your own animals. Fishing, canoeing, ranch trails, wildlife tours, cattle drives, branding, calving. Nearby: Halsey National Forest, Fort Hartsuff, Nebraska's Big Rodeo (Burwell), Calamus Dam and Fish Hatchery, National Country Music Festival (August in Ainsworth), Willow Lake, Sandhills scenic drives.

*A*sk real estate agents about the value of a piece of property and they'll tell you that only three things really count: "Location, location, location." If that's true, then Sandhills Country Cabin might be worth a million dollars. Just for its views. It's located in the heart of Nebraska's Sandhills region, the world's largest vegetated sand dunes. Oceans of empty, hilly, sandy-soiled grasslands stretch from horizon to horizon, often with not so much as an outbuilding or barn desecrating the scenery. Just wandering cattle dot the landscape.

Good Ol' Boys

When my brother, Mark, and I visited here, all was deserted, as the ranchers/innkeepers were out on the prairie doing chores. (Even their cabin brochure cautions that the "best time to call for reservations is between 6:00 A.M. and 8:00 A.M.") But that didn't stop us from enjoying the solitude of the open prairie, looking over cows, walking down to the river, and just plain having a good old country-boy time.

But this north-central Nebraska cabin has even more going for it than that. It's surrounded by four beautiful rivers—the Dismal, Middle Loup, North Loup, and Calamus—and plunked down in the middle of a huge cow ranch.

In fact, the cabin nestles on the banks of the North Loup River, where you're more likely to see wandering deer, coyotes, and migrating sandhill cranes than you are to see other people. It is rustic, with antique barnboard siding adding to its country decor. There's comfy furniture, a full kitchenette, and plenty of peace and quiet—except for the lowing of the cows.

Beverly DeGroff serves a full ranch breakfast to cabin guests. Then you can choose to wander around the ranch yourself, take a tour with the owners, or even help out with ranch duties during roundup and branding times.

The newest addition to this western outpost is another cabin, done in weathered barnboard to give it that Wild West feel. The three-bedroom, two-bath cabin also boasts a living and dining room. Yee-hah! Bring the entire family!

HOW TO GET THERE: From North Platte, take U.S. 83 north to Nebraska 2 (at Thedford); then go east about 27 miles to Dunning. Continue east on Nebraska 91 to Brewster, then turn north on Nebraska 7, at the northeast edge of town. Turn left on the first oiled country road, and proceed ½ mile to the cabin.

The Cambridge Inn
Cambridge, Nebraska 69022

INNKEEPERS: Mike and Elaine Calabro

ADDRESS/TELEPHONE: 606 Parker, P.O. Box 239; (308) 697–3220

ROOMS: 4; all with private bath. No smoking inn.

RATES: $60 to $75, single; $75 to $90, double; EPB.

FACILITIES AND ACTIVITIES: Lunch and dinner available by arrangement. Parlor, library, dining room, front porch. Nearby: golf, museums, antiques stores, Medicine Creek State Recreation Area, hunting, fishing, boating, biking.

" "We always said it'd take a lot to get us out of Colorado," noted Elaine Calabro. "But once we stepped inside this house, we knew it had to be ours."

"It" is The Cambridge Inn, a historic 1907 Neoclassical Revival house that's been a landmark in Cambridge for as long as anyone can remember. Built by W. H. and Anna Faling (he helped incorporate the town), the magnificient house retains the elegant features of an era long past.

These include luxurious cherry, oak, and pine woodwork; stained and beveled glass; and hand-grained walls and ceilings created by Danish craftsmen.

Actually, it was Mike Calabro, Elaine's husband and fellow innkeeper, who first spotted the house, then for sale, on a return trip from visiting his son's college in Galesburg, Illinois. He drove around the block a few times, then told Elaine about it on his return home to Colorado. They made the five-hour drive from Loveland on a pleasant day in October, walked inside the house . . . "And that was it," Elaine said.

The Calabros have fashioned an elegant inn full of Victorian charm. An entrance hall showcases a magnificent oak staircase leading to second-floor guest rooms; above the landing is an incredible stained-glass window original to the house. The parlor features twin oak columns at least 10 feet high. Memorable breakfasts in the dining room, itself a showplace, with its 10-foot-tall built-in fruitwood and leaded-glass sideboard, might include French toast stuffed with cream cheese and walnuts.

Among the guest rooms, Ivy Court is my favorite. Originally the home's master bedroom, it retains a high Victorian ambience. Its antique furnishings include a writing desk. There's a sitting room and a bay window gussied up with lace curtains. Its private bath also claims the home's original "water closet"— a claw-foot tub, pedestal sink, and unusual foot bath.

Choose Morningside, and you'll get a quilt-covered bed and antique oak armoire (see if you can find the signatures of those Danish workmen who crafted all the house's wood-grain appearances out of common oak). Or opt for the more simple Goldenrod, once the maid's room but now a bright, cozy retreat decorated with patterns of wildflowers.

Be sure to get out and explore the region during your stay here. The inn is located in the heart of the Republican River Valley (in fact, most of the river's bends take a hard right . . . just kidding!) of the Prairie Lakes region in Southwest Nebraska—a spot noted for great fishing, boating, and biking across its gently rolling hills.

HOW TO GET THERE: Take U.S. 6/34 into Cambridge (whose name changes to Nasby Street in town). Follow the road to the intersection of Nasby and Parker; the inn sits on the corner.

Fort Robinson State Park
Crawford, Nebraska 69339

INNKEEPER: Jim Lemmon, park superintendent

ADDRESS/TELEPHONE: 3200 Highway 20, P.O. Box 392; (308) 665–2900, fax (308) 665–2901

ROOMS: 22 lodge rooms, 24 cabins and adobes, 7 multiple-bedroom units, and 1 ranch house; all with private bath. Wheelchair accessible.

RATES: lodge rooms: $26 to $51, single or double; cabin/adobes: $52 to $83; multiple-bedroom units: $125 to $151; ranch house: $130; EP.

OPEN: Park open all year; lodging open April through late November; activities open Memorial Day through Labor Day.

FACILITIES AND ACTIVITIES: On the grounds of historic Fort Robinson. Full-service restaurant, museum, restored-buildings tour, activities center, sutler's store, swimming pool, horseback riding, Jeep rides, train tour, buffalo tours, stagecoach rides, biking, hay wagon rides, chuck wagon cookout, campfire programs, rodeo, Post Playhouse (live theater), picnic shelter, campgrounds. Nearby: golf at Legends Butte, hiking at Soldier Creek Wilderness Area.

*A*ny enthusiast of the Wild West has to love a stay at historic Fort Robinson. Established in 1874 near the site of the Red Cloud Indian Agency, which handed out supplies to 13,000 hostile Sioux as mandated by a "peace treaty," Fort Robinson was one of the most troubled spots on the Plains and "witness to the last tragic days of the Plains Indian wars."

It was the scene of the Battle of Warbonnet Creek in 1876, when Indians from Red Cloud attempted to flee and join legendary Sioux warrior Crazy Horse after the Battle of Little Big Horn; the place where Crazy Horse was killed "while trying to escape imprisonment"—actually, he was bayoneted in the back by a fort soldier. It also saw the epic 1879 Cheyenne Outbreak, led by Dull Knife, when Cheyenne warriors escaped from barracks at the fort, only to be killed or captured two weeks later.

Wander around the grounds to see original buildings, which tell the story of the fort's storied past. Visit the Post Headquarters, now a museum filled with artifacts from Indian Wars days; tour Adobe Officers' Quarters, some of the fort's oldest buildings, dating to 1874; stop by the Blacksmith Shop, where a muscled smithy will tell you how busy he was in the days of the U.S. Cavalry.

Guest rooms are snapshots of history. You can overnight in one of those original adobe officers' quarters; take a modest room at the Lodge, originally the Enlisted Men's Barracks; or rule the Peterson Ranch, a home on a designated wildlife preserve 3 miles west of the lodge that includes use of the barn and corral.

Kids love a ride in an original stagecoach, just like the ones that crossed the Plains. Jeep rides tour surrounding landscapes of buttes and grasslands and include a visit to the grounds of the infamous Red Cloud Agency, and buffalo treks offer up-close peeks at the American bison.

And tell me how anyone could resist a delicious buffalo-stew campfire cookout, with a sing-along under the stars.

HOW TO GET THERE: From Chadron, take U.S. 20 west; 2 miles past Crawford, you'll come to park headquarters; turn toward the parade grounds and you're there.

Plantation House Bed and Breakfast
Elgin, Nebraska 68636

INNKEEPERS: Merland and Barbara Clark

ADDRESS/TELEPHONE: RR2, P.O. Box 17 (401 Plantation);
(402) 843-2287

ROOMS: 5, 1 cottage; all with private bath.

RATES: $50 to $75, single or double; weekday, off-season, and length of
stay discounts. EPB.

OPEN: Year-round

FACILITIES AND ACTIVITIES: Family room, billiards room, garden
room with TV/VCR. Nearby attractions include: Neligh Mills historic
flour mill and museum; Ashfall Fossil Beds; Grove Lake (fishing); Fort
Hartsuff, restored Army fort with working exhibits; Flobert Springs.
Restaurants and antique shops. Golfing within 15-mile drive.

This century-old Greek Revival Mansion received its "plantation"
moniker because of its resemblance to an Old South estate. It
boasts twenty rooms filled with antique furnishings, and its family-style breakfasts are famous around these parts—consider freshly baked
breads and muffins, French toast with home-cured bacon, egg-and-cheese
puff pastries stuffed with sausage . . . and that's just some of the meal.

The five guest rooms are charming. You get fluffy robes for your down-
the-hall bathroom walk when overnighting in Mrs. Butler's Room. No, the
ol' gal doesn't come with the quarters, but her original mahogany furniture
does. Another favorite is the Stained Glass Room, which features . . . you
guessed it, a wall of stained-glass windows.

Then there's the Guest Cottage, perfect for a private getaway with or
without kids; of course, if you do bring the tykes along, they can frolic in the
inn's spacious backyard.

HOW TO GET THERE: From Norfolk, take U.S. 275 west/northwest to Neligh;
turn south on State Road 14 and go south to Elgin at State Road 70; go
about 2 ½ miles past 70 until coming to RR2, and turn to the inn.

TOP PICK
Inn

Meadow View Ranch
Bed & Breakfast Bunkhouse ¢¢
Gordon, Nebraska 69343

INNKEEPERS: Clyde and Billie Lefler

ADDRESS/TELEPHONE: HC 91, P.O. Box 29; (308) 282–0679 or
(308) 282–1359

ROOMS: 2-bedroom ranch bunkhouse; with private bath and kitchen.
No smoking inn.

RATES: $45, single; $75 double; $17 for each additional family member;
$8 for children under 12; free for kids under 6; EPB.

OPEN: June through Sep-
tember.

FACILITIES AND ACTIVI-
TIES: Horseback riding,
Sandhills scenic Jeep tour,
wagon rides, hiking, nature
photography, satellite TV,
VCR. Nearby: Old-Time
Cowboy Museum, Sandoz
Museum, rodeos, canoeing
on the Niobara River,

Chadron State Park, Fort Robinson, Fur Trade Museum, Bowring
Ranch, LaCreek National Wildlife Refuge, gateway to Black Hills of
South Dakota.

" ou'll have to excuse me," Billie Lefler said as she dusted herself off. "I just got in from a day of branding, and I can still
feel the sand in my boots." Billie and Clyde Lefler's cattle
ranch stretches across 5,000 acres of Nebraska's Sandhills region, noted for
sprawling prairie grasses and craggy, pine-dotted canyons. The original
ranch bunkhouse, where guests overnight, is smack dab in the middle of
these sandhills and lush meadows.

Along with 400 head of breeding cattle and "too many horses to count."

The amiable ranchers remind visitors that this is a working cattle ranch—
you can help out with the chores during your stay. Sign up for the ranch's

annual cattle drives and branding roundups. Or simply enjoy this scenic, quiet retreat deep in the country.

Billie explained that the ranch has been in the family since 1906, when their ancestors homesteaded here from Texas. The bunkhouse has two bedrooms, sitting room, full kitchen, full bath and shower, and more. In the Waddill Room, you'll find antique furniture that belonged to the ranch's first settlers.

Ranch breakfasts include a guest favorite, Billie's blueberry cakes, as well as fruit-filled French toast, pancakes, eggs, sausage, juices, and coffee. If you want a memorable ranch evening, try Meadow View's steak or hamburger cookouts. You'll feel like real cowboys and cowgirls out on the lonesome prairie.

HOW TO GET THERE: From Chadron, take U.S. 20 east past Gordon to Irwin Road, a dirt road just before mile marker 121 (if you pass this marker, you've gone too far). Follow Irwin 6 miles north, then go 2 miles west and continue to the ranch.

The Kirschke House ₵₵
Grand Island, Nebraska 68801

INNKEEPERS: Lois Hank and Kiffani Smith

ADDRESS/TELEPHONE: 1124 West Third Street; (308) 381-6851

ROOMS: 5; 1 with private bath, 3 with sink in room. No smoking inn.

RATES: $55 to $75; $145, suite; EPB.

OPEN: Year-round

FACILITIES AND ACTIVITIES: Can arrange for dinners. Sitting room,

Down Time

There's plenty to see in the area, including the Stuhr Museum of the Plains Pioneers, which even boasts Henry Fonda's birthplace home. But many guests are here to relax and would just as soon soak in the inn's wooden hot tub located in the lantern-lit brick wash-house, perfect for a late-night rendezvous with that special someone.

hot tub. Nearby: Fonner Park thoroughbred racing, sandhill-crane and whooping-crane migrations, Stuhr Museum of the Plains Pioneers, Piccadilly Dinner Theater, three public golf courses, L. E. Ray Beach and Park.

*L*ois Hank and Kiffani Smith have fashioned a country Victorian showplace in this historic 1902 two-story house, built by prominent contractor Otto Kirschke as his family home. (In case you're wondering why the house was made of brick—Kirschke owned the Grand Island Brick Works. In fact, his firm also constructed the ornate Hall County Court House and other prominent business blocks and private homes.)

The house's original features include a windowed cupola, turret tower, and beveled and stained glass. In the sitting room, guests can enjoy a tiled fireplace, Oriental rugs, and fine antiques. French doors lead to the dining room, where guests might take breakfasts of fresh fruit, egg-and-cheese casseroles with Canadian bacon, and homemade blueberry muffins. My favorite guest room is the Morning Glory Vine Room, with its 6-foot-high oak headboard, bed adorned with an antique star quilt, and Victorian dresser with 6-foot-long mirror. But the most romantic is the Roses Room, with its lace-canopied four-poster bed and seven vine-dappled windows that let the sunlight stream in.

HOW TO GET THERE: From I–80, take Grand Island's west exit 312 and continue north 9 miles on Nebraska 281; at the Nebraska 30 exit, turn east, over an overpass into the city of Grand Island. Follow Highway 30 east to a traffic light at Broadwell Street; continue 4 blocks past this light, then turn north on Washington Street and go 1 more block. The Kirschke House is located across the street, north of the Edith Abbott Memorial Library.

Memories Historic Bed and Breakfast
Lexington, Nebraska 68850

INNKEEPERS: Marv and Pat Goldsmith

ADDRESS/TELEPHONE: 900 North Washington; (308) 324–3290

ROOMS: 3; all with private bath. No smoking inn.

RATES: $50 to $55, single; $60, double; EPB.

OPEN: Year-round

FACILITIES AND ACTIVITIES: Sitting room, parlor, dining room, two porches, patio, fountain. Nearby: ten antiques shops, Dawson County Fairgrounds; "Annual Antiques Extravaganza" on Labor Day weekend.

*H*olidays are well represented at Memories, since each of the inn's five guest rooms is named for a seasonal celebration. The Thanksgiving Room is adorned with an antique 1840s hanging quilt on one wall, coverlets on the bed date to the 1800s, and primitive folk art is everywhere. Fourth of July will get every morning off to a star-spangled start. It has another antique quilt wall hanging, and there are a Victorian dresser and lots of folk art in red-white-and-blue motifs. The Christmas Room is the most heavily Victorian of all the guest rooms, with antiques and folk art crammed into every nook and cranny.

Breakfasts in the dining room, complete with its own set of French doors opening to the patio and original oak woodwork, are sumptuous affairs. Consider fresh juices; raspberries and cream; ham, bacon, and egg casseroles; and home-baked muffins.

HOW TO GET THERE: From I–80, get off at the Lexington exit and take U.S. 283 into town. Turn left (west) on Sixth Street, go 2 blocks to Washington, then turn north on Washington and proceed to the inn (located at Washington and Ninth Streets).

The Rogers House
Lincoln, Nebraska 68502

INNKEEPER:
Nora Houtsma

ADDRESS/TELEPHONE:
2145 B Street; (402)
476–6961

ROOMS: 12; all with private bath.

RATES: $68 to $135;
EPB.

OPEN: Year-round

FACILITIES AND ACTIVITIES: Library, sitting room with fireplace, sunrooms. Nearby: downtown Lincoln, University of Nebraska campus, Historic Haymarket District shops, New State Museum, State Capitol, University of Nebraska Museum, Antelope Park sunken gardens, Christlieb Western Art Collection, National Museum of Roller Skating. Short drive to seven Salt Valley State Recreation Areas, golf, swimming. Homestead National Monument about 50 miles south.

This 1914 Jacobean Revival house sits in the Historic Near South neighborhood of Lincoln, a quiet tree-lined respite off the beaten path from the city's University of Nebraska campus hubbub.

Built for its namesake banker, who hailed from Minden, The Rogers House, a local historic landmark, features leaded and beveled glass, French doors, polished hardwood floors, and antiques-filled guest rooms. If you overnight in the Hillsdale Room, you'll be staying in the mansion's original guest room; it has a four-poster bed and great views of the historic neighborhood. The Doctor's Retreat, originally the summer master bedroom, is adorned with a four-poster lace canopy bed and its own private sunroom.

Or perhaps you'd like to climb to third-floor tranquillity in the Jacobean Room, with its queen-sized antique bed, claw-foot bathtub, and window seat, where dancers used to sit awaiting appropriate suitors during mansion soirees in the house's ballroom (which originally took up the entire third floor).

Home-cooked breakfasts include such specialties as German baked eggs, just-made muffins, fruit dishes, and juices. Innkeeper Nora Houtsma also has four guest rooms in the historic 1909 West House next door; some of these feature whirlpool tubs.

HOW TO GET THERE: From I–80, take the downtown O Street exit and continue to Ninth Street; turn south (right), then proceed to A Street. Turn left and continue to Twenty-second Street; turn left again and go 1 block to B. The inn is on the corner of Twenty-second and B.

The Offutt House
Omaha, Nebraska 68131

INNKEEPER: Jeannie Swoboda

ADDRESS/TELEPHONE: 140 North Thirty-ninth Street; (402) 553–0951

ROOMS: 8, including 2 suites; 6 with private bath.

RATES: $75 to $115, single or double; EPB Sunday only; continental breakfast all other days.

OPEN: Year-round

FACILITIES AND ACTIVITIES: Sitting room, library, bar room, screened sunporch. Located in Historic Gold Coast neighborhood; a short drive to Old Market Area, Western Heritage Museum, Strategic Air Command Museum, Joslyn Art Museum, General Crook House, Omaha Playhouse, Fontenelle Forest, Pappillion Creek Dam Sites.

*J*eannie Swoboda was preparing the inn for a wedding reception upon our arrival. "It's beautiful weather for a bride," Jeannie said, referring to the bright sun and 84-degree temperature. It also was a great day to visit The Offutt House, a fourteen-room 1894 mansion built for its namesake legislator in elegant Château style.

Not a Drop

During the infamous Easter Sunday Tornado of 1913, when the Offutt House was one of only a handful of graceful homes that survived the terrible winds, a local source reported that "an open decanter of sherry was carried 35 feet from the dining room sideboard to the living room without spilling a drop."

Believe it or not!

Walk through a double set of double doors adorned with beveled glass to a greeting room with quarter-sawn oak woodwork. There are more fine woods in the rest of the house— rich mahogany graces the library (be sure to note the 10-foot-long fireplace mantel), and walnut fancies up the dining room.

Guest rooms offer several interesting features. The Fireside Room has its own fireplace, canopy iron-rail bed, and a deep claw-foot tub perfect for soaking away any worries. The Porch Suite has its own sleeping porch (of course!) surrounded by seven tall windows; it's a great place to cool off during hot Omaha summer nights. The third-floor Honeymoon Suite is a remote getaway in this big house, ensuring privacy for newlyweds.

Jeannie's Sunday breakfasts might include sausage and egg strata, homemade sweet rolls, and juices and other beverages. Maybe that's when you can get the innkeeper to fill you in on the house's most enduring legend (see sidebar).

HOW TO GET THERE: From downtown Omaha, take Dodge Street west to Thirty-ninth Street, turn north, and proceed to the end of the block and the inn.

The Blue Colonial ¢¢
Trenton, Nebraska 69044

INNKEEPERS: Peter and Marita Todd

ADDRESS/TELEPHONE: HC2, P.O. Box 120; (308) 276–2553

ROOMS: 3, with 1 two-bedroom suite; share 2 baths. No smoking inn.

RATES: $60 to 85; EPB. Packages available.

OPEN: Year-round

FACILITIES AND ACTIVITIES: Dinner and chuck wagon dinners available. Round-Up Room for television viewing, library, antiques store. Antiques and art collecting classes available. Hay rides. Hiking and picnicking can be arranged. Nearby: a short drive to Swanson Lake for swimming, fishing, boating. Golf course 6 miles away. Turkey, deer, pheasant, quail, geese, and duck hunting among the finest in state.

*M*y brother, Mark, and I arrived at the Blue Colonial just past 8:00 P.M. Peter Todd answered the door dressed in a Scottish clan kilt and its accoutrements.

We were slightly nonplussed, to say the least. After all, we were in the middle of Nebraska, miles from anywhere, and didn't expect to run into a traditionally garbed Highlander out on a llama ranch.

But proud Scotsman Peter explained that he and his wife, Marita, were serving a formal dinner to guests, and though quite unexpected, we were more than welcome to explore the inn as we wished.

Marita soon joined us and conducted a whirlwind tour of this cozy inn. Rather than a ranch house, this bed-and-breakfast feels more like an elegant little country house. Marita showed off the lovely Gathering Room, which is beautifully decorated with many of Peter's British antiques, including Scottish clan swords and coats of arms, and a magnificent 1820s English desk.

As you've probably already guessed, Peter, a retired clergyman, was born in Scotland.

Despite Highlander influences, other gathering rooms and guest rooms have a more Western ambience to them. The Round-Up Room (see what I mean?) offers a television and is crammed with Western art and curios. The library is another pleasant retreat, with its handsome brass chandelier and huge collection of books, seemingly covering every subject.

Of the guest rooms, Prairie Wolf might be the most impressive. That's because of its folk-art wolf headboard, which is just about life-sized. The Bison Room is another charmer, with its buffalo art, bronzes, and a buffalo-gun wall decoration. Even the shared bathroom is country cool, with its barnboard paneling, claw-foot tub, and mirror fashioned from a horse collar.

Breakfast can be enjoyed in your room, in the formal dining room, or (my favorite) in the small country dining room decorated with early-nineteenth-century Scandinavian furniture.

Later on take a hike with the mama llama, who'll pack a mean picnic lunch while you hike over the grasslands. Just watch out; those llamas can spit better than most big-league ballplayers.

HOW TO GET THERE: From Culbertson, take U.S. 34 west 6 miles past Trenton, then turn right on a ranch road (there's a small BLUE COLONIAL sign, but you've got to look hard for it); continue about 2 miles to the inn.

Select List of Other Inns in Nebraska

Sunset Motel
1210 East NE 2
Alliance, NE 69301
(308) 762-8660

Behrens Inn
605 East Third Street
Beemer, NE 68716
(402) 528-3212

Arrow Hotel
509 South Ninth Avenue
Broken Bow, NE 68822
(308) 872-6662

Best Western Inn
1100 West Tenth Street
Chadron, NE 69337
(308) 432-5990

Cottonwood Inn Bed and Breakfast
P.O. Box 446
Chappell, NE 69129
(308) 874-3250

New World Inn
265 Thirty-third Avenue
Columbus, NE 68601
(402) 564-1492

Johnston-Muff House
1422 Boswell
Crete, NE 68333
(402) 826-4155

Parker House B&B
515 Fourth Street
Fairbury, NE 68352
(402) 729-5516

Monument Heights B&B
2665 Grandview Road
Gering, NE 69341
(308) 635-0109

Grandma's Victorian Inn
1826 West Third Street
Hastings, NE 68901
(402) 462-2013

Midlands Lodge
910 West J Street
Hastings, NE 68901
(402) 463-2428

Crow's Nest Inn
503 Grant
Holdrege, NE 68949
(308) 995-5440

The Atwood House B&B
740 South 17th Street
Lincoln, NE 68508
(402) 438-4567
(800) 884-6554

Cornhusker Hotel
333 South Thirteenth Street
Lincoln, NE 68508
(402) 474-7474

Home Comfort

1523 North Brown Street
Minden, NE 68959
(308) 832-0533

Lied Conference Center

2700 South Sylvan
Nebraska City, NE 68410
(402) 873-8733

The Shepherd's Inn

Route 3, P.O. Box 106A
Ord, NE 68837
(308) 728-3306
(800) 901-8649

Candlelight Inn

1822 East Twentieth Place
Scottsbluff, NE 69361
(308) 635-3751

J. C. Robinson House

102 Lincoln Avenue
Waterloo, NE 68051
(402) 779-2704

Ohio

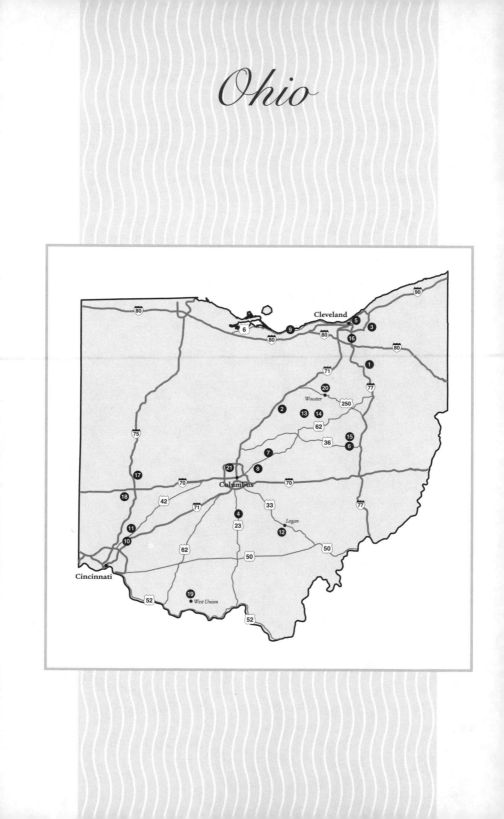

Ohio

Numbers on map refer to towns numbered below.

A Top Pick Inn

The Country Inn at Walden 💟
Aurora, Ohio 44202

INNKEEPERS: Manny Barenholtz, Robert Rosencrans, owners

ADDRESS/TELEPHONE: 1119 Aurora Hudson Road; (330) 562–5508 or (888) 808–5003

ROOMS: 25 suites; all with private bath, whirlpool. No smoking inn. Wheelchair accessible.

RATES: $150 to $295.

OPEN: Year-round

FACILITIES AND ACTIVITIES: Library, conference rooms, gathering rooms, restaurants; 31-stall, state-of-the-art horse barn; 78-seat theater; art gallery; pool and spa; situated on 1,000 acres.

*H*enry David Thoreau said that most people lead quiet lives of desperation. Obviously he never stayed at The Country Inn at Walden.

In fact, the Walden name alone is one thing this incredible inn shares with the aforementioned Thoreau, along with the love of nature. That's why owners Manny and Robert have fashioned a beautiful inn that almost brings nature inside this neoclassical getaway.

High tech meets rustic beauty in this impressive inn. The 1,000-acre tract is home to bucolic scenes that prominently feature horses—sleek purebred Arabians, Tennessee walkers and others—that stay at the inn's state-of-the-art, thirty-one stall stable. The stable is attached to the inn, so that owners never need go outside to see their steeds.

Guest suites feature everything from skylights, whirlpools, and separate showers to PC compatible writing desks with necessary ports, soothing tones of blue and green, and more. That "more" includes touch-screen telephones that control digital music and television, automatically turn on and off room lighting, check area attractions for ticket availability. Oh yes, these little wonders greet each guest by name and speak six languages.

Gourmet-style meals can be taken at the inn's Blue Ribbon Cafe. Its sophisticated offerings can include the likes of grilled Atlantic salmon with tangerine and olive oil and oven-dried Roman tomatoes, as well as an asparagus-and-poached pear salad. In fact, the restaurant has been rated one of the best in Northeast Ohio.

This is the epitome of quiet, elegant living.

HOW TO GET THERE: From the Cleveland metropolitan area, take I-77 south to the I-480 exit 156, toward Toledo/Youngstown; keep left in the fork at the ramp and merge onto I-480 east. Continue to the Ohio 14 east exit toward Youngstown, staying on I-480 east (and avoiding forks and ramps running into and out of it!). I-480 becomes Ohio 14. Then turn left onto Ohio 43 and go south; turn right (west) onto Mennonite Road and continue to South Bissell Road/Aurora Hudson Road. Turn left (south) and continue to the inn.

The Frederick Fitting House
Bellville, Ohio 44813

INNKEEPERS: Ramon and Suzanne Wilson

ADDRESS/TELEPHONE: 72 Fitting Avenue; (419) 886-2863

ROOMS: 3; all with private bath.

RATES: $60 to $70, single; $70 to $80, double; EPB.

OPEN: Year-round except Thanksgiving Day and Christmas Day.

FACILITIES AND ACTIVITIES: Picnic-basket lunch; candlelight dinner with wine, fresh flowers, music. Golf course, tennis courts nearby. Little shops and jogging trails in all directions. Canoeing and skiing (in season) within a few minutes' drive. Two state parks a short drive away. The Renaissance Theatre, the Mansfield Art Center, and the Kingwood Gardens within a half hour's drive. Mid-Ohio Raceway in Lexington is site of major sports-car races.

aby Kate originally discovered The Frederick Fitting House. It had been time for my then two-month-old daughter's midday feeding, so I drove down a quiet side street on this hot spring day looking for a parking spot bathed in shade. We stopped in front of a beautiful 1863 Italianate home and immediately were drawn inside.

It's completely furnished in American folk art and Ohio antiques; many are family heirlooms with interesting stories behind them, so be sure to get Ramon and Suzanne Wilson to weave their magic tales. Breakfasts are served on a big square table that invites conversation. (In summer, breakfast is outside in the gazebo.) Specialties include crepes, home-baked breads, and Dutch pastries, served along with Richland County honey, fresh fruit, and juice.

Walking up a magnificent freestanding spiral staircase of walnut, butternut, and oak, I found three charming guest rooms. The Colonial Room, with a canopy bed covered in lace, is perfect for romantics. Especially noteworthy among its many fine antique furnishings is a primitive pioneer coverlet. But my favorite is the Shaker Room, with its simple twin beds, antique writing desk, straight-back rocking chair, and wall pegs from which hang antique Shaker work utensils.

During the holiday season, the inn's two 10-foot Christmas trees are decorated with handcrafted ornaments, and luminarias glow along the outside walkway.

HOW TO GET THERE: Bellville is directly between Cleveland and Columbus. Leave I-71 at exit 165 and proceed east on State Route 97 into the village. Turn left onto Fitting Avenue. The inn is the last home on the left at the intersection of Fitting Avenue and Ogle Street.

The Inn at Chagrin Falls
Chagrin Falls, Ohio 44022

INNKEEPER: Mary Beth O'Donnell

ADDRESS/TELEPHONE: 87 West Street; (440) 247-1200, fax (440) 247-2122

ROOMS: 15, with 4 suites; all with private bath, several with fireplace and whirlpool. No smoking in rooms.

RATES: $135 to $225, double; subtract $15 for single; continental breakfast.

OPEN: Year-round

FACILITIES AND
ACTIVITIES: Gathering Room with fireplace; Gamekeeper's Taverne for fine dining. Nearby: walk to falls, browse quaint village shops, hike in Western Reserve surroundings. Eastern suburb of Cleveland only a short ride to Rock 'n' Roll Hall of Fame; Jacob's Field, home of Cleveland Indians; Severance Center, home to Cleveland Orchestra; The Flats, Cleveland's riverfront nightlife; and Sea World.

*D*riving to Chagrin Falls, I thought I'd entered a cinema time warp and arrived at Bedford Falls, home to Jimmy Stewart in the movie *It's a Wonderful Life.* See if you don't get the same feeling when you first arrive.

The inn is an elegant retreat fashioned from the historic Crane's Canary Cottage. Built in 1927, it still sports canary-colored clapboards. But inside, it boasts English-style antiques and early American reproductions from Colonial Williamsburg, Baker, Drexel, and other fine furniture houses.

Among the bedchambers, my favorite may be the Crane Suite, with its king-sized bed, Jacuzzi, and fireplace (original to the home) that has a massive hearth standing at least 6 by 4 feet. Daughters Kate and Dayne like the Philomethian Suite, with its four-poster mahogany bed, plantation-shuttered windows, corner fireplace, and whirlpool.

Are You Game?

Do try dinner at Gamekeeper's Taverne, attached to the inn. Where else might you sample char-grilled blackwing ostrich fillet, black buck antelope, or sautéed elk tenderloin? Other delicious entrees include herb-crusted rib pork chops, cedar-planked salmon, and penne pasta with smoked venison sausage.

Why you're at it, note that no inn visit would be complete without partaking in a village tradition: Buy yourselves ice cream cones and relax by the falls!

HOW TO GET THERE: From Cleveland, take I–77 south to I–480 east, then follow U.S. 271 north. The first exit on 271 is Chagrin Boulevard; get off and go west 9 miles to reach Chagrin Falls. As you continue into town there will be a large hill *before* reaching the stoplight at the bottom of the hill, turn right on West Street to the Inn.

Penguin Crossing Bed and Breakfast
Circleville, Ohio 43113

INNKEEPERS: Ross and Tracy Irvin

ADDRESS/TELEPHONE: 3291 State Route 56 West; (740) 477–6222 or (800) PENGUIN

ROOMS: 5; all with private bath. No smoking inn.

RATES: $100 to $225. EPB. One rooms wheelchair accessible.

OPEN. Year-round

FACILITIES AND ACTIVITIES: Concierge service. Short drive to Deer Creek State Park, A. W. Marion State Park/Hargus Lake, The Hocking Hill (for hiking), Paint Creek Stables, Tecumseh! (an outdoor historical theater). About 90 minutes to Paramount's King's Island amusement park.

*J*ust waddle into this charming inn where the rooms are named for different types of penguins. The King Penguin room boasts a king-size poster bed and king-size Jacuzzi for two. The Emperor Penguin rooms is all Victorian, with a heart-shaped whirlpool for two.

However, the rule of the roost goes to the Adelie Penguin room, with its Jacuzzi for two, wood-burning fireplace, and inviting four-poster queen bed.

You should know that the house itself is a former stagecoach stop, built in 1820 and lovingly restored into a romantic retreat by innkeepers Ross and Tracy Irvin. And even though the inn is located just 25 minutes south of downtown Columbus, you'll feel like you're miles away.

Maybe at the South Pole, with all the innkeepers' penguin collection around.

HOW TO GET THERE: From Columbus, take U.S. 23 south to Circleville, and turn west on State Route 56. The inn is 4 miles ahead.

Glidden House
Cleveland, Ohio 44106

INNKEEPER: Sharon Chapman, general manager

ADDRESS/TELEPHONE: 1901 Ford Drive; (216) 231–8900, fax (216) 231–2130

ROOMS: 60, including 8 suites; all with private bath, TV, radio, and air-conditioning. Wheelchair accessible.

RATES: $179, single; $189, double; $199 to $229, suites; continental breakfast.

OPEN: Year-round

FACILITIES AND ACTIVITIES: Dining room, sitting room. Stroll to Wade Oval. A short drive to Case Western Reserve University, Cleveland Garden Center, Little Italy, Museum of Natural History, Severance Hall, Institutes for Music and Art.

"Pa, are you sure this isn't some fancy mansion instead of a B&B?" asked my daughter Kate. Well, it's both. It's a 1910 mansion, built in distinctive French Gothic style by Francis Kavanaugh Glidden, son of the founder of the Glidden Paint Company (it was occupied by Glidden family members until 1953). Now the landmark building serves as a historic (and classy) bed-and-breakfast inn, painstakingly restored to its original grandeur and old world ambience.

The lobby itself is elegant and posh, with distinctive Victorian flourishes. The manse's original parlor, which now serves as the dining room, boasts a great stone fireplace, a fire blazing in the hearth. Floral wall coverings give a high Victorian feel to the room. So do the dark wainscoting and ceiling beams—all handsome hand-carved oak.

Our room was in the wing that was added in 1988 but designed to complement the house's historical significance and architectural integrity. Dayne, Kate's sister, especially liked the country Victorian decor. "This antique pine is a lot like our house," she said. "It makes me feel sort of like I'm at home."

Sort of.

Glidden House suites are on the upper floors; a few even retain original ornately carved fireplaces.

The next morning we were back in the parlor for a sprawling breakfast buffet of fresh fruits, juices, cereals, fresh-baked breads, muffins, croissants, preserves, and sweet rolls.

Kate and Dayne decided that it'd be "okay" to come back here someday.

HOW TO GET THERE: From I–90, exit at Dr. Martin Luther King Drive and go south to East Boulevard; follow the circle to Ford Drive and the inn.

Inn at Roscoe Village

Coshocton, Ohio 43812

INNKEEPER: Steve Hansen, manager

ADDRESS/TELEPHONE: 200 North Whitewoman Street; (740) 622–2222 or (800) 237–7397

ROOMS: 50; all with private bath, air-conditioning, phone, and TV. Wheelchair accessible.

RATES: $89, single or double, Sunday through Thursday; $100, single or double, Friday and Saturday; continental breakfast. Several seasonal weekend packages.

OPEN: Year-round

FACILITIES AND ACTIVITIES: Full-service restaurant, tavern, sitting rooms. Nearby: Roscoe Village, 1830 canal town, includes canal boat rides, craft shops, five exhibit-museum buildings, four restaurants, horse-drawn trolley, Johnson-Humrickhouse Museum. Amish country nearby. Pro Football Hall of Fame in Canton. Scenic countryside of Ohio River Valley.

BUSINESS TRAVEL: Located about 75 miles from downtown Columbus. Corporate rates, meeting rooms, fax.

*T*he inn's choppy brick exterior design borrows heavily from other Greek Revival canal-era structures in the village of Coshocton. Inside, the second-floor parlor is a favorite with guests. It's easy to see why: It has exposed wood beams, a huge fireplace fronted by high-back sofas, a beautiful wrought-iron chandelier, and tall windows. Wonderful crafts are sprinkled throughout the inn (including hand-stitched quilts)—native Ohio folk art reflecting the village's heritage.

Rooms have sturdy, handcrafted wood furniture made by Amish craftsmen in nearby Holmes County. Four-poster beds, high-back chairs, and more tall windows add to the charm.

A full-service dining room, complete with china and silver, offers meals to guests in an atmosphere of Early American elegance. The inn's master chef prepares the most exciting culinary delights, which have been featured in many magazines. Selections might include veal, sea scallops, and roast duckling. Breakfasts offer terrific choices as well, including whole-wheat griddle cakes and hazelnut whole-wheat waffles, served along with farm-fresh eggs, honey, and sweet butter.

After I'd been there awhile, I walked along the historic Ohio & Erie towpath north from town to where the *Monticello III,* a reconstructed canal boat, floats passengers to Mudport Basin. Don't miss all the antiques and specialty stores

The Legend of Charlie

I became curious about the Roscoe Village Inn's King Charlie's Tavern. Turns out it's named after Charlie, the first white settler in these parts. Legend has it that an heir to the throne of England stopped in the village tavern on his way across the country and made quite a fuss about how towns were so much more interesting in Europe. Charlie made things a lot more interesting for him right then and there, hiking him up by the seat of his pants and throwing him out the door.

along Whitewoman Street, which gets its name from the Walhonding River—*walhonding* is the Delaware Indian word for "white woman."

Innkeeper Steve Hansen can custom-tailor your schedule for your complete relaxation and enjoyment and will set up one- to three-day itineraries to suit your level of fun.

HOW TO GET THERE: From Cleveland to the north, take I–77 south to exit 65. Follow Route 36/16 west into Coshocton. Turn west on Ohio 541, then north on Whitewoman Street to the inn. From Columbus and Indianapolis to the southwest, take I–70 and exit north on Route 60. Then turn east on Route 16 and follow into Coshocton. Follow the directions listed above.

The White Oak Inn
Danville, Ohio 43014

INNKEEPERS: Ian and Yvonne Martin

ADDRESS/TELEPHONE: 29683 Walhonding Road; (740) 599–6107

WEB SITE: www.whiteoakinn.com

ROOMS: 10; all with private bath and air-conditioning, 3 with fireplace. No smoking inn.

RATES: $85 to $140, weekends; EBP. $25 for additional person or bed in room. Two-night minimum on weekends in May and October, and all holiday weekends. Special weekday rates. Archaeology, wildlife, theater, and murder-mystery packages available.

OPEN: Year-round

FACILITIES AND ACTIVITIES: Dinner available; at extra cost, a four-course gourmet meal. BYOB. Expansive grounds, lawn games, screen house. Nearby: good antiques in area stores. Kokosing River offers some of best smallmouth bass fishing in Ohio; also canoe livery. Thirty minutes from Millersburg, center of Amish culture in the United States; 35 minutes from Malabar Farm State Park; 25 minutes from Roscoe Village in Coshocton, restored canal-era town with own canal boat and towpath, specialty shops, and craft stores.

*I*an and Yvonne Martin are from Ontario, Canada, and their inn is already renowned for dinner menus reflecting their Canadian-Scottish heritage. In fact, the White Oak has made newspaper headlines as "the country inn that fosters foreign tastes."

Yvonne, the inn's superb chef, is a native of Scotland. She blends the best of her native and Canadian gustatory specialties into deliciously pleasing, almost exotic, dining experiences. Consider a few of her Euro-styled country-gourmet delights: Mulligatawny soup, a curried chicken soup; French Canadian tourtière, a double-crusted meat pie laced with spices and served with sweet chutney or chunky tomato sauce; and for sweet tooths, Canadian Nanaimo Bars, a tortelike obsession of chocolate, custard, coconut, and walnuts.

Yvonne's also been chosen as one of only fifty country inn chefs in the United States to be on the DuPont Corporation's Country Inn Chefs Advisory Panel, an honor based on her superior cuisine and hospitality.

Ian is the inn's primary decorator/contractor/landscaper and all-around good guy. Seemingly always looking for ways to improve the inn, he's most recently succeeded in acquiring an antique pump-organ case refinished and

Be Indiana Jones for a Weekend

Another interesting White Oak attraction: Several Native American artifacts have been unearthed on inn property. Perhaps you'd like to be in on one of Ian's digs during "archaeology weekends." Led by a Kenyon College archaeology professor, you'll help with everything from digging up the ground to washing artifacts and labeling them.

fitted as a front desk. "It makes a statement," he said.

So do the inn's guest rooms. Those in the main building, complete with everything from antique headboards to hand-carved washstands, boast all kinds of hardwoods, including oak, maple, walnut, cherry, and poplar. In fact, I defy you to find a more beautiful shade of red maple than in the Maple Room.

Downstairs in common rooms, all the magnificent woodwork is white oak; the floor, red oak. It was fashioned from timber on this very land, cut just across the road, Ian said.

Additional rooms in the Guest House, just a short walk from the main building, offer spacious bedchambers closer to the woods; these include queen-sized beds and cozy fireplaces, perfect for romantics of the inn-wandering crowd. All guests can enjoy Ian's screened porch, a perfect way to take advantage of summer's cool breezes without becoming mosquito fodder.

And here's an honor for the inn. The PBS series *Country Inn Cooking with Gail Greco* featured the inn and highlighted Yvonne's recipe for French Canadian pork tourtière. Yummm!

HOW TO GET THERE: The inn is closer to Millwood than Danville. From Columbus, take U.S. 62 northeast to the junction of U.S. 36 and U.S. 62. Go east on U.S. 36 for 1 mile to Ohio 715, then 3 miles east to the inn.

The Buxton Inn 🪙
Granville, Ohio 43023

INNKEEPERS: Audrey and Orville Orr, owners; Cecil Snow, manager

ADDRESS/TELEPHONE: 313 East Broadway; (740) 587–0001

ROOMS: 25, including 3 suites; all with private bath, air-conditioning, phone, and TV. Wheelchair accessible.

RATES: $75 to $85, single; $85 to $95, double; continental breakfast or discount on full breakfast. Children under 5 free.

OPEN: Year-round except Christmas Day and New Year's Day.

FACILITIES AND ACTIVITIES: Full-service restaurant with nine dining rooms; full-service bar. Nearby: tennis, golf, biking, swimming, horseback riding, art galleries, antiques shops, specialty boutiques, museums, historic sites. Also near Ye Olde Mill of 1817 and Hopewell Indians' Newark earthworks.

Cecil Snow, manager of The Buxton Inn, and I sat in the charming basement dining room of the inn, built in 1812 as a tavern by a pioneer from Granville, Massachusetts. "Stagecoach drivers would stop at the tavern during their journey across the frontier and would sleep down here on beds of straw," he said. He pointed out original rough-hewn beams and stone walls that are still sturdy after all these years, as is the great open hearth where the drivers cooked their meals.

The Buxton is Ohio's oldest continuously operating inn. Look closely and you'll see that the pegged walnut floors were laid with hand-forged nails. "Those windows were laid into foot-thick walls for protection from Indians," Cecil said. Black walnut beams and timbers frame walls and ceilings; fireplaces are scattered throughout the house.

The main inn building has four guest rooms. The Eastlake and Victorian Rooms are two-room suites. One features nineteenth-century Eastlake antiques; the other has elegant Victorian beds, an exquisite settee, and an antique crystal chandelier. The Empire Room is my favorite because of its large

Dining Delights

Delicious dining fare at the Buxton includes wholesome breakfasts with farm-fresh eggs, sausage, and flapjacks. Lunch specialties lean toward Colonial-style fare—old-fashioned beef potpie topped with a flaky crust and Osie Robinson's Chicken Supreme, a puff pastry filled with chicken in mushroom and pimiento sauce.

Loosen up your belt before you get to the dinner table. Inn favorites include French pepper steak with brandy, Louisiana chicken with artichoke hearts, and calf sweetbreads with Burgundy-mushroom sauce.

Cecil even makes dessert a difficult decision. Shall I choose Daisy Hunter's hot walnut-fudge cake a la mode, gingerbread with hot lemon sauce, homemade pecan pie topped with whipped cream, or "olde tyme" vanilla-velvet ice cream?

sleigh beds and fine silver chandelier.

Did you know that President William Henry Harrison supposedly rode a horse up the inn stairs to the second-floor ballroom during some spirited nighttime revelry?

Down the block, on the corner, stands the 1815 Warner House, with eleven more rooms similarly decorated. And nearby is Ty-Fy (Welsh for "my mother"), with four more guest quarters and Founder's Hall, with six bedchambers.

Oh yes. Ask Cecil about the inn ghost who was once a light-opera star.

HOW TO GET THERE: From Columbus, take I–70 to Ohio 37. Then go north to Ohio 661 and proceed into Granville. From Cleveland, take I–71 to Route 13 through Mansfield. Go south on Route 13 until you reach Ohio 661 just outside Mansfield. Head south on Ohio 661 into Granville and the inn.

Captain Montague's
Huron, Ohio 44839

INNKEEPERS: Judy and Mike Tann

ADDRESS/TELEPHONE: 229 Center Street; (419) 433–4756 or (800) 276–4756

ROOMS: 7; all with private bath and air-conditioning. No smoking inn.

RATES: $95, single or double, weekdays; $125 to $150, weekends; EPB. Seasonal rates available. Two-night minimum on summer weekends.

OPEN: Year-round

FACILITIES AND ACTIVITIES: Outdoor in-ground swimming pool, gazebo/carriage house, manicured gardens. Nearby: short walk to Lake-front Park, beach on Lake Erie, Huron's famous mile-long pier. Browse historic architecture of Old Plat neighborhood. Cedar Point Amusement Park 7 miles away. Golf, tennis, wildlife estuaries, summer stock theater close by. Boat transportation to Lake Erie islands 8 miles away.

My 15-year-old daughter, Kate, an award-winning Irish dancer herself, noticed lots of Celtic "stuff" at the Captain's. "I married an Irishman," chuckled innkeeper Judy Tann. "And he's very proud of his roots."

Judy noted that there's usually Irish music playing throughout the inn. "If it was on now, I'd ask to see a little bit of your dancing, Kate."

That's all the encourage-
ment Kate needed. She took
her pose and pranced
through parts of a jig and
reel. "Mighty impressive,"
Judy said and gave Kate a big
hug.

The inn is mighty impres-
sive, too. Built around 1878
by the town's shipbuilder
and owner of the local lum-
beryard, the stately home
boasts exquisite woods. Con-
sider the mantels in the parlor and dining rooms, as well as the intricately
carved front staircase: They are all solid black walnut.

Yet the inn takes its name from the home's second owner—a Great Lakes sea
captain who hauled ore and coal over their treacherous waters.

Kate's 13-year-old sister, Dayne, visited the Captain's with us, too. She
loved the antique rockers and period reproductions, especially two rockers in
the parlor. After a long day's drive through Ohio, Dayne relished the chance
to stretch out on the comfy chair.

The girls adored the guest rooms. Me, too. I especially liked the room
named for the captain, a manly retreat with a four-poster bed, a sea chest at the
bed's foot, one of the home's original gas lamps, and pictures of sailing ships
everywhere.

Kate and Dayne were taken by Sarah, the room named for the captain's
wife. I think it was the brass bed with frilly Battenburg lace canopy that got
them. Or maybe it was the Victorian sitting couch. I liked the original coal
gate over the fireplace hearth.

I would have missed the angel figurines sitting atop the mantel, though,
if the girls hadn't pointed them out.

You can enjoy breakfast in a huge Victorian dining room served at a ten-
chair harvest table. Or opt for summer breakfast in the charming gazebo,
converted from the home's carriage house. Judy's morning treats include
cinnamon coffee, Irish Cottage scones (the inn's specialty), egg bakes, and
baked French toast.

As we were saying our good-byes, Judy pointed out the inn's original
"ruby" glass on the front doors. "These were the forerunners of one-way
glass," she explained. "Especially when it gets darker outside, you can see out
perfectly well, but it's almost impossible to see anything inside the house."

"Cool," said Kate and Dayne. And it was.

HOW TO GET THERE: From Sandusky, take U.S. 6 east to Huron, then continue straight ahead on Cleveland Street as U.S. 6 jogs right. Follow Cleveland Street to Center Street and the inn.

Kings Manor Inn 🏨
Kings Mills, Ohio 45034

INNKEEPERS: Dan and Sue Koterba, Adele Molinaro, Bob Molinaro

ADDRESS/TELEPHONE: 1826 Church Street; (513) 459-9959

ROOMS: 4, including 1 suite; all with private bath and air-conditioning.

RATES: $70 to $80, single; $80 to $90, double; EPB.

OPEN: Year-round

FACILITIES AND ACTIVITIES: Sitting and dining rooms, library sunroom, porch. Nearby: minutes from Paramount's Kings Island, one of Ohio's premier theme/amusement parks; The Beach waterpark; Jack Nicklaus's Golden Bear Sports Center (golf). A short drive to Lebanon and Waynesville antiques shops. Bike the Little Miami Scenic Bike Trail, starting in town. Cincinnati is about 30 minutes away.

*I*t wouldn't be an exaggeration to say that my daughters, Kate and Dayne, rated this handsome inn as one of their very favorites. That's because it felt more like the country house of a beloved aunt. Besides, the innkeepers' country-style hospitality had us feeling as if we were staying in our home away from home.

Kings Manor Inn, built in 1903 by Col. George King, is nestled in the quaint village of Kings Mills. It's a spacious manor-style house, graced with original hand-rubbed hardwood moldings, leaded-glass windows, and antique furnishings that include family heirlooms and pieces from the original King estate.

The girls had their favorite inn spots, especially the Sun Room, just across the hall from our bedchambers. Surrounded by tall windows, we plopped down into wicker chairs and sofas to share Kings Island stories. We lingered here for two straight days. Kate arranged for all of us to enjoy cool glasses of iced tea; her reward was another game of checkers, followed by a Monopoly marathon.

Guest rooms are delightful. Ours was the Audrenia Suite, with its hand-carved manteled fireplace and antique mahogany furnishings. Another favorite is the Scarlet Room, with its own whirlpool bath. Kings Manor breakfasts are fancy affairs, with fine china, a silver table service, and fabulous meals. We loved  the heaping helpings of egg and cheese casseroles, crisp slices of bacon, home-baked muffins, fresh fruit plates, juices, milk, and more.

It was really hard for the girls to leave, since they'd made friends with Emily (Sue Koterba's daughter) and Maria (Sue's sister-in-law's daughter). They all posed for pictures while sitting on the porch, frolicking on the lawn, making funny faces . . .

We really miss this place.

HOW TO GET THERE: From Cincinnati, take I–71 north to Exit 25 (Kings Mills Road); get off and proceed east on Kings Mills Road into the village. Turn south (right) on Walnut and go to Church Street. Then turn left and continue to the inn.

The Golden Lamb
Lebanon, Ohio 45036

INNKEEPER: Paul Resetar

ADDRESS/TELEPHONE: 27 South Broadway; (513) 932–5065

ROOMS: 18, with 1 suite; all with private bath.

RATES: $67 to $90, single; $80 to $103, double; $115 to $125, suite; EP.

OPEN: Year-round

FACILITIES AND ACTIVITIES: Full-service restaurant with wheelchair access, nine dining areas, and tavern. Upstairs museum with Shaker furniture collection. Large gift and crafts shop. Nearby: Lebanon

Antique Center featuring 150 dealers. A short drive to Warren County Museum, Kings Island amusement park, Jack Nicklaus golf center, town of Waynesville (more than forty antiques shops).

*E*arly 1800s stagecoach drivers and travelers (many of whom couldn't read) were simply told to drive to the sign of The Golden Lamb for a warm bed and a good meal. I saw the large wooden sign depicting a golden lamb still hanging in front of this charming and historic inn.

"It's a real friendly place," innkeeper Paul Resetar said, "the kind of place people like to come back to again and again."

I heartily agree with him. From its beginning in 1803, The Golden Lamb has offered warm hospitality to its guests. Samuel L. Clemens paced through its hallways while in rehearsal for a performance at the Lebanon Opera House. Charles Dickens eloquently complained about the "lack of spirits" at the then-temperate hotel, circa 1842. Benjamin Harrison, Ulysses S. Grant, and eight other presidents stayed here.

The inn is famous for its Midwestern cooking prepared by its European-trained chef and its antiques-laden guest rooms named for illustrious visitors. I walked up creaking stairs and along squeaking hallway floorboards to marvel at the antique furniture gracing the second- and third-floor rooms.

Anyone can do the same; the doors to all unoccupied rooms are kept open. "We want people just coming to dinner to enjoy the antiques collection of our inn, too," Paul said. "We encourage them to walk through the halls and look inside."

I couldn't resist bouncing up and down on the replica of the massive Lincoln bed in the Charles Dickens Room, resplendent in its Victorian finery. Another favorite was the huge four-poster Boyd bed in the DeWitt Clinton Room.

All the rooms are spacious. Besides a rocking chair, a tall secretary stuffed with books, and other antique furnishings, mine had two four-poster beds.

My family dined in the Shaker Room, with wall pegs holding all kinds of antique kitchen gadgets, pots, and pans. I thought that the roast Butler County turkey with dressing and giblet gravy was almost like Mom's—a special treat. My wife was delighted by another inn favorite, pan-fried Kentucky ham steak (specially cured and aged), glazed with bourbon. Our youngest, Kate was fed well, too—with all the cooing and attention she received from the friendly wait-resses.

The inn's display of authentic antique Shaker furniture is said to be one of the largest private collections of its kind. On the fourth floor are glass-enclosed display rooms featuring many fine pieces.

HOW TO GET THERE: Lebanon is midway between Cincinnati and Dayton. From I-75, take Ohio 63 east 6 miles to Lebanon. From I-71, take Ohio 123 west 3 miles to Lebanon. The inn is at the juncture of Ohio State Routes 63 and 123.

The Inn at Cedar Falls
Logan, Ohio 43138

INNKEEPER: Ellen Grinsfelder

ADDRESS/TELEPHONE: 21190 State Route 374; (740) 385-7489

WEB SITE: www.innatcedarfalls.com

ROOMS: 9, plus 6 cabins; all with private bath and air-conditioning, 1 with wheelchair access.

RATES: $65 to $75, single; $80 to $95, double; $140 to $150, Sunday through Thursday; $185 to $240, Friday and Saturday, for cabins; EPB.

OPEN: Year-round

FACILITIES AND ACTIVITIES: Dinner. Log-house common room, corner library, porch, log and patio dining areas. Gift shop. Special-activity weekends. Nearby: wildlife watching, hiking, cross-country skiing, photography. A short drive to canoeing and fishing on the Hocking River; geologic marvels including Cedar Falls, Ash Cave, Cantwell Cliffs, Conkle's Hollow, Rock House, Hocking Valley Scenic Railway, Lake Logan.

*S*outhern Ohio's Hocking Hills offer some of the most spectacular vistas in the Appalachian foothills. Sitting squarely in the center of this magnificent landscape is The Inn at Cedar Falls.

Surrounded on three sides by Hocking State Park, the inn is a nature retreat—a wonderland of eighty acres filled with wildlife and whispering trees. Mink, red fox, and white-tailed deer abound. Woodpeckers and wild turkeys thrive in the dense forest. Spring brings a splash of colorful wild-flower blossoms. Autumn hues are astounding.

One of the inn's log houses dates from 1840. Innkeeper Ellen Grinsfelder pointed out the 18-inch-wide logs and original plank floors. "When my mother first purchased this cabin, we discovered the original mud and horsehair chinking between the logs," she said, "so we had some work to do." The log houses have common rooms and porches filled with rockers, mountain-style folk furniture, game tables, and a special room stuffed with books.

Meals often are served on the patio, where gourmet-style food vies with the scenery for guests' attention. Visit during a "guest chef" weekend and you might be treated to everything from ratatouille in eggplant shells and grilled garlic shrimp to a chocolate torte with hazelnuts. And where else can you find a cabin in the woods featuring such delicacies as apple-smoked pork loin, bean soup, bread pudding with whiskey sauce, and homemade breads, muffins, and desserts?

Guest rooms, located in the recently added "barn" are country cozy, furnished with antiques, rag rugs on plank floors, and rocking chairs. Windows offer scenic views, and fragrant wildflower bouquets are placed in each room. It's no surprise that the governor of Ohio has stayed here.

Cabins are restored 1800s structures; one has a fireplace, and two have full decks. Each has a distinct personality—Colonial, Shaker, or antique.

Breakfasts might include a fruit compote and country ham with red pepper relish and chutney. After your meal you can browse among locally made crafts in the inn's small gift boutique.

HOW TO GET THERE: From Columbus, take U.S. 33 south through Lancaster to the Logan–Bremen exit, which is State Route 664; turn right, go about 9½ miles to State Route 374, then turn left and continue 1 mile to the inn, located on the right side of the road (parking on the left).

The Blackfork Inn
Loudonville, Ohio 44842

INNKEEPERS: Sue and Al Gorisek

ADDRESS/TELEPHONE: 303 North Water Street; (419) 994-3252

ROOMS: 8, with 2 suites in adjacent Landmark building; all with private bath and air-conditioning.

RATES: $65 to $80, single or double for rooms; $100 to $125 for suites; continental breakfast.

OPEN: Year-round

FACILITIES AND ACTIVITIES: In Ohio Amish country. Nearby: Mohican State Park, historic Malabar Farm. A short drive to restaurants and Snow Trails ski area.

*S*ue Gorisek will show you the handsome secretary that was brought to Ohio from Connecticut in a covered wagon by her great-great-grandfather. "He thought he'd be living in the wilderness with the Indians," Sue told me, "so he was determined to bring at least one piece of fine furniture along with him."

In fact, there are several beautiful antique pieces that can be traced to Sue's family back East, including a Pembroke table in the parlor that dates from 1760. The lovely Victorian walnut bedroom suite in the Josephine Room was made in Painesville, Ohio. It's a family heirloom. "My great-grandmother was born in that bed," Sue said. A photograph of her great-grandmother hangs on the wall.

The house itself dates to 1865, when it was built by Phillip Black, a Civil War merchant who brought the railroad to town. That family used the house until the mid-1940s.

The inn's downstairs common rooms almost resemble a museum, so stunning are the antique furnishings. Guest rooms are more informal and are named for members of the Black family. Several have big brass beds and Victorian-style trappings, except for the whimsical Margaret Room—with its

tropical feel contributed by an antique wardrobe displaying a Tahitian princess stencil.

There's another building at the Blackfork. It's called the Landmark, built in 1847 by the namesake feed people. Two suites are the attraction here, boasting fireplaces and large baths.

Sue offers a hearty breakfast with some unusual choices. There are blueberry pancakes, apple fritters, cinnamon rolls, home-grown raspberries with Swiss cream, and Amish products such as trail bologna and specially made cheeses. She can also arrange evening meals at the inn, prepared by one of the fine local chefs.

HOW TO GET THERE: From Columbus, take I–71 north and exit on U.S. 30 east. Then take Ohio 60 south into Loudonville (it turns into Main Street). Turn north on North Water Street and continue a few blocks to the inn.

The Inn at Honey Run
Millersburg, Ohio 44654

INNKEEPER: Marge Stock

ADDRESS/TELEPHONE: 6920 County Road 203; (330) 674–0011; toll-free in Ohio (800) 468–6639

WEB SITE: innathoneyrun.com

ROOMS: 39, with 1 suite and 2 guest houses; all with private bath and air-conditioning, most with TV.

RATES: $90 to $150, rooms; honeycomb rooms, $130 to $150; $225, cabins; single or double; continental breakfast. Two-night minimum Friday and Saturday. Special winter rates.

OPEN: Year-round

FACILITIES AND ACTIVITIES: Full-service dining room (closed Sunday) with wheelchair access. BYOB. Meeting rooms host movies and table tennis on weekends, library, game room, gift shop. Hiking trails, sheep and goats in pastures, nature lecture and walks most weekends, horse-shoes, croquet, volleyball. Nearby: Holmes County antiques and specialty stores, cheese factories, quilt shops, nine-hole golf course. A short drive to Roscoe Village canal-era town and Warther Wood Carving Museum.

"Just look at that," Marge Stock said, pointing to a black Amish carriage clip-clopping down a winding country road just below a room deck of The Inn at Honey Run. "That's why I love spring, fall, and winter here. You can still see sights like that through the trees. It takes you back to the 1800s."

To get here I had driven down a hilly, twisting road that I thought would never end. "We're hard to find," Marge admitted. Her graceful inn is situated on sixty hilly, wooded acres in the middle of Ohio Amish country. Its wood and stone construction blends magnificently with the gorgeous landscape.

"Birding here is great," Marge said, as she pointed to countless feeders surrounding the inn. "Visitors have recorded about thirty different species."

I was eager to see the rooms, and I wasn't disappointed. They're done in a potpourri of styles: Early American, contemporary with slanted ceilings and skylights, and Shaker—my favorite—with many pegs on the walls to hang everything from clothes to furniture.

Marge uses Holmes County folk art to highlight each room. Handmade quilts adorn walls and beds (which are extra long), and there are comfortable chairs with reading lamps.

"I love books," Marge said, "so I made certain each room has a reading light and a chair that rocks or swivels, where you can put your feet up on the window-dowsill and read, or just stare out at the birds."

More surprises: Twelve "Honeycomb Rooms" are the "world's first commercial earth-shelter rooms," built under and into Holmes County hills. "It's the perfect place for overstressed executives," Marge said of these almost cave-like retreats, which each feature a wood-burning fireplace, a whirlpool bath, and breakfast delivered to the door. There are also two wonderful cabins perched high on a hill, with panoramic views of Holmes County landscapes.

Food is made from scratch, with pan-fried trout from Holmes County waters a dinner specialty. Marge's full country breakfast features juice, eggs and bacon, French toast with real maple syrup, and homemade breads.

After breakfast you might want to take a hike on the grounds, perhaps followed by Luke, the inn's coon hound, or by Sandy, the beagle. Willy (a white cat) can be borrowed for room visits.

HOW TO GET THERE: From Millersburg it is 3³⁄₁₀ miles to the inn. Go east on East Jackson Street in Millersburg (Routes 39 and 62). Pass the courthouse and gas station on the right. At the next corner, turn left onto Route 241, which makes several turns as it twists out of town. Nearly 2 miles down the road, while proceeding down a long, steep hill, you'll cross a bridge over Honey Run. Turn right immediately around another small hill onto County Road 203, which is not well marked. After 1 mile, turn right at the small inn sign. Go up the hill to the inn.

Valley View Inn
New Bedford, Ohio 43824

INNKEEPERS: Dan and Nancy Lembke

ADDRESS/TELEPHONE: 32327 State Road 643; (330) 897–3232 or (800) 331–8439

ROOMS: 10; all with private bath and air-conditioning. No smoking inn.

RATES: $80 to $95, single or double; EPB Monday through Saturday; EP Sunday.

OPEN: Year-round

FACILITIES AND ACTIVITIES: Sitting room, dining room, game room, large porch overlooking valley. Nearby: Amish crafts shops, food stores and restaurants; cheese factories; antiques stores; hiking, biking; wildlife tours.

"Look, Pa," Kate shouted. "Horses!" A team of Percherons was hitched up to a plow tilling the fields under the steady hand of an Amish farmer, the broad brim of his straw hat billowing in the wind. Kate and her sister, Dayne, waved to the plowman, and he tipped his hat to them.

For the girls that was quite a start for our visit to the Valley View Inn. Nestled in the midst of Ohio Amish country (and one of the most tranquil areas of the state), the Valley View Inn is true to its name. It overlooks a far-reaching valley crisscrossed by tidy Amish farm fields, pastures, and woodlands. The vistas from its porch are among the Midwest's most beautiful.

Inside, there's more country-perfect peacefulness. Guest rooms have furniture handmade by local Amish craftsmen, and each bed is adorned with a hand-pieced quilt made by one of the inn's Amish neighbors. In fact, rooms are named for the pattern of quilt displayed on the bed.

We stayed in the Country Song Bird, a delightful retreat with two double beds and roomy quarters. After unpacking we headed out to the inn's corral, where innkeepers Dan and Nancy Lembke keep a number of their horses.

Kate and Dayne made sure that we revisited the porch to watch a terrific sunset; then we came back inside, sat down with a checkerboard, and played a few games. Dayne opted for looking at magazines found in the living room, curled up in front of the fireplace. Evening snacks included homemade cookies, juices, and milk. We couldn't go to sleep without a trip to the family room, where an old-fashioned player piano produced a toe-tapping melody.

Breakfast time is another eye-opener. Nobody can go away hungry, that's for sure—a full family-style breakfast is prepared by the inn's Amish cook. Goodies might include fresh fruit salad, ham puffs (a meat, cheese, and egg casserole dish), hash-brown casserole, homemade muffins, lemon bread, juices, and other beverages. (A continental breakfast is offered on Sunday.)

It's also fun to drive along the country roads in search of Amish specialties. Homemade pies in little shops hidden in the driveways of Amish farms are worth the search. And if you've got room in your vehicle for an authentic, hand-made Amish rocking chair, buy one. They can't be matched for comfort.

HOW TO GET THERE: From Cleveland, take I-77 south to the Dover exit, then turn west (right) onto Ohio 39; go about 9 miles to Ohio 93 at Sugarcreek and turn south (right). Continue 3 miles to Ohio 643/557. Stay on Ohio 643 to New Bedford; proceed south on Ohio 643 for about 3 miles to the inn, which is on the right.

The Inn at Brandywine Falls
Sagamore Hills, Ohio 44067

INNKEEPERS: George and Katie Hoy

ADDRESS/TELEPHONE: 8230 Brandywine Road; (330) 467–1812 or 650–4965

WEB SITE: www.innatbrandywinefalls.com

ROOMS: 6, with 3 suites; all with private bath. No smoking inn. Wheelchair accessible.

RATES: $130 to $190, or $262 to $240, two nights/two people. EPB.

OPEN: Year-round

FACILITIES AND ACTIVITIES: Located on 33,000 acres of parkland known as Cuyahoga Valley National Park. Porch swings, chairs overlooking gorge. Short hike to boardwalk to falls and down into gorge. Bike and hike trails yards away.

" *L*ook at the wonderful waterfall, Pa," said Dayne. "It's got to be 100 feet high."

My daughter was close—Brandywine Falls checks in at 67 feet. But the hike on the boardwalk to the falls, then down deep into the gorge itself, seems much greater.

Maybe that's because Dayne, Kate (my other daughter), and I were so taken by the grandeur of nature at Brandywine Falls, part of the massive Cuyahoga Valley National Park. We had been marveling at the natural beauty for miles before we came upon this handsome inn.

Easy Does It

A visit to Brandywine Falls offers you a chance to walk and to marvel at nature. Relax. Visit the falls. Doze in the sun. Ride a bike. Breathe in the aroma of wildflowers in the forest.

Just be.

The Inn at Brandywine Falls turned out to be among my girls' favorite on our swing through eastern Ohio. Not only does it boast a waterfall, hiking and biking trails, and expansive grounds perfect for running, jumping, and rolling about, but it also has horses and goats.

"A perfect combination," opined Kate.

The inn, a Greek Revival beauty built in 1848 by James Wallace, was the centerpiece of a once-thriving community with a sawmill and gristmill, thriving businesses along the falls.

Today all that is left of the village are some mill foundations and the inn. But the inn (and the falls) are more than enough.

Suites here are among my favorites on the Midwest country inn landscape. The Granary offers towering windows overlooking a hemlock grove, as well as rustic, wide-plank pine floors and handhewn wooden beams. Then there are the king-sized bed, wood-burning stove, two-person whirlpool, microwave, and fridge.

The Loft, which began as a small barn in the 1800s, has been transformed into another rustic wonder. It also features a wall of windows overlooking the hemlock grove, as well as a romantic loft area with bed and oversize whirlpool. Downstairs you can marvel at all the country geegaws decorating the suites. There's even a model train that circles the ceiling—something kids especially love.

In the main house, the James Wallace Parlor has an elegant double sleigh bed, Axminster carpeting, English armoire, hand-painted lamp shades, and an antique chair (oldest original piece of furniture in the house) that came from 1820s Maryland.

But I might opt for Adeline's Room, a charming and romantic second-floor room with double sleigh bed, claw-foot tub, and the only guest quarters with glimpses of the falls.

Guests take breakfast in the dining room, where a portrait of James Wallace gazes down over the festivities. Goodies include fruited oatmeal soup, fresh juices, homebaked breads, and hot beverages.

Did I mention that's a candlelight breakfast?

HOW TO GET THERE: From the Ohio Turnpike, take exit 12, then continue on Highway 8 for 1½ miles to Twinsburg Road. Turn west (left) and drive another 1½ miles to a dead end at Brandywine Road. Turn right and cross the bridge. The inn is on the left.

The H. W. Allen Villa
Troy, Ohio 45373

INNKEEPERS: Bob and
June Smith

ADDRESS/TELEPHONE:
434 South Market Street;
(937) 335–1181

ROOMS: 6, with 1 suite; all
with private bath, air-
conditioning, TV, and
phone.

RATES: $75, single; $80,
double; EPB. Cribs and baby beds available.

OPEN: Year-round

FACILITIES AND ACTIVITIES: Double parlor, dining room, and library.
Nearby: Hayner Cultural Center, Historical Courthouse, Overfield Tav-
ern, Museum of Troy History. A short drive to golf course, Dayton Art
Institute, U.S. Air Force Museum.

*B*ob and June Smith's villa brochure carries a translation of *bed-
and-breakfast* in Japanese. That surprised me, but June explained
that the nearby Panasonic plant regularly sends visiting Japanese
executives here. In fact, two Japanese businessmen were checking in during my
visit. In heavily accented English, they marveled at the "big, beautiful house."

It is very big and extremely beautiful. Built in 1874 by Henry Ware Allen,
part owner of the largest flour mill in the county, the three-story Victorian
mansion has fourteen rooms, 12-foot-high ceilings, seven fireplaces, and
white and black walnut woodwork throughout. The Smiths opened the inn
to travelers in 1986, filled with their bounty of twenty years of antiques collecting. The furnishings are remarkably distinctive; the home seems more
museum than wayfarer station.

Guest rooms are bathed in Victorian antiques, but I can't help marveling at the Allen Room, with its four-poster Gamblers brass bed and
extremely unusual gold-domed lamps that would seem at home in a
maharajah's palace. A breakfast of cinnamon French toast, vegetable
omelettes, or bacon, tomato, and egg dishes is served on a 15-foot-long
antique table.

HOW TO GET THERE: From Dayton, take I–75 north to the Troy exit (exit 73, which is Ohio 55), and proceed 1 mile east, then 2 blocks north on South Market Street to the inn.

Twin Creek Country Bed and Breakfast
West Alexandria, Ohio 45381

INNKEEPERS: Dr. Mark and Carolyn Ulrich

ADDRESS/TELEPHONE: 5353 Enterprise Road; (937) 787–3990 or (937) 787–4264.

ROOMS: 4, with 1 suite; all with private bath.

RATES: $69 to $179; EPB.

OPEN: Year-round

FACILITIES AND ACTIVITIES: Located on 170 acres of rolling hills and scenic woods. Walk to fine dining at Twin Creek Tea Room in Florentine Hotel and five minutes from Tomsmaze, a state-renown corn maze that you can walk through. Short drive to Hueston Woods State Park, Air Force Museum, Germantown Nature Center and Hiking Trails; a fifty-minute ride to Paramount's King's Island.

*N*ot many people can say that their home is located on part of a historic land grant signed by Thomas Jefferson. But that's the truth here at Twin Creek, an 1830s farmhouse (one of the oldest in the country) that sits on 170 acres of the Ulrich Home Farm.

So your major concern here should be to relax. It's not hard, considering that the farm's hiking trails wind through more than seventy acres of peaceful woods filled with wildlife. Of course, it's easy to relax back at the inn, too. The front porch is a great conversation starter, and the back deck has served as headquarters for many a picnic.

Guest rooms are comfortable and country perfect, as are the full farm breakfasts. I guess I didn't mention that Dr. Ulrich is a large-animal vet, with his office located in another building on the farm. So there are always some interesting critters around, including a resident horse and pony.

HOW TO GET THERE: The inn is located halfway between Dayton, Ohio, and Richmond, Indiana. From I–70, take the State Route 503 exit. Go left off the exit on SR 503. Follow this south for about 4 miles into the village of West Alexandria. In the middle of town at the traffic light, go east (left) on State Route 35 (Dayton Street) and follow it about 1 mile out of town to the first road on the right, which is Enterprise Road. Go right (south) on Enterprise for about 5 miles. The inn is located on the right (west) side at the back of a country lane. There is a white reflective sign at the end of the lane that reads: DR. MARK ULRICH, VETERINARIAN and TWIN CREEK COUNTRY BED AND BREAKFAST. Please go to the back of the white house where the innkeepers will check you in and take you to your room in the historic brick farmhouse.

Murphin Ridge Inn
West Union, Ohio 45693

INNKEEPERS: Sherri and Darrell McKinney

ADDRESS/TELEPHONE: 750 Murphin Ridge Road; (937) 544–2263

ROOMS: 10, 3 cabins; all with private bath and air-conditioning. Wheelchair accessible. No smoking inn.

RATES: $100, single or double, Wednesday and Thursday; $115, single or double, Friday through Sunday with a two-night minimum Friday and Saturday; cabins, $150 to $175. EPB.

OPEN: Year-round except January; closed Mondays and Tuesdays.

FACILITIES AND ACTIVITIES: Three-room 1810 farmhouse converted into full-service dining rooms; inn common room with cable television, VCR, books, and magazines; porch with rockers; heated swimming pool; horseshoe pit; outdoor basketball and tennis courts; 10 miles of hiking trails. Nearby: Serpent Mound and remote forest preserves for hiking; biking on backcountry roads; Amish stores.

*I*t didn't take long for my pa and me to fall in love with the Murphin Ridge Inn. Located in the heart of Adams County and tucked in the foothills of the Appalachian Mountains, this handsome and historic homestead has everything most country inns only dream of:

History: It's located on the 600-acre site of a Virginia land grant awarded to a Revolutionary War soldier.

Scenery: The inn sits high on a ridge overlooking Peach Mountain at the edge of Appalachia's quiet woodlands and sweeping valleys.

Local color: Adams County is also the heart of Amish country, where horse-drawn buggies can be spotted along rural lanes.

Great accommodations: The ten-room inn boasts handmade Shaker reproduction furnishings that are nearly museum quality. Two rooms feature fireplaces; two offer private balconies overlooking the Appalachian hills. Then there are wonderful cabins out back of the inn, with two-person whirlpools, fireplaces, and the ultimate in country romance.

Local lore: Get the innkeepers to tell you how Morgan's Raiders swept down Wheat Ridge Road during the Civil War in retaliation for its abolitionist activities, including its part in the Underground Railroad, which helped runaway slaves escape to the north.

A day after we left Murphin Ridge, Pa and I already missed the place badly.

HOW TO GET THERE: From Cincinnati, take Ohio 32 east to Unity Road. Turn right on Unity and follow to the stop sign. Turn left onto Wheat Ridge Road for 3 miles, then turn left onto Murphin Ridge Road and continue to the inn.

The Wooster Inn
Wooster, Ohio 44691

INNKEEPER: Andrea Lazar

ADDRESS/TELEPHONE: Wayne Avenue and Gasche Street; (330) 264–2341

ROOMS: 16, with 2 suites; all with private bath, air-conditioning, and phone. Pets welcome.

RATES: $70 to $120, single; $85 to $135, double. Special weekend packages available.

OPEN: Year-round except Christmas Day.

FACILITIES AND ACTIVITIES: Wheelchair access to dining room. Sitting area, outside patio. Nearby: access to many Wooster College activities and sports facilities. Ohio Light Opera special on weekends.

*I*magine an evening of professional light opera, maybe Offenbach's *La Belle Hélène*—which might be described as a Woody Allen–type soap opera with ravishing waltzes—and you'll get the idea of the flair of the Ohio Light Opera. Now imagine following your musical evening with a delicious meal featuring champagne and a juicy steak served in a Colonial-style dining room.

That's just some of the fun you'll have at the wonderful Wooster Inn. Owned and operated by the College of Wooster and located right on its beautiful campus, the inn is surrounded by tall trees and green fields. In fact, I watched a little friendly competition on the college's golf course right from the dining room window.

The inn has an English country feel to it. The lobby is spacious and casually gracious, with a large sitting area of high-back chairs and sofas. A stately grandfather's clock softly chimes on the hour. French doors open onto the Colonial-style dining room and terrace, which overlook the aforementioned links.

Guests may also use many of the facilities at the college. These include tennis courts and the golf course just out the back door. You can even use the library. Bedchambers are spacious, comfortable, and cheery, with windows overlooking the inn grounds, muted flowered wallpaper, oak and cherry furniture, quaint bedspreads, and a couple of wing chairs. Be sure to make reservations well in advance. College guests adore the inn.

Breakfast specialties include blueberry pancakes with Ohio maple syrup. Dinner offers a wide selection of choices, including beef tenderloin in Burgundy wine and pepper sauce, sherry-basted pork chops with rosemary, fresh rainbow trout or salmon, and veal cutlets.

The Wooster Inn

HOW TO GET THERE: Five principal highways run through Wooster: U.S. 30 and 250, and State Routes 3, 585, and 83. From Cleveland, exit the 250 bypass at Burbank Road and continue south to Wayne Avenue. Turn east on Wayne to the inn.

The Worthington Inn
Worthington, Ohio 43085

INNKEEPER: Steve Hanson, general manager

ADDRESS/TELEPHONE: 649 High Street; (614) 885-7700

ROOMS: 26, with 7 suites; all with private bath, air-conditioning, TV, and phone.

RATES: $150 to $175, single or double; $215 to $260, suites; EPB. Also special "without breakfast" rates.

OPEN: Year-round

FACILITIES AND ACTIVITIES: Four dining rooms, pub, ballroom. Located in historic Old Worthington Village. Free maps for walking tours of area, which include several homes built as early as 1804. Nearby: antiques shops, specialty stores, and boutiques.

BUSINESS TRAVEL: Located about 20 miles north of downtown Columbus. Corporate rates, conference rooms, fax.

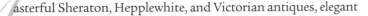

*M*asterful Sheraton, Hepplewhite, and Victorian antiques, elegant stained glass and crystal, bath mirrors imported from France, triple sheeting on beds, turndown service, and a complimentary split of champagne transport you back to a more graceful style of traveling. I bet you never would have guessed that this magnificent inn, completed in 1831 and then known as the Central House, was originally a stagecoach stop.

A $4 million restoration in 1983 transformed what had become a white elephant into a luxurious and romantic turn-of-the-century–style getaway. Every room's decor is different; some sport an early American motif, complete with hand stenciling on walls and ceilings and elegant pine period pieces, while others are Victorian, featuring fine walnut, mahogany, and cherry antique furnishings.

The Presidential Suite is a descent into pampered decadence. It offers more than 800 square feet of pomp and luxury. On one of the walls are framed papers that set the terms of an indentured servant. Those valuable documents were found within the walls during the restoration. Four more suites, located in the 1817 Snow House just across the street, offer more elegance. The center hall staircase is black walnut, and you can notice unpeeled log joints in the cellar.

HOW TO GET THERE: From Cleveland, take I–71 south to Ohio 161. Exit west to Worthington, then turn left on High Street and continue to New England Avenue and the inn.

Pub Talk

Treat yourself to a cold quaff in the Pub Room. The splendid marble-topped bar, with its leaded- and stained-glass accoutrements, seemingly stretches on forever. Made in Austria, it originally was used as a soda fountain in Baltimore at the turn of the century. Ask the bartender to explain how the interesting Cruvinet wine decanter system works.

Select List of Other Inns in Ohio

The Cincinnatian Hotel
601 Vine Street
Cincinnati, OH 45202
(513) 381-3000
(800) 942-9000

Prospect Hill B&B
408 Boal Street
Cincinnati, OH 45210
(513) 421-4408

50 Lincoln B&B
50 East Lincoln Street
Columbus, OH 43215
(614) 291-5056

Red Fox Country Inn
26367 Danville Amity Road
P.O. Box 717
Danville, OH 43014
(740) 599-7369

The Russell-Coper House
115 East Gambier Street
Mount Vernon, OH 43050
(740) 397-8638

Heartland Country Resort
2994 Township Road 190
Fredericktown, OH 43019
(419) 768-9300
(800) 230-7030

Bailey House
112 North Water Street
Georgetown, OH 45121
(937) 378-3087

English Manor B&B
505 East Linden Avenue
Miamisburg, OH 45342
(937) 866-2288
(800) 676-9456

Ravenwood Castle
65666 Bethel Road
New Plymouth, OH 45654
(740) 596-2606
(800) 477-1541
Web site:
www.ravenwoodcastle.com

Wisconsin

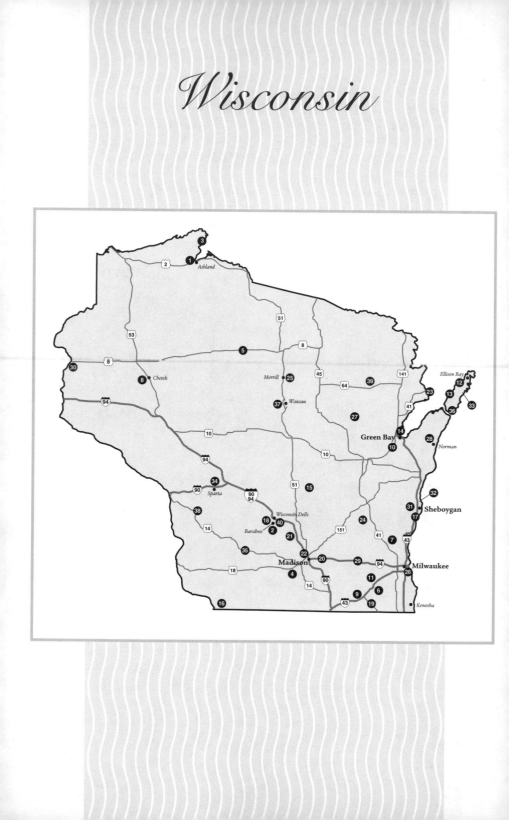

Wisconsin

Numbers on map refer to towns numbered below.

*A Top Pick Inn

*A Top Pick Inn

Hotel Chequamegon 🖼 📱
Ashland, Wisconsin 54806

INNKEEPER: Mary Ellen Margetta, general manager

ADDRESS/TELEPHONE: 101 West Front Street; (715) 682–9095

ROOMS: 62, with 20 suites; all with private bath, air-conditioning, TV, and phone.

RATES: $90 to $135, single or double, rooms; $135 to $155, single or double, suites; EP. Senior citizens' discount of 10 percent. Low-season rates from October 1 through May 1.

OPEN: Year-round

FACILITIES AND ACTIVITIES: Spa, indoor pool, restaurant, lounge. Overlooks waters of Lake Superior and twenty-five-slip marina. Nearby: historic fishing village of Bayfield, with specialty and antiques shops; historic-home tours; ferry to Madeline Island, part of Apostle Islands National Lakeshore. Several downhill-ski hills a short drive away, including Blackjack, Big Powderhorn, Indianhead, and Telemark.

BUSINESS TRAVEL: Corporate rates, meeting rooms, fax.

he Hotel Chequamegon resembles one of those grand resort hotels that sprang up on Great Lakes shorelines around the turn of the century. Its massive white-clapboard styling harkens back to more

Shuqauwaumekong

The Hotel Chequamegon is not a historic inn, although it rests upon a historic site. Opened in 1985 and built at a cost of $12.5 million on the site of the first hotel of the same name (which burned down in 1908), it returns visitors to the days when Ashland was a booming lumber mecca. It derives its name from an Indian word, the Chippewa's *shuqauwaumekong,* which means "a narrow strip of land running into a body of water."

elegant times. It is crowned on each end by rounded towers and capped out back by an expansive veranda with two cupola gazebos overlooking the water.

Oak woodwork is everywhere, with posts and columns and high ceilings adding to the charm. Especially luxurious is the Northland Parlor Room, with its ornate, many-columned fireplace, brass chandelier, and high-back chairs; the room opens onto the huge veranda.

Simple but dramatic guest rooms are examples of understated elegance. Floral prints, fluffy quilts, comfortable sofas and chairs, and great views from lakeside rooms provide special touches. Executive suites each have a large whirlpool bath, a wet bar, an antique-style mahogany sleigh bed, balloon drapes, and lace curtains.

Fifield's, the inn's elegant restaurant, features such entrees as planked whitefish, fresh Lake Superior trout, blackened walleye, and an assortment of steaks and pastas. Molly Cooper's, fashioned to resemble a 1930s speakeasy, is an interesting spot for a nightcap.

HOW TO GET THERE: The hotel is located at the intersection of Highways 2 and 13, easily accessible from any direction.

The Gollmar Guest House
Baraboo, Wisconsin 53913

INNKEEPER: Thomas Luck

ADDRESS/TELEPHONE: 422 Third Street; (608) 356-9432, fax (608) 356-3847

WEB SITE: www.golmar.com

ROOMS: 3, all with private bath, central air. No smoking inn.

RATES: $80 to $130; EPB.

OPEN: Year-round

FACILITIES AND ACTIVITIES: Dining room, parlor library, patio, veranda, gardens. Short drive to Circus World Museum, International Crane Foundation, Lake Delton, Wisconsin Dells, Devil's Lake State Park.

*T*he beautiful 1889 home boasts original hand-painted ceiling murals, beveled glass windows, fancy chandeliers, oak woodwork, and shiny oak hardwood floors—part of the charm that Benjamin and Isabelle Gollmar instilled in this home upon its construction. Innkeeper Tom Luck also can boast that the house is filled with original furniture and antiques. So you're really living history when visiting the inn.

Guests rooms are charming and quaint, too. Isabelle's Gollmar Guest Room was the house's original guest bedchambers. I especially like Viola's Attic, tucked away for even more privacy.

You can exchange Baraboo stories with guests in the parlor library. Or breathe in the fresh air on the patio—unless a chair on the veranda, overlooking the gardens, is more your style.

HOW TO GET THERE: From the south, take I-90/94 to exit 106 (Highway 33) and go west to Baraboo. Highway 33 in Baraboo is Eighth Street—at the first stop light at East Street turn left; go 5 blocks and turn left on Third Street. The inn is on the right about 1½ blocks from East Street.

Old Rittenhouse Inn
Bayfield, Wisconsin 54814

INNKEEPERS: Jerry and Mary Phillips

ADDRESS/TELEPHONE: 301 Rittenhouse Avenue (mailing Address: Box 584); (715) 779-5765 or (888) 561-4667

WEB SITE: www.rittenhouseinn.com

ROOMS: 17, in three Victorian homes; all with private bath, 9 with fireplace, 13 with whirlpool, some with wheelchair access.

RATES: $99 to $159, single or double; $249, suite; continental breakfast. Special off-season packages.

OPEN: Year-round

FACILITIES AND ACTIVITIES: Three romantic dining rooms. Recreational activities of all kinds available: fishing, sailing, Apostle Islands

National Lakeshore; fur-trading museum and other attractions on Madeline Island; canoeing on Brule River; annual festivals; cross-country skiing.

*I*sat in an elegant Victorian dining room in the early morning as an immaculately dressed Jerry Phillips, resplendent in a black velvet vest and a wide bow tie, served me an exquisite breakfast.

After sipping freshly pressed apple cider, I started on brandied peaches and blueberries in sour cream. Next came delicious New Orleans–style cinnamon French toast.

The sound of classical music wafted through the room, which was adorned with rich Victorian-print wallpaper, brass chandeliers, and antique oak and mahogany tables and chairs. I pulled my seat closer to the roaring fire in the hearth.

"I think it's important that the feeling inside a home fits the personality of the house," Jerry said as we talked about what made a good country inn, "and it must deliver personal service that makes it a special place to stay."

The Old Rittenhouse Inn scores well on both points. It's an opulent 1890 Victorian redbrick and wood-shingle mansion, not far from the spectacular shoreline of Lake Superior, with historic islands nearby to explore—an almost perfect destination. It has a long wraparound veranda and gabled roof; elegant dining rooms and sitting areas are done in formal prints, with fine Victorian furnishings and all kinds of period lamps.

The guest rooms are immaculate. Many have four-poster beds, marble-topped dressers, and vanities; some have a fireplace to take the chill off cold winter days. Several boast tall windows looking out toward blustery Lake Superior. There's also complimentary champagne in each room in the evening.

Recently added inn rooms are incredibly spacious; I don't think it would be an exaggeration to say that they're the largest I've seen in any country inn. Big brass, iron-rail, and walnut beds are inviting. Then there are pretty stained-glass windows depicting Bayfield lakeshore scenes. All the new rooms have their own fireplaces.

The inn also offers delicious multicourse gourmet meals. Here Mary Phillips is the genius. Her specialties include steak Bercy stuffed with oysters, fresh trout poached in champagne, and pork ragout. Homemade breads are served steaming in heaping baskets. Save room for some incredible desserts, such as Jerry's white-chocolate cheesecake.

Check out the Phillipses' other two Bayfield inns. The elegant Le Chateau Boutin, a 1907 Queen Anne mansion, boasts fabulous appointments with seven guest rooms. The 1888 Grey Oak Guest House, a Gothic Victorian, offers four more bedchambers.

What an elegant "hat trick!"

HOW TO GET THERE: From Minneapolis–St. Paul, take I–94 east to U.S. 63. Take 63 north to State Route 2 and go east to Route 13. Take 13 north to Bayfield. The inn is on the corner of Rittenhouse and Third.

Cameo Rose Bed and Breakfast
Belleville, Wisconsin 53508

INNKEEPERS: Dawn, Gary, and Jennifer Bahr

ADDRESS/TELEPHONE: 1090 Severson Road; (608) 424–6340

WEB SITE: www.cameorose.com

ROOMS: 5; all with private bath. No smoking inn.

RATES: $99 to $149, single or double; EPB

OPEN: Year-round

FACILITIES AND ACTIVITIES: Cathedral great room, porches, rose gazebo, flower gardens, 120 acres of hills, woods, hiking trails. Nearby: fifteen minutes from Madison, the University of Wisconsin, the State Capitol, State Street (shops and specialty stores), Dane County Coliseum, golf courses, water sports on Lakes Medota and Monona.

*I*f there is a more attractive Victorian-style inn than this one, let me know about it. I'll put my money on the Cameo Rose, a hostelry that's blossoming into one of the finest little getaways in the Midwest.

"We built the house specifically for a bed-and-breakfast," Dawn Bahr told me. She and husband Gary adapted plans from a "House of the Week" design in the local paper. It was completed in 1991, though it has the Victorian-era complement of ornate gingerbread, slashing gables, and an imposing tower.

Dawn does all the decorating—and it is exquisite. Of course, roses are everywhere, especially in the Tower Room, graced with Cameo Rose wall coverings, Battenburg lace, handsome quilts, and a double whirlpool whose win-

dow looks out over the surrounding valley.

The breakfasts here are tops. Served in the formal dining room on antique china with crystal goblets, consider hot breakfast fruit compote, eggs Benedict, berry streusel muffins ("Wild berries grow everywhere around here," Dawn said), and homemade cinnamon rolls—a house specialty.

The inn is located on 120 acres of hills and trees. Part of the renowned Ice Age Trail edges across the property. There are also miles of hiking paths that loop to hilltops, through maple and oak groves, and into the valley. Or relax among the rose and flower gardens, a blaze of colors in the growing season.

The Cameo Rose is a special place. But don't take my word. See for yourself.

HOW TO GET THERE: The inn is located 5 miles south of Verona, 3 miles north of Belleville (and about 12 miles southwest of Madison) in unincorporated Basco. From Madison, take Highway 151 (Verona Road) west and use the Paoli exit. Basco, the town, is basically a sign and a small group of houses at Henry Road along Highway 69 about 1 mile past Paoli, on the way to Belleville. You'll see the Cameo Rose to the left on a hill, a bit more than 1 mile down Henry Road.

Palmquist's The Farm 🏨
Brantwood, Wisconsin 54513

INNKEEPERS: Jim, Helen, Anna, Toinie, and Art Palmquist

ADDRESS/TELEPHONE: N5136 River Road; (715) 564-2558 or (800) 519-2558.

ROOMS: 8 in 2 buildings, with 4 suites; suites with private bath. Four other buildings for couples or families; all with private bath. No smoking inn.

RATES: Weekends, daily: $78 adults, $39 children 5–11, $31 children 3–4; weekdays: $55, $27, and $22, respectively; AP. Bed and Breakfast only: adults $42.50; children 3–12, $21.

OPEN: Year-round

FACILITIES AND ACTIVITIES: Sauna house, warming house with ski rentals, hiking on private nature trails, fishing in farm ponds and in the Somo River, children's farm activities, log cabin-building seminars, hayrides, sleigh rides. Nearby: bike the Bearskin Trail, hike the Ice Age Trail, visit Timm's Hill County Park (highest point in Wisconsin).

"*A*re you Finnish?" asked Jim Palmquist, whose grandfather came to the United States from that country. "Puhala is a pretty common Finnish name, you know."

Maybe. My mother's family came from Armagh, Northern Ireland. But we hit a dead end for my pa's relatives as soon as we reach Austria. Could the Puhalas have migrated from Finland to Austria on the way to America?

Enough about me. Jim and his wife, Helen, boast a premier bed-and-breakfast experience on their 800-acre cattle ranch. You can hike its nature trails through maple groves and up hardwood ridges. Or help your kids with farm chores such as feeding with the calves, chickens, and horses—and spend some time with Barney, one of the friendliest yellow Labs you'll ever meet.

Perhaps the ranch's most spectacular digs are in the White Pines Inn, a massive log building built by Jim and a noted local log builder. A huge great room is the place to relax, then enjoy the porch and gaze up at the stars before retiring to your handsome suite.

I also like the Sauna House (just like a Finn), a two-bedroom building with its own private sauna, and the River Cabin, which sits on the bank of the Somo.

Helen's food is legend in these parts and includes Finnish dishes such as creamed rice with raspberry sauce, oven pancakes with real maple syrup, and

Finnish whole-wheat bread. It will be difficult to leave this place, so I'm warning you ahead of time.

HOW TO GET THERE: From the east or west, take U.S. 8. The ranch is located 12 miles east of Prentice and 20 miles west of Tomahawk off U.S. 8. Look for the Palmquists' THE FARM sign at the intersection of U.S. 8 and River Road; turn on River Road and continue 1 mile to the inn.

The Hillcrest Inn and Carriage House
Burlington, Wisconsin 53105

INNKEEPERS: Mike and Gayle Hohner

ADDRESS/TELEPHONE:
540 Storle Avenue;
(262) 763–4706

WEB SITE:
www.thehillcrestinn.com

ROOMS: 6; all with private bath. No smoking inn.

RATES: $95 to $185, single or double; EPB.

OPEN: Year-round

FACILITIES AND ACTIVITIES: Magnificent parlor with panoramic water views, flower gardens, walking path to water, private shoreline. Nearby: watersports on Echo Lake and the Fox and White Rivers; antiques shops, boutiques, and art galleries in town.

*S*ituated high on a hill overlooking the water, this four-acre estate has a very English feel to it. It was very Edwardian.

The guest rooms are a little piece of jolly old England. The Kensington Room, with its green, burgundy, and gold, feels like quarters at an exclusive English gentleman's club. There's a large double whirlpool that's great for relaxing with that special someone while watching the fireplace blaze away.

A weekend in the Windmere Suite means you have the entire second floor of the Carriage House to yourselves. Of course, there's a large whirlpool for your ultimate soaking pleasure.

A favorite guest activity is to relax on the inn's upper and lower porches. We walked through the garden down to the water, just across the street. If there's a prettier spot for a city inn in all the Midwest, I'd like to know about it.

HOW TO GET THERE: From downtown Burlington, take Highway 11 about 7 blocks to Pleasant Avenue. Turn south on Pleasant and continue for 2 blocks; then turn right on Storle Avenue and the inn.

Stagecoach Inn
Cedarburg, Wisconsin 53012

INNKEEPERS: Liz and Brook Brown

ADDRESS/TELEPHONE: W61 N520 Washington Avenue; (262) 375-0208 or (888) 375-0208

WEB SITE: www.stagecoachinn-wi.com

ROOMS: 12, including 6 suites; all with private bath and air-conditioning; suites with double whirlpool bath and TV. No smoking inn.

RATES: $80 to $140; continental breakfast.

OPEN: Year-round

The Old and New

Look for these inn originals: The heavy front door dates from 1853; the intricate woodwork on the door and window frames, as well as the crown molding above the front door, is made of single pieces of wood carved to look multilayered; and the handsome cherry staircase banister is authentic and impressive.

A newer addition—a historical annex to the main inn—is the Weber Haus. This 1847 frame building is one of the oldest operating structures in Cedarburg. Honeymoon couples love the privacy, and its three suites are decorated with four-poster beds, wicker, and antiques. It also has a garden and picnic area.

FACILITIES AND ACTIVITIES: Stagecoach Pub, candy store. In heart of historic Cedarburg. Nearby: walk to Cedar Creek Settlement; the old Woolen Mill; Stone Mill Winery; antiques, craft, and specialty shops; restaurants and art galleries. Also nearby: bike trails, golf, fishing, cross-country skiing, River Edge Nature Center, museum, Ozaukee Pioneer Village, Ozaukee Covered Bridge (last remaining covered bridge in Wisconsin).

*S*tagecoach drivers slept on the basement's dirt floor in bunks made of stone rubble and straw. The chimney that took the flue for the driver's pot-bellied stove still stands.

The stagecoach-stop charm carries over to the guest rooms, which are decorated with period antiques. "We wanted to keep the inn authentic," Liz Brown said. "This community is restoration-minded."

That's an understatement. The Stagecoach Inn is in the heart of the historic downtown district, which was anchored by the Wittenburg Woolen Mills, now restored and called the Cedar Creek Settlement. (The mill provided wool uniforms for soldiers during the Civil War.) More than 150 rare "cream city" brick and stone buildings stand throughout town, many dating to the mid-1800s.

Everything at the inn is cozy and cheery, with many special touches. Liz created the pretty stencils on the walls and reconditioned the original pinewood plank floors. Her antique four-poster and brass beds are covered with Laura Ashley comforters. Suites are decorated with more antiques, wicker, and Laura Ashley fabrics and have two-person whirlpool tubs.

The Stagecoach Pub is located on the inn's first floor. I had an imported beer from a massive antique oak cooler at a century-old bar. The tin ceiling adds to the frontier charm. Folksingers entertain here on evenings twice a month. Liz serves breakfast here, too, at antique tavern tables. (Or you can take your breakfast on the back deck.) She offers hot croissants, juice, cereal, fresh fruit, bran muffins, coffee, and herbal teas, and she'll recommend a good spot for dinner in the historic town. You can play games and cards here at night, in a warm coffeehouse atmosphere. Late-night sweet tooths can find a candy shop on the first floor.

HOW TO GET THERE: From Chicago, take I–94 to I–43 and get off at exit 17 (Cedarburg). Take Pioneer Road 3 miles to Washington Avenue and turn right on Cedarburg. The inn is located on the right side of the street.

The Washington House Inn
Cedarburg, Wisconsin 53012

INNKEEPER: Wendy Porterfield, manager

ADDRESS/TELEPHONE: W62 N573 Washington Avenue; (262)
375-3550 or (800) 554-4717

WEB SITE: www.washingtonhouseinn.com

ROOMS: 34, including 15 suites; all with private bath, air-conditioning,
TV, and phone; 31 rooms with whirlpool bath. Wheelchair accessible.

RATES: $69 to $119, single or double; $79 to $209, suites; continental
breakfast. Special packages available.

OPEN: Year-round

FACILITIES AND ACTIVITIES: Situated in the heart of historic Cedarburg. Nearby: walk to restaurants and Cedar Creek Settlement: old
Woolen Mill; Stone Mill Winery; antiques, craft, and specialty shops.
A short drive to Ozaukee Pioneer Village, Ozaukee Covered Bridge (last
remaining covered bridge in Wisconsin).

Cedarburg is a historic woolen mill town, with many rare "cream
city" brick and stone buildings dating from the mid-1800s. In fact,
the downtown area alone has more historic structures than any
other city west of Philadelphia.

One of these is The Washington House Inn, a country-Victorian "cream
city" brick building completed in 1886. The tall front doors and authentic
frontier ambience are softened by a long lobby featuring Victorian furnishings,
rich parquet floors, brass chandeliers, and a marble fireplace.

I looked at the original hotel
register, which recorded visitors
during the months of 1895. How
did anyone ever have the time to
write in that fancy scroll? I also
noticed an unusual display: a
"wedding brick" discovered during
restoration with the date "1886"
and the names of the happy couple
scratched on it.

The guest rooms are named for leading citizens of historic Cedarburg. The country-Victorian decorations are absolutely charming, with floral wallpapers, fancy armoires, cozy down quilts, fresh flowers, and more. I really like the leaded-glass transom windows of some rooms.

In the newly restored rooms, there's more of a plain country feeling, but there's nothing plain about the decor. The exposed brick walls and beamed ceilings are spectacular.

Then there are some very deluxe quarters. My favorite has country-style antiques, loft beds cozied by their own fireplace, and another loft area that boasts a 200-gallon spa tub warmed by a second fireplace.

Or perhaps you'd like a room at the inn's other building, the 1868 Schroeder House, located about four doors down from the main inn. Fireplaces are part of the romance here.

It's fun to eat breakfast in a dining room with white pressed-tin ceilings, oak tables and chairs, and tall windows that wash the room in light. (Of course, you may have breakfast in bed, too.) Home-baked breads, cakes, and rolls are made from recipes found in an authentic turn-of-the-century Cedarburg cookbook. Cereal, fresh fruit, and beverages also are offered.

One of manager Wendy Porterfield's favorite times of the day is the afternoon social hour in the dining room, with an opportunity to share with guests her love of this historic town. A manteled fireplace with Victorian sofas and chairs just off the main dining area makes things more cozy.

HOW TO GET THERE: From Chicago, take I–94 to I–43, just north of Milwaukee, and get off at the Cedarburg exit. This road eventually changes to Wisconsin 57; follow it into town (where it becomes Washington Avenue). At Center Street, turn left and park in the lot behind the hotel.

Canoe Bay
Chetek, Wisconsin 54728

INNKEEPERS: Dan and Lisa Dobrowolski
ADDRESS/TELEPHONE: W16065 Hogback Road; (715) 924–4594 or (800) 568–1995

E-MAIL: mail@canoebay.com

WEB SITE: www.canoebay.com

ROOMS: 19 in 9 buildings, including inn and lodge rooms and deluxe cottages, all with private bath, double whirlpool, air-conditioning, and audio/video centers. No smoking inn.

RATES: $270 to $420, single or double; Rattenbury Cottage, $700; EPB. Gourmet dinners.

OPEN: Year-round

FACILITIES AND ACTIVITIES: Located on private 280 acres: two private lakes, hiking paths, nature trails, cross-country ski trails, cross-country rentals, bike rentals, fishing, swimming, canoes, rowboats, and more. Sitting room, video room, library. Spa services: theraputic massage, body wraps, facials, hand and feet care. About 45 minutes west of St. Paul, Minnesota.

Gourmand Demands

Just how spectacular are those gourmet meals served at this Relais et Chateaux inn restaurant, which itself boasts incredible views of the lake and surrounding woodlands? Judge for yourself—here's a sample menu for a typical prix fixe "taste of Canoe Bay" menu:

- carmelized acorn squash bisque
- pan-seared salmon with smoked corn and radish salsa
- Summerfield Farm's dry-aged beef tenderloin au jus, shitake and oyster mushrooms, carmelized shallot mashed potatoes
- dark chocolate terrine with port wine reduction and toasted hazelnuts

To make sure your dinner is a satisfying experience, Canoe Bay offers one of the largest wine lists in the Midwest, from Australian Shiraz to Bordeaux reds, Chilean Merlots to German Rieslings, Côte Roties to Caymus Special Selection Cabernet Sauvignon.

Bon appetit!

*D*an and Lisa Dobrowolski's inn has perhaps set new standards in luxury. I've always considered this elegant country retreat possibly the best Mid-America has to offer discerning guests, but don't take my word for it.

Canoe Bay is the first Midwest lodging establishment to become a member of the prestigious Paris-based association Relais et Chateaux, which includes many of the finest hotels and lodgings in the world. The inn also has received a four-star rating from the *Mobil Travel Guide,* the only lodging in the Midwest to be so honored.

Now you can't have any doubts when I say Canoe Bay is an experience that shouldn't be missed.

Dan (a former TV weatherman for WFLD–Channel 32 in Chicago) and Lisa built their inn on the shore of crystal-clear Lake Wahdoon, a fifty-acre spring-fed body of water surrounded by 280 acres of private oak, aspen, and maple forests. The inn provides breathtaking views, incomparable service, and complete privacy besides many opportunities for outdoor recreation and relaxation, including wildlife watching.

The main building's centerpiece is a great room, with soaring natural-cedar cathedral ceilings, a wall of windows, and a 30-foot-tall, hand-constructed fieldstone fireplace. Inn rooms here are exquisite, like something out of *Architectural Digest.*

Also sprinkled through this grand country estate are luxurious cottage suites, featuring Frank Lloyd Wright's signature Prairie-style architecture along with "every possible creature comfort with the ultimate in privacy." Even Canoe Bay's exterior spaces have received what Wright called "organic architecture" treatment, with natural prairie, woodland grasses, and wildflowers designed and installed by a nationally renowned consulting ecologist.

The innkeepers spared no expense in re-creating the great architect's distinctive style. For example, the Oak Park Suite boasts a 14-foot-high wall of casement windows overlooking the lake; the Wood Grove Suite allows guests to observe natural surroundings from their platform two-person Jacuzzi through wraparound windows. Also count on a river-rock fireplace, a stereo/TV/VCR/CD, a wet bar with refrigerator and microwave oven, and a huge private deck.

Or how about staying overnight in the Rattenbury Cottage, a hilltop retreat with the inn's best views of the lakes. Designed by the Taliesin Architects, Frank Lloyd Wright School of Architecture, this masterpiece includes a massive stone fireplace, cathedral ceilings with clerestory windows, double whirlpool, unique "wet room" shower, and all the finest appointments available.

Mornings bring pampering, with breakfast baskets delivered to your room or brought out to the patio overlooking the lake, where you can enjoy scores of chirping songbirds. Canoe Bay also offers dinner featuring gourmet cuisine that would be difficult to beat even when considering Chicago or Minneapolis's best restaurants, thanks to Culinary Institute of America–trained staff.

The inn's standout season could be autumn, with its incomparable colors, but holidays receive special treatment, too. Thanksgiving and New Year's Day guests can enjoy guided cross-country ski tours, ice skating, ice fishing, and a 14-foot-tall Christmas tree with all the trimmings.

Then again, anytime at Canoe Bay is special. You might even receive a free, personal weather forecast from prognosticator Dan, who's often heard to say, "If there's a better place on Earth, I don't know it."

Forget Earth. This is heaven.

HOW TO GET THERE: Once in Chetek, Highway 53 becomes Second Street. Follow that through town, over a bridge, and turn right on County Road D (there's a cemetery at this intersection). Go about 1½ miles to Hogback Road (look for a CANOE BAY sign here); turn left and continue for about 7 miles to the inn.

Allyn Mansion Inn
Delavan, Wisconsin 53115

INNKEEPERS: Joe Johnson and Ron Markwell

ADDRESS/TELEPHONE: 511 East Walworth Avenue; (262) 728–9090

WEB SITE: www.allynmansion.com

ROOMS: 8, 5 with private bath, 3 share four baths; all with air-conditioning. No smoking inn.

RATES: $75 to $125, single or double, weekends; EPB. Midweek discounts and corporate rates available. Two-night minimum, end of May through Columbus Day.

OPEN: Year-round

FACILITIES AND ACTIVITIES: Evening social hour on weekends. Three formal parlors, library reading room. Patio, Victorian rose, and herb garden. Nearby: restaurants, Circus Hall of Fame. A short drive to Lake Geneva resort, Kettle Moraine State Park, Alpine Valley Music Center, skiing, antiquing.

his 1885 Queen Anne mansion has one of the most elaborate restorations of "high Victorian" style in the Midwest. Walnut woodwork, frescoed 13-foot-high ceilings, and ten Italian marble fireplaces will delight inn lovers and house preservationists alike. Eye-catching stained, leaded, and etched glass, parquet floors, and brass chandeliers add even more elegant touches. I felt like royalty when ascending the magnificent three-story walnut staircase that rises to a stunning horseshoe window.

Marvelous antique furnishings predate 1900, the bounty of Joe Johnson and Ron Markwell's multiyear collection. I especially liked the Wave Crest glass (New England, circa 1890s); it's one of the finest sets of its kind in the Heartland.

Guest rooms are spectacular re-creations of Victorian splendor. Besides a photograph of the home's matriarch "trying to smile," according to Joe, Mrs. Allyn's Room features a piece original to the house (and my favorite Victorian gadget to date), a Murphy-type bed that resembles a fine walnut wardrobe, finials and all.

Mr. Allyn's Room has black print Victorian wallpaper, besides a marble fireplace and a mahogany canopy bed. "People gave me funny looks when I chose this pattern," Joe said. "But I thought it would match the house's architectural character." It sure does.

It's difficult not to admire the 60-foot-high Eastlake tower built to the original architectural plans, which the innkeepers found in an old basement safe. Guests may climb up the open tower, accompanied by the innkeepers. And the innkeepers are justifiably proud that the inn is a grand prize winner of the National Trust's Great American Home Awards.

HOW TO GET THERE: From Milwaukee, take Wisconsin 50 west into Delavan and continue west on Wisconsin 11 to the inn.

James St. Inn
De Pere, Wisconsin 54115

INNKEEPER: Kevin C. Flatley, manager

ADDRESS/TELEPHONE: 201 James Street; (920) 337–0111,
fax (920) 337–6135

ROOMS: 30; all with private bath

RATES: $69 to $159, single; $79 to $169, double; continental breakfast.

OPEN: Year-round

FACILITIES AND ACTIVITIES: Fireplace in gathering room, library, river
promenade. Nearby: minutes from St. Norbert College, National Railroad Museum, Heritage Hill State Park, Hazelwood, Lambeau Field
(home of the Green Bay Packers), Green Bay Packer Hall of Fame.

BUSINESS TRAVEL: Data ports in rooms, fax machine, conference room,
corporate rates.

*T*he historic four-story 1892 Columbian Mills, originally built by
prominent Wisconsinite John Dousman, didn't close until 1982.
Today, a restoration company has transformed the old mill into
a luxurious bed-and-break-
fast inn, with brick walls
and archways, beamed ceilings, antique brass light fixtures, and other elegant
amenities.

All guest rooms are
comfortable, mostly done
in elegant Shaker-style
appointments. But check
out the suites. Some boast
whirlpools, fireplaces, private balconies, and views of the Fox River. I particularly like Suite 106, with its mahogany and walnut furniture—and riverside
location.

I like some of the "extras," too. Morning newspapers are free at the front
desk—including Sunday's; fresh-perked coffee is always ready for guests in the
lobby; and wine and cheese are served every afternoon from 4:00 to 9:00 P.M.

There's another interesting aspect to the James St. Inn: The river flows
under it.

So when they tell you here that your "room is on the water," they really
mean it.

HOW TO GET THERE: From Green Bay, take Wisconsin 57 south into DePere. At James Street, turn right and continue to the river and the inn.

Eagle Centre House
Eagle, Wisconsin 53119

INNKEEPERS: Riene Wells-Herriges and Dean Herriges

ADDRESS/TELEPHONE: W370 S9590 Highway 67; (262) 363–4700

WEB SITE: eagle-house.com

ROOMS: 5, including 2 suites; all with private bath and air-conditioning, suites with whirlpool tub. No smoking inn.

RATES: $95 to $155, single or double; EPB.

OPEN: Year-round

FACILITIES AND ACTIVITIES: Parlor, taproom, front and side porches overlooking hills and meadows, hiking trails. Nearby: Old World Wisconsin, nationally acclaimed pioneer living-history museum; Kettle Moraine State Forest South, with Ice Age landforms, lakes, hiking and cross-country ski trails; riding stables; sleigh rides. A short drive to downhill skiing, antiques shops, golf course.

*W*hen Riene Wells-Herriges and Dean Herriges, local historians and preservationists, began talking about moving from their 1880s farmhouse, Riene said, "I won't move into a new home unless it's like Hawks Inn."

No problem. Dean, a sixth-generation master carpenter whose family emigrated to Wisconsin from Germany in the 1840s, drew up plans to replicate Hawks Inn, an authentic 1846 stagecoach stop located in nearby Delafield.

What a job they've done. Their classic Greek Revival house is built atop a hill overlooking twenty acres of prairie plants and meadow. Dean used nineteenth-century building methods to fashion period architectural details such as hand-built window sashes, eyebrow windows, and pine plank floors, along with other labors of love.

"People don't realize that Wisconsin once had six hundred stagecoach inns," Dean said. "We wanted today's travelers to experience what staying at a stagecoach house was really like."

Riene personally greeted us at the door. Inside we felt heat from two wood-burning stoves that warm double parlors on the first floor: The Tap Room offers tavern tables for card games, books and magazines, and part of the antique collection that Riene has collected for more than twenty years; the formal parlor boasts a straw-filled Victorian couch and other handsome period furnishings.

Our third-floor room was huge, with pine plank floor, an 1840s rope bed (well strung, so I did "sleep tight"), and beautiful rag rugs made by Dean's grandmother.

Other guest rooms are equally handsome and spacious, including two suites offering something that nineteenth-century travelers never knew— whirlpool tubs.

For breakfast we feasted on Dean's cranberry and walnut pancakes, homemade raisin and cranberry breads, fresh fruits, and yogurt. The meal is served on Riene's antique English stoneware—part of a 700-piece collection— in the inn's dining room.

Hear the tick-tock of the clock in the dining room? That's coming from a pre–Civil War timepiece that still tells accurate time. And here's more pioneer-style fun: Riene's special 1800s weekends, with innkeepers (and guests) in period costumes and a six-course dinner that includes everything from quail with forcemeat stuffing to rabbit pie.

HOW TO GET THERE: From Milwaukee, take I–94 west to Wisconsin 67, then go south through Eagle to the inn, located about ½ mile north of Old World Wisconsin.

The Ephraim Inn
Ephraim, Wisconsin 54211

INNKEEPERS: Nancy and Tim Christofferson
ADDRESS/TELEPHONE: Route 42, P.O. Box 247; (920) 854–4515
ROOMS: 17; all with private bath, air-conditioning, and TV.
RATES: $95 to $175, single or double; EPB. Two-night minimum

throughout year with advanced reservations.

OPEN: April through October; weekends during winter.

FACILITIES AND ACTIVITIES: Across the street from bay and beach. Next to Wilson's Ice Cream Parlor. Nearby: a short walk to specialty shops and studios, sports facilities and activities (boating, sailboarding). A short drive to restaurants, golf, hiking trails, ski trails, Peninsula Players Theater, and Birch Creek Music Center.

I believe Ephraim has the most beautiful harbor in all Door County. The Ephraim Inn, located in the heart of this charming village's historic district, faces that harbor, affording guests one of the finest vistas around.

The inn itself, despite its conspicuous setting right next to the always packed Wilson's Ice Cream Parlor, is a haven for relaxed hospitality. Just about a decade old, it exudes the warmth of a fine country home, and its wood beams, exposed brick, and country antique reproductions add to the charm.

More than half of the guest rooms provide a magnificent view of the harbor and the tiered green bluffs that rise above it. Each is identified by a hand-carved and hand-painted wooden plaque affixed to the door.

Tulip Heart is one of my favorites, with its four-poster pine bed, fluffy bed quilt, and country cupboard for clothes. I especially liked the Shaker-style wall pegs that circle the room. An antique jelly cupboard keeps modern conveniences like the television out of sight.

Forget-Me-Not has more of the same, including an iron-and-brass-rail daybed and hand stenciling; and Tulip Star, on the second floor, boasts a four-poster English bed and an alcove window that affords more great harbor views.

For breakfast, count on fresh fruit and juices, Colombian coffee, homemade granola, freshly baked muffins, and egg dishes, all served in cozy din-

ing areas. Perhaps you'd enjoy a table across from a crackling fire on a brisk fall morning.

The inn's common room also faces the harbor and exudes a very masculine feeling. It's all oak paneling and exposed brick, with another fireplace and soft sofas for night talk.

Then get set for some wandering. Start next door at Wilson's Ice Cream Parlor, a Door County landmark since 1906, and where I first caught a glimpse of my wife-to-be. We were each staying at different country inns at the time.

HOW TO GET THERE: From Sturgeon Bay, take Wisconsin 42 into Ephraim. The inn is just past Wilson's Ice Cream Parlor.

White Gull Inn
Fish Creek, Wisconsin 54212

INNKEEPERS: Andy and Jan Coulson

ADDRESS/TELEPHONE: 4225 Main Street, P.O. Box 160-C; (920) 868-3517, fax (920) 868-2367

WEB SITE: www.whitegullinn.com

ROOMS: 13, plus 3 cottages and 2 buildings for multiple couples; all with private bath and air-conditioning. No smoking inn.

RATES: Main Lodge, Cliff House: $99 to $190, single or double; cottages: $200 to $275; EP. Midweek winter packages. Two-night minimum on high-season weekends, three-night minimum on some holidays.

OPEN: Year-round

FACILITIES AND ACTIVITIES: Wheelchair access to dining room; famous Door County fish boil featured on Wednesday, Friday, Saturday, and Sunday nights. Situated in the heart of historic Fish Creek: short walk to art galleries and specialty and antiques shops. Peninsula State Park, Peninsula Players (Shakespeare theater), and golf nearby.

he inn's "Master Boiler" sits perched on a small chair in the dining room, pumping a concertina and singing "oompah" songs to guests as they devour the latest fish boil—whitefish, potatoes, and a secret recipe boiled outside in a huge cauldron with flames darting toward the sky. Served with hot loaves of bread, homemade coleslaw, and mugs of ice-cold beer, it's a Door County institution. A tasty extra is home-baked cherry pie for dessert.

I like the casual atmosphere of the White Gull Inn; it makes me feel right at home. The landmark 1896 white clapboard also looks New England picture-perfect.

Local legend says that the inn originally sat on the other side of Green Bay, 18 miles away, in Marinette, Wisconsin. During a frigid Door County winter around the turn of the century, it was dragged on a crudely fashioned log sled by draft horses across the frozen waters to its present location—sort of a Victorian mobile home. Innkeeper Andy Coulson, however, says that he believes the White Gull, unlike its sister inn, the Whistling Swan, was built where it stands today.

Some guest rooms are comfortably furnished with country-Victorian antiques that create an intimate, romantic retreat. I loved the iron-rail beds that Andy has painted a cheery white. There are also high ceilings and plank floors covered with braided scatter rugs. Other cottages and houses call to mind family times.

The lobby has a large fireplace, often with a blazing fire to take the chill off a typically nippy Door County morning. There's also a common room with gas fireplace and color television.

Besides famous fish boils, the dining room serves dishes like beef Wellington, baked whitefish (a local favorite), and chicken piccata.

But don't miss the fish boil, especially you first-timers. It's not just a dinner; it's a real happening.

Also check out the Whistling Swan, a sister inn across the street. I love the quaint rooms and the enclosed porch overlooking Main Street.

HOW TO GET THERE: From Milwaukee, take Wisconsin 43 north. Near Manitowoc, take Wisconsin 42 north past Sturgeon Bay into Door County. In Fish Creek, turn left at the stop sign at the bottom of a hill along the twisting road and proceed about 3 blocks to the inn.

The Astor House
Green Bay, Wisconsin 54301

INNKEEPERS: Greg and Barbara Robinson

ADDRESS/TELEPHONE: 637 South Monroe Avenue; (920) 432-3585 or (888) 303-6370

WEB SITE: www.astorhouse.com

ROOMS: 5 suites; all with private bath. No smoking inn.

RATES: Weekend: $85 to $152, single or double; weekdays: $79 to $99, single or double; continental breakfast.

OPEN: Year-round

FACILITIES AND ACTIVITIES: Guest parlor, wraparound veranda. Located in Astor Historic District—take self-guided walking tour of notable homes. Short drive to Lambeau Field, Green Bay Packer Hall of Fame, Heritage Hill State Park, Oneida Casino, Weidner Center for the Performing Arts. Bay Beach Wildlife Sanctuary, Arena Expo Center.

*G*reen Bay's only bed-and-breakfast inn boasts a tony three-diamond rating. Not hard to understand once you've visited this gracious 1888 Victorian beauty.

Just look at the craftsmanship: the exterior boasts fishscale shingles, vertical boards, sunbursts, and circle motifs—all decidedly Victorian. Inside, there are leaded glass, 9-foot-tall oak pocket doors, original silver crystal chandelier, and a grand staircase with octagonal-carved spindles.

The Marseilles Garden suite is like a Monet flower garden come to life and perfect for lovers. Consider its ivy-laced headboard, arbor trellis, gas-log fireplace, and double-whirlpool room.

The Hong Kong Retreat is nearly 4,000 square feet of space, reached by a spiral staircase leading to the third floor. Luxuriate in the double jade whirlpool; the black tile fireplace is guaranteed to keep things cozy.

And the Vienna Balconies is a two-level suite with another double whirlpool in its bedroom and a private third-floor balcony overlooking the gardens.

Breakfast is delivered to your room or may be taken in the guest parlor. It might include scones, apple tortes, and baked apples and pears. Recipes are taken from renowned bed-and-breakfast cookbooks.

There's even turndown service at the Astor House. Finally, a reason for this rabid Chicago Bears fan to think of Green Bay and not envision those evil Packers.

HOW TO GET THERE: Located at the junction of Highways 54 and 57, 8 blocks from Green Bay's City Centre. From Milwaukee (Port Washington), take Wisconsin 57 north into Green Bay; it turns into Monroe Street in town. Watch for Wisconsin 54 and the inn.

Schneider's Oakwood Lodge
Green Lake, Wisconsin 54941

INNKEEPER: Mary Schneider

ADDRESS/TELEPHONE: 365 Lake Street; (920) 294-6580

ROOMS: 12; 9 with private bath, some with balcony.

RATES: $85 to $101, single; $101 to $120, double; EPB. Children, cribs, $10 extra per night. Two-night minimum on weekends; three-night minimum on holiday weekends. Off-season rates available.

OPEN: Year-round except November and March.

FACILITIES AND ACTIVITIES: Family room, room balconies, patio, private lake pier and raft. Water sports and activities. Will arrange mid-week golf packages. Nearby: three golf courses, including renowned Lawsonia; horseback riding; specialty shops in town; cross-country skiing.

The huge white cottage with the arched second-floor balcony jumped out at me as I approached the bend in the country road. It was surrounded by tall trees, perched lakeside in a perfect getaway setting.

I discovered that this is one of only a few buildings that remain of the original massive Oakwood Hotel complex built in the 1860s. Now it's a charming inn with "the best view of Green Lake."

I sat outside on the back-porch dining terrace, just a stone's throw from the lake, devouring some excellent breakfast specialties: homemade buttermilk pancakes. There were also hearty helpings of homemade breads and

rolls, and cakes and sweet rolls for morning sweet tooths. What a fabulous way to enjoy the day's first meal—lakeside alfresco. In cold weather breakfast in the dining room is also delightful.

There are twelve charming rooms in this historic building; my favorites are upstairs facing the lake. I like just to sit and watch all the colorful sails bob along the waters. Some of the rooms have high walnut headboards and brass beds.

HOW TO GET THERE: Travel Wisconsin 23 west to Business 23 and then turn left on South Street. Take South to Lake Street and turn right. Oakwood Lodge is at the intersection (bend of the road) of Lake Street and Illinois Avenue.

Wisconsin House Stage Coach Inn
Hazel Green, Wisconsin 53811

INNKEEPERS: Ken and Pat Disch

ADDRESS/TELEPHONE: 2105 East Main Street; (608) 854–2233

ROOMS: 8; 6 with private bath and 2 suites.

RATES: $65 to $125; EPB.

OPEN: Year-round

FACILITIES AND ACTIVITIES: Parlor, library, dining room, veranda, Crawford Garden. All the attractions of historic Galena, Illinois, are just 10 minutes away, including the U.S. Grant home, historic architecture, boutiques, craft and antique shops. Dog racing, riverboat rides in Dubuque, 15 minutes away.

*T*his 1846 stagecoach inn served boomtown travelers on the Milwaukee to Galena, Illinois, stage. They came here for business, and the business was lead mining.

The inn was purchased in 1853 by Jefferson Crawford as a residence for his family. He was a good friend of U. S. Grant, who visited here ofter, the last time being August 1868, at the occasion of Crawford's death.

Today, eight guest rooms offer respite for weary modern travelers to this new boomtown region—and the business this time is tourism. Best bet here is the Two-Bit Suite, which occupies the entire third floor, boasts a king-size canopy bed, and overlooks the garden. Though the Jefferson Crawford Suite, with its grand views south and west, is another charmer.

HOW TO GET THERE: From Galena, Illinois, take U.S. 20 west to Highway 80 north into Wisconsin and continue to Hazel Green. In town, the name of the street changes to North Percival. Turn right on Fairplay and go to East Main Street. The inn is on the corner.

The American Club 🧡 👥
Kohler, Wisconsin 53044

INNKEEPER: Susan Porter Green, vice president

ADDRESS/TELEPHONE: Highland Drive; (920) 457–8000 or (800) 344–2838, fax (920) 457–0299

WEB SITE: www.destinationkohler.com

ROOMS: 236; all with private whirlpool bath, air-conditioning, TV, and phone. Wheelchair accessible.

RATES: $220 to $950 for summer season (May 1 through October 31) rates. Off-season rates available. Two-night minimum on weekends from July through September. Several packages available.

OPEN: Year-round

FACILITIES AND ACTIVITIES: Nine restaurants and full-service dining rooms. Renowned for extravagant buffets, special-event and holiday feasts; large Sunday brunch. Ballroom. Sports Core, a world-class

health club. River Wildlife, 500 acres of private woods for hiking, horseback riding, hunting, fishing, trapshooting, canoeing. Cross-country skiing and ice skating. Also Kohler Design Center, shops at Woodlake, Kohler Arts Center, Waelderhaus. Nearby: antiquing, lake charter fishing, Kettle Moraine State Forest, Road America (auto racing).

BUSINESS TRAVEL: Located 5 minutes from downtown Sheboygan. Corporate rates, conference rooms, fax services.

*J*ust 4 miles from the shoreline of Lake Michigan, amid tall pines, patches of white birch, scrubbed farmhouses, and black soil, is one of Wisconsin's best-kept secrets. It's The American Club, a uniquely gracious guest house.

I found an uncommonly European ambience at this elegant inn. With its Tudor-style appointments of gleaming brass, custom-crafted oak furniture, crystal chandeliers, and quality antique furnishings, The American Club looks like a finely manicured baronial estate. It's also the only five-diamond resort hotel in the Midwest.

Built in 1918 as a temporary home for immigrant workers of the Kohler Company (a renowned plumbing manufacturer, still located across the street), the "boarding house" served as a meeting place where English and citizenship classes were taught—a genuine American Club.

Some rooms feature a four-poster canopied brass bed and huge marble-lined whirlpool bath. Special suites contain a saunalike environmental enclosure with a push-button choice of weather—from bright sun and gentle breezes to misty rain showers. And consider these guest room amenities: fluffy bathrobes, scales, twice-daily maid service, daily newspapers—the list goes on.

West-wing rooms are equally gracious. The Club's Inn on Woodlake offers sixty additional rooms ($139 to $300) that include continental breakfast and privileges at the Sports Core and Blackwolf Run.

The inn's showcase restaurant is The Immigrant, where I dined on a gourmet meal of smoked Irish salmon. The wine list was impressive, too. For dessert I walked to the Greenhouse in the courtyard. This antique English solarium is a perfect spot for chocolate torte and other Viennese delights.

The hotel's Pete Dye–designed Blackwolf Run golf course, comprising two very distinct eighteen-hole courses, is one of the most dramatic links around. On its opening in 1988, it was named the "Best New Public Course in the Nation" by *Golf Digest*. It's now rated one of the top three courses in the nation. I cannot get there often enough.

Another new course, Whistling Straits, looks like Scotland along Wisconsin's Lake Michigan Coastline. It boasts two layouts: the Straits course, all along the coast; and the Irish course. They are ranked 35th and 67th respectively on *Golf Magazine*'s prestigious "Top 100 Courses in the World."

HOW TO GET THERE: From Chicago, take I–94 north and continue north on I–43, just outside of Milwaukee. Exit on Wisconsin 23 west (exit 53B). Take 23 to County Trunk Y and continue south into Kohler. The inn is on the right. From the west, take I–94 south to Wisconsin 21 and go east to U.S. 41. Go south on 41 to Wisconsin 23, then head east into Kohler.

Frank Lloyd Wright's Seth Peterson Cottage
Lake Delton, Wisconsin 53940

INNKEEPER: Audrey Laatch, Preservation Board Chairperson

ADDRESS/TELEPHONE: Fern Dell Road (write c/o Sand County Service Company, Box 409, Lake Delton 53940); (608) 254–6551, fax (609) 254–4440

ROOMS: 1 cottage, with living room, dining room, kitchen, bedroom, bath. No smoking inn.

RATES: $250, single or double; EP.

OPEN: Year-round

FACILITIES AND ACTIVITIES: Located deep in the woods, high on a bluff overlooking Mirror Dells, Ho Chunk Casino, Mid-Continent Railway Steam Train. Nearby: skiing, fishing, hiking, biking, boating.

*H*ere's your only chance to overnight in a Frank Lloyd Wright original. The cottage sits on a wooded bluff overlooking Mirror Lake. It is much smaller than it looks in photos. But its austere Prairie stylings are unmistakably Frank Lloyd Wright.

In 1958 Seth Peterson, a lifelong Badger State resident and enthusiast of the master architect, convinced the ninety-year-old Wright to design a cottage. The famed architect allotted a tre- mendous amount of space in the limited area available.

The floor plan follows Wright's architectural philosophy, which he enunciated in 1954: "Organic architecture must come from the ground up into the light by gradual growth. It will itself be the ground of a better way of life."

The result: an elegant and simple building, often described as containing "more architecture per square foot than any other building Wright ever designed."

The cottage, perched atop a wooded bluff, is made of native sandstone. It boasts a dramatic sandstone floor that "mirrors the craggy cliffs on the lake and surrounding terrain."

A wall of windows lets natural light suffuse the interior while allowing a constant awareness of the closeness of nature—trees virtually surround the cottage. French doors opening onto a terrace allow breathtaking views of the water below. The structure also boasts the Wright signature—a massive sandstone fireplace in the living room.

An overnight here is something that won't soon be forgotten. It's like participating in history.

HOW TO GET THERE: From Chicago, Milwaukee, or Madison, take I–94 north to Wisconsin 23; go south to Shady Lane Road and turn left (east); proceed to Mirror Lake Road and turn left (north); then follow as the road turns into Fern Dell and proceeds east. Watch for the inn on the left side of the road. (If you come to Mirror Lake State Park headquarters, go back— you've gone too far east.)

French Country Inn
Lake Geneva, Wisconsin 53147

INNKEEPER: John Cole

ADDRESS/TELEPHONE: Highway 50 West, Route 4, P.O. Box 690; (262) 245–5220

ROOMS: 32, including 1 suite; all with private bath, air-conditioning, TV, and phone. All rooms have lake views.

RATES: Sunday through Thursday: $120 to $245, single or double; Friday and Saturday: $150 to $265, single or double; EPB. Two-night minimum on weekends. Special holiday and low-season rates.

OPEN: Year-round

FACILITIES AND ACTIVITIES: Full-service restaurant and bar, afternoon tea, outdoor swimming pool. Nearby: golf, horseback riding, and winter ski areas. A short drive to Lake Geneva specialty shops, boat tours, water activities.

*W*hat looks like a modest lakeside retreat from the outside reveals itself to be a magnificent showplace. I marveled at the lobby's intricate parquet floors, hand-carved solid oak staircase, and rich chandeliers—all shining and sparkling from rays of the sun filtering through a large skylight.

The inn's main house, including that magnificent staircase, was completely hand built by master craftsmen in Denmark in the 1880s. Later it was dismantled in piecemeal fashion, shipped by boat and rail to Chicago, and reassembled as the Danish Pavilion for the 1893 Columbian Exposition. After that the building was purchased and moved to its present site.

Eager to see the guest rooms, I wasn't disappointed. Located in annexes just steps from the main building, the rooms are gracefully done in country French styles, with brass beds, high-back chairs, and balloon drapes. Some have cathedral ceilings and skylights; all have their own gas fireplaces and private balconies overlooking Como Lake. In fact, the balconies are only 25 feet from the shoreline.

Late-afternoon tea, featuring samples from the inn's kitchen, is served in the parlor, itself a warm retreat dominated by a fireplace and more country French furnishings. A full breakfast of cheese and sausage omelettes, fresh fruit, juice, and homemade croissants should leave no one hungry.

HOW TO GET THERE: From Chicago, take I–94 to Wisconsin 50 west and proceed about 3 miles out of Lake Geneva. Then turn north at the inn sign off Highway 50 and proceed down the winding road to the inn.

The Geneva Inn
Lake Geneva, Wisconsin 53147

INNKEEPER: Richard Treptow, general manager

ADDRESS/TELEPHONE: N2009 State Road 120; (800) 441–5881

ROOMS: 37, including 4 suites. Wheelchair access.

RATES: $150 to $250, single or double; $350, lakeside suites; continental breakfast.

OPEN: Year-round

FACILITIES AND ACTIVITIES: Full-service restaurant, lounge, sitting room with fireplace, dock and marina. Nearby: a short drive to Geneva Lake Cruise Line docks; K. J. Flemings, Ltd. (Irish imports); Yerkes Observatory; Uncle John's Fun Park; downtown shops; golf courses, public beach, fishing. Hike the 26-mile path around the lake for up-close glimpses of multimillion-dollar mansions. Alpine Valley downhill ski area, horseback riding, dog track, Green Meadow Farm.

When the inn's pianist played Disney's "Beauty and the Beast" and "A Whole New World" for daughters Kate and Dayne, their candlelit dinner was complete. Prettied up in fancy dresses, the girls beamed, softly sang along with the music, and blushed as the musician nodded a smile their way.

This pampering was only the beginning of personal touches and extras served up by this elegant retreat on the shores of Lake Geneva. In fact, the Geneva Inn might be the best-kept secret in this old resort town. Resonating with the peaceful atmosphere and luxurious decor of an English inn, the thirty-seven-room hotel most closely resembles a dignified British gentlemen's club.

The hotel gleams with mahogany, oak, and other fine woods. Waverly wall coverings add rich textures, and hunter green dominates the color scheme. The centerpiece of the common rooms is a three-story, glass-topped atrium dominated by a massive brick fireplace.

Our girls loved their guest room, with its English pencil-post beds, brass lamps, refrigerator, and wet bar. But it was the oversize double whirlpool bath that got most of their attention, its bubbly waters providing almost as much fun as a Wisconsin Dells water park.

Pampering includes turndown service with complimentary cognac and chocolates; thick, fluffy bathrobes; specially made quilts adorning beds; a refrigerator fully stocked with all kinds of late-night treats; and a free newspaper waiting outside the door in the morning. The inn's breakfast buffet reminded us of morning meals in Europe: mounds of fresh fruits and melons, croissants, morning meats and cheeses, and fragrant teas that start the day off right.

Whatever Floats Your Boat

Two in-town recommendations: Our girls love the "ice cream social" boat float, offered by the Geneva Lake Cruise Line, located at the Riviera docks on Wrigley Drive. The seventy-five-minute cruise offers Lake Geneva history narration and Wisconsin-made ice cream.

Or take a float on the mail boat, one of the few remaining marine mail deliveries in the United States. What make this so interesting? Well, the boat never actually stops—the mail carrier must jump off the boat, deposit mail in boxes on the dock, and leap back onto the boat without ending up in the drink.

HOW TO GET THERE: From I-94, exit at Wisconsin 50 and go west to Lake Geneva. At the intersection of Wisconsin 50 and 120, turn south on 120 and continue 2 miles to the inn.

Fargo Mansion Inn
Lake Mills, Wisconsin 53551

INNKEEPERS: Tom Boycks and Barry Luce

ADDRESS/TELEPHONE: 406 Mulberry Street; (920) 648-3654

WEB SITE: www.fargomansion.com

ROOMS: 5, including 2 suites; all with private bath and air-conditioning; phone and TV on request. No smoking inn.

RATES: $89 to $170, single or double; EPB.

OPEN: Year-round

FACILITIES AND ACTIVITIES: Parlor, sitting room. Perennial flower garden. Bicycles-built-for-two available to guests. Nearby: Rock Lake beaches, boating, swimming. A short drive to restaurants, hiking trails, Native American burial grounds, Aztalan State Park, Drumlin Bike Trail, golf, tennis, trapshooting.

*I*arrived on a warm spring day to find the grounds of the inn masked by a cover of bright blue flowers. "Mr. Fargo planted the scilla more than one hundred years ago," Tom Boycks said. "They only last about two weeks, but they continue to come up every year."

Tom and Barry Luce have done a masterful job restoring this 1881 mansion built by Enoch J. Fargo, a local entrepreneur and descendant of the famed Wells Fargo family. The foyer alone is a stunning masterpiece of Queen Anne architecture, with a 30-foot-high ceiling and a handsome winding staircase of quarter-sawn oak.

Guest rooms, named for Fargo relatives and friends, are elegant and comfortable. The Elijah Harvey Suite celebrates that period when Victorians became fascinated with Turkish stylings. Earthy colors, Turkish rugs, an ornate Victorian double bed with marble-topped washstand, and a reading nook are inviting enough. But the bathroom includes a whirlpool surrounded by hand-cut Italian marble done in earth-tone colors that carry out the Turkish theme to the hilt. It's addictive, so don't be surprised if you begin to utter remarks such as "Take me to the Casbah." You'll also enjoy its private balcony.

It's one of my favorite getaway spots.

Tom and Barry call the E. J. Fargo Suite their "grandest." It has an 8½-foot Victorian queen-sized bed, a working marble fireplace warming a cozy sitting area, ceiling-to-floor bay windows providing a panorama of the grounds, and a private porch done up in wicker furniture during summer weather, perfect for sunset watching and relaxing.

Where's the bathroom? Go to the bookcase and "remove" a title called *The Secret Passage*. The bookcase swings open to reveal a secret passageway and a bathroom done entirely in Italian marble, with a whirlpool bath built for two and an oversize glass-enclosed shower. The effect is memorable.

Breakfast—which includes egg casseroles, morning meats, croissants, juice, and coffee—is often taken in the music room; the massive table can seat twenty. For dinner there are several restaurants nearby; the innkeepers will recommend one to suit your tastes.

On a walk after our meal, Barry said that the sidewalks surrounding the inn were the first in the state of Wisconsin. Fargo himself went to Germany to learn how to mix the concrete for them.

HOW TO GET THERE: From Milwaukee, take I–94 west to Lake Mills exit (Wisconsin 89). Go through town to Madison Street, turn left, then turn left on Mulberry Street and proceed to the inn.

Victorian Treasure Bed and Breakfast 💗

Lodi, Wisconsin 53555

INNKEEPERS: Kimberly and Todd Seidl

ADDRESS/TELEPHONE: 115 Prairie Street; (608) 592–5199 or (800) 859–5199

WEB SITE: www.victoriantreasure.com

ROOMS: 8, including 4 suites; all with private bath and air-conditioning. No smoking inn.

RATES: $89 to $199, single or double; EPB, afternoon wine, cheese, and fruit.

OPEN: Year-round

FACILITIES AND ACTIVITIES: Sitting rooms, porch. Nearby: water activities on Wisconsin River and Lake Wisconsin. Hiking, rock climbing, bird-watching on Baraboo Range. Also nearby: restaurants; downhill and cross-country skiing; Devil's Lake State Park, with 500-foot bluffs; American Players (Shakespearean) Theater in outdoor amphitheater; Taliesin, home of Frank Lloyd Wright; golf; bald eagle watching.

BUSINESS TRAVEL: Located about 20 miles north of Madison, 20 miles south of Baraboo. Corporate rates, meeting room, fax.

*I*t's hard to imagine that the rambling Bissell Mansion Victorian, with its expansive wraparound veranda, was built for only $3,000 in 1897 by lumber baron and Wisconsin state senator William G. Bissell. Snooping traced a great-granddaughter to Rockford, Illinois, and she gave the innkeepers some early-1800s photos of the house. These now hang on the inn walls.

Many original chandeliers, brass door fittings, and woodwork hark back to fine Victorian-era craftsmanship. The tulip-drop brass chandelier in the sitting room, which casts a warm glow over Victorian high-back chairs and a sofa, is one of the home's original gas fixtures.

I walked up a grand staircase, coming to a wide hallway that leads to the guest rooms. The handsome Queen Anne's Lace Room has a queen-sized four-poster lace canopy bed in front of three floor-to-ceiling windows draped with antique lace panels for privacy. It also has an expansive bath featuring a two-person whirlpool.

In the Victorian Rose Suite, an elegant queen-sized bed with antique Eastlake headboard and footboard is set amid a blaze of bold Victorian printed wall coverings. The effect is light and airy, with three huge windows that allow sunlight to filter into the room.

Oops. I forgot to mention this suite's parlor, which boasts a two-person corner whirlpool, topped with a mood inducing canopy, tucked away in a romantic alcove.

The Wild Ginger Room has handsome furnishings (especially the hand-carved walnut bed and bureau) and a porch perfect for stargazing.

All beds have down comforters, four pillows, and luxurious linens—real European style.

Kimberly Seidl's five-course gourmet breakfast might include fresh fruit with ginger syrup, home-baked nut breads and cinnamon rolls, vegetable frittata, omelettes, and locally "grown" sausages. The "house" specialty: pecan cream cheese-stuffed French toast topped with fresh fruit sauces.

Another choice—stay at the inn's other property, the Hutson House; it's an 1893 Queen Anne Victorian with four luxury suites that include whirlpool bath, fireplace, stereo, and wet bar. Perhaps the Angelica suite is the inn's finest. It boasts three rooms of Eastlake elegance, with steps leading up to a mahogany tester bed, double whirlpool, oak-manteled fireplace—even a private front porch.

I also like the Magnolia Suite, with its two-person corner whirlpool facing its own oak-manteled fireplace. Things can't get much better at this award-winning treasure.

HOW TO GET THERE: From Chicago or Milwaukee, take I–90/94 to Wisconsin 60 and go west into Lodi. In town take Route 60 (now called Lodi Street) 1 block west, then turn right on Prairie Street. The Bissell Mansion is the second house on the left.

Arbor House
Madison, Wisconsin 53711

INNKEEPER: John and Cathie Imes

ADDRESS/TELEPHONE: 3402 Monroe Street; (608) 238–2981

ROOMS: 8; all with private bath. No smoking inn.

RATES: $89 to $10, weekdays; $105 to $210, weekends. EPB.

OPEN: Year-round

FACILITIES AND ACTIVITIES: In the midst of Madison. Near State Capitol, all the shops and boutiques of downtown Madison, University of Wisconsin campus, Camp Randall Stadium. Walking distance to Lake Wingra. Near Lakes Monona and Mendota.

his award-winning environmentally responsible inn proves that you can be socially aware and still be an elegant ecological showplace. But first some history.

The 1853 house originally served as a stagecoach stop. Visitors would hitch their horses outside, drink and dance in what is now the sitting room, and sleep it off in an upstairs bedroom. It was known for its rough, rowdy characters and frequent John Wayne-style barroom brawls.

These days, the only fight that's put up here is to become even more urban-ecologically responsible. Water efficiency, nontoxic products, sustainable harvested woods, organic natural cottons, biodegradable cleaners, and more are the hallmark of the Arbor House

However, you won't be roughing it, Greenpeace style. In fact, many of the guest rooms are spectactular. Consider the Aldo Leopold, with its romantic poster bed, chapel ceiling, and arboretum window view. The John Muir boasts a pine sleigh bed and a balcony literally in the trees. And The Studio features a skylit whirlpool tub and stove fireplace.

HOW TO GET THERE: In Madison, go east on University Avenue toward North Park Street; turn right onto North Park; then turn right on Regent Street. Regent Street becomes Speedway Road, so continue west-southwest until Glenway Street; turn south (as marked) to Monroe, then turn left to the inn.

Canterbury Inn
Madison, Wisconsin 53703

INNKEEPERS: Trudy and Harvey Barash

ADDRESS/TELEPHONE: 315 West Gorham; (608) 258–8899 or (800) 838–3850

WEB SITE: www.madisoncanterbury.com

ROOMS: 6; all with private bath, wheelchair accessible. No smoking inn.

RATES: $130 to $375; special events (UW home football weekends, graduation weekends, holidays, art fair, etc.) rates slightly higher; continental breakfast.

OPEN: Year-round

**FACILITIES AND ACTIVI-
TIES:** Bookstore, coffeehouse, coffeehouse jazz
sessions, author readings,
afternoon teas, chamber
music, chess club, kids'
reading. Short walk to State
Street, State Capitol. Short
drive to Dane County Coliseum.

" "Y ou spend so much time in bookstores, you should live in one." This is an oft-repeated refrain in the Puhala household. So we did the next best thing. We spent the weekend in one. Officially called a bed, book, and breakfast, the Canterbury Inn boasts a decidedly English ambience. Its handsome bookstore, with arched interior doorways and comfy chairs for serious book browsings, rambles into several rooms, with stacks of tomes almost reaching the ceiling. And something's always happening on the other side of the store, home to Canterbury's coffeehouse.

Guest rooms are exquisite, each named for a traveler to Canterbury (from Chaucer's *Canterbury Tales*, of course). All boast handcrafted stencils that elaborate on their character's stories. I like the Merchant's Room especially for an entrance into the bath—its fanciful whimsy bespeaks of medieval artistry.

Can you sleep in the bed of the Knight's Room while Palamon and Arcite look longingly at you from their prison tower?

Maybe the Miller's Room is more your style; it has a painting of the poor lad known as Nicolas the Gallant, "and making love was his secret talent."

HOW TO GET THERE: From John Nolan Drive in Madison, take Broom Street west past Gotham (it's one-way the wrong way) to Gilman; turn right and go to Henry; turn right and proceed to Gorham; turn right to the inn.

Mansion Hill Inn
Madison, Wisconsin 53703

INNKEEPER: Anke Cramblit

ADDRESS/TELEPHONE: 424 North Pinckney Street; (608) 255–3999 or (800) 798–9070

WEB SITE: www.mansionhillinn.com

ROOMS: 11, including 2 suites; all with private bath, air-conditioning, cable TV, stereo, VCR, and minibar.

RATES: $120 to $340, single or double. Midweek rates available. Continental breakfast.

OPEN: Year-round

FACILITIES AND ACTIVITIES: Victorian parlor, dining room (with catered dinners available), belvedere, private wine cellar, garden. Access to health spa, private dining club. Mansion Hill Historic District invites touring, especially Period Garden Park. Madison is state capital; many fine ethnic restaurants, specialty shops, art galleries, recitals, theaters, nightclubs. Nearby: University of Wisconsin main campus; swimming, fishing, boating in surrounding lakes.

*A*n extraordinary inn! I knew it would be special as soon as a tuxedo-clad manservant opened a tall door, graced with elegantly stenciled glass, to greet me officially.

This 1858 building is an architectural showplace. Its fine construction materials include white sandstone from the cliffs of the Mississippi, Carrara marble from Italy, and ornamental cast iron from Sweden. The original owner imported old-world artisans to do all the construction work. It shows.

Nearly $2 million has been spent to restore the mansion to its former magnificence. I loved the handsome arched windows and French doors that let the sunlight spill in. Hand-carved white marble fireplaces blaze with warmth, and a spectacular spiral staircase winds four floors up to the belvedere, which provides a panoramic view of the city.

All the rooms are exquisitely furnished in beautiful antiques—some of the finest I have ever seen. I stayed in the McDonnell Room, which evokes a bold Empire atmosphere. I felt like royalty in these surroundings: arched windows, French doors, a large crystal chandelier, and an incredible 10-foot-tall tester bed that one might find in the sleeping quarters of the Prince of Wales. It also had an oval whirlpool tub, where I soaked in the swirling hot waters with a set of tubside stereo headphones clamped on my ears.

Another extraordinary room has floor-to-ceiling bookcases with a hidden door opening into an incredible bathroom with arched windows, classical Greek Revival columns, and a huge marble tub.

A deliriously romantic retreat is the Turkish Nook, swathed in Victorian silks, strewn with pillows and ottomans, and featuring a tented sultan's bed— all evoking the sensual delights and intrigues of the mysterious Middle East.

It's easy to understand why "Too much is not enough" is the inn maxim. You can dine on gourmet meals, which are specially arranged on request. Or explore Madison's gustatory delights on your own, perhaps at L'Etoile, L'Escargot, or The White Horse Inn.

HOW TO GET THERE: From Milwaukee, take I–94 west to Madison. Exit west on Wisconsin 30 to Wisconsin 113. Go south to Johnson, then west to Baldwin. Turn south on Baldwin to East Washington, then west toward the capitol building. At Pinckney Street, turn north. The inn is on the corner of Pinckney and Gilman.

Lauerman Guest House Inn
Marinette, Wisconsin 54143

INNKEEPERS: Sherry and Steve Homa, Tony and Doris Spaude

ADDRESS/TELEPHONE: 1975 Riverside Avenue; (715) 732–7800

ROOMS: 7; all with private bath, air-conditioning, TV, and phone.

RATES: $75 to $80; EPB.

OPEN: Year-round

FACILITIES AND ACTIVITIES: Menominee River marina 2 blocks away.

Two golf courses within 2 miles. Restaurants, Theater on the Bay, University of Wisconsin at Marinette a short drive away.

With towering Corinthian pillars, a commanding balcony overlooking the Menominee River, and an ornate portico that once welcomed horse-drawn coaches bringing formally attired gentlemen and their handsomely dressed ladies, the Lauerman Guest House Inn was hailed as one of the most outstanding examples of Colonial Revival architecture in this part of the Midwest. Built in 1910 by its namesake—a local businessman who was grossing more than $1 million a year from his department store—the inn exhibits all the special touches of turn-of-the-century elegance.

Guest rooms are charming. One of my favorites is the Bow Room, with its silk-screened wallpaper done in an English garden floral pattern. Through the huge window I could gaze at the stately black walnut trees that dot the grounds. I even liked the bath, with its original soaking tub, pedestal sink, and cameo window. Freda's Room has handsome mahogany woodwork as well as a whirlpool bath; the Master Suite offers more mahogany and bird's-eye maple woodwork and French doors that open to an expansive private porch overlooking the Menominee River.

For breakfast consider waffles, eggs, sausage, juice, and coffee. Then just get out and enjoy the countryside.

HOW TO GET THERE: From Green Bay, take U.S. 41 north into Menominee. Turn left on Riverside Avenue and continue 1½ blocks to the inn.

The Audubon Inn
Mayville, Wisconsin 53050

INNKEEPER: John K. Peterson

ADDRESS/TELEPHONE: 45 North Main Street; (920) 387–5858

WEB SITE: www.classicinns.com

ROOMS: 17; all with private bath, air-conditioning, TV, and phone. Pets OK.

RATES: $109.50 to $119.50, single or double. EPB on weekends; continental breakfast weekdays.

OPEN: Year-round

FACILITIES AND ACTIVITIES: Lunch, dinner, Sunday brunch. Sitting rooms, bar with lounge. Nearby: Horicon Marsh, spring and fall geese migration; Kettle Moraine State Forest, hiking, biking, and backpacking; golfing; cross-country skiing; lake activities.

*I*t's difficult to articulate the scope of this elegant renovation. An 1896 hotel that had fallen into disrepair now sparkles as a community showplace thanks to Wisconsin country inn king Rip O'Dwanny.

Rip and his partners invested more than $500,000 in handsome woodwork alone, then imported hand-dyed carpets from Great Britain and commissioned fourteen fabulous stained-glass windows that adorn the dining room and bar. They also commissioned a master craftsman from Wisconsin

Wisconsin's Most Beautiful Bar

The bar is quite special. Consider that Rip had the second and third floors above the bar removed to the ceiling. Then he fashioned skylights on the third-floor roof and opened the second floor completely so that natural light could fall on a massive, hand-etched glass depiction of geese in flight over the marsh (the hallmark of this wetland bordertown) that is the lounge's incredible centerpiece and ceiling. It's already been called the most beautiful bar in Wisconsin.

to create marvelous handmade etched-glass panels that decorate the inn. Did I say decorate? These are not mere decorations, but fine works of art.

Guest rooms are superbly crafted, boasting four-poster canopy beds handmade in New Hampshire and adorned by handcrafted quilts, Victorian-inspired wall coverings "imported" from California, double whirlpool tubs, Shaker-inspired writing desks, brass lamps, and wooden window blinds.

"I feel that this is the ultimate country inn," Rip said. "Not only does the inn offer luxurious comfort and privacy but it's also a great restaurant that employs four master chefs and a pastry chef."

In fact, my gourmet dinner rivaled anything I've ever tasted in a fancy New York restaurant. The menu changes monthly, but when offered, I highly recommend the swordfish moutarde (a charbroiled steak served atop a mustard cream sauce and wonderfully presented). Also impressive: grilled barbarie breast of duck, served with raspberry sauce, and New York strip steak au poivre, adorned with cracked peppercorn sauce.

You'll be sorry if you don't sample an incredible strawberry dessert tart.

HOW TO GET THERE: From Milwaukee, take U.S. 45 north to Wisconsin 67; then go west into Mayville's downtown district and the inn.

Candlewick Inn
Merrill, Wisconsin 54452

INNKEEPERS: Ken and Jane Oswald

ADDRESS/TELEPHONE: 700 West Main Street; (715) 536–7744 or (800) 382–4376

WEB SITE: //members.aol.com/thewick89/index.htm

ROOMS: 5; all with private bath. No smoking.

RATES: $60 to $95, single or double; continental weekdays, EPB weekends.

OPEN: Year-round

FACILITIES AND ACTIVITIES: Living room, dining room, screened porch, library. Short ride to bicycle trails, Council Grounds State Park, cross-country skiing, downhill at Rib Mountain State Park, Wisconsin River canoeing, fishing.

*O*ne of the main reasons my brother, Mark, and I come to Merrill is to thunder down the Underdown, a 21-mile-long bushwacking mountain bike trail that winds through some of the most rugged terrain in northern Wisconsin. It follows old logging paths and unbroken tall-grass switchbacks and is named, by the way, for Bill, a moonshiner who based his still operations deep in these woods during Prohibition days.

Now the only thing that'll get you high up here is fresh air, blue skies, and a great biking challenge that also includes other world-class routes like the Harrison Hills Trails, the Hiawatha Trail, Parrish Highlands Trail, Augustyn Springs Trail, Jack Lake Trail, Bearskin State Trail—the list seems endless.

While you're biking the area, you can overnight at the Candlewick Inn, a historic 1880s home transformed into a comfortable bed-and-breakfast. The old lumber baron–era house is an elegant, grace-filled refuge from the biking trails, with five guest rooms decorated with antiques, handmade quilts, and cozy comforters.

And don't miss breakfast. You'll need those homemade breads, muffins, and sweets to carry you on two wheels for another day.

HOW TO GET THERE: The inn is located on Highway 64 in the west section of Merrill. It's at the intersection of West Main (Highway 64 in town) and State Street, just north and east of the Wisconsin River. If you're on Highway 64 at the Historic Courthouse or museum, you've gone too far east.

County Clare
Milwaukee, Wisconsin 53202

INNKEEPER: Cary "Rip" O'Dwanny

ADDRESS/TELEPHONE: 1234 North Astor Street; (414) 272–5273, fax (414) 290–6300

ROOMS: 41; all with private bath and double whirlpools, four-poster bed, cable TV.

RATES: $119.50 to $129.50, single or double.

OPEN: Year-round

FACILITIES AND ACTIVITIES: Great restaurant, Irish pub bar, live Irish entertainment. Short walk/drive to Lake Michigan shoreline; downtown shopping, Milwaukee Art Museum, Cathedral Square; running paths; Summerfest grounds, which hosts all kinds of massive festivals, including Irish Fest.

Me mother, herself, would love to visit this wonderful Irish inn, which is a little bit of Auld Sod plunked down near the magnificient Milwaukee lakefront on the city's fashionable East Side. Her family comes from County Armagh, St. Patrick's Day is always a big deal, and she loves Notre Dame.

In other words, Ma sounds perfect for this place.

Why County Clare in Suds City? As Innkeeper Rip O'Dwanny notes, during his frequent visits to Ireland, he's not only acquired many friends but has gained a better understanding of what it means to be Irish.

"I've concluded that it's as much a state of mind as it is a nationality," he said. "County Clare has been created to provide our guests with an Emerald Isle experience."

It sure does. Much resembling an Irish inn, County Clare exudes warmth, charm, and Irish character. Guest rooms are elegant, with four-poster beds, Axminster carpeting, and baths that boast a double whirlpool and a separate, large vanity. The inn restaurant is another slice of Ireland, where you can enjoy great Irish pub food, feel the warmth of a peat fireplace in the hearth, and listen to the lilting brogues of Irish patrons and staff.

Irish Logic

I love the old Guinness posters displayed throughout the bar and restaurant, as well as the Gaelic sayings on both walls and menu. Some of the best are "When the blossom grows white, the potatoes are good," "Don't praise the bread until it's baked," and "Laughter is the gayest where the food is best."

But here's one even me dear old Ma can't explain to me: "Never sell your hens on a wet day."

Note the twenty stained-glass windows that circle the restaurant: Each bears the colorful crest of Ireland's many counties.

Let's get back to food for a moment. As the menu says, Irish cooking is like an Irish song—it's simple and tasty on the tongue, while filling and wholesome for body and spirit. But these selections are anything but "simple." Consider tenderloin Shannon as an appetizer: fried curry tenderloin with a light orange marmalade and mustard sauce; smoked Irish salmon salad with goat cheese; County Clare Meatloaf, with carmelized onions and Worchestire Irish Cream gravy; or even a corned beef sandwich, done the Dublin way.

Then there's a wonderful bar serving Guinness on tap—perhaps the world's most wonderful thirst quencher. At nights you're likely to hear plenty of Irish music, much of it performed by artists from Ireland.

Everyone will wake up to a bright "top o' the mornin'" after a stay at County Clare.

HOW TO GET THERE: From Chicago, take I-94 west to I-794 east in Milwaukee, and exit on Van Buren; follow for 8 blocks to Knapp, turn right, and the inn is 3 blocks ahead.

The Pfister 🎭 📱
Milwaukee, Wisconsin 53202

INNKEEPER: Rosemary Steinfest, general manager

ADDRESS/TELEPHONE: 424 East Wisconsin Avenue; (414) 273-8222 or (800) 678-8946, fax (414) 273-0747

ROOMS: 307, including historic hotel rooms and suites; all with private bath, air-conditioning, and phone. Wheelchair accessible.

RATES: Rooms: $264, single or double; suites and specialty rooms: $314 to

$450; EP. Special packages available.

OPEN: Year-round

FACILITIES AND ACTIVITIES: The Greenery, a full-service restaurant, lunch buffet in Cafe Rouge, The English Room, 24-hour room service; swimming pool, massage therapy, hotel shops, famed fireplace room for drinks and gatherings. Nearby: Grand Avenue Mall, Bradley Center (Milwaukee Bucks NBA basketball games). A short drive to Miller Park (Milwaukee Brewers MLB baseball games).

BUSINESS TRAVEL: Located in the heart of downtown Milwaukee, a few minutes walk from City Hall, Mecca Convention Center. Corporate rates, conference rooms, fax.

*E*lvis stayed here. So did Buffalo Bill, Jack London, and Arturo Toscanini. Ditto for nearly every president since William McKinley. Luciano Pavarotti was enamored of the towels. And it's one of the few places where Rodney Dangerfield got respect.

Seems just about anybody who's anybody stays at the Pfister, Milwaukee's grande dame hotel as well as one of the Midwest's most distinguished hostelries. What's the secret?

"People come to the Pfister to come to the Pfister," said Peter Mortensen, chief concierge. That's true since a five-year, multimillion-dollar restoration has returned the 1893 hotel to its former grandeur. There are hand-painted murals on the ceiling, terra-cotta angels guarding a turn-of-the-century fireplace, ornate marble columns, gold-leaf detailing, brass and gilt chandeliers—and that's just in the lobby.

Each of the 307 rooms has a marble bathroom, complete with hair dryer and mini-television. Brass and mahogany are everywhere. Many suites, including those in the historic wing, feature a whirlpool tub and three telephones—bedside, deskside, and in the bathroom.

Similar rooms in the twenty-three-story Pfister Tower, added to the original building in 1966, offer breathtaking views of Lake Michigan. (Its Presidential Suite, where I once spent a memorable weekend, resembles a posh penthouse apartment, complete with master bedroom and wet bar.) Guest room furnishings include everything from Chinese Chippendale cabinets to elegant Renaissance chairs.

Of course, the rationale for going to an elegant hotel is to see and be seen. So get out of your room and head to the hotel's English Room, where you can dress to the nines for a "grand hotel" dining experience.

Winner of numerous culinary awards, this Milwaukee institution offers selections such as breast of pheasant prepared with a peppered game sauce and celery chips, and sautéed twin tenderloins of beef with roasted garlic potato puree and grand mustard sauce, all served by tuxedoed waiters. And who can pass up a dessert of bananas Foster or cherries jubilee?

Need some exercise after all that food? Walk around the lobby and second-floor mezzanine, graced with what's claimed to be the largest hotel collection of Victorian art in the world.

Or head to the glass-encased, twenty-third-floor swimming pool for laps and a sweeping panorama of the city. Forget about bringing towels—there are plenty of fluffy ones available. Before leaving, lounge around the lobby's historic fireplace. Rediscovered during restoration, it's where hotel guests and full-time Milwaukeans used to gather in the hotel's grand turn-of-the-century days. "I like to think of it as Milwaukee's living room," Peter said.

HOW TO GET THERE: From Chicago, take I-94 (Tri-State Tollway) to Milwaukee; exit at I-794/Downtown Milwaukee (get in the right-hand lane). Follow that to the Van Buren/Jackson exit; get off and follow that exit (as it veers left) to Mason Street. Turn left and go 2 blocks to Jefferson; finally, turn left and continue to the hotel.

WinterGreen
Mountain, Wisconsin 54149

INNKEEPERS: Joyce Mahlik and Bob Gale

ADDRESS/TELEPHONE: 16330 Thelen Road; (715) 276-6885

ROOMS: 4; all with private bath, 2 with whirlpool tubs.

RATES: $75 to $115; EPB.

OPEN: Year-round

FACILITIES AND ACTIVITIES: Gathering room, library, gift shop. In the midst of the Nicolet National Forest. Short drive to fish hatchery, historic logging camp, canoeing outfitters, cross-country ski, biking and hiking trails.

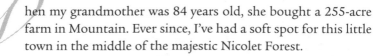 hen my grandmother was 84 years old, she bought a 255-acre farm in Mountain. Ever since, I've had a soft spot for this little town in the middle of the majestic Nicolet Forest.

That's where tranquil WinterGreen is nestled, surrounded by tall pine, aspen, birch, and maple trees and overlooking a secluded lake. Inside, Bob's handcrafted furniture is a welcome respite for hikers and bikers resting up in the handsome gathering room.

Guest rooms also are country elegant. The White Pine Room boasts a wrought-iron lace canopied bed with a luxurious down-filled comforter that'll keep you warm on both chilly summer and winter nights. The Teaberry Room boasts its own whirlpool tucked in a private alcove. You can catch a glimpse of the inn's private lake from the Loon Room. And there's another whirlpool with a forest view in the Trillium Room.

HOW TO GET THERE: The inn is located about 72 miles northwest of Green Bay. From Green Bay, take U.S. 41 north to State Road 64 and go west; proceed to State Road 32 and go north. The inn is 6 miles north of Mountain on Highway 32 and go north. The inn is 6 miles north of Mountain on Highway 32 and Thelen Road.

Norman General Store
Norman, Wisconsin 54216

INNKEEPERS: Anne and Jerry Sinkula

ADDRESS/TELEPHONE: E3296 Highway G; (920) 388–4580

ROOMS: 4; all with private bath, 2 with whirlpool. No smoking inn.

RATES: $65 to $95, single or double; EPB.

OPEN: Year-round

FACILITIES AND ACTIVITIES: Music room, dining room. Short drive to Lake Michigan, fishing in East Twin River, biking and hiking through countryside on Ice Age and Ahnapee Trails, Gree Bay, Door County, Fos Cities, agricultural tours.

*T*his little charmer is located in a tiny crossroads village in the heart of Wisconsin's Czech community—a picturesque dairy farm hamlet like several that still dot the Badger State landscape. Jerry and Anne Sinkula, former dairy farmers themselves, lovingly restored the historic structure, whose store was built in 1882 while the attached house was added in 1904. It was some project; the door leading into the General Store alone was covered with ten layers of old paint.

Today as you stroll through the house, you might think you've stepped back in time. Many of the furnishings belonged to families who had homes in the area. Guest rooms boast more antiques; of course, there's a nod to the modern in two bedchambers—whirlpool baths.

Two of the guest rooms—Valley View and Maple View—overlook miles of farmland and the graceful lines of the East Twin River Valley. The Summer Kitchen, originally located behind the General Store, also has been completely renovated and is perfect for two couples or families with older kids.

Anne cooks up a dairyman's breakfast for guests: farm-fresh eggs, made-from-scratch breads and muffins, homemade coffee cakes, and more.

And as former dairy farmers, the innkeepers can help you discover authentic rural treasures. Want to visit a working dairy farm? No problem, they'll arrange it. How about tours of the area's ethnic Czech heritage? Again, your wish is their pleasure.

HOW TO GET THERE: From Green Bay, take I–43 south to Highway 29. Go east to Highway 42 and turn north; continue until reaching County Road G, then turn left (west), and continue into Norman and the inn, located on County Road G.

Inn at Pine Terrace
Oconomowoc, Wisconsin 53066

INNKEEPER: Rich Borg

ADDRESS/TELEPHONE: 371 Lisbon Road; (262) 567–7463

WEB SITE: www.innatpineterrace.com

ROOMS: 13; all with private bath, air-conditioning, phone, and TV, 6 with double whirlpool bath. Wheelchair accessible. No smoking inn.

RATES: $65.51 to $160, single or double; continental breakfast.

OPEN: Year-round

FACILITIES AND ACTIVITIES: Sitting room, swimming pool, breakfast room, conference room. Nearby: short walk to Lac La Belle for swimming, fishing, boating, and three beaches. Restaurants and Olympia Ski Area, with downhill and cross-country skiing, a short drive away.

Cary O'Dwanny and his wife, Christine, two of the principal owners, greeted me outside their inn, an impressive three-story Victorian mansion built in 1884 by the Schuttler family, well-known wagon makers from Chicago. In fact, two Schuttler sons married girls whose families used those wagons to haul barrels of beer for their breweries; one was an Anheuser, another a Busch.

The restoration, which took more than two years to complete, is an accomplished one. Cary spent more than $750,000 in millwork alone to bring back the elaborate butternut and walnut moldings that are everywhere. Furniture, done in antique Eastlake style, was custom made especially for the inn. A curving walnut handrail that crowns the three-story staircase is valued at $55,000.

Most bathrooms have a marble-lined two-person whirlpool bath. Guestroom doors have brass hinges and hand-carved wooden doorknobs. Custom wall coverings and brooding Victorian paint colors evoke the period as almost no other inn has before.

Once the town was an exclusive vacation spot for wealthy Southern families escaping the summer heat. "The mansion was the 'in' place to be," Cary said. "Five U.S. presidents were guests here, beginning with Taft." Other notables included the likes of Mark Twain and Montgomery Ward.

Elegant guest rooms are named for historic residents of Oconomowoc. Most are huge by inn standards, with the first-floor beauty perhaps the showpiece. It features a massive bedroom area with a crowning touch: marble steps leading to a marble platform, upon which sits a white enamel, claw-foot bathtub illuminated by a bank of three ceiling-to-floor windows—shuttered for privacy, of course.

Rooms on the third floor are smaller, since these are the old servant's quarters; however, they are no less attractive. My room, named for Captain Gustav Pabst, was a charming hideaway with slanting dormer ceilings that created a small sitting-room alcove. Its brass lighting fixtures, rich woodwork, deep green wall coverings, double whirlpool tub, and tiny window offer a view of Lac La Belle.

A breakfast buffet, served in the dining room on the lower level, means cereals, fresh fruits, home-baked muffins, and coffee.

Later you can lounge at the inn's swimming pool or take a dip in the refreshing water while already making plans for your return visit here.

HOW TO GET THERE: From Milwaukee, take I–94 west to U.S. 67. Exit north and continue through town to Lisbon Road. Turn right; the inn is just down the street.

St. Croix River Inn 💚
Osceola, Wisconsin 54020

INNKEEPER: Sonja Smith

ADDRESS/TELEPHONE: 305 River Street; (715) 294–4248 or (800) 645–8820

WEB SITE: www.stcroixriverinn.com

ROOMS: 7; all with private bath and air-conditioning, 2 with TV.

RATES: Friday and Saturday, $100 to $200; Sunday through Thursday, $85 to $150; single or double; EPB. Gift certificates available.

OPEN: Year-round

FACILITIES AND ACTIVITIES: Outdoor porch, sitting room overlooking St. Croix River. Nearby: several area antiques shops, canoeing, fishing, downhill and cross-country skiing at Wild Mountain or Trollhaugen. A short drive to restaurants and Taylors Falls, Minnesota—a lovely little river town with historic-homes tours and cruises on old-fashioned paddle wheelers.

*T*his eighty-plus-year-old stone house is poised high on a bluff overlooking the scenic St. Croix River. It allows unsurpassed, breathtaking views while providing one of the most elegant lodgings in the entire Midwest.

I'm especially fond of a suite with a huge whirlpool bath set in front of windows, allowing you to float visually down the water while pampering yourself in a bubble bath.

The house was built from limestone quarried nearby which belonged to the owner of the town's pharmacy and remained in his family until a few years ago.

Now let's get right to the rooms (suites, really), which are named for riverboats built in Osceola. Perhaps (and this is a big perhaps) Jennie Hays is my all-time favorite inn room. It is simply exquisite, with appointments that remind me of exclusive European hotels. I continue to rave about a magnificent four-poster canopy bed that feels as good as it looks and a decorative tile fireplace that soothes the psyche as well as chilly limbs on crackling-cool autumn or frigid winter nights.

Then there is the view! I'm almost at a loss for words. A huge Palladian window, stretching from floor to ceiling, overlooks the river from the inn's bluff-top perch. It provides a romantic and rewarding setting that would be hard to surpass anywhere in the Midwest. The room has a whirlpool tub, and there's a private balcony with more great river views.

The G. B. Knapp Room is more of the same: a huge suite, with a four-poster canopy bed adorned with a floral quilt, tall armoire, its own working gas fireplace, and a whirlpool tub. Walk through a door to the enclosed porch (more like a private sitting room), with windows overlooking the river. There are also exquisite stenciling, bull's-eye moldings, and private balconies.

Pampering continues at breakfast, served in your room. It might include fresh fruit and juices, omelettes, waffles, French toast, or puff pastries stuffed with ham and cheese, as well as home-baked French bread and pound cake.

The innkeeper also delivers to your room a pot of steaming coffee and the morning paper a half hour before your morning meal. Sonja can recommend a great place for dinner, but you simply may never want to leave your comfortable quarters.

Let's face it: This is one of the Midwest's most romantic retreats—pure grace and elegance.

HOW TO GET THERE: From downtown Osceola, turn west on Third Avenue and follow it past a hospital and historic Episcopal church (dating from 1854, with four turreted steeples). The inn is located on the river side of River Street.

52 Stafford
Plymouth, Wisconsin 53073

INNKEEPER: Sean O'Dwanny

ADDRESS/TELEPHONE: 52 Stafford Street, P.O. Box 565;
(920) 893-0552 or (800) 421-4667

WEB SITE: www.classicinns.com

ROOMS: 20; all with private bath, air-conditioning, TV, and phone.
Wheelchair accessible. Well-behaved pets OK.

RATES: $89.50 to $139.50, single or double; EPB on weekends;
continental breakfast weekdays. Two- or three-night minimums on
Road America race weekends.

OPEN: Year-round

FACILITIES AND ACTIVITIES: Dinner. Sitting room, Irish folksinger/
entertainment in bar. Nearby: Road America in Elkhart Lake; state parks
with hiking, biking, nature trails, cross-country skiing (in season), Old
Wade historic site, swimming and fishing at local lakes, charter fishing
on Lake Michigan.

*S*ean's dad, Cary O'Dwanny, better known as Rip, has created a little bit
o' Ireland in the middle of cheese country: 52 Stafford, an "authentic"
Irish country house complete with imported European appointments,
classy guest rooms, and Guinness Stout on tap.

"I wanted the feeling of casual elegance," Rip told me as we shared a pint
of bitters, "where you could feel at home in blue jeans or a tuxedo.

"I also decided to use only the
finest materials when decorating
the inn," he said. First-floor hardwoods are all solid cherry, with
crown moldings and solid-brass
chandeliers (weighing eighty
pounds apiece) adding classical
touches.

Rip picked the yarn colors for
the handmade floral carpet
imported from England that

graces the inn. Much of the leaded glass came from Germany. Chinese silk adorns lobby wing chairs. The bar is imposing. It's solid cherry, stretching almost to the ceiling. Green and white tiles cover the footrest. Then there's beautiful hand-sandblasted etched glass, with deep-relief designs of harps and wreaths done by a local craftsman. The glass gave off a lilting greenish glow. Just pull up a bar stool, order a Guinness on tap, and you'll be close to heaven.

All rooms are individually decorated. Mine had a handsome English four-poster bed and fox-hunt wall prints, tall shuttered windows, crown ceiling moldings, and an elegant brass chandelier. Another special inn feature is a first-floor antique leaded-glass window—above a fireplace. It has more than 400 jewels and beads in it, while the fireplace flue must swing to the left, around the window.

Rip's breakfast, served in the inn's handsome dining room, offers huge omelettes, French toast, homemade muffins, and much more.

The inn's chefs have fashioned quite a gustatory reputation for 52 Stafford and one of its sister inns, The Audubon Inn, located in Mayville, Wisconsin. Consider Guinness brisket (a beef brisket simmered in Irish stout and served with boiled carrots, Kilkenny potatoes, leeks, and cabbage). Or try the Stafford steak (a certified eight-ounce black Angus beef tenderloin served with a shiitake mushroom sauce). And how can you resist Bailey's Irish cheesecake for dessert?

A final note: 52 Stafford's Saint Patrick's Day celebrations have been known to last for an entire week before March 17 and culminate with a huge parade.

HOW TO GET THERE: From Milwaukee, take I-43 north, switching to Wisconsin 57 just past Grafton. At Wisconsin 23, turn west and drive into Plymouth. At Stafford Street, turn south. The inn is on the right side of the street.

The Rochester Inn
Sheboygan Falls, Wisconsin 53085

INNKEEPERS: Sean and Jaquelyn O'Dwanny

ADDRESS/TELEPHONE: 504 Water Street; (920) 467-3123

WEB SITE: www.rochesterinn.com

ROOMS: 6, including 4 suites; all with private bath, air-conditioning, TV, and phone. Well-behaved pets OK.

RATES: $99.50 to $169.50, single or double, Sunday through Thursday;

$89.50 to $139.50, single or double, Friday and Saturday; EPB. Two-night minimum on special festival weekends.

OPEN: Year-round

FACILITIES AND ACTIVITIES: Nearby: a short drive to restaurants, Kettle Moraine State Forest for biking and hiking, Lake Michigan fishing and boating, Road America (automobile racing), Blackwolf Run for golfing, Kohler Design Center.

*A*n elegant creation, this 1839 National Historic Landmark has been transformed from a pioneer general store into a den of opulence. Inn rooms are quite breathtaking, each with its own parlor, fashioned with quality antique reproductions that include wing chairs, Chippendale-style sofas, and finely polished armoires.

Though each has its own distinctive look, they are similar in their Victorian-inspired stylings. For example, the Charles D. Cole Room (named after the Sheboygan Falls settler who built this structure) is swathed in handsome wall coverings produced in California and features a pencil-post bed adorned

Green Dining

For dinner wander to Sean O'Dwanny's father's flagship inn, 52 Stafford, for wonderful gourmet meals. Or just enjoy the Irish folk music performed by artists brought directly from the Auld Sod. Might as well take a pull on a Guinness, since your stay at the Rochester entitles you to two complimentary drinks from the 52 Stafford bar.

(By the way, early settlers named this town Rochester, only to discover that a village in New York claimed the same name—so they changed it to Sheboygan Falls.)

Sean's father calls this "the classiest little inn in America." He may be right. And we may have the makings of a country inn family dynasty.

with a handmade quilt, its own wet bar, and a double whirlpool bath.

Breakfast treats, taken in a small dining room, include a choice of quiche, French toast or pancakes, scrambled eggs with ham or sausage, cinnamon and butter croissants, and fresh fruit. Innkeeper Jacquelyn O'Dwanny also offers specialties such as poached pears, stuffed French toast, and pecan waffles. She can arrange a prebreakfast sip of juice or coffee in your room.

Take a peek at the photo hanging above the dining room table. It shows the building in its early days. Note that there seem to be no sidewalks—not even a road.

HOW TO GET THERE: From Milwaukee, take I–94 to U.S. 43 north and continue to the Sheboygan Falls exit (exit 51); turn west and proceed about 8/10 mile to County Road A, turn north until reaching Wisconsin 28, and take Wisconsin 28 west into the town and to the inn.

Church Hill Inn
Sister Bay, Wisconsin 54234

INNKEEPERS: Paul and Joyce Crittenden

ADDRESS/TELEPHONE: 425 Gateway Drive; (920) 854–4885

ROOMS: 34; all with private bath. Wheelchair accessible.

RATES: Weekdays: $124 to $164, single or double; weekends: $134 to $174, single or double; EPB. Three-night minimum on summer weekends. Special packages available.

OPEN: Year-round

FACILITIES AND ACTIVITIES: Sauna, whirlpool, exercise room, heated outdoor pool. Located in heart of Door County peninsula, one of the

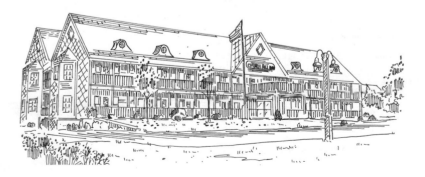

Midwest's premier vacation spots. Nearby: golf courses, water sports, shopping, antiques, orchards, shoreline. Country Walk specialty stores steps away. Town's beach, dock, and downtown 2 blocks away.

*T*his inn sits high on a hill, glistening in the Door County sunlight like a regal jewel in the crown of the royal family. It is designed and decorated in English country style, striving to blend the best of an elegant small hotel with the intimacy of a European bed-and-breakfast inn. Masterful guest rooms are beautifully done in antiques and reproductions. In fact, many of the antiques were purchased in England and brought back especially for the inn.

Each of the inn's stately wings features its own separate sitting areas, complete with fireplace, high-back chairs, and books and magazines; there are also a wet bar and a porch. These areas feel much like the library of an English country estate and are nice places to unwind and relax.

That is, if you ever leave your room. They are handsome; many feature a four-poster canopy bed done in rich mahogany, queen-sized mattress, Empire-style dresser, and private balcony. For total luxury enjoy a room with double whirlpool bath, fireplace, refrigerator, and huge bay windows with quaint bench seats that might offer a view of the flower-filled terrace. Or maybe you'd like a room that has delicate French doors opening directly onto the inn's swimming pool and its elegant sunbathing deck.

HOW TO GET THERE: From Sturgeon Bay, go north on Wisconsin 42 and continue into Sister Bay. The inn is on a hill near the intersection of Wisconsin 42 and 57.

Justin Trails B&B Resort
Sparta, Wisconsin 54656

INNKEEPERS: Donna and Don Justin

ADDRESS/TELEPHONE: 7452 Kathryn Avenue on County J, Route 1, P.O. Box 274; (608) 269-4522 or (800) 488-4521

WEB SITE: www.justintrails.com

ROOMS: 4, with 1 suite; 1 cottage, 2 log cabins—all with private bath. No smoking inn.

RATES: $75 to $250, single or double; EPB.

OPEN: Year-round

FACILITIES AND ACTIVITIES: Parlor, dining room, porch; hiking and biking trails, farm pond, novice ski hill. Groomed and tracked cross-country ski trails, ice-skating pond. Short drive to Elroy–Sparta bicycle trail.

The last time I visited this rural getaway (a 213-acre Holstein farm that has been in the same family since the turn of the century) there was about a foot of snow on the ground and Don Justin had just gotten done with scores of chores. But he and wife Donna still took time to show me their wonderful place.

I came in winter. There are 12 miles of Nordic ski trails crisscrossing the landscape, as well as an ice-skating pond. In summer it's also a great place, especially for kids, since Don welcomes children of all ages to ride on the tractor with him and pitch in with farm duties.

At any time of the year, it's a relaxing rural getaway.

Guest rooms are country quaint, with antique furnishings, Laura Ashley coverlets, and more. I like the Maple Room's bird's-eye maple sleigh bed. Kate and Dayne liked the cow memorabilia all about. Or perhaps you'd rather stay in Little House on the Prairie, a Scandinavian log house with a loft sleeping area, whirlpool, and skylight; or a hand-hewn log cottage with locally made Amish furniture and its own whirlpool.

All beds have nine pillows each, a luxurious and romantic touch.

Donna cooks up a hearty farm breakfast for everybody. It might include French toast, eggs, bacon, homemade apple sauce, juices, and hand-ground coffee.

Did I mention that Sparta is a trailhead for the Elroy–Sparta bicycle trail, one of the finest in the Midwest?

HOW TO GET THERE: East I–90 at Sparta (Highway 27) and turn left; go for about 5 miles to County J, then turn right. Proceed for 1½ miles to Katherine Drive and the inn.

The Springs 📱
Spring Green, Wisconsin 53588

INNKEEPER: Tom van Duursen, general manager

ADDRESS/TELEPHONE: 400 Springs Drive; (608) 588-7000 or (800) 822-7774, fax (608) 588-2269

ROOMS: 80 suites; all with private bath, whirlpool, cable TV, balcony, or patio. Wheelchair accessible.

RATES: $195 to $205, single or double, June through September; off-season rates available; continental breakfast. Special lodging and golf packages available.

OPEN: Year-round

FACILITIES AND ACTIVITIES: Full-service dining room, casual restaurant, snack bar, swimming pool, lap pool, spa tub, full-service health club, sitting area with fireplace facing woods, world-class golf course (twenty-seven holes), hiking trails, cross-country ski trails. Nearby: a short drive to Taliesin (Frank Lloyd Wright's home), American Players Theater (Shakespearean company), House on the Rock, Tower Hill State Park, Spring Green art galleries and crafts shops, horseback riding, biking, Wisconsin River canoe rides.

BUSINESS TRAVEL: Located about 45 minutes west of Madison, 3 minutes from downtown Spring Green. Corporate group rates, conference rooms, fax.

*T*he Springs is a luxurious Frank Lloyd Wright–inspired resort nestled among the rolling wooded hills of the picturesque Jones Valley on land once owned by the famed architect.

Faithful to Wright's vision of organic architecture, the resort neatly blends in with the verdant countryside, full of low-to-the-ground horizontal lines, inspiring vistas through long rows of windows, and massive terraces of natural stone.

Inside, the resort boasts more Wright-inspired surprises. Cherokee reds and other earth tones add touches of understated elegance. Furnishings might have come directly from Wright's own studio, full of unexpected lines and angles.

Our suite was a handsome paean to Wright's genius as well as a luxurious

oasis. My wife, Debbie, loved the original art adorning the walls. Our daughters, Kate and Dayne, couldn't wait to test the whirlpool bath. I was drawn to the balcony, which overlooks the beautiful award-winning Robert Trent Jones Golf Course.

The girls lobbied for a quick swim, so we headed to the pool. They were thrilled to discover a massive pool shaped by three intersecting circles, along with a huge lap pool and spa tub. I went to the fitness room for a quick workout on fabulous equipment. Then we hiked around the golf course, planning my future assault on these nationally renowned links.

Dinners are exquisite culinary events, thanks to chef Scott Finley. His mushroom strudel (wild mushrooms sautéed in white wine and heavy cream and nestled in a pastry puff shell) is heavenly. A favorite entree is grilled filet mignon topped with a small pat of blue cheese butter and a tarragon-rich béarnaise sauce. Desserts of chocolate chambord or crème caramel can excite the palate of anyone.

It's almost impossible to visit The Springs without challenging the links. I took on the resort's newest nine, designed by PGA golfer Andy North, himself a Wisconsin native. He envisions this layout as the "Pinehurst of the Midwest."

Could be. I got bitten by the narrow fairways and big-hitter challenges (not to mention mosquitoes—bring insect repellent). In fact, I probably left more balls in the woods than on the greens. The par four, 371-yard number six offers one of the prettiest views in the state.

HOW TO GET THERE: From Madison/Middleton, take U.S. 14 west to Spring Green. Just outside Spring Green, you'll see directional signs for THE SPRINGS; follow the signs to the resort.

The Inn at Cedar Crossing 🖤
Sturgeon Bay, Wisconsin 54235

INNKEEPER: Terry Smith

ADDRESS/TELEPHONE: 336 Louisiana Street; (920) 743-4200

WEB SITE: innatcedarcrossing.com

ROOMS: 9; all with private bath and air-conditioning, TV on request. No smoking inn.

RATES: $110 to $180, single or double; continental breakfast. Two-night minimum on weekends when Saturday night is included. Three-night minimum on most holiday and peak fall weekends. Special winter/spring packages available November through April.

OPEN: Year-round

FACILITIES AND ACTIVITIES: Full-service restaurant, two dining rooms, pub with mahogany bar. About 3 blocks from waterfront. Short walk to quaint shops, restaurants, Miller Art Museum, historic district, downtown area. Half-hour's drive to beaches, antiques shops, tip of Door County peninsula. Cross-country ski rentals available at inn through local outfitter.

This handsome inn, housed in an 1884 merchant building modeled after European markets, is one of my Door County favorites. Debbie and I especially liked all the elegant guest rooms.

And they are exquisite—some of the most luxurious in the Midwest. Consider the Corner Suite, which reflects the inn's 1880s heritage in grand fashion. An ornately carved archway, with two tall columns, frames the handsome bedchamber, whose queen-sized bed is adorned with a down-filled European comforter. Golden-oak furniture surrounds a cozy fireplace in the "sitting room," a perfect spot for romantic whispers.

There are two other rooms I must mention: The Anniversary Room offers a king-sized, hand-carved mahogany canopy bed, with period furnishings, fireplace, and whirlpool tub. A Touch of Williamsburg

features its own private porch, as well as a pencil-post bed, massive whirlpool bath, fireplace, and hand-painted armoire.

No visit to the inn would be complete without dinner at its heralded restaurant, rated by *Milwaukee Journal* magazine as one of the twenty-five best in Wisconsin. Dinners might include tart cherry-stuffed pork loin, whitefish baked in brown butter with capers and pine nuts, and grilled New York strip steak with pungent cherry chutney. Among sinfully decadent desserts are double diablo chocolate tortes and the inn's famous "mile-high" cherry pie—it weighs seven pounds whole!

Of course, menus continue to change; no telling what kind of delectable meals you'll enjoy on your next visit.

HOW TO GET THERE: Go north on Wisconsin 42/57, around Sturgeon Bay, over the new bridge. Turn left on Michigan Street and go about 1 mile to the first stop sign. Then turn right on Fourth Avenue, go 1 block, then left on Louisiana. The inn is just before the stop sign, on the right.

White Lace Inn ♥
Sturgeon Bay, Wisconsin 54235

INNKEEPERS: Bonnie and Dennis Statz

ADDRESS/TELEPHONE: 16 North Fifth Avenue; (920) 743–1105 or (877) 948–5223

ROOMS: 19, in 4 historic houses; all with private bath and air-conditioning, some with fireplace, whirlpool, TV. Wheelchair accessible.

RATES: $99 to $179, single or double, weekdays; $109 to $239, Friday and Saturday. Special winter or spring fireside rates and packages available November through May. EPB.

OPEN: Year-round

FACILITIES AND ACTIVITIES: Five blocks to bay shore. Nearby: specialty and antiques shops, restaurants, Door County Museum, Miller Art Center; swimming, tennis, and horseback riding. A short drive to Whitefish Dunes and Potawatomi State Parks, Peninsula Players Summer Theater, Birch Creek Music Festival. Cross-country skiing and ice-skating in winter. Gateway to the peninsula.

*B*onnie and Dennis Statz call their award-winning inn "a romantic fireside getaway." I can't think of a better place to spend a cozy, pampered weekend for two.

Things have only gotten better since my last visit. Now the White Lace Inn resembles a private Victorian-era park, with three handsome historic buildings connected by a redbrick pathway that winds through landscaped grounds filled with stately trees, wildflower gardens, and a rose garden  featuring varieties dating from the 1700s. You will also enjoy the Vixen Hill gazebo, a great place to pause among the inn's many gardens; it is a beauty from Pennsylvania.

The Main House was built for a local lawyer in 1903; what's surprising is the extensive oak woodwork put in for a man of such modest means. Stepping into the entryway, I was surrounded by magnificent hand-carved oak paneling.

Bonnie has a degree in interior design and has created guest rooms with a warm feel, mixing Laura Ashley wallpaper and fabrics with imposing, yet comfortable, antique furnishings like rich Oriental rugs and high-back walnut and canopied beds. Fluffy down pillows are provided, handmade comforters and quilts brighten large beds, and lacy curtains adorn tall windows.

The 1880s Garden House has rooms with their own fireplace. They're done in myriad styles, from country elegant to the grand boldness of over-sized Empire furniture.

This time my wife and I stayed in the Washburn House, the third and most recent "old" addition to the White Lace. All rooms here are luxurious; ours had a canopy brass bed with down comforter, fireplace, and two-person whirlpool. It was graced with soft pastel floral chintz fabric and white-on-white Carol Gresco fabrics that tell a story (in fact, some of her work is part of the Smithsonian Design Institution collection). The bath's Ralph Lauren towels are heavenly.

Next time, I want a room in the Hadley House—maybe one with a huge whirlpool, fireplace, and private balcony.

Back in the main house, Bonnie's homemade muffins are the breakfast treat, along with juice, coffee, and delicious Scandinavian fruit soup (a tasty concoction served cold) or old-fashioned rice pudding. Blueberry soup and apple crisps are summer specials. It's a great time to swap Door County stories.

For dinner the innkeepers will recommend a restaurant that suits your tastes. I'm always pleased with the Inn at Cedar Crossing. Or try Oliver Station, a restored railroad station converted into a casual restaurant and microbrewery that serves great beer and beer/cheese soup.

HOW TO GET THERE: From Milwaukee, take U.S. 41 north to Wisconsin 42, toward Sturgeon Bay. Just outside the city, take Business 42/57 and follow it into town, cross the bridge, and you'll come to Michigan Street. Follow Michigan to Fifth Avenue and turn left. White Lace Inn is on the right side of the street. Or you can take the 42/51 bypass across the new bridge to Michigan Street. Turn left on Michigan, go to Fifth Avenue, and take a right on Fifth to the inn.

Rosenberry Inn
Wausau, Wisconsin 54401

INNKEEPERS: Barry and Linda Brehmer

ADDRESS/TELEPHONE: 511 Franklin Street; (715) 842–5733

WEB SITE: www.rosenberryinn.com

ROOMS: 9, including 2 suites; all with private bath, air-conditioning, TV, and phone. No smoking inn.

RATES: $55 to $75, single; $70 to $90, double; $120 to 160, suites; continental breakfast.

OPEN: Year-round

FACILITIES AND ACTIVITIES: Gathering room, porch. Nearby: downtown Wausau and the Mall, Washington Square shopping complex, antiques shops, boutiques, restaurants, Leigh Yawkey Woodson Art Museum. A short drive to Dells of Eau Claire nature trails, rock climbing, rappelling, fishing, and canoeing. Rib Mountain skiing; cross-country ski trails.

I have just arrived at the Rosenberry Inn early on a weekend morning. Inside on the guest book stand rests a cowbell to alert the innkeepers of new arrivals.

It's library quiet in the house. I just know I'll wake the entire place if I ring that bell, and I don't want a guilty conscience—especially on Sunday.

Oh, what the heck. Cllaaannnnggggg!

After everyone was awake, I discovered that all guest rooms are graced with Victorian antiques and some country primitives; four have a fireplace. In the rose-colored room, I like the iron-rail beds and the working fireplace—good to take away the chill after skiing at nearby Rib Mountain. Another has antique Victorian bedspreads, homemade comforters, and a fireplace that transforms the room into a cozy retreat.

There is an additional home, located in the Historic District just 1½ blocks away. Rooms in the DeVoe House have a fireplace and whirlpool bath. These are cozy retreats for big-city visitors.

HOW TO GET THERE: From Milwaukee, take I-94 west to U.S. 51 and head north until you reach Wausau. At Highway 52, go east to Franklin Street and turn left to the inn.

Westby House Victorian Inn ¢¢
Westby, Wisconsin 54667

INNKEEPERS: Mike and Marie Cimino

ADDRESS/TELEPHONE: 200 West State Street; (608) 634-4112 or (800) 434-7439

WEB SITE: www.westbyhouse.com

ROOMS: 7, including 1 suite; 6 with private bath, all with air-conditioning, TV, and phone. No smoking inn.

RATES: $75 to $165, single or double; continental breakfast.

OPEN: Year-round

FACILITIES AND ACTIVITIES: Full-service restaurant. Short walk to specialty stores and antiques shops. In Wisconsin Amish country, with quaint back-road exploring. Winter cross-country skiing, major ski-jump park and training site. Town celebrates many Norwegian holidays.

*T*his charming Queen Anne–style inn, located in a Norwegian community, is a Westby landmark. The eighteen-room mansion, built in the 1890s, has all the special Victorian touches: a tall tower, stained-glass windows, gingerbread finery, and elegant interior woodwork.

Guest rooms are small-town charming. The spacious Anniversary Suite has a large brass bed, lacy curtains on windows, and a Victorian love seat and chair; it's a guest favorite. There are two white iron-rail beds in the Greenbriar Room. And the Squire

Room has cheery country accents, such as eyelet lace curtains and a hand-painted queen-sized bed, which looks awfully inviting.

The inn's most recent addition is the Fireplace Room. This two-room suite has regal antiques (including a fainting couch), lots of lacy finery, a

Try the Torsk

Dinner also looked pretty inviting, with choices such as fresh trout and sautéed shrimp with mushrooms and onions. (Of course, everything at the inn is made from scratch, right down to the salad dressing.)

I suggest that you try the torsk, an inn specialty. It's eight ounces of Norwegian cod baked in lemon butter and served with egg noodles. Then opt for a luscious dessert—the Victoriannie—a homemade brownie topped with ice cream, whipped cream, and a cherry.

Remember that Westby's Olympic-style ski jump draws top athletes to its winter competitions every year. It's a great time to enjoy the Westby House hospitality.

fireplace, and a cozy nook inside the home's tall tower—high Victorian and very romantic.

Downstairs, the busy Victorian dining room draws people from all over town for its delicious, hearty food. I sat in front of a manteled fireplace at an antique table complete with bentwood chairs and devoured my lunch: a hot crabmeat sandwich with tomato slices and jack cheese.

HOW TO GET THERE: The inn is located halfway between Chicago and the Twin Cities. From La Crosse, take U.S. 14/61 southeast into Westby. Turn west onto West State Street and continue to the inn.

Jesse's Historic Wolf River Lodge
White Lake, Wisconsin 54491

INNKEEPER: Joan Jesse

ADDRESS/TELEPHONE: White Lake; (715) 882–2182

ROOMS: 9, 8 with private bath, plus 1 carriage house; 2 rooms and carriage house with private bath.

RATES: Weekends: $90, single; $110, double; weekdays: $75, single; $95, double. Carriage house $160 per night with four people. EPB. Most reservations are made at week long or weekend package rates. Special ski-season rates (Christmas season to mid-March).

OPEN: Year-round

FACILITIES AND ACTIVITIES: Full-service dining room, bar, wine cellar, parlor and game rooms, gift shop, outdoor hot tub. Located on Wolf River, with world-class whitewater rapids during high-water periods. River is runnable April through October. Excellent trout fishing May and June. Ideal terrain for cross-country skiing, horseback riding.

here can you find world-class whitewater rapids, kayaking, and fly-cast trout fishing in a spot where eagle and osprey soar overhead and roadsides are smothered by early summer wildflowers? The Wolf River Lodge, of course.

This rustic lodge is a center for river rafting on the Wolf River. In the majestic Nicolet National Forest country, frothing whitewater rapids tumble over boulders and ledges, dropping 12 feet per mile for 25 miles. The crystal-clear water is often icy cold. Guest rooms are small but cozy, with pine furniture and country finery. I like the brightly colored quilts and braided rugs that add color to the rustic charm. George Washington didn't sleep here, but a senator who became our thirty-fifth president did.

The food is simple but delicious. Breakfast means a morning treat: the lodge's renowned crepes. Most evening meals feature delectable trout; delicious roast duck; thick, juicy steaks; and baked stuffed pork chops with pine-nut dressing.

The lodge's newest attraction is a carriage-house loft (with its own private bath) that sleeps two to six people; this handsome log home should be a real family pleaser.

HOW TO GET THERE: From Milwaukee, take I–43 north to Green Bay; then take U.S. 41/141 north to Wisconsin 64. Head west to White Lake. Turn north on Wisconsin 55 and watch for the Wolf River Lodge signs that direct you to the inn.

Hawk's View Bed & Breakfast 🖤
Wisconsin Dells, Wisconsin 53965

INNKEEPER: Carol Moeller

ADDRESS/TELEPHONE: E11344 Pocohontas Circle; (608) 254–2979

WEB SITE: www.bbonline.com/wi/hawksview

ROOMS: 4; all with private bath, 2 with whirlpool. No smoking inn.

RATES: $125 to $175, single or double; EPB.

OPEN: Year-round

FACILITIES AND ACTIVITIES: Deck/shoreline overlooking Wisconsin River and Dells scenery, one acre of forested grounds. Great eagle watching. Short drive to downtown Wisconsin Dells and all its attractions, Circus World Museum, International Crane Foundation, Devil's Lake State Park, Ho-Chunk Casino, Cascade Mountain Ski Area.

*T*his chalet, perched atop one of the Dells' signature rock formations overlooking the Wisconsin River, is true to its name. It boasts a hawk's-eye view of the Dells' fascinating natural wonders. If you want an up-close view of the river and its environs, just take the inn's boardwalk down to the shoreline.

Very quiet, very secluded, located on one acre of dense pine forest. No crowds. No noise. No miniature golf. This can't be Wisconsin Dells.

But it is!

Not only do you enjoy spectacular vistas at Hawk's View, but guest rooms are equally enticing. Victorian Garden, with its panoramic river view, offers Victorian antiques as well as a two-person whirlpool and fireplace; Yesteryear features an antique brass bed and two-person whirlpool.

If a suite is your desire, try Forest's Edge, two rooms with its own private house entrance and deck. Inside you'll enjoy elegant North Woods lodge decor: bedroom with king-sized bed, two-person whirlpool, and fireplace.

The Country Retreat is a two-story private guest cottage with quaint country charm.

Breakfasts are a treat, too. The candlelit fireside meal is served in the dining room, with incredible river views. For those who want a morning commune with nature, take your meal out on the private deck.

HOW TO GET THERE: Take I–90/94 to exit 87 in the Dells. At the second stoplight turn right onto Highway 12/23, then at the first stoplight turn left onto County Road A. Go about 1¾ miles to Hillside Drive, turn left, and proceed ½ mile to Pocahontas Circle and the inn.

Thunder Valley Inn 🪙 🎴
Wisconsin Dells, Wisconsin 53965

INNKEEPERS: Anita Nelson, Kari and Sigrid Nelson

ADDRESS/TELEPHONE: W15344 Waubeek Road; (608) 254–4145

WEB SITE: www.lb.com/tv

ROOMS: 9 rooms, plus 1 cottage; all with private bath. Wheelchair accessible. No smoking inn.

RATES: $55 to $100, single; $55 to $105, double; EPB. Two-night minimum on weekends and holidays.

OPEN: Year-round (inn), May to October (restaurant).

FACILITIES AND ACTIVI-TIES: Full-service restaurant with folk music performances, gift shop, children's farm tours. Nearby: a short drive to Noah's Ark Water Park, Country Legends Music Theater, Ripley's Believe It or Not Museum, Storybook Gardens, Biblical Gardens, Stand Rock Winnebago Indian Ceremonial, Wisconsin River boat cruises, the Ducks (amphibious World War II vehicles) Wisconsin River tours, gift shops, boutiques, golf, fishing, horseback riding, and more.

his 130-year-old homestead, run by descendants of the original Norwegian immigrants who settled here, dishes out the finest home-cooked farm-style meals in the Dells.

Everything's organically grown, home-ground, and made from scratch, including the most delicious whole-grain griddle cakes (topped with lingonberries) this traveler has ever tasted. Also try scrambled eggs with Ole's Norwegian white sauce. Breakfast meats include delicious turkey ham.

Daughters Kate and Dayne ordered the "animal pancakes" offered for kids. They squealed with delight when everything from lions to rhinos appeared on their plates.

And massive cinnamon rolls—*Detergodt!* They are good! In fact, we ordered twice as many the next day.

During the meal owner Anita Nelson introduced daughters Sigrid and Kari, dressed in traditional folk costumes, who fiddled Norwegian folk tunes and pioneer songs. Their serenade was a lovely way to start the day.

After breakfast children can help "Farmer Benson" collect eggs in the hen house, feed goats, pet chicks, and watch peacocks fan their colorful feathers. Dayne, however, got a little nervous when asked to pick up some of the chicks and return them to the hen house.

"Would you please do it?" she asked Farmer Benson. "After all, you're the farmer."

Besides a Friday night fish fry, Thunder Valley also offers Saturday evening dinners and chautauquas. Home-style food includes slow-cooked beef pot roast sautéed with onions, mashed potatoes, and fresh garden vegetables. Entertainment might be anything from the Grieg Norwegian Men's Chorus to a quilt show or ice cream social.

The Norwegian hospitality extends to charming guest rooms. The original Farm Hus has six of them: Lena's Room offers an antique iron double bed; Wildflower features two full-sized beds with goose-down comforters and a kitchenette; and the Norskevalley is a spacious bedchamber with California king bed, feather-filled comforter, antique Norwegian desk, and claw-foot bathtub. The Hus's gathering room boasts a Franklin stove, sitting room, and dining room.

Another inn building, the Guest Hus, features rustic knotty-pine interiors. It's especially good for families. And the Wee Hus, a cottage that's perfect for romantic getaways and honeymooners, is adorned with colorful folk art accents.

VELKOMMEN TO THUNDER VALLEY INN, say all the signs. Here, they really mean it!

HOW TO GET THERE: The inn is located just north of Wisconsin Dells on Highway 13. Best way there is to take exit 87 (Highway 13) from I–90/94. Go east through downtown Wisconsin Dells to the stoplight (junction of Highways 16, 23, and 13); turn left on Highway 13 and go about 1 mile. Watch for the inn's sign on the right.

Select List of Other Inns in Wisconsin

Oak Hill Manor
401 East Main Street
Albany, WI 53502
(608) 862-1400

Cooper Hill House
33 South Sixth Street
Bayfield, WI 54814
(715) 779-5060

The Creamery
1 Creamery Road
Downsville, WI 54735
(715) 664-8354

Thorp House Inn and Cottages
4135 Bluff Road
Fish Creek, WI 54212
(920) 868-2444

Lazy Cloud Lodge
N2025 North Lake Shore Drive
Fontana, WI 53125
(414) 275-3322

Mascione's Hidden Valley Villas
1584 East Shore Drive
Hillsboro, WI 53257
(608) 489-3443

The 1884 Phipps Inn
1005 Third Street
Hudson, WI 54016
(715) 386-0800

Martindale House
237 South Tenth Street
La Crosse, WI 54601
(608) 782-4224

Jamieson House
407 North Franklin
Poynette, WI 53955
(608) 635-2277

The Stout Trout B&B
W4 244 County F
Springbrook, WI 54875
(715) 466-2790

The Barbican Inn
132 North Second Avenue
Sturgeon Bay, WI 54235
(920) 743-4854

The Grey Goose Bed and Breakfast
4258 Bay Shore Drive
Sturgeon Bay, WI 54235
(920) 743-9100

The Reynolds House
111 South 7th Avenue
Sturgeon Bay, WI 54235
(920) 746-9771

Hamilton House Bed & Breakfast
328 West Main Street
Whitewater, WI 53190
(414) 473-1900

Indexes

Alphabetical Index to Inns

Inns with Full-Service Restaurants

Bed-and-Breakfast Inns
(serve breakfast only)

Riverside Inns

Inns on Lakes

Inns with a Swimming Pool

Inns near Downhill or Cross-Country Skiing

Inns Especially Good for Kids

Historic Inns (Hotels)

Inns with a Hot Tub

No Smoking Inns

Inns with Wheelchair Access
(to at least one room)

Inns for Business Travelers

About the Author

Bob Puhala is a Chicago-area writer who has authored nearly thirty travel books, wrote a travel column for the *Chicago Sun-Times* for fifteen years, and has written newspaper and magazine articles for publications ranging from *USA Today* to the *Columbia Journalism Review*. Bob is currently working on special media projects.